www.wadsworth.com

wadsworth.com is the World Wide Web site for Wadsworth and is your direct source to dozens of online resources.

At *wadsworth.com* you can find out about supplements, demonstration software, and student resources. You can also send email to many of our authors and preview new publications and exciting new technologies.

wadsworth.com
Changing the way the world learns®

Teaching with Technology

Designing Opportunities to Learn

SECOND EDITION

PRISCILLA NORTON
George Mason University

KARIN M. WIBURG
New Mexico State University

THOMSON

WADSWORTH

Australia • Canada • Mexico • Singapore • Spain • United Kingdom • United States

THOMSON

WADSWORTH

Education Editor: Dan Alpert
Development Editor: Tangelique Williams
Editorial Assistant: Lilah Johnson
Technology Project Manager: Jeanette Wiseman
Marketing Manager: Dory Schaeffer
Marketing Assistant: Neena Chandra
Advertising Project Manager: Bryan Vann
Project Manager, Editorial Production: Trudy Brown

Print/Media Buyer: Robert King
Permissions Editor: Bob Kauser
Production Service: Carlisle Publishers Services
Copy Editor: Carlisle Publishers Services
Cover Designer: Jennifer Dunn
Compositor: Carlisle Communications, Ltd.
Text and Cover Printer: Webcom, Ltd.

Printed in Canada

1 2 3 4 5 6 7 06 05 04 03 02

For more information about our products, contact us at:
Thomson Learning Academic Resource Center
1-800-423-0563
For permission to use material from this text, contact us by:
Phone: 1-800-730-2214
Fax: 1-800-730-2215
Web: http://www.thomsonrights.com

Library of Congress Control Number: 2002101172

ISBN 0-534-60309-2

Wadsworth/Thomson Learning
10 Davis Drive
Belmont, CA 94002-3098
USA

Asia
Thomson Learning
5 Shenton Way #01-01
UIC Building
Singapore 068808

Australia
Nelson Thomson Learning
102 Dodds Street
South Melbourne, Victoria 3205
Australia

Canada
Nelson Thomson Learning
1120 Birchmount Road
Toronto, Ontario M1K 5G4
Canada

Europe/Middle East/Africa
Thomson Learning
High Holborn House
50/51 Bedford Row
London WC1R 4LR
United Kingdom

Latin America
Thomson Learning
Seneca, 53
Colonia Polanco
11560 Mexico D.F.
Mexico

Spain
Paraninfo Thomson Learning
Calle/Magallanes, 25
28015 Madrid, Spain

To our mothers:
Kathleen Mullarky Norton
and
Carolyn Anfinsen Weightman

Contents

Chapter 9

Designing Systems of Assessment   219

Chapter 10

Designing Learning Environments   251

An Introductory Note to Readers

What does it mean to be literate in a technological age? How can learners use technology to become thinkers and problem solvers? How do we learn to live and work in a society with new electronic media constantly exposing us to cultures and values different from our own? How can teachers use technology to design learning that supports rather than hinders living in a world challenged by such questions?

This book explores answers to questions such as these. It has been written to assist potential and practicing educators to use technology to design the types of learning experiences needed by students in our rapidly changing world. To tap the power of technology for learning it is not enough for teachers to know about hardware and software and how to use them. Nor will the power of technology for learning be realized by offering prescriptions for practice. Instead, *Teaching with Technology* is based on a vision of classrooms governed, not by scope and sequences or traditional teaching practices, but by educators skilled in the art of design and knowledgeable about effective technology use. This approach rests on our belief that the best teaching occurs when educators make choices about learning environments, learning tools, and learning experiences based on strategies drawn from a broad knowledge base. Thus, the term design is used in this book to refer to the process educators use to intentionally plan learning experiences that are appropriate for their students.

We believe that understanding how to design effective technology-based learning opportunities requires comprehending how profoundly changes in technology have impacted society, schooling, and curriculum. Therefore, the book is bound together by the notion that the new electronic technologies are one of the primary, if not the primary, stimuli shaping new socio-cultural contexts and that these resulting contexts demand new educational environments and new ways of designing instruction. Although the electronic technologies are shaping these changes, they also create opportunities for educators to design the type of learning needed to respond to current challenges. We believe that, if integrated into the learning experiences of today's students, the electronic technologies can assist in helping students learn to make decisions, model the results of scientific investigations, provide scenarios for family living, experiment with the dimensions of art, solve real problems, and participate in a variety of human communities.

Education is an important carrier of culture. A large part of what students learn about life's options is linked to the decisions that educators make as they shape the experiences of learners. Student learning is not accidental; it is the direct result of students' experience of the learning opportunities teachers design. New ways of designing learning are needed. The way it has always been done no longer serves to prepare today's students. Industrial models for the design of learning that rely heavily on the technology of print are increasingly inconsistent with the world students bring with them to school or will meet upon graduation.

This book presents an alternative process for thinking about designs for learning—a process influenced by the consequences of today's electronic technologies while simultaneously using the power of these same technologies as an integral tool in the designing of learning. This text, whether used in educational technology courses or curriculum and instruction courses, provides a new way to view the design of improved and effective learning environments for the future.

We have used scenarios throughout the book to present concrete examples in order to assist readers to see the relationship of theory to practice. We have used this approach in the hope that it adds life to the text and provides another lens readers can use to reflect on the design of teaching and learning. The narrative is the vehicle humans use not to search for empirical truth but to inform the conduct of life (Bruner, 1986). Embedded in the study of lived lives are themes that can inform future decisions. If Margaret Mead (1971) is correct in her assessment that young people everywhere share a kind of experience that none of the elders have ever had, we believe that it is within the life stories of the young that the impact of technology in shaping aspects of our social, cultural, cognitive, and epistemological lives might best be uncovered. If teachers are to respond to the new experiences learners bring to school, we believe it is important to study the stories of teachers who are seeking new directions in their educational practice.

So, as you read this book, you will encounter a number of stories about learners, educators, and classrooms. They are real stories. We hope these stories bring to life alternatives that inform the decisions you make about the learning experiences you design for students—experiences that capitalize on the possibilities of today's technologies.

The Ten Chapters

To explore the ways in which you can intentionally construct learning opportunities for students that reflect contemporary contexts and integrate technology to support learning, this book is organized in ten chapters. Chapter 1, "Today's Technological Challenges," places schooling, curriculum, and instructional design within the larger context of transformations that have occurred as society has moved from a print-dependent, industrial age to a postmodern era deeply influenced by electronic media. Chapter 2, "Designing Opportunities for Learning," reviews traditional notions of design, presents emerging criticisms of these traditional approaches, and offers two ideas—multiple intelligences and constructivist learning—and an educational dilemma—translating these views of learning into a theory of teaching. The chapter concludes by posing six design questions.

Chapter 3, "The FACTS of Design," develops the model of design offered by this book and is new to this edition. Starting with the premise that teachers are and ought to be designers, this chapter presents the art of design as putting together pieces of a puzzle. The puzzle pieces of the FACTS Model of Design include Foundations (knowledge, problem solving, literacy, information use, and participating in a community), Activities, Contents, Tools, and a System of assessment all set within the frame of an appropriately constructed learning environment.

Each of these puzzle pieces has a unique shape and combination of colors. Each can fail to fit with the others, fit only when artificially shoved into place, or blend smoothly into an elegant pattern of inquiry and learning. Each time educators design an opportunity for learning the puzzle pieces must be shaped and colored differently. Yet, each time they must smoothly join with the other pieces.

Chapter 4, "Designs for Knowledge," explores four animating ideas that shape the design of opportunities students have to build knowledge: teaching the *structures* related to content areas as opposed to isolated packets of information, teaching *processes* related to content area understanding, using a variety of *discourse forms* to support content area learning, and assisting students to do history, economics, biology, and geology by anchoring a learning design with an authentic problem.

Chapter 5, "Designs for Problem-Solving," explores how thinking and problem solving can become part of the ongoing educational process. The chapter focuses on how the educational applications of new understandings of cognition and intelligence can support productive thinking, how promoting students' thinking about thinking—metacognition—can facilitate higher order thinking skills, how problem solving is best developed within a culture and community of thinkers, and how using problem-centered learning can serve as a framework for designing opportunities for learning.

Chapter 6, "Designs for Literacy," presents a framework for creating learning opportunities that promote students' ability to derive knowledge from and participate fully in a symbolic world. This framework centers on design that assists students to develop an understanding of how symbols are used to represent ideas, what cognitive processes are useful in interpreting messages inherent in symbolic forms, and how broader patterns of discourse are used to organize information.

Chapter 7, "Designs for Using Information," explores how teachers can design opportunities for students to learn to use a wide range of information resources to become searchers, sorters, creators, and communicators in a world where we are at risk of drowning in information. It explores a framework for assisting students to transform information into ideas that can be communicated in order to influence their lives. Finally, the chapter explores the world of online learning.

Chapter 8, "Designs for Community," focuses on how educators can design learning experiences that are responsive to the needs of a wide range of diverse students, that create communities of learners who can both collaborate and cooperate, and that promote students' abilities to participate in civic actions as they learn to shape the context in which they live. The chapter concludes with an exploration of the ways in which online communities extend students' interactions beyond the classroom and promote their abilities to participate in virtual communities.

Chapter 9, "Designing Systems of Assessment," presents assessment strategies that support the development and implementation of the educational practices proposed in this book. It also suggests how technology can be used to support this implementation. After discussing the teacher's role in assessment and the alternative assessment movement, the chapter is organized around specific ways that technology can be used to support designs for learning including expanding the types of assessment and the audience involved, using technology to support the observation and documentation of new kinds of learning, and developing a culture of assessment supported by electronic networks and opportunities for teachers, students, and communities to exchange and access exemplary work.

Chapter 10, "Designing Learning Environments," examines how educators can design learning spaces more appropriate to emerging visions of teaching and learning. It promotes a vision of the environment as an instructional strategy and suggests that how the environment is designed communicates to students messages about what is important. Particular attention is paid to the design of learning environments conducive to the integration of the electronic technologies into the ongoing teaching and learning processes of the classroom.

The FACTS Web-Based Design Tool

We have tried to build several features into the book to support your learning. First, each chapter begins with a short, context-setting story that is followed by a short summary of the chapter. Second, each chapter ends with a bulleted Chapter Ideas section. The Chapter Ideas highlight the important points embedded in the text of the chapter. Despite these two features, we decided as we worked on the revision that yet another support system was necessary. So, the third feature of this book is an extensive Web-based design tool.

The FACTS Web-Based Design Tool is an online interactive environment that supports the transition from the design process presented in this book to designs of action that can be implemented in classrooms. Even though the FACTS design model appears as a linear process when captured by the structure of this book's text, it is, in reality, a dynamic, iterative process. The FACTS Web-Based Design Tool supports and models this dynamic process better than a more static paper-pencil environment because an online, linked environment is more flexible and interactive. You can sign on to the FACTS Web-Based Design Tool, establish a permanent log-in and password, and use the tool anytime you want—even after you are finished reading the book and/or taking a course.

On the opening Web page for the Web-based design tool there are four puzzle pieces that link to the Design Mentors, the Design Challenges, and to Design Examples, respectively, as well as a puzzle piece that enables you to Create Your Own Design. Using the process of modeling, coaching, and fading, these links support learning to use the FACTS Design model. The Design Mentors provide you the opportunity to observe teachers using the design model. The Design Examples allow you to examine a variety of completed learning designs. The Design Challenges present instructional dilemmas and coach you as you experiment with using the design model. The Create Your Own Design link takes you to the FACTS Web-Based Design Tool environment that you can use to solve your own instructional dilemmas. We will refer to this tool throughout the chapters.

Acknowledgments

Without the assistance of many others, the original book and this second edition would not have been possible. We would like to thank Dr. Carmen Gonzales of New Mexico State University, Dr. Debra Sprague of George Mason University, and Dr. Elizabeth Willis of Northern Arizona University who lent valuable insights and were willing to try drafts in their classes as we worked on the first edition. Conversations with Dr. Debra Sprague, Dr. Jerry Miller at Alliant International University, and Dr. Penny Garcia at the University of Wisconsin-Oshkosh provided additional assistance with the second edition. Doctoral students at the University of New Mexico, Penny Garcia and Barbara Jones, provided valuable assistance on the first edition. Susan Estrada, a graduate student at the University of New Mexico, obtained all the copyright permissions for the first edition. Doctoral students at George Mason University, William Warrick and Nancy Farrell, provided invaluable assistance on the second edition. Monique Lynch, a doctoral student at George Mason University, obtained all the copyright permissions for the second edition.

We would like to thank the following reviewers whose thoughtful comments helped us shape this edition: John Caruso, Western Connecticut State University; Charles Dickens, Tennessee State University; Robert Gillian, Northwestern State University; and Douglas Hansen, Saginaw Valley State University. We also wish to acknowledge the useful suggestions of the reviewers of the first edition of this text: David M. Crossman, University of Pittsburgh; Wallace Hannum, University of North Carolina, Chapel Hill; Richard Howell, Ohio State University; Al P. Mizell, Nova Southeastern University; Ron Pahl, California State University, Fullerton; and Jerry Summers, Indiana State University.

We would also like to thank the many teachers who allowed us to visit their classrooms and who provided us with insights about teaching and learning, both as we visited schools and during our university courses. Without their help and their willingness to welcome us into their classrooms and their lives as graduate students, neither the first nor the second edition would have been possible.

For this second edition, there are some special acknowledgments. The second edition was Dan Alpert's idea. As an editor at Wadsworth, he had the vision and recognized the potential of the Web-based design tool and supported its development. Trudy Brown and Mary Jo Graham shepherded the book from manuscript to finished product. Watts Conrad designed the early graphics for the Web-based design tool. Monique Lynch took over from Watts and created the final look and feel for the tool with creativity and insight. She spent endless hours getting all the puzzle pieces just right. Mike Belcher was the designer and programmer for the Web-based design tool. He is the genius behind all of its functionality.

Last, we would like to thank our families, particularly our husbands Marve Wiburg and Mike Belcher. Collectively, they supported our work on the manuscripts, listened to us as we wrestled with ideas, read drafts, helped with the bibliography, and took on additional household responsibilities. Mike never thought he would be "donating" his considerable system design and programming skill but happily and without complaint spent hours and hours of his weekend time making the vision of a Web-based design tool a reality.

Today's Technological Challenges

I can remember the day my parents bought their first television. I was three years old. I remember the first time I answered the telephone. It was very late at night. Our new puppy was crying, and I was holding her. The phone rang. It was for my father. After that phone call, he left for two weeks. I know now he was called to respond to the Cuban Missile Crisis, but then I thought phones only brought bad news. I was in eighth grade when I got a transistor radio. I remember it sitting in the middle of the dining room table as my family listened to President Johnson's announcement that he would not seek a second term. My friend bought one of the first calculators available for over $400. We spent a whole evening testing its capacities. I ordered my first computer from a local Radio Shack store and taught myself to use it.

Today's students will never remember their encounters with the electronic technologies in the same way I do for these technologies are a natural part of their living and learning environment. It always shocks me to walk into classrooms and see either very limited access or no access to telephones, computers, television, and, often times, calculators. Doesn't technology have a place in education?

Maria Chavez
A Middle School Parent

When the Ancient Greeks debated the invention of the alphabet, as they do in the opening scenario of this chapter, they feared that the use of letters might lead to a decline in the capacity of humans to use their memory and to an erosion of "truth." Despite their fears, the technology of letters changed their oral culture into a scribal culture. When Gutenberg invented the printing press in 1452, he had no idea that his invention would bring about "the most radical transformation in the conditions of intellectual life in the history of Western Civilization" (Eisenstein, 1979). Yet, his invention was to change a scribal culture into a print culture. As a consequence of the printing press, editors and printers would standardize texts, reorder their parts, and develop a static, linear medium, mass produced and accessible to all. Now, in the twenty-first century, with the invention and spread of the electronic technologies yet another revolution has occurred.

Each new technology—the alphabet, the printing press, the electronic technologies—profoundly changes the way humans come to know and interact with the world. The reinvention of knowledge as a result of our interactions with computers is already occurring and is changing our life options and the kinds of educational opportunities required for students to succeed in this new knowledge environment. This chapter explores technology, its deep impacts on society, and the challenges it presents to educators.

SOCRATES' TALE

No one knows for sure on which day it happened or even which year. Maybe it never happened and is only a story fabricated by Plato's imagination. It is an important story, nevertheless.

It must have been early morning in the city of Athens when Socrates stepped out to begin his customary practice of journeying to the marketplace, the gymnasiums, the palaestrae, or the workshops of artisans to engage any person who presented the potential of a stimulating intelligence. Wearing his one simple and shabby robe, he was probably barefoot. His face was unusual for a Greek, with a spacious spread, a flat, broad nose, thick lips, and a heavy beard. He confessed to an unduly large paunch and hoped to reduce it by dancing. As he encountered Athenians engaged in their early morning preparations, he professed to know nothing. He often told fellow Athenians that he knew only questions, not answers. They, however, were not convinced. When one of them asked the oracle at Delphi if there was any man wiser than Socrates, the oracle is reported to have replied, "No one."

It was Socrates' habit to question all men's beliefs, prodding them with questions, demanding precise answers and consistent views, and generally making himself a terror to all who could not think clearly. His method was simple: he called for the definition of a large idea and then examined the definition to reveal its incompleteness, its contradictions, or its absurdity. He posed question after question after question, seeking a fuller definition. Sometimes he proceeded to a general conception by investigating a long series of particular instances. Other times, he used irony to point out the unintended consequences embedded in a definition or opinion (Durant, 1939).

On the morning in question, Socrates was employing his now famous "Socratic method" as he dialogued with his student, Phaedrus. Phaedrus was applauding the wonders of the alphabet; Socrates summarily challenged Phaedrus's enthusiasm. "Would it not be wiser," he must have queried that morning as the two of them strolled through the plaza, "to fear the disciples of the written word? Would they not have the 'show of wisdom' by knowing the letters without the reality of wisdom, being unable to grasp true ideas?" When Phaedrus persisted in his accolades for this new invention, Socrates illustrated his concerns with an allegory. It went something like this.

Theuth, the god of Naucratis, was the inventor of many arts, but his greatest discovery was the use of letters. Theuth, desiring that all Egyptians might have the benefit of his discovery, went to the god, Thamus, king of all Egypt, to share his discovery. In his enthusiasm, Theuth told Thamus that letters would make the Egyptians wiser and give them better memories. To Theuth's surprise, however, Thamus replied that Theuth had attributed to his invention a quality that did not exist. Instead, Thamus believed, the discovery of letters would create forgetfulness since others would trust to the external written characters and not remember themselves. Worse yet, letters would give their users not truth but only the semblance of truth. Users of letters would appear omniscient but would actually know nothing.

Having related the story of Theuth and Thamus, Socrates cautioned Phaedrus:

> He would be a very simple person, and quite a stranger to the oracles of Thamus, who should leave in writing or receive in writing any art under the idea that the written word would be intelligible or certain; or who deemed that writing was at all better than knowledge or recollection of the same matters. (Plato, 1928, pp. 323–324)

Sufficiently chastened and perhaps feeling a bit "simple," Phaedrus was left to reconsider his enthusiasm for alphabetic writing. Yet, even as he and Socrates pondered the implications of this newly invented alphabetic system, professional schoolmasters were establishing schools for the freeborn with a curriculum divided into three parts—music, gymnastics, and writing. Everyone learned to play the lyre, and much of the material of instruction was put into poetic or musical form for easy remembering. No one was considered educated who had not learned to wrestle, swim, and use the bow and sling. Writing included reading and arithmetic, which used letters for numbers. Slowly but consistently, these schoolmasters began promoting written text as a serious competitor to oral literature as the primary vehicle for storing and transmitting the cultural store of knowledge. The fact that we remember Socrates at all is proof of their success. "No one" may have been wiser than Socrates, but on this particular morning at least, it seems that Socrates may have missed the mark.

Writing and books remained the province of the guild of master scribes and of the church well into the Medieval Ages. Most medieval Europeans relied primarily on oral traditions for social, political, and economic interchange. As late as 1661, the French High Court passed a decree that scribes must not teach reading and that schoolmasters must not teach writing and that neither should be allowed to teach mathematics (Aries, 1962). But neither Socrates nor the French High Court could stem the tides of inevitable change.

With the development of the printing press and the production of paper in the mid-fifteenth century, the use of print spread rapidly. In less than a century, reading and writing had been added to traditional studies in religion and etiquette as the basis of an enlarged and extended elementary school. Although religion and etiquette are no longer an integral part of most educational settings, reading and writing have come to play a role in schools that might horrify Socrates and would surely enrage the French High Court.

Was Socrates the first technology phobic—the first to fear new technologies? Or was Socrates simply attempting to prompt Phaedrus to look beyond his enthusiasms and seek "truth" as it might apply to the often hidden consequences of human inventions? Perhaps Socrates was only hoping to push Phaedrus (and us) to ask questions about the ways in which technology impacts and shapes our lives. For just as the printing press played an important role in changing Western Civilization from a scribal to a print culture, the electronic technologies are playing a pivotal role in our transformation from a print culture to an electronic culture—the Information Age. As that transformation proceeds in every aspect of our lives, we have yet to fully realize the implications of these changes. Nevertheless, as Tapscott (1998, pp. 1–2) has written:

> For the first time in history, children are more comfortable, knowledgeable, and literate than their parents about an innovation central to society. And it is through the use of the digital media that the N-Generation will develop and superimpose its culture on the rest of society. Boomers stand back. Already these kids are learning, playing, communicating, working, and creating communities very differently than their parents. They are a force for social transformation.

TECHNOLOGY'S PLACE IN EDUCATION

The technology of the printing press provided a new social and intellectual context for modern schools. The technology of print became the "defining" technology of schools. A defining technology is a technology that results in fundamental changes in how people see themselves and their world. A defining technology serves as a filter, structuring and directing people's interpretations of their experiences (Bolter, 1984). For instance, the defining technology of the ancient world was the simple but elegant technology of the hand. Ancient craftsmen manipulated their world with tools that were extensions of their hands. Thinking "through" the technology of the hand, ancient philosophy was firmly rooted in a concrete world, examined with a craftsman's practical experience.

With print as a defining technology, the design and delivery of instruction has become firmly rooted in print-oriented practices. Most classrooms have reading books, language arts books, science books, social studies books, and math books. Most schools have a library and at least a part-time librarian or library aide. Most school districts and state departments of education have established elaborate mechanisms for adopting textbooks. Most schools teach a standardized, centralized, step-by-step curriculum while simultaneously promoting analytical habits of thinking. Schools depend on scientific, statistically analyzed, instructional design and assessment techniques.

Today's defining technologies, claims Bolter (1984), are the electronic technologies. Thinking "through" the electronic technologies, we are presented with alternate means of communicating, informing, and knowing. This leads to accelerated change and uncertainty while simultaneously opening up a wide range of possibilities. The challenge confronting today's global community is to design learning opportunities that prepare both young and old alike to benefit from and contribute to contemporary culture. We must choose whether we will reject the electronic technologies as Socrates and the French High Court rejected print or whether we will open ourselves to their possibilities and meet the challenge.

Modern education has sustained a long-term interest in the use of the electronic technologies as a remedy for educational problems. Teachers and parents are accustomed to hearing forecasts of an impending educational revolution each time a new technological innovation arrives on the scene. Fifty-five years ago, radio broadcasting was supposed to revolutionize education. Soon thereafter, teaching machines such as those proposed by Skinner were predicted to bring sweeping changes. Next, the television was touted as the medium that would solve problems facing education. Now, the microcomputer is often hailed as the next technological innovation to have a major curative impact on the educational process.

Consider the following:

- Wilbur Schramm (1960) writing about the new tutorial machines and instructional television in 1960 stated, "It seems uncommonly good fortune that such devices should come into use just at the time when our schools are being challenged both in quantity and quality."
- In 1970, the Commission on Instructional Technology stated its conviction that "technology can make education more productive, more individual, and powerful, make learning more immediate, give instruction a more scientific base and make access to education equal" (Tickton, 1970).
- In 1983, the National Commission on Excellence in Education, declaring a "nation at risk," recommended the teaching of computer science (programming) as one of the Five New Basics.
- The National Association of Secondary School Principals declared, "Yes, the electronic classroom is both an enduring and a potentially revolutionizing development in education" (Cromer, 1984).

These examples point to our growing awareness that the new electronic technologies have an important place in contemporary educational practice. These technologies will not replace print anymore than print replaced spoken language. Instead, as we learn about their possibilities and how to design learning opportunities that capitalize on those possibilities, the electronic technologies can and are becoming an integral part of the teaching and learning process. They can and are serving as "engines of change."

TODAY'S TECHNOLOGY USERS

Technological innovation, in the process of fulfilling its promise, generally passes through three stages (Naisbitt, 1982). The first stage follows the line of least resistance; technology is applied in ways that do not threaten people. During this stage, the chance that a new technology will be abruptly rejected is reduced. For instance, the vacuum tube that played such an important role in the development of the computer was originally only a parlor toy—"lightning in a bottle." Likewise, many of us had our first exposure to the microchip through digital watches, microwave ovens, and video games. They were fun and sometimes captivating but of little real consequence in the conduct of our daily life except as they served to familiarize us with the microchip. The first computers in classrooms were used for little more than free time activities or as reinforcement for those who had finished their work early.

The second stage of technological innovation begins when a new technology is merged with older technologies to perform functions we are already able to do but which may be done more efficiently with a new technology. Thus, some of the first books were nothing more than the tales of the traveling bard written down and more closely reflect the structure of oral language than that of more modern books (Jaynes, 1976). Educational television of the 1960s was often little more than a lecture on film—"a talking head." The computer was, at first, perceived only as a number cruncher popularly introduced as a pocket calculator. People have long been capable of calculation; a pocket calculator simply makes calculation more efficient. Many teachers' first use of the microcomputer was to keep an electronic version of their grade book or to assign simple drill programs for practicing math facts or spelling words—"electronic workbooks."

Most educational uses of computers in schools today are solidly second-stage applications. Word processors are used as sophisticated typewriters. Databases are large storage systems of information that students search to find answers to questions designed by the teacher and presented in worksheet format. Drill and practice programs designed to teach a myriad of isolated skills are common.

The third stage of technological innovation points to new directions and uses for technology that grow out of the technology itself. This occurs when individuals and eventually the culture at large discover ways to use a new technology to meet emerging needs and to satisfy new goals. Increasingly, today's students are third-stage technology users, discovering and inventing the many ways in which the new electronic technologies support their goals and offer them new possibilities for learning and connecting with others. Because the electronic technologies are distributed, interactive, malleable, and lacking central control, they are a vehicle for revolutionary change in every discipline, attitude, and social structure. Third-stage users recognize the new uses and new goals inherent in these electronic technologies and are learning to capitalize on their possibilities. When these third-stage users enter schools that ignore the information world that shapes their nonschool experiences, they often find school remote from their lives and somewhat irrelevant.

> Maggie is a Kindergartner. At her school, students are scheduled to go to the school's computer lab once a week for about 45 minutes. When Maggie's class goes to the computer lab, they use the mouse to double click on the folder with the "K" for Kindergarten. The teacher tells the children which program they are to work on that week. Usually, they are asked to use one of the programs that provides learning activities related to letter recognition, color recognition, or number recognition. Sometimes the programs are organized in a game format where a certain number

of correct responses result in completion of a puzzle or an animated, cartoonlike character dancing a jig. Other times, the program is much like an electronic workbook with students responding to a series of items presented in sequence.

One day about four months into the school year, Maggie's teacher was absent on "computer" day, and the substitute took the children to the computer lab. The substitute did not know much about computers and, after telling the children which program they were to use, left them to work alone. Maggie, bored with the assigned program, began to explore. In another folder, she stumbled upon a program called *Kid Pix*® program. Double clicking with her mouse on the program's icon, Maggie discovered a wonderful world for drawing. There were stamps to place multiple images of such things as trees or people or different animals on the monitor. She could select colors and draw brilliant shapes. She could select letters from an alphabet bar to invent the spelling of words to go with her pictures (Figure 1.1).

When Maggie went home that day, she told her parents about the program. Her father, knowing that Maggie's aunt had access to software for children, suggested that perhaps she might be able to get a copy of the program if she called her aunt. Maggie went to the phone and selected "Memory 2"—the code she had learned for calling her aunt. Maggie's aunt was not home. An answering machine responded to Maggie's call, asking for a message. Maggie left a brief message.

Later that night, when Maggie's aunt returned home, she listened to the messages on the answering machine. One of the messages was a quiet voice saying "I have a question. Please call me." Fortunately, Maggie's aunt recognized the voice. Unfortunately, it was well past Maggie's bedtime.

Early the next morning before Maggie left for school, Maggie's aunt returned the call. Maggie told her aunt about the program and asked if she had *Kid Pix®* program. Her aunt had a copy and agreed to send it. When the software arrived, Maggie and her father installed it on their computer. At five, Maggie had used the telephone, left a voice message, and asked not for a Barbie doll but software. She had used a variety of electronic technologies to meet her learning needs.

Increasingly, students who attend school are like Maggie. They are part of the Net Generation—"a generation of children, who in 1999, will be between the ages of two and twenty-two, not just those who are active on the Internet" (Tapscott, 1998, p. 3). Like Maggie, this generation of children is using the new electronic technologies to help create a culture of learning, where the learner enjoys enhanced responsibility, interactivity, and connections with others. Rather than relying on teachers and other adults to serve as the source of facts and theories, N-Geners partner with peers and adults to learn socially. They construct narratives to make sense of their experiences. They use electronic media to brainstorm, debate, and influence each other.

As they exploit the new electronic media, these students are creating a new, more powerful and more effective learning paradigm. These learners bring to learning a new and different set of expectations. Tapscott (1998, pp. 142–149) describes N-Geners' changing expectations about learning using the following eight shifts.

From Linear to Hypermedia Learning.   Traditional approaches to learning are linear and reflect the structure of books as the central learning tool. Most textbooks are written to be read from beginning to end. N-Geners' access to information is more interactive and nonsequential. They navigate back and forth between TV, books, video games, and the Internet. They typically participate in several activities at once.

From Instruction to Construction and Discovery.   As Papert (1996, p. 67) states, "The scandal of education is that every time you teach something, you deprive a child of the pleasure and benefit of discovery." Today's learners seek a shift away from teaching toward learning partnerships and learning cultures. They want to learn by doing, experiencing, inventing, and creating rather than consuming prepackaged instruction.

From Teacher-Centered to Learner-Centered.   The new media support shifting learning to the learner and away from the transmitter. This does not suggest, however, that teachers suddenly play lesser roles. Teachers remain critical and valued. Teachers remain essential to the creation and structuring of the learning experience. N-Geners are challenged by teachers who engage them in discussing, debating, researching, and collaborating on projects instead of by teachers who seek to "pass along" information.

From Absorbing Material to Learning How to Navigate and How to Learn.   N-Geners assess and analyze. More importantly, they synthesize. They engage information sources and people to build or construct higher-level structures and mental images.

From School to Lifelong Learning.   Previous generations divided life into the school years and the work years. Today's learners understand that in a world of constant and rapid change with knowledge doubling annually, learning is a lifelong process. They are not motivated by the prospect of "finishing" school. Rather, they are motivated by a challenge to master or a problem to solve.

From One-Size-Fits-All to Customized Learning.   Mass education was a product of the industrial economy. In an industrialized society, it made sense to assume that a large proportion of students at any given grade level would "tune in" and be able to absorb the information. Today's students expect to be treated as individuals—to have highly customized learning experiences based on their background, talents, and cognitive and interpersonal styles. After all, that is the way they structure their nonschool learning experiences.

From Learning as Torture to Learning as Fun.   One of the design goals of redesigned schools should be to make learning fun. Entertainment has always been a profound part of the learning process and teachers have, throughout history, been asked to convince their students to entertain ideas. From this perspective, the best teachers are entertainers. Entertainment builds enjoyment, motivation, and responsibility for learning.

From Teacher as Transmitter to Teacher as Facilitator.   As N-Geners assume more and more responsibility for their own learning, understand learning to be a social act, and use the new technologies available to them, they need teachers who can act as a resource and consultant to their learning. They seek teachers who can support their emerging competence as collaborators, researchers, analyzers, presenters, and resource users.

Finding a way to rethink today's schools in light of these shifting learner expectations will not come easily. Doing so will be a challenge not just because of our resistance to change but also because of the current atmosphere of cutbacks, high-stakes testing, reliance on standards to define the educational enterprise, lack of time as a result of the pressures of increased workloads, and reduced retraining budgets. Nevertheless, concludes Tapscott (1998, p. 149), "a whole generation of teachers needs to learn new tools, new approaches, and new skills."

REALIZING TECHNOLOGY'S PROMISE

How should learning be redesigned for today's learners? In January 1993, ABC television aired a special on education titled *Common Miracles: The New American*

Revolution in Learning, which was hosted by Peter Jennings and Bill Blakemore. At its conclusion, Peter Jennings stated:

> Education is how a society hands out its life chances; how it gives people options. Philosophers sometimes say the best definition of freedom is a good range of options. So, if this new revolution of learning is welcomed and done well, it will give many more Americans real freedom.

What are today's life chances and life options? Where do they come from, and how are they defined? The options that any educational system offers originate within the cultural context. Each culture shapes experience and assigns meaning to those experiences. Each culture creates a vision of what it means to be human and what can and ought to be part of the human experience. Individuals can benefit from and contribute to that vision when the mechanisms society invents for handing out life chances—its educational system—reflect the social context. And, as we have seen, the social context is in large part shaped by the technologies invented and used by a society.

In his 1992 book, *School's Out,* Lewis Perelman challenged readers to imagine that it is near the end of the nineteenth century and that a

> national task force on "excellence in horses" has issued a report exclaiming that America is "at risk" because its horse breeding and training are afflicted by a "rising tide of mediocrity." . . . the task force suggests, since the "horseless carriage" seems to be becoming pretty popular, all horses and their trainers should take a course in "automobile literacy" so they won't be scared by the noise of these curious contraptions. . . . Imagine, too, that top business leaders, instead of investing in Ford and Delco and Goodyear, instead of lobbying for paved roads and traffic lights and parking lots, put millions of dollars in "business-stable partnerships," "wrangler-of-the-year" awards and "break-the-mold" horse breeding demonstrations (pp. 19–20).

As ridiculous as this parody of the 1983 *Nation at Risk* report and contemporary school reform efforts might sound, Perelman claims it is an accurate reflection of how technologically blind recent educational reform efforts have been. One of the examples Perelman uses to communicate his vision of the way technology can inform learning is General Motors' CAMS Project. At the core of the CAMS Project is a mainframe computer programmed to know how to maintain and repair GM cars.

> Linked by a telecommunications network to computer terminals right in the repair bay of a dealer's garage, CAMS is constantly available to help the mechanic figure out what's wrong with the customer's car and how to fix it. CAMS can take data directly from electronic testing instruments, ask and answer questions, prescribe cures for automotive maladies. . . . CAMS, like any good expert system, is not engraved in stone—or even in silicon—but is continually upgraded and improved. In effect, it too is a "learner." . . . Most new CAMS users relied on the automatic mode for just a few weeks, then gradually shifted to the manual mode as their experience grew. In other words, the mechanic learned from the computer expert, and became more expert and effective themselves. So CAMS turned out,

completely inadvertently, to be a highly effective, automatic training system, a *teacher* in its own right. (pp. 26–27)

From examples like this, Perelman concludes that "teaching" and "learning" are being fused and transformed. Machines help humans to learn. Humans help machines to learn. Nobody calls or thinks about this kind of learning as education or training or school. Yet, for Perelman, the CAMS Project is a harbinger of "a new kind of learning system that will comprise the brains and nerves of the entire twenty-first century's economy" (p. 27). And, as such, it represents a vision of what ought to replace schools—hyperlearning tools contextualized in apprentice-style situations.

> Maybe folks who have been haranguing us to "save our schools" just don't understand that the classroom and teacher have as much place in tomorrow's learning enterprise as the horse and buggy have in modern transportation. Maybe they don't see that for the twenty-first century and beyond, learning is in and school is out. . . . The nations that stop trying to "reform" their education and training institutions and choose instead to totally replace them with a brand-new, high-tech learning system will be the world's economic powerhouses through the twenty-first century. (p. 20)

It would not be difficult for us to support Perelman's call for a more insightful consideration of the impacts of and roles for technology in planning educational experiences for today's learners. Nor would it be difficult for us to challenge inadequacies in the way technology is used in today's schools or the way learning opportunities are designed. It would also not be difficult for us to support the proposition that in contemporary society, learning is "in." These notions are well supported by the literature and are increasingly entering popular perceptions. What disturbs us is Perelman's assertion that using the new electronic technologies to promote learning implies that "school is out." If learning is in, then schooling is in.

Perhaps in the domain of workplace training, CAMS represents a viable alternative to schools. But we wonder how the mechanics learned to ask questions that the CAMS program might answer? How did they learn to answer the questions asked by the CAMS program? Where did the mechanics learn to interpret the symbols represented on the CAMS computer monitor? Where did they learn to understand the abstract, symbolic environment of the expert system and apply that understanding to their concrete experiences? Where is the expert system that helps mechanics learn to make political decisions, to develop their views about values, ethics, life, and death? Where is the expert system that teaches the nature of relationships and connections to others within the broader sociocultural context? Is it possible to design learning opportunities with hyperlearning tools that engage learners with nonoccupational learning? How can we ensure that all learners encounter these tools if there are no schools? How do a culture's young learn of their options?

Unlike Perelman, we believe a culture's ability to answer these questions depends on embracing the notion of school. Technology does indeed have a role in

Do you agree?

☆

learning but, for us, that role is not as a replacement for schools or teachers. Instead, we believe the electronic technologies can and should become an integral part of the teaching and learning process in schools just as they are being integrated throughout nonschool learning experiences. In this way, knowledgeable adults can support emerging learners as they struggle to become caring, knowledgeable, contributing members of their culture. In this way, skillful adults can help emerging learners develop the foundational habits and dispositions necessary for lifelong learning. In this way, caring adults can shape the contents of learning just as technology-using N-Geners are shaping the processes. In this way, thoughtful adults can make sure that learners who do not have technology access in their homes do not become know-nots and do-nots. As Tapscott (1998, p. 13) writes: "Our responsibilities are to them [N-Geners]—to give them the tools and opportunity to fulfill their destinies."

We recognize that educational change is a difficult and complex process. "It is easier to put a man on the moon," Massachusetts Institute of Technology professor Jerold Zachiarias said in 1966, "than to reform public schools." Almost two decades later, retired Admiral Hyman Rickover (1983) said, "Changing schools is like moving a graveyard." Yet, reformers keep trying. With each new technology, some see new possibilities and new urgencies. Claims predicting changes in teacher practice and student learning begin to dominate the literature in a wave of enthusiasm for the new technology, and efforts are made to bring these technologies and visions to classrooms. Not long after each innovation is introduced, academic studies to demonstrate the effectiveness of envisioned changes are conducted to compare changes with conventional instruction. These studies invariably "prove" that the innovation is better than conventional practice. Then, as Cuban (1986b, p. 5) wrote:

> Marring the general favor and scientific credibility enjoyed by the innovation, however, would be scattered complaints from teachers or classroom observers about the logistics of use, technical imperfections, incompatibility with current programs, or similar concerns. At a later point, surveys would document teacher use of the particular tool as disappointingly infrequent. . . . blaming intransigent teachers for blocking improvements through modern technology.

This cycle of exhilaration/scientific credibility/disappointment/teacher bashing describes the fate of motion pictures, radio, and instructional television. Will it also describe the fate of the newer electronic technologies—cable television, camcorders, VCRs, and a range of computer tools? The answer to this question lies, for us at least, in understanding the origins of the practices that these newer electronic technologies challenge.

Schools—their physical arrangements, the organization of content, the allocation of tasks and time, the rules that govern student and adult behavior—are designed to support the original mandate established for public schooling. Cuban (1986b, p. 57) defines this mandate as a charge to educators to "get a batch of students compelled to attend school to absorb certain knowledge and values while maintaining orderliness." Thus, teachers have developed and passed on strategies to maintain control, teach a prescribed content, capture student interest in that content, match levels of instruction to differences among students, and show tangible evidence that students are performing satisfactorily. Teachers have learned to ration their time and energy to cope with these demands, and certain teaching practices have emerged as resilient, simple, and efficient solutions.

For example, rows of desks provide easy access and surveillance. Teaching the entire class at one time is an efficient and convenient use of a teacher's time. Lecturing, recitation, seatwork, and homework drawn from texts are direct, uncomplicated ways of transmitting knowledge and directions to groups. The tools that teachers have added to their repertoire are ones that are simple, durable, flexible, and responsive to teacher-defined problems in meeting the demands of daily instruction. A chalkboard, then, is an integral component of classroom practice because it solves the problem of writing, erasing, and keeping material for days as well as the problem of providing easy access for all students to information. A textbook is an integral part of classroom practice because it solves other instructional problems. It is portable, compact, and durable. It can be read for hours or a few minutes, skimmed or read carefully. All students can be assigned the same sections. It travels easily.

Projectors, radios, television, and computers do not easily solve these problems. They are sometimes scarce, sometimes undependable. We are not always skilled at their use. We have few if any experiences seeing the ways in which others use these tools to promote learning. Thus, writes Cuban (1986b, p. 59): "The simplicity, versatility, and efficiency of those aids such as the textbook and chalkboard in coping with problems arising from the complicated realities of classroom instruction far exceed the limited benefits extracted from using machines."

Still, there are some teachers who do use a variety of tools as part of their instructional repertoire. There are teachers, for example, who believe that films, television, and Internet resources enhance textbook reading. There are teachers who are deeply concerned over visual illiteracy and seek to use television to enhance critical viewing skills. There are teachers who believe that using camcorders to produce video helps students to understand the anatomy of the media. There are some teachers who believe that teaching students to express content understanding with desktop publishing and Web page designs helps students structure and communicate their understanding and teaches them the ways in which these mediums can be used to persuade or entice. For such teachers, television, camcorders, and a variety of computer tools solve their daily problems of motivating students to learn and of supplying relevant and meaningful content that gets students to reason and solve problems. "In effect, the practical criteria these teachers use in deciding what is best for them and students are broader than ones used by their colleagues" (Cuban, 1986b). And, perhaps most importantly, these teachers recognize the possibilities inherent in the new electronic technologies to solve the problem of designing opportunities for student learning that mirror the tools and practices embedded in the larger technology context from which today's students come.

Because teaching with technology is never simply a matter of just using technology, practical criteria for designing learning opportunities for today's students depend on our ability to reach beyond time-honored design considerations. To capitalize on the possibilities of using technology to meet the challenge of our technological world, we must embrace new student urgencies, emerging views of learning, and new curricular opportunities as well as a range of technology possibilities. The remainder of this book explores a model for the design of learning opportunities for students that centers on a cluster of interacting considerations—foundations, contents, activities, tools, assessments, and environments. We begin this exploration in Chapter 2 by reviewing traditional models of design, identifying potential limitations inherent in these models, and introducing the elements of an alternative set of design criteria.

CHAPTER IDEAS

- The new electronic technologies have an important place in contemporary educational practice. These technologies will not replace print anymore than print replaced spoken language. Instead, as we learn about their possibilities and how to design learning opportunities that capitalize on those possibilities, the electronic technologies can and are becoming an integral part of the teaching and learning process. They can and are serving as "engines of change."
- Technological innovation, in the process of fulfilling its promise, generally passes through three stages (Naisbitt, 1982). The first stage follows the line of least resistance; technology is applied in ways that do not threaten people. The second stage of technological innovation begins when a new technology is merged with older technologies to perform functions we are already able to do but which may be done more efficiently with a new technology. The third stage of technological innovation points to new directions and uses for technology that grow out of the technology itself.
- Increasingly, today's students are third-stage technology users, discovering and inventing the many ways in which the new electronic technologies support their goals and offer them new possibilities for learning and connecting with others. Because the electronic technologies are distributed, interactive, malleable, and lacking central control, they are a vehicle for revolutionary change in every discipline, attitude, and social structure. Third-stage users recognize the new uses and new goals inherent in these electronic technologies and are learning to capitalize on their possibilities.
- Today's students are part of the Net Generation—"a generation of children, who in 1999, will be between the ages of two and twenty-two,

not just those who are active on the Internet" (Tapscott, 1998, p. 3). This generation is using the new electronic technologies to help create a culture of learning, where the learner enjoys enhanced responsibility, interactivity, and connections with others. Rather than relying on teachers and other adults to serve as the source of facts and theories, N-Geners partner with peers and adults to learn socially.

- These students are creating a new, more powerful and more effective learning paradigm. These learners bring to learning a new and different set of expectations. Tapscott (1998, pp. 142–149) describes N-Geners' changing expectations about learning as shifts from linear to hypermedia learning, from instruction to construction and discovery, from teacher-centered to learner-centered, from absorbing material to learning how to navigate and how to learn, from school to lifelong learning, from one-size-fits-all to customized learning, from learning as torture to learning as fun, and from teacher as transmitter to teacher as facilitator.

- Finding a way to rethink today's schools in light of these shifting learner expectations will not come easily. Nevertheless, concludes Tapscott (1998, p. 149), "a whole generation of teachers needs to learn new tools, new approaches, and new skills."

- Technology has a role in learning but not as a replacement for schools or teachers. Instead, the electronic technologies can and should become an integral part of the teaching and learning process in schools just as they are being integrated throughout nonschool learning experiences. In this way, knowledgeable adults can support emerging learners as they struggle to become caring, knowledgeable, contributing members of their culture. In this way, skillful adults can help emerging learners develop the foundational habits and dispositions necessary for lifelong learning. In this way, caring adults can shape the contents of learning just as technology-using N-Geners are shaping the processes. In this way, thoughtful adults can make sure that learners who do not have technology access in their homes do not become know-nots and do-nots.

- Schools—their physical arrangements, the organization of content, the allocation of tasks and time, the rules that govern student and adult behavior—are designed to support the original mandate established for public schooling. Cuban (1986b, p. 57) defines this mandate as a charge to educators to "get a batch of students compelled to attend school to absorb certain knowledge and values while maintaining orderliness."

- Projectors, radios, television, and computers do not easily solve these problems. They are sometimes scarce, sometimes undependable. We are not always skilled at their use. We have few if any experiences seeing the ways in which others use these tools to promote learning. Still, there are some teachers who do use a variety of tools as part of their instructional repertoire. For these teachers, television, camcorders, and a variety of computer tools solve their daily problems of motivating students to learn and of supplying relevant and meaningful content that gets students to reason and solve problems. "In effect, the practical criteria these teachers use in deciding what is best for them and students are broader than ones used by their colleagues" (Cuban, 1986b).

- Because teaching with technology is never simply a matter of just using technology, practical criteria for designing learning opportunities for today's students depend on our ability to reach beyond time-honored design considerations. To capitalize on the possibilities of using technology to meet the challenge of our technological world, we must embrace new student urgencies, emerging views of learning, and new curricular opportunities as well as a range of technology possibilities.

DESIGNING OPPORTUNITIES FOR LEARNING

When I became a teacher, I was pretty sure I knew exactly what it meant to be an educator. After all, I had seen others teach for sixteen years. My experiences told me that teachers follow a prescribed curriculum defined by the textbooks chosen by the school district and neatly laid out as a sequential series of facts, concepts, and skills. If they were secondary teachers, they taught a particular subject usually in an hour period. It they were elementary teachers, they neatly divided the day into segments and taught a series of subjects. Helping students learn consisted of following the text, creating worksheets, asking questions, and checking students' work. The strategies I learned as part of my teacher preparation program reinforced these notions and helped me develop effective ways to continue this tradition of learning.

Then I met Alex. Alex is my son, and, although he has always been willing to do what he was told to do at school, he often asks some very hard questions. At six, after a long day of sounding out words in his reading circle, Alex asked why he had to learn all that. We tried to explain that it was part of learning to read. Alex pointed out that he wanted to read so he could learn things. He couldn't see what sounding out words had to do with it. When he was in high school, he asked for help with algebra. He was working on factoring equations. He told us he had to master factoring equations but that he did understand why. Neither his mother nor I were very helpful. To this day, I'm not sure either Alex or I have ever had to factor an equation.

Knowing Alex has challenged me to rethink the approaches I use to design learning opportunities for my students.

Richard Druxman
High School Teacher

Student learning is not accidental; it is the direct result of the process that educators use to intentionally plan appropriate learning experiences for students. Yet, designing learning opportunities that meet today's technological challenges while simultaneously using technology as part of the solution is one of today's most pressing demands. Traditional strategies for the design of learning were developed to meet the needs of an industrialized, print-dependent society. Critics of these strategies suggest that students actually learn lessons that detract from their ability to fully participate in today's society and that these lessons, in fact, interfere with learning. If educators are to design more appropriate learning opportunities for students, they must look beyond the voices of current practice, curriculum guides, and educational fads. They must seek deeper answers to the question: What are the emerging principles and guidelines for the design of learning opportunities?

This chapter looks at the history of curriculum and instruction and, specifically, at traditional models for designing learning opportunities. It examines some of the criticisms of traditional instructional design and presents two considerations that can serve as the basis of an alternative model of design. Finally, this chapter poses six questions that must guide the construction of a more contemporary model of design.

Contemporary historians do not attribute the invention of computers to any particular individual. Nor have they affixed a date to its invention. Yet, someday, someone will write with authority: "In the second half of the twentieth century, a disparate collection of scientists, mathematicians, and engineers brought together a cluster of concepts and rendered those concepts in silicon and plastic. A group of enterprising entrepreneurs made this invention readily accessible, changing a print culture into an electronic culture. Once again, human learning was reinvented."

In 1990, Paul and Denise Martinez elected to become part of a pilot program sponsored by their local school district. This pilot established an alternative school where families could choose to send their children to school for half of the instructional day and then "home school" their children for the remainder of the day. Two of their children, Amber and Brandon, are now middle school age, and two of their children, Heather and Joshua, are high school age. From 8 o'clock until noon, Amber, Heather, Brandon, and Joshua gather at their neighborhood school with other children in the program. They participate in an instructional program designed to cover the traditional curriculum. They use a programmed series to complete exercises in each of the subject areas. Teachers at the alternative school help them to decipher the concepts presented by each lesson, to complete the assigned questions, and to correct their errors. The children understand that this is a necessary part of their educational program, but it is not their favorite part of their learning day.

When morning lessons are over, the children return home for lunch. After lunch, the children's learning activities take on a completely different flavor. Sometimes, the family joins other families for field trips, learning exchanges, and social events. Other times, Amber, Heather, Brandon, and Joshua pursue their own learning projects. This month, Heather and Joshua have chosen to participate in the organization of the upcoming regional home-schooling conference. This yearly event brings together home-schooling families from a four-state region to share their experiences and to participate in a wide range of seminars presented by educators, politicians, and other experts.

Paul and Denise have been elected Program Chairs for this year's conference. Heather and Joshua volunteered to design databases to keep track of registration and to send out confirmation letters. They will also use Quicken, an accounting program, to keep track of the money received for registration and spent for speakers and facilities, and to orchestrate the design and publication of the conference brochures and program. As part of their work, they have researched accounting principles like debits and credits. They have mastered desktop publishing and editing principles. They have studied principles of layout and design from the advertising world. They were amazed at the amount of reading, writing, mathematics, and art they learned and are proud of their publications and contributions to the conference.

Amber and Brandon were not particularly interested in the upcoming conference. Instead, they had recently begun to wonder if they wanted to continue with home schooling. Amber at 13 is concerned that she might not meet anyone she wanted to date when her parents finally decided she was old enough. Brandon at 12 was wondering if participating in school sports would be more fun than playing on the family's intramural church team. Paul and Denise were willing to consider Amber and Brandon's growing interest in public school but wanted them to make informed decisions.

With help from their parents, Amber and Brandon designed a plan to study the pros and cons of home schooling. First, Amber and Brandon used the Internet to make connections with a number of other home-schooled students throughout the United States. Second, using the Internet, they made connections with a number of middle school classes. Third, they constructed a survey that asked both home-schooled students and public school students questions about their school experiences. They designed their survey and e-mailed it to all the students they had contacted. As survey responses were returned, Amber and Brandon tallied the data and constructed comparison graphs for each of their questions. Fourth, Amber and Brandon undertook a robust reading program. They used the World Wide Web to search for articles and studies related to home schooling and joined online discussions about home schooling. In addition, their parents helped them obtain a number of classic books on education (e.g., Rousseau's *Emile* and Whitehead's *The Aims of Education*). Amber and Brandon's parents wanted them to think deeply about the purposes and processes of education as well as popular opinion and home-schooling practices.

Bringing the results of all their studies, conversations, and surveys together, Amber and Brandon wrote a position paper on the pros and cons of home schooling from a student's perspective. They notified everyone who had answered their survey when the position paper was done, and many students requested an "electronic" copy. Brandon decided that he would like to continue with the part-time home-schooling program; Amber is still trying to decide.

The world of learning that Amber, Heather, Brandon, and Joshua are experiencing in the afternoons is dramatically different from the world of school they experience in the mornings. Their afternoon world is rich with information, with new and interesting technologies, with experiences directly connected to their lives, desires, and interests, and with meaningful, socially oriented learning. Their afternoon learning experiences are not governed by the need to master a collection of facts or isolated, segmented skills. Heather and Joshua learn mathematics through productive, real-world applications. Amber and Brandon are connected to a wide range of students among whom they can always find someone with common interests and the desire to form collaborations. Their afternoon learning experiences occur in a social context enhanced by interactions with others who can model more advanced learning. They are third-stage technology users, learning in ways not possible without the new electronic technologies.

How will students who do not have resources similar to those available to Amber, Heather, Brandon, and Joshua learn to participate in this technology-rich world? How can schools design learning opportunities that reflect the information-rich, technology-rich world of today's students? Educators today often find themselves between two cultures, wondering how this astonishing tapestry of technological resources might weave thoughts and ideas into a subtle, rich learning environment even as they continue to design learning experiences for students that reflect more traditional educational practice. Many educators find that designing learning opportunities that meet the challenges presented by these technologies while simultaneously using them as part of the solution is one of today's most pressing dilemmas.

THE EFFICIENCY MODEL OF LEARNING

Modern educational strategies for designing learning experiences for students were developed to meet the needs of an industrialized, print-oriented society. In the second half of the nineteenth century, European scholars theorized that it was possible to develop methods that would make the study of human behavior more scientific. The ideas of Wilhelm Wundt in Germany and Francis Galton in England heavily influenced the development of a new American School of Psychology and, along with it, the emerging field of educational psychology. Edward Thorndike, a student of two influential American psychologists of the time, Stanley Hall and William James, enthusiastically applied the new scientific psychology to the control of learning.

In his still-influential book, *Principles of Learning* (1921), Thorndike suggested that learning would occur if subject matter was carefully refined and sequenced and students appropriately reinforced. The learning he advocated was primarily connectivist, an extension of Pavlovian classical conditioning. His prescription for intense practice as a condition of learning remains popular today, and his work supporting empirical investigation as the basis of scientific instruction continues to influence the educational community.

The popularity of theories that advocated the scientific control of human behavior in education reflected larger reform efforts in society and business. Frederick Taylor, an industrialist, developed a method for studying the movements of workers on assembly lines. This method, which used a process of measurement and control, led to increased production. This efficiency movement in industry became increasingly popular as industrialists argued that the scientific method could be used to control human behavior and eliminate production problems. Elliot Eisner (1994) wrote:

> What one sees here is a highly rationalized managerial approach to the production process. The worker's job is to follow the procedures prescribed. In this system, individual initiative and inventiveness by workers were regarded as sources of error, like sand in a motor, they impeded the operation of a smooth running machine that depended on adherence to formula. (p. 10)

Although Frederick Taylor was not an educator, when schools faced criticism in the early 1900s related to "inefficient" practices and poor learning by students, his educational disciples turned eagerly to scientific management as a way to improve schools. In 1911, for instance, the High School Teachers Association of New York City invited Harrington Emerson, an efficiency expert with the Santa Fe railroad, to speak at its December meeting on the topic "Scientific Management and High School Efficiency." In his speech, Emerson defined the four essential elements necessary for efficiency as (1) definite and clear aims, (2) an organization capable of attaining these aims, (3) equipment adequate to achieve the aims, and (4) a strong executive who could achieve the aims. He further enunciated twelve principles of efficiency: high ideals, common sense, competent advisors, discipline, fair dealing, standard records, planning, standard conditions, standardized operations, standard instructions, standard schedules, and efficiency reward (Kleibard, 1995).

Gagne (1987) describes these early efforts in instructional design as the confluence of the scientific study of human learning first practiced by Thorndike and his followers and the availability of new technologies. The technologies of interest included both procedures and tools. New techniques, such as programmed learning and audiovisual materials, were conceptualized as a way to increase the efficiency of learning. These two fields, the study of optimal conditions for human learning and the use of well-developed procedures and tools, combine to create the context in which educational decisions are made and, thus, influence most traditional approaches to the design of instruction.

The Efficiency Model and Designs for Learning

For today's educators, "efficiency" principles coupled with the "science" of exact measurement and precise standards remain central guides for the design of learning. Among the many models based on this approach to instructional design are Programmed Instruction (Skinner, 1958), Instructional Objectives (Mager, 1962), Mastery Learning (Bloom, Madaus, & Hastings, 1981), Gagne's Conditions of Learning (1965), and ADDIE (Fardouly, 1998).

Programmed Instruction. B. F. Skinner, the father of operant conditioning, is usually credited with the development of programmed instruction. Skinner (1954) believed conditions in the typical classroom were aversive to learning. In such settings, he stated, a diverse group of people at different levels of understanding are forced to listen to the same presentation. Skinner further argued that under these conditions, learning progress is slow since it is difficult to reinforce each individual's learning. A single teacher, states Skinner, cannot adequately reinforce 30 or more students.

Skinner's solution was programmed instruction. Programmed instruction is instruction designed to present information in a sequential series of small steps or frames, each requiring a response from the learner. If correct, the learner is given the next step and reinforced positively for the response. If incorrect, the learner is retaught the concept. In the late 1950s and early 1960s, large numbers of print-based programmed instructional materials were developed for both industrial training and the public schools. In the early days of computer use in education, the programmed instruction model led to large numbers of drill and practice programs.

Specifying Behavioral Objectives.

Designing learning opportunities from a conventional approach requires the identification of specific, observable behaviors that are to be performed by the learner. While objectives were advocated in teaching as early as the 1900s, the behavioral objectives movement gained momentum in the 1950s and 1960s along with programmed instruction. In Tyler's (1975) famous eight-year study of schools, he reported that many of the problems of instruction seemed to be related to the fact that schools did not specify objectives. Teachers were unclear about what they were to be teaching, and students were not aware of what they were supposed to be learning.

The major implementation of behavioral objectives occurred when Bloom published the *Taxonomy of Educational Objectives* (1956). The use of behavioral objectives to design opportunities for learning was further supported by Mager (1962) when he wrote: "Before you prepare instruction, before you choose materials, machine, or method, it is important to be able to state clearly what your goals are" (p. viii). To clearly state educational goals, Mager developed a procedure for writing complete and precise objectives. According to this procedure, well-written objectives state the terminal behavior to be displayed by the learner, the criterion or standard by which the behavior will be evaluated (e.g., 70 percent of items correct on the test), and the conditions under which the behavior will be displayed.

Since his original work in 1962, Mager has continued to elaborate his system for the design of instruction. He believes that his system ensures that instruction correctly solves instructional problems, derives from demonstrated needs, is appropriately adjusted to the needs of each student, and contributes to student eagerness to learn more. For Mager, there are four broad phases in the instructional design process: analysis, development, implementation, and improvement. Analysis seeks to identify key skill outcomes. The development phase includes the drafting of measurement instruments, the design of relevant practice, and the selection of content derived to support learning objectives. Implementation includes showing students how the course objectives and instructional modules are related as well as collecting materials and arranging the environment. The final phase, improvement, centers on a continuous determination of how well the instruction works (Mager, 1962).

Mastery Learning.   The "learning for mastery" approach (Bloom, Madaus, & Hastings, 1981) is based on the idea that learners will succeed in learning a task if given the exact amount of time they need. Mastery Learning opposes the practice of assuming that only about a third of a class will learn the material taught, suggesting that "this set of expectations, which fixes the academic goals of teachers and students, is the most wasteful and destructive aspect of the present educational system" (p. 51). In contrast, Bloom, Madaus, & Hastings suggested that at least 90 percent of students can master learning goals if given the time and appropriate methods and materials.

Thus, Mastery Learning proposes a test, teach, retest, reteach model. Using this model, design of instruction creates opportunities for students to learn a concept or skill, tests to identify those learners who have not mastered the concept or skill, reteaches the concept or skill, and retests for mastery. This process is repeated until the concept or skill is learned. Bloom et al. suggested a variety of strategies to provide conditions for Mastery Learning including the use of tutors, small group study, peer tutoring, programmed instruction, audiovisual materials, and games.

The Conditions of Learning Model.   Gagne's (1965) "conditions of learning" model is based on an understanding of human learning and its relationship to instruction. Prior to Gagne, learning was often conceptualized as a single, uniform concept. No distinction was made between learning to load a rifle and learning to solve a complex mathematics problem. Gagne's "conditions of learning" model suggests that there are various types of human learning and that each type requires different kinds of instructional strategies. For example, while Thorndike advocated continuous practice as the key to learning, Gagne suggested practice was effective only for certain types of learning (e.g., learning involving kinesthetic skills, such as typing or playing ball). Conversely, when learning cognitive strategies, the learner must be presented with and assisted in solving puzzling problems. For this type of learning, practice without a change in perception can be counterproductive.

Gagne's model for the design of instruction includes a sequence of external, instructional events that guide the design of instruction. Instructional events, according to Gagne's framework, must first gain the student's attention and then provide a means to share the goals of instruction. Next, instructional events must be designed that stimulate recall, provide presentations in all modalities, and create linkages to meaningful frameworks. The final three instructional events must monitor and adjust student learning, require application, and bring closure to learning. For each of these phases, Gagne has aligned internal learning events with each of the external instructional events.

Although Gagne's approach does not address affective conditions for learning, Wiburg has added conditions that must be present inside the learner for learning to occur. If students are unable to attend to stimuli or are emotionally not ready for learning a specific subject, for example, it may be necessary to redesign learning appropriate to these affective or cognitive conditions. Table 2.1 summarizes Gagne's original conditions of learning model and adds Wiburg's affective/cognitive conditions.

TABLE 2.1	RELATIONSHIP OF INSTRUCTIONAL EVENTS TO LEARNING EVENTS		

Instructional Events	Affective/Cognitive Conditions	Internal Learning Events
Gain attention	Ability to attend	Attend
Share goals of instruction	Emotional desire for learning	Expectancy
Stimulate recall	Ability to retrieve	Recall of related info
Present in all modalities	Auditory and visual processing ability	Perception
Provide meaningful frameworks	Learner schema relevant to new concept	Encoding in long-term memory in meaningful ways
Monitor and adjust	Feeling of getting it	Oh, I see. I get it.
Require application	Intellectual confidence	Secure schema
Closure	Satisfaction	Retention

ADDIE.   Recently, with the advent of the capacity for designers to create technology-based instructional materials, designers have formalized the design process, integrating elements from all the previous efficiency models. Although this model of design is most often applied to workplace training, it is being used to design instruction throughout K–12 education.

ADDIE represents a systematic approach to **A**nalysis, **D**esign, **D**evelopment, **I**mplementation, and **E**valuation. The ADDIE process begins with a detailed analysis of who the learners are, what they already know, what their learning characteristics are, what they need or want to learn, why they need it, and in what environment the learning will be applied. Once the analysis is complete, design and development begin. Design and development depend on careful and systematic articulation of the objectives that will govern instruction, what skills are to be developed, what resources and strategies will be used, how content will be sequenced, and what techniques will be used to ascertain that objectives have been met. The next step, implementation, involves teaching learners how to make the best use of learning materials, presenting classroom instruction, and/or coordinating and managing instruction either locally or from a distance. The final step, evaluation, is the assessment of both teachers and learners in order to form a basis for improvement and further development of instruction (Fardouly, 1998).

Integrated Learning Systems: A Case Study

One way in which the principles of traditional instructional design have been translated into practice involves the use of computers to create Integrated Learning Systems (ILSs). Integrated Learning Systems are software programs designed around the identification of a series of identified skills. Developers of integrated learning systems analyze the content to be learned, breaking it down into its fundamental subskills, ordering them sequentially. The teacher's manual accompanying the system usually has a diagram similar to those found in teacher's manuals for textbooks called a scope and sequence. For instance, ILSs associated with reading instruction often begin with word recognition objectives divided into initial consonants and vowels moving on to the basic patterns of letter configuration associated with simple words. Later lessons move to instruction in blends, diphthongs, and digraphs. Vocabulary lessons are designed using words associated with grade-level instruction. Comprehension lessons reflect the basic skills of comprehension such as following directions, determining cause and effect, detecting sequence, distinguishing between fact and fiction, and finding the main idea. Numerous multiple-choice items for each comprehension skill have been designed at each grade level to be presented to students when appropriate.

Math lessons often begin with simple counting, move to one-digit addition, two-digit addition with no carrying, two-digit addition with carrying, and on through the computational skills of subtraction, multiplication, division, fractions, and so on. Word problems reflecting these computational skills have also been designed at grade level–appropriate reading levels. The software for the Integrated Learning System is, thus, comprised of a large bank of questions related to each of the identified tasks and a set of programmed rules for determining which questions are presented to which student when.

Although many Integrated Learning Systems are designed to run from a school or district server with students completing assigned items at the computer, some ILSs bypass the expense of networked computers and individual student workstations. Renaissance Learning, Inc. has created integrated learning systems for both math and reading that support teachers' planning and management of instruction using a single classroom computer. To use *Accelerated Math®* and *Accelerated Reader®,* all that is needed is a classroom computer, a printer, and an AccelScan® optical mark reader. Ms. Archer's story may help to illustrate how ILSs might shape instruction. It was originally presented in Norton and Sprague's (2001) *Technology for Teaching.*

> Nicki Archer teaches middle school mathematics. In their efforts to ensure that all students master mathematics skills and to support teachers in achieving this goal, Ms. Archer's school has purchased *Accelerated Math®* for grades 6 and 7 as well as the Pre-Algebra programs. The local high school has purchased the Algebra 1, Algebra 2, Geometry, Pre-Calculus, Calculus, and Basic Math software for use in its math program.
>
> Students in Ms. Archer's class participate in whole- and small-group instruction, textbook activities, and real-life problem-solving situations two days a week. The other three days students work individually or in small groups on exercises printed with the *Accelerated Math®* software. As they solve the problems on the printed worksheets, they fill in bubbled scan sheets to reflect their answers. When a worksheet is complete, students scan their answers back into the computer and their work is automatically scored. The next practice assignment is printed for students, taking into consideration the objectives mastered and new objectives to be

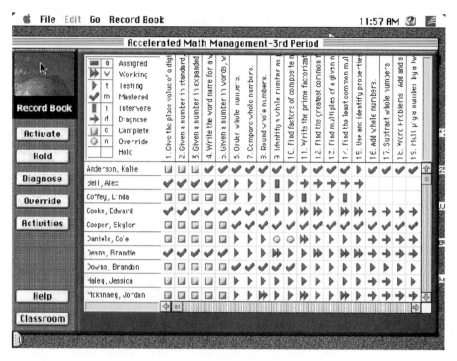

FIGURE **2.1**

A SAMPLE ASSIGNMENT BOOK FROM *ACCELERATED MATH*—GRADE 6.
Source: *Accelerated Math*® is a registered trademark of Renaissance Learning, Inc. Used with permission.

learned. Ms. Archer is able to identify objectives she thinks are important for students and choose or eliminate some of the objectives included in the software using a computer-based Assignment Book (see Figure 2.1).

In preparing for the days when students will be working with *Accelerated Math*, Ms. Archer must spend her planning time monitoring student progress, printing out worksheets to avoid backlogs during class, and grouping students who are working on common objectives. She makes extensive use of the 31 different reports available. In particular, Ms. Archer depends on the Diagnostic Report that provides her with a summary of each class and reports the highest mastered objective, total objectives mastered, problems attempted, and percentage scores on both the practice sheets and the objective test. She also prints monthly Parent Information Reports for students to take home. These reports provide parents with information about the objectives students have mastered each month and the objectives that are currently targeted. It includes students' test scores as well.

An Excerpt from Priscilla's Journal:

I talked with my niece, Kate, today. It was her first day in fifth grade. When I asked her how the day went, she was enthusiastic. She liked her teacher. She knew many of the children from last year. When I asked her what she had learned, she told me about the "rule" that all fifth graders had to remember all the states and capitals in the United States. They would get a certificate at the end of the year if they knew them all. She said they had started learning them that day but that it was kind of boring since she already knew them all. So, I mentioned several states and she named the capitals. I mentioned several capitals and she named the states. I asked her how come she knew all that. "I learned it from the *Geo Safari*™ that you gave me last Christmas," she told me. "I guess," reflected Kate, "everyone else doesn't have one."

For those of you unfamiliar with the lore of computerized toys, a *Geo Safari* is a tabletop, computerized console with a keyboard on the base and a backrest for game cards. It comes with a package of game cards on geography, and Kate's gift had included two additional packages. Children place the cards on the backrest and enter the code from the card into the computer. They can then select up to three players and up to 99 seconds for length of response time. When the Go button is pushed, a word is presented to the player, and the player identifies the number of the correct response and types it on the keyboard. Players get up to three chances to enter the correct answer. This software, like that of the ILS's, clearly rests on the efficiency model of learning and includes concepts like division of content to be learned into isolated sets of facts and skills, sequencing of instruction, providing appropriate reinforcement, programmed instruction, and learning for mastery.

Using the state card that presents a map of the United States with numbers and names on each of the states, Kate had mastered the name and location of each state and learned its capital. Priscilla's journal entry ended with the following:

> Poor Kate. It's going to be a dull year in social studies. If toys like *Geo Safaris* can support educational goals like memorizing all the states and capitals, why don't schools just buy a few *Geo Safaris* for every fifth-grade classroom and let children play their way to knowing? It doesn't take weeks of memorizing flash cards and filling out worksheets. It doesn't take a sophisticated, expensive Integrated Learning System. Why do students get the whole year? If the solution is as simple as Kate thinks (just get a *Geo Safari*), why do we value knowing the states and capitals enough to make it a fifth-grade goal? Instead, if given the opportunity, I wonder what Kate and her friends could figure out about why cities are located where they are, how geographic circumstances might shape the way we conduct our lives, and even why states have capitals in the first place. The process of figuring that out has got to be more important than memorizing states and capitals.

Questioning the Efficiency Model

Notions about learning associated with the efficiency model focus attention on individual learning. The completion of individual assignments, individual grading systems, and single desks in rows communicate that learning is something students must do by themselves. These notions focus instructional attention on the learning of small, isolated skills and facts. In many elementary schools, morning instruction consists of an hour of reading, an hour of language arts, and an hour of mathematics. In the afternoon, instruction often includes an hour of social studies and an hour of science. For middle and high school students, instruction is generally divided into one-hour periods or 90-minute blocks. Each period or block is dedicated to a subject—Algebra, U.S. History, or Biology. Little or no time is spent connecting separate subject areas in either elementary, middle, or high schools.

Notions about learning associated with the efficiency model focus attention on books as the primary source of information. Students are given a reading book, a science book, or a mathematics book and told to "read the book and answer the questions." These texts focus attention on the "overt curriculum"—the content to be covered. They do not attend to what students learn about learning—the "covert curriculum."

Notions about learning associated with the efficiency model focus on methods or techniques for analyzing and presenting what should be learned, not on learning goals. Teachers are conceptualized as technicians charged with the job of increasing the speed of learning. These notions view knowledge as independent of the situations in which it is learned and used. Yet, researchers who have studied learning in everyday situations and different cultural settings suggest that knowledge is not some kind of independent phenomena, but rather that it is situated in the activity, context, and culture in which it is learned (Brown, Collins, & Duguid, 1989). In short, how something is learned is just as important as what is learned.

Critics of the efficiency model express concern that the principles of learning associated with the model may actually detract from learners' ability to fully participate in today's society. Educators who plan to design learning experiences for today's students must design for the whole of learning. They must recognize that much of learning is social, that learning is not for later life but for living, and that students are not vessels to be filled but constructors of their knowledge. They must create environments that promote problem solving, cooperation, communication, critical thinking, and learning how to learn—the same attributes reported as necessary for participating in evolving, nonschool contexts (e.g., Committee for Economic Development, 1985).

Even as teachers continue to depend on the efficiency model as a guide for designing learning opportunities for students, their students know that outside of school they are learning from their peers, from television, and, for an increasing number of them, from and with computers. Outside of school they experience a fast-paced, varied, ever-changing world of information, ideas, and beliefs. The answers to their dilemmas are not always found on the pages of their textbooks or in the lectures of their teachers.

Learning in School and Learning Outside of School

Resnick (1987) notes four categories that differentiate learning in school from learning in contemporary social contexts outside of school. One, school learning depends on individual cognition while learning outside of school depends on shared cognition. The conventional classroom with its methods of interaction and testing is designed with the assumption that learning is an individual process. This has become, Resnick writes, the dominant view even though most other human activity includes learning that is highly social. People learn communally but are taught individually.

Second, school learning centers on pure mentation while learning in broader social contexts depends on tool manipulation. Schools support the belief that thought is a process that happens in one's head. Environmental supports—either social or physical props—are occasionally allowed in learning but are almost always denied in testing. This ignores the innovative and productive ways in which people deploy their environment in order to take advantage of tools that can help spread the burden of cognition.

Third, school learning centers on symbol manipulation while learning in broader social contexts depends on reasoning with "stuff." Conventional school-work involves students in abstract symbol manipulations that are often divorced from connections between the symbols and the real world to which they refer. Out-side school, people either manipulate the stuff of the real world directly, or if that is not possible, they work with symbols closely connected to their activities. Symbols in school are opaque and disconnected and are often ends in themselves rather than tools to help achieve ends defined by authentic activity.

Last, school learning focuses on generalized learning while learning in broader social contexts centers on situation-specific competencies. School learning is designed to be abstract and general in order to assure maximum transference. Recent research (Lave, 1988) indicates that abstract knowledge is both difficult to learn and difficult to apply. Less abstract, situation-specific knowledge appears to be much more easily acquired and can be transferred more readily to provide scaffolding for additional knowledge. This permits the construction of connections between disparate situations.

As we move farther into the twenty-first century, schools must begin to prepare students for a world rooted in information and technology. Such a world calls for students with the kinds of skills and understandings that enable them to function within and contribute to this emerging world. Students must have opportunities to participate in problem-oriented learning activities relevant to their interests and worthy of their investment of time and effort. Their learning must depend on more than symbol manipulation, generalized learning, pure mentation, and individual cognition. It must lead to competence acquired through authentic activity presented in an environment that encourages collaboration. Students have the right to expect that the knowledge and technology capabilities commonplace in their homes and communities are accessible in their schools. They have the right to a learning environment rich with resources both printed and electronically generated.

RETHINKING THE DESIGN OF LEARNING OPPORTUNITIES: TWO IMPORTANT IDEAS AND AN EDUCATIONAL DILEMMA

The efficiency model found its expression in perceptions of learning that pivoted on stimulus-response learning and in instructional practices that adopted programmed instruction, behavioral objectives, mastery learning, and a consideration of the relationship between the conditions of learning and a sequence of external instructional events. Using this model, the design of opportunities for learning rested on the clear identification and articulation of a sequence of objectives, taught systematically, chained together over time, and reinforced through repeated practice. As we search for a new design model, there are two important considerations that can serve as a platform for beginning. These considerations include an emerging view of learning potentials and abilities and a vision of learning called constructivism.

A View of Intelligence

What are humans capable of in their intellectual lives? Answers to this and many similar questions are generally dominated by a collection of ideas that stress the existence and importance of mental powers—capacities variously termed *rationality, intelligence,* or *mind.* The search for the essence of humanity has led to a focus on knowledge and those capacities that figure in knowing. Through the ages, some have explained this essence as a single, unitary function often summarized as intelligence or IQ. Others have explored this essence as a collection of many capacities. Franz Gall identified 37 human factors or powers of mind. J. P. Guilford favored 120 vectors of mind.

The debate continues. There are those who believe that different portions of the nervous system mediate diverse intellectual capacities; there are those who believe that major intellectual functions are the property of the brain as a whole. For most educational practice, however, the unified theory of a single intellectual power, an IQ, has dominated our perception of humans' capacity to know and think.

Against this backdrop of competing perceptions, Gardner (1983) has convincingly argued for the existence of several relatively autonomous human intellectual competencies. He freely admits that the exact nature and breadth of each intellectual competency has not been satisfactorily established nor has the precise number of intelligences been fixed. Yet, Gardner believes firmly in the existence of at least some intelligences that are relatively independent of one another and that these competencies "can be fashioned and combined in a multiplicity of adaptive ways by individuals and cultures . . ." (p. 9).

Gardner proposed seven distinct intelligences: linguistic intelligence, musical intelligence, spatial intelligence, logical-mathematical intelligence, bodily-kinesthetic intelligence, interpersonal intelligence, and intrapersonal intelligence. Recently, Goleman (1997) has added an eighth—emotional intelligence. Each intelligence proposed by Gardner meets eight criteria: (1) potential isolation by brain damage, (2) the existence of idiots savants, prodigies and other exceptional individuals, (3) an evolutionary history and evolutionary plausibility, (4) support from experimental psychological tasks, (5) support from psychometric findings, (6) an identifiable core operation or set of operations, (7) a distinctive developmental history along with a definable set of expert "end-state" performances, and (8) susceptibility to encoding in a symbol system. It is this last criterion—susceptibility to encoding in a symbol system—that is of particular interest to educational practitioners.

"Much of human representation and communication of knowledge," writes Gardner (1983), "takes place via symbol systems—culturally contrived systems of meaning which capture important forms of information" (p. 66). Language, mathematics, visual representation, musical notation, dance, and print are all culturally valued systems. They mediate between our thoughts about the world and our experiences of the world. They support our ability to abstract, to manipulate, to analyze, to conceptualize, to remember, and to synthesize. They are tools of thought.

Innovative design of learning experiences for students capitalizes on the human potential to use these symbolic forms to tap multiple learning modalities. Using drawing, painting, writing, and multimedia authoring tools, students can generate information using all intelligences. In social studies classes, students can synthesize findings and present reports that utilize sound, images, animation, charts, and graphs to explain what they have learned. In a bilingual classroom, students can record or present information in two languages. As students begin to process concepts using multiple modalities, they also increase retention and develop a broader range of intellectual strategies.

The multiple intelligences are not, however, tidy, discrete categories. Rather, they are "useful fictions . . . for discussing processes and abilities that (like all of life) are continuous with one another" (Gardner, 1983). The multiple intelligences serve as an analytic tool for thinking about the potentials of a learner, but they do not dictate an instructional process. The intelligences do not exist in isolation. Rather, they are encountered in a cultural setting that exerts control over their development and their use. These intellectual processes or abilities create possibilities; combining them in culturally valued ways creates a multiplicity of possibilities.

Understanding that all learners are able to know the world through language, logical-mathematical analysis, spatial representation, musical thinking, the use of the body to solve problems or to make things, an understanding of others, and an understanding of ourselves points to the many ways in which learners can be approached. It also points to the need to challenge the assumption that everyone will learn the same materials in the same way. Rather, the theory of multiple intelligences argues that learners possess different kinds of minds and therefore learn, remember, perform, and understand in different ways. Thus, things to be learned need to be presented in a number of ways. Writes Gardner (1991, p. 11):

> While the recognition of different ways of representing and acquiring knowledge complicates matters in certain ways, it is also a hopeful sign. Not only are chances of acquiring understanding enhanced if multiple entry points are recognized and utilized, but in addition, the way in which we conceptualize understanding is broadened. Genuine understanding is most likely to emerge, and be apparent to others, if people possess a number of ways of representing knowledge of a concept or skill and can move readily back and forth among these forms of knowing.
>
> . . . an education built on multiple intelligences can be more effective than one built on just two intelligences [linguistic and logical-mathematical]. It can develop a broader range of talents, and it can make the standard curriculum accessible to a wider range of students. (p. 81)

Constructivist Learning

Constructivist notions of learning contrast sharply with traditional notions of learning that depend on presenting students with limited facts and concepts and then asking them to memorize those facts. Constructivist notions of learning start with a simple proposition: Individuals construct their own understandings of the world in which they live. Students search for tools to help them understand their experiences. Their experiences lead them to conclude, for instance, that some people are generous and others are cheap of spirit, that representational government either works or it does not, that fire burns if we get too close, that rubber balls usually bounce. These and hundreds of thousands of other understandings, some more complex than others, are constructed by learners through reflection on their interactions with objects and ideas (Brooks & Brooks, 1999).

Constructivism rests on four central tenets (Fosnot, 1989). First, knowledge depends on past constructions. We can only know the world through our mental framework. We use this framework to transform, organize, and interpret new information. This mental framework is constructed and evolves as we interact with our environment and attempt to make sense of our experiences. It is the teacher's role to assist students in making sense of the input in the classroom by structuring the learning environment, but learners must structure their own understanding of it, checking and elaborating on their understanding through inputs drawn from social interaction.

Second, constructions come about through systems of assimilation and accommodation. We assimilated information, integrating it into our existing mental framework. When information is incongruent with our mental frameworks, it cannot be assimilated and added to our store of knowledge. When this occurs, we accommodate, that is, we develop a higher-level theory or logic to encompass the information.

Third, learning is an organic process of invention, rather than a mechanical process of accumulation. Knowledge is not just an accumulation of facts. Instead, learners must be provided with experiences of hypothesizing and predicting, manipulating objects and data, researching answers, imagining, investigating, and inventing in order to construct knowledge.

Fourth, meaningful learning occurs through reflection and resolution of cognitive conflict, negating earlier, incomplete levels of understanding. Teachers can only mediate in this process.

In addition to these four tenets, an understanding of learning recognizes the learner's cognitive developmental abilities as a major factor in the process of constructing understanding. Students' developmental abilities range from being able to do something with assistance to being able to do something alone. This is referred to as a learner's "zone of proximal development" (Vygotsky, 1978). Teachers cannot expect students to learn below their level of development—a child who knows no Spanish will not suddenly converse in Spanish. At the same time, a child who already knows much of the common vocabulary in Spanish should not spend days filling out worksheets with common words or engaging in recitation. It makes no sense to teach students what they already know or to teach them what they are not yet ready to learn.

A constructivist view of learning suggests at least five instructional principles. Brooks and Brooks (1999) identify these instructional principles as:

1. Posing Problems of Emerging Relevance to Students—Relevance does not have to be preexisting for students. Not all students arrive at the classroom door interested in learning verb constructs, biological cycles, or historical timelines, but most students can be helped to construct understandings of important topics. Relevance emerges through teacher mediation and often begins with the posing of a good problem.
2. Structuring Learning around Primary Concepts—When designing curriculum, constructivist teachers organize information around conceptual clusters of problems, questions, and discrepant situations because students are most engaged when problems and ideas are presented holistically rather than in separate, isolated parts.
3. Seeking and Valuing Students' Points of View—Students' points of view are windows into their reasoning. Awareness of students' points of view helps educators challenge students, making learning experiences both contextual and meaningful. Each student's point of view is an instructional entry point that sits at the gateway of personalized education.
4. Adapting Curriculum to Address Students' Suppositions—Learning is enhanced when the curriculum's cognitive, social, and emotional demands are accessible to students. Some sort of relationship must exist between the demands of the curriculum and the suppositions that each student brings to learning. Students will find lessons bereft of meaning unless their suppositions are addressed and honored.
5. Assessing Student Learning in the Context of Teaching—Creative assessment of learning from a constructivist perspective values the cognitive functioning of students, the dispositions of students, and the status of the teacher/student relationship. Student conceptions, rather than indicating rightness or wrongness, become entry points for teachers. Student conceptions become places to begin the sorts of intervention that lead to the learner's construction of new understandings and the acquisition of new skills. Assessment is used in service of the learner, rather than as an accountability device.

Numerous others have identified attributes of constructivist learning environments. Jonassen (1994), for instance, summarizes the implications of constructivism for instructional design as:

1. Provide multiple representations of reality;
2. Represent the natural complexity of the real world;
3. Focus on knowledge construction, not reproduction;
4. Present authentic tasks (contextualizing rather than abstracting instruction);
5. Provide real-world, case-based learning environments, rather than predetermined instructional sequences;
6. Foster reflective practice;

7. Enable context- and content-dependent knowledge construction; and
8. Support collaborative construction of knowledge through social negotiation (p. 35).

To Brooks and Brooks' (1999) and Jonassen's (1994) principles, we add another. Educators who understand learning as construction choose tools and activities that afford a variety of opportunities for constructing knowledge. Polin (1992) suggests that when selecting tools to support the construction of knowledge educators should look for the following characteristics: (1) the tool promotes learning as a whole, meaningful task, not a subskill; (2) the tool carries some of the burden of the task—it "scaffolds" the elements of the task the learner cannot accomplish alone; and (3) the tool allows for increasingly complex versions of the task to be carried out by gradually turning back some of the task burden to the learner.

The electronic technologies can and should be a vital part of constructivist approaches to learning. Yet, schools all too often emphasize the first order effects of technology as they struggle to use technology to support traditional learning goals. Technology is viewed as useful only in so much as particular applications can be taught and used. Viewed thusly, technology's effects are minimal. When schools look to second-order effects of technology—its effects on social organization—classrooms are significantly impacted. Salomon (1991) states:

> Not allowing computers to serve as the trigger for the design of new learning environments, holding the environment constant and only changing the means of delivery, is a wasteful abuse of powerful technology, resulting in underwhelming yield. System-wide changes may be the most important opportunities afforded by computers. These entail new designs of whole curricula and socially-based inquiry opportunities; interdisciplinary, authentic learning tasks; changing roles for teachers; and new modes of assessment. (p. 44)

Today's world is one of rapidly expanding knowledge with concurrent demands to integrate that knowledge with new skills and new jobs. Technology, integrated into the ongoing educational process, can play a significant role in creating educational environments that reflect the way people interact with the real world, sharing representational and computational task burdens. It can assist in creating environments that reflect the real-world contexts in which both users and tools are embedded. It can support creative and divergent thinking by allowing learners to deploy inventive problem-solving strategies in situated learning tasks. It can be used to honor the construction of knowledge by supporting conversations, reflection, and shared exploration rather than as a tool for delivering rote definitions and answers. It can provide a vehicle for moving beyond conventional problem solving by enabling issues, dilemmas, and problems to emerge from authentic activity. We have summarized principles for learning taken from the efficiency model and from a constructivist perspective in Table 2.2.

An Educational Dilemma

For educators and students who find the structure of traditional learning structures organized around the principles of the efficiency model limiting and insufficient for

TABLE 2.2	EFFICIENCY LEARNING AND CONSTRUCTIVIST LEARNING
Efficiency Learning	**Constructivist Learning**
Teachers present; students listen.	Teachers facilitate; students do, present, think, construct.
Working together is cheating.	Working together facilitates learning and problem solving.
Subjects are presented separately.	Subjects are integrated into a learning whole.
Learning is fact-centered.	Learning is problem-centered.
The teacher is the source of all knowledge.	There are many rich resources for learning.
Print is the primary source of information.	Concepts are explored using a variety of communication tools.
Assessment is based on how much is memorized and can be given back to the teacher.	Assessment is based on each student's developing abilities to solve problems, communicate ideas, present information, and learn how to learn.
Schools are isolated and separate from the rest of the community.	Technology connects the world to the classroom and the classroom to the world.

meeting today's learning needs, a theory of multiple intelligences and constructivism are both appealing and consistent with intuitive impressions about learning. As Von Glasersfeld (1995) wrote: "Constructivism does not claim to have made earth-shaking inventions in the area of education; it merely claims to provide a solid conceptual basis for some of the things that, until now, inspired teachers had to do without theoretical foundation." Moving from theory to practice, however, presents challenges since "models are rarely developed to the point where they can be more or less operationalized" (Mendelsohn & Dillenbourg, 1994).

Thus, for example, one often hears that constructivist approaches to teaching reject rote learning, memorization, telling, and lecturing on the basis that students "ought" to be constructing their own meaning. Yet, students can construct knowledge, even from lectures, if they listen to, and think about, what is appropriate for them (Clements, 1997). Even memorization that at first glance appears to be a passive absorption of data takes place with a framework of constructive cognitive ability. Such activity includes decisions as to what the learner commits to memory, the match between the original material and the way the learner perceives it, the purposes and duration for which the learner retains the information, the ways the learner does or does not apply the information, and the links to other knowledge that are made or not made (Brooks & Brooks, 1999; Perkins, 1992).

Similarly, educators who claim to be constructivist often fault local, state, and national standards for difficulties in helping students develop deep understanding, claiming that standards demand coverage instead of depth. Yet, even if they wanted, teachers cannot ignore the curriculum prescribed by local, state, and national agencies. The educational system demands that students master a specified body of information, viewed by a culture as both valid and important.

Standards are also attacked for their "rightness." Demanding that students master conventional knowledge, claim some, is anathema to the constructivist principal of knowledge construction. Ackerman (1995) asks: "How can a teacher give reason to a student . . . by appreciating the uniqueness and consistency of his or her thinking, while, at the same time, giving right to the expert whose views coincide with more advanced ideas in a field?" (p. 341). To this query, Jonassen, Peck, and Wilson (1999) reply, "Not all meaning is created equally." If individual ideas are discrepant from community standards, they are not regarded as viable unless new evidence supporting their viability is provided. Students' must also learn to judge their constructions by the same rigorous standards of viability and evidence.

Constructivism and multiple intelligences are not theories of teaching; they are theories of learning. They inform us about how students learn, not about how to teach. They do not prescribe a particular way of teaching. While these theories of learning are suggestive of teaching strategies as we have seen in the previous two sections, they do not provide a framework for the design of learning opportunities for students—for creating an instructional plan. We turn our attention now to six questions whose answers can build a bridge from notions of learning and learner potential to the design of classroom instruction.

> Successful teaching of complex skills greatly depends on an instructional plan that carefully considers what is to be learned, what the technology contributes, and what the learning environment and the teacher must provide. The instructional plan must ensure that students receive ongoing guidance—guidance that often comes from the teacher but that may come from instructional materials or other students as well. Student collaboration is often an important aspect of the learning process. Teachers are called upon to play a variety of roles; to be a learning environment manager as well as an information provider. (Sivin-Kachala & Bialo, 1996, p. 3)

SIX GUIDING QUESTIONS

In this book's Preface, we defined *design* as the process of intentionally planning learning experiences for students. Carefully reflecting on the following six guiding questions, adjusting answers to fit together as though assembling pieces of a puzzle, can result in robust, authentic, timely, and rigorous opportunities for students to construct meaningful, socially valued knowledge and understanding.

1. What foundations of learning do today's students most need to learn?
2. What activities should designers choose to ensure that students become actively engaged in learning through construction?
3. What contents, ideas, and/or concepts afford a context for student learning?
4. What tools might a designer choose to best support and enhance student learning?

5. What system of assessment might a designer construct to appropriately assess student learning?
6. How might learning environments be constructed to complement the overall learning design?

These six questions frame a design process that recognizes the limitations of the efficiency model and the ways in which learning outside of school differs from traditional school learning. Answers to these questions can and, we believe, should embrace a view of intelligence that is not unitary as well as constructivist notions of learning and the power of technology to support learning. In Chapter 3 we turn our attention to using these questions as a guide to a model for designing opportunities for learning.

CHAPTER IDEAS

- Educators today often find themselves between two cultures, wondering how this astonishing tapestry of technological resources might weave thoughts and ideas into a subtle, rich learning environment even as they continue to design learning experiences for students that reflect more traditional educational practice. Many educators find that designing learning opportunities that meet the challenges presented by these technologies while simultaneously using them as part of the solution is one of today's most pressing dilemmas.
- Modern educational strategies for designing learning experiences for students were developed to meet the needs of an industrialized, print-oriented society and were derived from principles of efficient production and management.
- For today's educators, "efficiency" principles coupled with the "science" of exact measurement and precise standards remain central guides for the design of learning. Among the many models based on this approach to instructional design are Programmed Instruction (Skinner, 1958), Instructional Objectives (Mager, 1962), Mastery Learning (Bloom, Madaus, & Hastings, 1981), Gagne's Conditions of Learning (1985), and the ADDIE model (Fardouly, 1998).
- Programmed instruction is instruction designed to present information in a sequential series of small steps or frames, each requiring a response from the learner. If correct, the learner is given the next step and reinforced positively for the response. If incorrect, the learner is retaught the concept.
- Writing complete and precise behavioral objectives includes stating the terminal behavior to be displayed by the learner, the criterion or standard by which the behavior will be evaluated (e.g., 70 percent of items correct on the test), and the conditions under which the behavior will be displayed. Designing instruction around the clear articulation of behavioral objectives

ensures that instruction correctly solves instructional problems, derives from demonstrated needs, is appropriately adjusted to the needs of each student, and contributes to student eagerness to learn more.

- The instructional design process derived from specifying behavioral objectives includes four phases: analysis, development, implementation, and improvement. Analysis seeks to identify key skill outcomes. The development phase includes the drafting of measurement instruments, the design of relevant practice, and the selection of content derived to support learning objectives. Implementation includes showing students how the course objectives and instructional modules are related as well as collecting materials and arranging the environment. The final phase, improvement, centers on a continuous determination of how well the instruction works (Mager, 1962).

- Mastery learning is based on the idea that learners will succeed in learning a task if given the exact amount of time they need. It proposes a test, teach, retest, reteach model. Using this model, design of instruction creates opportunities for students to learn a concept or skill, tests to identify those learners who have not mastered the concept or skill, reteaches the concept or skill, and retests for mastery. This process is repeated until the concept or skill is learned. Student attention is then turned to the next concept or skill.

- Gagne's conditions of learning model for the design of instruction includes a sequence of external, instructional events that guide the design of instruction. Instructional events, according to Gagne's framework, must first gain the student's attention and then provide a means to share the goals of instruction. Next, instructional events must be designed that stimulate recall, provide presentations in all modalities, and create linkages to meaningful frameworks. The final three instructional events must monitor and adjust student learning, require application, and bring closure to learning. For each of these phases, Gagne has aligned internal learning events with each of the external instructional events.

- Recently, with the advent of the capacity for designers to create technology-based instructional materials, designers have formalized the design process, integrating elements from all the previous efficiency models. Although this model of design is most often applied to workplace training, it is being used to design instruction throughout K–12 education. ADDIE represents a systematic approach to **A**nalysis, **D**esign, **D**evelopment, **I**mplementation, and **E**valuation.

- One way in which the principles of traditional instructional design have been translated into practice involves the use of computers to create Integrated Learning Systems (ILSs). Integrated Learning Systems are software programs designed around the identification of a series of identified skills. Developers of integrated learning systems analyze the content to be learned, breaking it down into its fundamental subskills, ordering them sequentially. This software clearly rests on the efficiency model of learning and includes concepts like sequencing of instruction, appropriate reinforcement, programmed instruction, and learning for mastery.

- Notions about learning associated with the efficiency model focus attention on individual learning. These notions focus instructional attention on the learning of small, isolated skills and facts. Notions about learning associated with the efficiency model focus attention on books as the primary source of information. Notions about learning associated with the efficiency model focus on methods or techniques for analyzing and presenting what should be learned, not on learning goals.

- These notions view knowledge as independent of the situations in which it is learned and used. Yet, researchers who have studied learning in everyday situations and different cultural settings suggest that knowledge is not some kind of independent phenomena, but rather that it is situated in the activity, context, and culture in which it is learned (Brown, Collins, & Duguid, 1989). In short, how something is learned is just as important as what is learned.

- Critics of the efficiency model express concern that the principles of learning associated with the model may actually detract from learners' ability to fully participate in today's society. Educators who plan to design learning experiences for today's students must design for the whole of learning. They must recognize that much of learning is social, that learning is not for later life but for living, and that students are not vessels to be filled but constructors of their knowledge. They must create environments that promote problem solving, cooperation, communication, critical thinking, and learning how to learn.

- Four categories differentiate learning in school from learning in contemporary social contexts outside of school. One, school learning depends on individual cognition while learning outside of school depends on shared cognition. Second, school learning centers on pure mentation while learning in broader social contexts depends on tool manipulation. Third, school learning centers on symbol manipulation while learning in broader social contexts depends on reasoning with "stuff." Last, school learning focuses on generalized learning while learning in broader social contexts centers on situation-specific competencies.

- The efficiency model found its expression in perceptions of learning that pivoted on stimulus-response learning and instructional practices that embraced programmed instruction, behavioral objectives, mastery learning, and a consideration of the relationship between the conditions of learning and a sequence of external instructional events. As we search for a new design model, there are two important considerations that can serve as a platform for beginning. These considerations include: an emerging view of learning potentials and abilities and a vision of learning called constructivism.

- "Much of human representation and communication of knowledge," writes Gardner (1983), "takes place via symbol systems—culturally contrived systems of meaning which capture important forms of information" (p. 66). Language, mathematics, visual representation, musical notation, dance, and print are all culturally valued systems. They mediate between our thoughts about the world and our experiences of the world. They support our ability to abstract, to manipulate, to analyze, to conceptualize, to remember, and to synthesize. They are tools of thought.

- Innovative design of learning experiences for students capitalizes on the human potential to use these symbolic forms to tap multiple learning modalities. Using drawing, painting, writing, and multimedia authoring tools, students can generate information using all modalities.

- Constructivist notions of learning contrast sharply with traditional notions of learning and start with a simple proposition: Individuals construct their own understandings of the world in which they live. Constructivism rests on four central tenets (Fosnot, 1989). First, knowledge depends on past constructions. Second, constructions come about through systems of assimilation and accommodation. Third, learning is an organic process of invention, rather than a mechanical process of accumulation. Fourth, meaningful learning occurs through reflection and resolution of cognitive conflict, negating earlier, incomplete levels of understanding. Teachers can only mediate in this process.

- Educators who design learning experiences for students using constructivist notions of learning base their designs on five instructional principles: (1) Posing Problems of Emerging Relevance to Students, (2) Structuring Learning around Primary Concepts, (3) Seeking and Valuing Students' Points of View, (4) Adapting Curriculum to Address Students' Suppositions, and (5) Assessing Student Learning in the Context of Teaching.

- Educators who understand learning as construction choose tools and activities that afford a variety of opportunities for constructing knowledge. The electronic technologies can and should be a vital part of constructivist approaches to learning.

- "Not allowing computers to serve as the trigger for the design of new learning environments, holding the environment constant and only changing the means of delivery, is a wasteful abuse of powerful technology, resulting in underwhelming yield. System-wide changes may be the most important opportunities afforded by computers. These entail new designs of whole curricula and socially-based inquiry opportunities; interdisciplinary, authentic learning tasks; changing roles for teachers; and new modes of assessment" (Salomon, p. 44).

- In this book's Preface, *design* was defined as the process of intentionally planning learning experiences. Six questions must lie at the heart of any contemporary model of design: What foundations of learning do today's students most need to learn? What activities should designers choose to ensure that students become actively engaged in learning through construction? What contents, ideas, and/or concepts afford a context for student learning? What tools might a designer choose to best support and enhance student learning? What system of assessment might a designer construct to appropriately assess student learning? How might learning environments be constructed to complement the overall learning design?

- These six questions frame a design process that recognizes the limitations of the efficiency model and the ways in which learning outside of school differs from traditional school learning. Answers to these questions embrace a view of intelligence that is not unitary as well as constructivist notions of learning and the power of technology to support learning. In the process of intentionally planning learning experiences for students, answers to these six questions cannot be viewed sequentially. Instead, effective design requires educators to attend to the complex interplay of these considerations.

The FACTS
of Design

Can you remember an instance in which you "borrowed" an idea for an activity or project that had worked well in another classroom? The idea might have been successful with students of similar ages, backgrounds, and interests as our students'. The curricula for both groups of pupils might have been comparable. And yet, think back and remember what happened when you last tried to "plug and play" an idea from another classroom into your own. How well did it work? How well did it really work? Not so well, eh?

When we are asked to wade through large collections of lesson plans, replicate projects from other classrooms, or follow overly-prescriptive directions for educational activities written by folks who can't possibly know our students as we do, we are asked to ignore much of what experience and reflection have taught us. Using Internet tools and resources in our classrooms in ways that will benefit students and teachers—in ways that are truly worth the time, effort, energy, and expense—calls upon us to function more as *instructional designers* than direction-followers. Creating and implementing learning activities as a designer is an artisan's endeavor. I speak to you as that artisan; analogously, as chef rather than cook; conductor rather than metronome; educator rather than automatron.

Judi Harris (1998b)
University of Texas,
Austin

A teacher's most important role is that of instructional designer. The design of learning opportunities permits teachers to construct opportunities to learn for their students that are responsive to the unique learning, contextual, and personal characteristics of a classroom. We turn first to a look at teachers as designers. We then present a design model, using puzzle pieces as a design metaphor. Next, we introduce the six puzzle pieces using the six guiding questions. Finally, we present a Web-based design tool as two teachers begin the process of designing learning opportunities for students in their classrooms.

THE TEACHER AS DESIGNER

There is some controversy and a great deal of discussion these days about the role of the classroom teacher. Some say, in a rather pejorative way, that the role of teachers has traditionally been that of a "sage on the stage." By this they mean that a teacher stands before the class "telling" students what they need to know and expecting students to "spit" it back on objective tests. While newer understandings about learning—constructivism and multiple intelligences—suggest that a teacher's role ought to be a bit different, it is a myth that a teacher ought not to be a sage. How are students to develop expertise if there is no expert present? How are we to know if students' constructions are viable and rigorous if there is no sage in the classroom? Deep content understanding is a prerequisite to good teaching.

Others would describe the role of a teacher as a "director." Once again, this role would be discouraged. Yet, all organisms—and the classroom is an organism with a life and a pace unique to it—need a head. Someone must lead the organizing, planning, and directing functions. That does not mean that all the other constituent parts of the organism do not have a vital and crucial role or a part in these functions. It simply means that even though all are equal and learning members of a community of learners, someone must be a bit more equal.

In the last 20 years, various alternative descriptors of the educator's role have emerged. A teacher is a facilitator; a teacher is a coach; a teacher is a cognitive mentor. These descriptors of an educator's role reflect the notion that students not the teacher are the locus of the learning act. This suggests that as learners what students need is a "guide on the side"—a provocateur and support system.

Regardless of which of these versions or combination of versions of what a teacher ought to be, there is a much more fundamental but less discussed role. That is, the teacher as designer. The teacher as a designer recognizes the centrality of planning, structuring, provisioning, and orchestrating learning. Although the role of designer may be the least observed or recognized teacher role, the intellectual analysis of content filtered through an understanding of learning and learners and the subsequent construction of learning opportunities for students underpins all robust and worthwhile learning opportunities. It is possible for teachers to rely on the learning designs of others—the textbook publisher, the instructional materials provider, or the lesson plan idea book. Yet, only teachers know their particular community of learners, the unique personalities of their learners, and the content and requirements of their context. Only the classroom teacher understands the conditions of their classroom, the prior experiences and content-related comprehension of both teacher and student, the group dynamics of a particular group of learners, and the resources available for teaching and learning. Taking static instructional designs and trying to shove them into your own context is not nearly as satisfying as designing opportunities for learning that meet the unique learning needs of your classroom.

Teachers are and ought to be designers. And, the art of design focuses on the ways in which we craft answers to six guiding questions. We stated those questions in Chapter 2 as:

- What **F**oundations of learning do today's students most need to learn?
- What **A**ctivities should designers choose to ensure that students become actively engaged in learning through construction?
- What **C**ontents, ideas, and/or concepts afford a context for student learning?
- What **T**ools might a designer choose to best support and enhance student learning?
- What **S**ystem of assessment might a designer construct to appropriately assess student learning?
- How might learning environments be constructed to complement the overall learning design?

With these questions as guides, an educator can begin the dynamic process of designing opportunities for students to learn. Answers to each of these questions become pieces in a puzzle. They have a unique shape and combination of colors. Each puzzle piece can fail to fit with the others, fit only when artificially shoved into place, or blend smoothly into an elegant pattern of inquiry and learning. Each time educators design an opportunity for learning the puzzle pieces must be shaped and colored differently. Yet, each time they must smoothly join with the other pieces. We portray this design process in Figure 3.1.

Our design puzzle has five major pieces—**F**oundations, **A**ctivities, **C**ontent(s), **T**ools, and **S**ystems of assessment. As a memory aid, we refer to these as the FACTS of Design. These five pieces form the core considerations for the design of learning opportunities. Each of the five pieces is, in reality, a cluster of puzzle pieces themselves. For instance, the **A**ctivities puzzle piece is a whole composed of four categories of activity—authentic activities, building knowledge activities, constructing activities, and sharing activities. Once each piece is assembled from its constituent parts, it must fit smoothly with the other pieces. These five pieces, in turn, must fit smoothly into the learning environment—a cluster of physical, intellectual, and values spaces. The learning environment over which we have some control is represented by the sixth puzzle piece. It remains jagged on its exterior because all learning environments that educators craft are also part of a larger local, state, national, and global community—environments over which we have little control but that influence our classrooms nevertheless.

FIGURE **3.1**
THE FACTS OF DESIGN

Unfortunately, the design process is not as tidy as it first appears. Sometimes we design pieces carefully, crafting combinations of tabs and insets, colors, and shapes, only to find that they do not fit with the other pieces we have created or that some pieces are incomplete when aligned with others. This dynamic, interactive process of design then is iterative, moving from additions and subtractions to one piece to changes in another to additions to another to subtractions in yet another. This interaction must proceed until the whole finally emerges.

In short, these questions cannot be answered in sequence. They are not like items on a test—one leading to another. They are not a list of considerations but interacting parts of a larger whole—a design for learning. As we built and experimented with this model and then our students who are classroom teachers began experimenting with the model to create their own designs, we learned that paper and pencil was too static a medium for adding and subtracting to designs as each question was asked, answered, related to other questions, and then revised. To aid teachers in the use of this model, it occurred to us that an interactive Web-based design tool would be an appropriate design environment. We will introduce that Web-based tool to you in the final section of this chapter.

THE FACTS OF DESIGN

Before we introduce the Web-based design tool, however, we first need to introduce the puzzle pieces more completely.

What Foundations of Learning Do Today's Students Most Need to Learn?

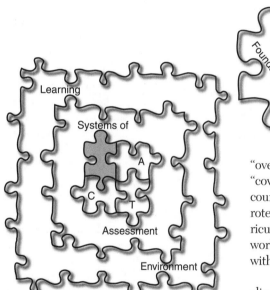

What is schooling for? What do we hope for all learners as they progress toward the end of their K–12 learning experience? Education has both an overt curriculum—that which is articulated and visible—and a covert curriculum—that which is not articulated but is the underlying message of schooling. For instance, Toffler (1980) writes that in the traditional, industrial school basic reading, writing, and arithmetic, a bit of history and other subjects constituted the "overt curriculum." Beneath it, however, lies an invisible or "covert curriculum" that is far more basic. It consists of three courses: one in punctuality, one in obedience, and one in rote—repetitive work. This cluster of overt and covert curriculums is the result of an industrialized society's demand for workers willing to take orders from a management hierarchy without questioning.

While this may be a rather harsh indictment of industrialized schooling, it illustrates the differences between the overt and covert curriculum. Those who design learning opportunities for today's students must not only think about and design the overt curriculum, they must hold in their minds a set of foundations or habits of mind that they want students to take from their learning experiences. What do we hope for our students? What foundational habits of mind should students be developing over time? What are the fundamentals that transcend topics, projects, assignments, assessments, and grades? These are difficult questions, and there are a number of viewpoints.

Hirsch's (1996) notion of the need for a shared body of knowledge represents one major response to the question about the foundations of learning. Echoing Thomas Jefferson's call for public schooling that would "diffuse knowledge more generally through the mass of the people," the notion of shared knowledge as the foundation of learning states that there is a body of lasting knowledge that should form the core of the curriculum. Such knowledge includes, for example, the basic principles of constitutional government, important events of world history, essential elements of mathematics and of oral and written expression, widely acknowledged masterpieces of art and music, and stories and poems passed down from generation to generation. By clearly specifying important knowledge in language arts, history and geography, math, science, and the fine arts, teaching for shared knowledge presents a practical answer to the question, "What do our children need to know?"

Another school of thought centers on the processes of intellect more than on the contents of intellect. Perhaps the best example of the ways in which this school of thought defines the foundations of learning is the SCANS Report (1991). Produced by the Secretary's Commission on Achieving Necessary Skills (SCANS) appointed by the Secretary of Labor, the objective of this report was to help teachers understand how curriculum and instruction must change to enable students to develop those high performance skills needed to succeed in the high performance workplace. The commission identified a solid foundation in basic literacy and computational skills, thinking skills necessary to put knowledge to work, a cluster of personal qualities, and a set of workplace competencies as central to success in a high performance workplace. Included among the basic literacy and computational skills were reading, writing, arithmetic/mathematics, listening, and speaking skills. Thinking skills included creative thinking, decision making, problem solving, seeing things in the mind's eye, knowing how to learn, and reasoning. Personal qualities included responsibility, self-esteem, sociability, self-management, and integrity/honesty. The five workplace competencies identified by the commission were the ability to identify, organize, plan, and allocate resources, work with others, acquire and use information, understand complex interrelationships, and work with a variety of technologies.

We have chosen to collapse the SCANS report criteria and add the notion of shared knowledge. Thus, we believe students must have varied opportunities to become knowledgeable; they must have varied opportunities to become problem-solvers; they must learn to use a wide range of literacies to link the symbolic world with meaning; they must have varied opportunities to use information to inform the conduct of their lives, and, as technology links the world in intricate webs of connections, students must learn to be active participants in a range of communities. By developing a deep understanding of the ways in which learners develop these habits of mind, educators can help students adopt them as their own. We will explore these five foundations of learning—knowledge, problem solving, literacy, information using, and community—in Chapters 4, 5, 6, 7, and 8 as we pursue the many ways in which the FACTS design model can be used to design opportunities for learning.

What Activities Should Designers Choose to Ensure that Students Become Actively Engaged in Learning Through Construction?

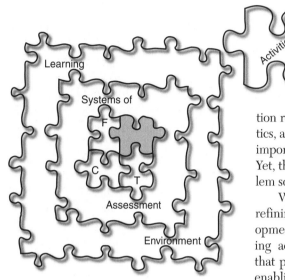

Educators must design opportunities for students to engage in the kinds of activities that support and shape the ability to think and problem-solve. These activities should help students become competent with at least four categories of cognition: memory, information extending processes, information rearranging processes, and metacognition. These heuristics, as general problem-solving strategies are often called, are important in the problem-solving process and can be learned. Yet, these general heuristics tell only part of the story of problem solving.

While it is possible to create designs for developing and refining these heuristic processes, it is likely that their development is better facilitated when anchored in broader learning activities. Anchored instruction creates environments that permit sustained exploration by students and teachers, enabling them to understand the kinds of problems and opportunities experts in various areas encounter and the knowledge that these experts use. One way to plan for anchored instruction is to use problem-based or problem-centered learning. A problem-centered curriculum is one that is built around the solution to a real-world problem of interest. Placing the problem at the center emphasizes students' "doing" rather than their mastery of discrete pieces of information or skills.

Once a design for learning has been anchored in a problem, students must be challenged with appropriate activities that support and direct their ability to solve problems in a robust and comprehensive manner. A design must present opportunities for students to enter the community and culture of practitioners who solve similar problems and engage in a range of activities that mirror the activities used by problem solvers. If student learning is to be contextualized in a culture of practice and anchored with a problem of significance, opportunities for student learning must be bolstered by students' participation in authentic activities, building knowledge activities, constructing activities, and sharing activities—the ABCS of Activity. These activities are introduced in this section and more completely developed in Chapter 5.

Authentic Activities.   Learning activities and contexts are not distinct or even neutral with respect to what is learned. The activities through which knowledge is developed and deployed cannot be separated from what is learned. Rather, activity is integral to what and how knowledge is learned and must be authentic. *Authentic activity* is defined as the ordinary practices of a culture. *Authentic activity* is important for learners because it is the only way they gain access to the standpoint that enables practitioners to act meaningfully and purposefully in solving problems related to their practice. It is activity that shapes and hones emerging knowledge. Authentic activity provides experience for subsequent activity. Authentic activity provides the bridge from "inert" knowledge to entrance into a culture of practice.

Building Knowledge Activities.   Teaching a generous number of carefully chosen exemplary facts within a meaningful explanatory context is important for engaging in insightful thinking and problem solving. However, "usable knowledge" is not the same as a list of facts. Experts' knowledge is connected and organized around important concepts. It is specifically tied to the contexts in which it is applicable. It supports understanding and application to other contexts rather than only the ability to remember. Thus, it is clear that students need opportunities to engage in knowledge building activities that include, for example, reading and discussing ideas, watching demonstrations, viewing films, responding to questions, and completing structured experiments. Building knowledge does not mean avoiding facts, but primacy is given to the kinds of activities that connect these facts into webs of meaning.

Constructing Activities.   Students need opportunities to test their knowledge with nonroutine problems, problems that may have many right answers, and problems that have no predetermined path for their solution. Learners really understand when they test what they have come to know against what they want to do. Constructing activities push students beyond building knowledge to using emerging knowledge to make or form something that represents their deepening understanding. Moving from knowledge to understanding involves performances of understanding. Constructing activities are performance activities that ask students to expand, reform, apply, or extend their knowledge by making something, producing something, building something, or creating something. The outcomes of constructing activities serve as observable performances of understanding. What learners make, produce, build, or create demonstrate what they are able to "do" with their knowledge.

Sharing Activities.   When students build knowledge and construct products that reflect their understanding in situations that mirror the authentic activities of practitioners, they need opportunities to test their knowledge and judge their products. Sharing activities allow students to test their understanding in public arenas, to receive feedback that supports their successes, or to be challenged with new evidence or missing evidence or faulty connections and applications. Students need opportunities to compare the meanings they have built about knowledge domains with those of others.

What Contents, Ideas, and/or Concepts Afford a Context for Student Learning?

When educators design learning opportunities for students, they must select the "something" of learning. This "something" can be selected from the interests and

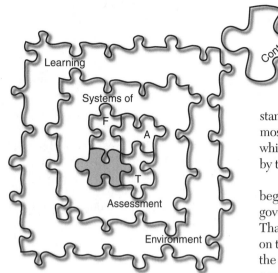

urgencies of students themselves. It can be part of the prescribed curriculum, reflecting the history, literature, science, and values judged by the learning community as fundamental to living in and contributing to that community. It can be drawn from events in the news or from professional standards created by curriculum and disciplinary experts. For most educators today, the source of the "something" around which a design for learning pivots is the standards established by their state.

The standards movement, as a way of defining content, began with President George Bush's 1989 invitation to state governors to join him at a national summit on education. That meeting produced agreement among the participants on the need for national education goals. A few months later, the governors and the president agreed on a set of goals. As a result, one by one, the national disciplinary societies, from the National Council of Teachers of Mathematics to the National Council of Teachers of English, and others, like the National Science Board and the American Association for the Advancement of Science, produced standards for their disciplines. At the same time, state after state was gathering its citizens together to build a statewide consensus on the right standards for the state, drawing on the work of the disciplinary societies and experts in the field. As we write this book, 49 of the 50 states have passed and implemented standards.

Tucker and Codding (1998) state that the importance of these standards centers on the fact that they are (1) high and for all students, (2) rigorous and world-class, (3) useful for developing what is needed for citizenship, employment, and lifelong learning, (4) focused on what is most important in each discipline, (5) consistent with the time it takes to teach and to learn the subject, (6) clear and usable, (7) adaptable without sacrificing clarity, and (8) reflect a broad consensus on what is truly important (p. 57). Write Tucker and Codding (p. 44): "These standards actually require that students know the things that lie at the heart of the core subjects in the curriculum as well as the core concepts in the disciplines."

While many challenge the adoption of these standards and/or their concomitant systems of assessment (e.g., Ohanian, 1999; Meier, 2000), they are the realities of current educational practice. They are the "something" of education. But only when seen through the lens of the efficiency model do they become a list of objectives to be taught, tested, and retaught. Instead, when viewed as the "something" of learning and placed within a larger design frame they become the content of learning—the vehicle for subsequent deeper understandings about the physical, social, and intellectual world in which we all live. All designs must have a "something" for it is not possible to learn to solve problems. We must learn to solve problems about something. It is not possible to be knowledgeable; we must become knowledgeable about something. It is not possible to be literate; one must be literate about something. It is not possible to use information; we must learn to use information about something.

What Tools Might a Designer Choose to Best Support and Enhance Student Learning?

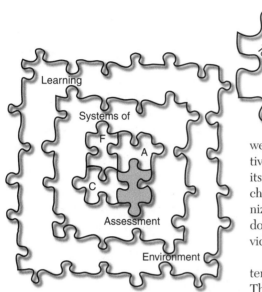

Technology is most often thought of as the machines or tools humans use to extend their physical and sensory capabilities. As Freud (1961) wrote: "Man has, as it were, become a kind of prosthetic god. When he puts on all his auxiliary organs he is truly magnificent; but those organs have not grown on to him and they still give him much trouble at times." Technology is, however, more than just a thing we attach to ourselves. It is a means to an end; it is human activity (Rybczynski, 1983). In fact, the word *technology* derives its meaning from the root word, *technique.* Making wise choices about the use of technology, then, depends on recognizing the ways in which it facilitates the things humans can do. The tools made available to members of a community provide opportunities for shaping the world in which they live.

Technology creates a bridge between an individual's potentials and their ability to act on and influence our world. Thus, a variety of machines enable us to use particular techniques to respond to, manipulate, and understand our concrete surroundings. The invention of the microscope and telescope, for example, allowed us to see beyond our natural visual range. We have used these tools to examine the very small and the very large aspects of our physical world.

Just as machines enable us to act on the environment, information tools provide techniques for constructing our cognitive and social worlds. Thus, for example, the invention of the printing press served as the impetus for radical transformations in the conditions of intellectual life in Western civilization. Its effects were sooner or later felt in every department of human activity and eventually changed a scribal culture into a print culture. The use of the printing press encouraged editors and printers to standardize texts by reordering their parts, dividing them into coherent sections, and indexing citations. This process made the ancient texts accessible, stylistically intelligible, and internally consistent, which is to say, the subject was reinvented. The format of books—their particular way of codifying information—helped to reorder the thoughts of all readers, whatever their profession. Because of its increased ability to reproduce and disseminate information, the printing press increased the amount of information to which a person was exposed. People were provided a kind of prefabricated, often abstract, experience necessary for the creation of expertise. In addition, print increased creativity by making food for thought much more abundant and allowing mental energies to be more efficiently used (Eisenstein, 1979). Its general acceptance, however, was neither easy nor smooth.

The second half of the twentieth century saw the invention and spread of an incredible range of electronic tools. These tools have become important extensions of our cognitive and social worlds. The electronic technologies have their most important consequence in the creation of a variety of knowledge environments with which humans can interact. Whatever the environment, human interaction with these electronic technologies models, engages, and challenges the user to think. As knowledge environments, these technologies provide a new window on human and physical nature. With them, we begin to see reality differently simply because they produce knowledge differently from more traditional information technologies. As Pagels (1988) wrote: "as a new mode of production, the computer creates not only a new class of people struggling for intellectual and social acceptance, but a new way of thinking about knowledge."

Every technology has properties—affordances—that make some activities easier and some activities more difficult and some activities impossible. Each technology creates a mind-set, a way of thinking about it and the activities to which it is relevant. This mind-set soon pervades those touched by it, and the more successful and widespread a technology, the greater its impact on the thought patterns of those who use it and, consequently, the greater its impact on all of society. Technology is not neutral; it dominates (Norman, 1993).

A chair affords support for sitting. A toothbrush affords brushing between the teeth. A classroom environment may afford competition or cooperation. Both television and reading are display mediums, but they provide quite different affordances. Television captures the watcher with a sequential presentation of images and sound. It is fairly easy to use but provides no user control. Reading may be more difficult but affords self-pacing. Reading allows random access to information and the ability to stop and reflect. Television affords experience; reading affords reflection. Yet, neither are interactive in the sense that a conversation or a hypermedia environment can be interactive.

The design of opportunities to learn must include the careful consideration and selection of tools. The kinds of tools offered to students as they interact with content, engage in activities, and develop competence with the foundations of learning determine, to a large extent, the kinds of learning outcomes possible. Understanding the relationship between tools, activities, and intellectual possibilities allows designers to support student learning in robust and creative ways. In the remainder of this section, we will review the range of tool options available to educators, concentrating on the electronic technologies. This is not intended to be an exhaustive list. Rather, it points to some of the more common tools and the ways in which they uniquely support learning. For a more comprehensive examination of tools and strategies for capitalizing on the possibilities afforded by a range of tools, we recommend *Technology for Teaching* by Norton and Sprague (2001).

Books—Ordering and Informing.   Perhaps the most common tools in today's classrooms are books. They come as textbooks, reference books, novels, and anthologies. They serve as the predominant source of information and provide robust opportunities for students to gain insights and overviews of selected material. As we have seen, books present ordered, sequential, abstract concepts and stories. They offer students opportunities to encounter descriptions and discussions about the topics they are studying. Books are well chosen when a design for learning requires students to access information so organized. They serve educators well for presenting an introduction or overview for building background information prior to engaging in other activities.

Television, Film, and Video—Patterns and Emotion.   Television, film, and video (hereafter referred to as video) were once very popular educational tools. They have lost some of their allure and are often used as entertainment, filler, or reinforcement. Yet, carefully selected and embedded in designs for learning, choosing video offers educators several compelling reasons for choosing them. Video provides richer sources of information than are available in books. Gestures, affective states, scenes, music, and so on always accompany dialogue. Therefore, there is more to notice. The ability to perceive dynamic, moving events facilitates comprehension. Learning to recognize patterns of events or patterns of behavior is facilitated by video. Abstractions become complex webs of interaction when presented visually. Films are good for setting contexts, for showing the social and emotional consequences of events and ideas, and for introducing topics.

Skills Software—Drilling and Practicing.   When students need opportunities to practice a skill or test their prowess at a skill (e.g., multiplication facts, vocabulary words, and memory tasks like states and capitals), a skills software program offers interactive experiences, generally with immediate feedback about performance. Skills software is well chosen when students need time to develop skills or to remember information. It is important to remember, however, that if this knowledge goes unused in richer contexts of inquiry, it remains little more than inert information and will not be used when and where appropriate.

Computer Graphics—Seeing and Rendering.   When teachers and students understand and use computer graphics tools, image making becomes a significant part of the learning process. When students learn with computer graphics, they learn to convey a host of things about their experience of the world that are not easily conveyed by verbal and print language. Shape, size, proportion, relationship, scale, surface, texture, and rhythm are all expressed more readily through image making than through using words. Computer graphics programs provide educators with a wide range of opportunities for helping students to become makers, observers, and inquirers. Computer graphics in education can be used in at least three ways: (1) to gain insight through interaction with, and visualization of, data and simulations; (2) to provide information to others through publication and presentation materials; and (3) to create a medium for creative and artistic expression (Brown, 1992).

Choosing a computer graphics program allows designers to support students' use of images to decorate, represent, organize, explain, and transform. Decorative images are images intended to make documents, Web pages, hypermedia stacks, and displays appear visually appealing. Representational images reshow information in a different form or add information that can best be captured in an image as opposed to other forms such as words. Organizational images are images that point out the relationship within a structure like a flow chart or an organizational hierarchy, presenting a visual map of steps or sequences and showing the relationship between elements. Explanative images are multidimensional images that show interrelated elements. These images visually explain a concept, how a system works, and/or changes that occur in parts of a system. Transformational images are images that illustrate a change process or an evolutionary process.

Word Processors, Desktop Publishers, and Web-Based Editors— Informing and Publishing. Until the advent and relatively easy availability of computers and a range of varied software applications, the process of "writing" and "reading" depended primarily on handheld utensils like paintbrushes, pens, pencils, paper, or canvas. Yet, a variety of computer tools can now be part of anyone's arsenal of tools for writing. Word processors are computer programs that allow the user to write, edit, revise, format, and print text as well as offering more capability and versatility than either a typewriter or writing by hand. Desktop publishing (DTP) refers to the ability to produce documents that closely resemble those produced by professional printers. Through the ability to control the precise placement of text and graphics on the page, writers can become publishers too. Web-based editors allow writers to create Web pages for publication on the Internet. When choosing one or more of these publication tools, five important principles should guide the design of learning opportunities for students: viewing writing as a process, understanding the role of writing across the curriculum, learning from models, choosing the right tool, and following good design principles.

- Using writing as an instructional strategy makes learning active as individual students or groups of students create something of their own. Across the curriculum writing removes students from their passivity. Active learners become active thinkers. These projects use writing as a means of engaging the mind, body, and spirit of students in the activity of learning a particular subject matter.
- Good writing instruction includes the reading and study of examples of excellence because students learn the conventions and the power of particular organizational patterns from observing and studying powerful examples. Students need to study examples of excellence so that they learn to formulate messages of quality.
- Students need to learn to choose the right tool for the kind of message they wish to communicate. Word processors should be a writer's tool of choice when the message is best conveyed primarily as text. Desktop publishers are environments for bringing together messages composed in other environments and organizing those elements to effectively communicate a message. When students wish their message to have longevity, a desktop publisher is a good choice. Web-based editors are good for messages that serve a broad, undefined readership. Web-based editors are a good choice for communicating a message in which timeliness, a broad audience, interactivity, feedback, multiple forms of representation (pictures, sound, animation, and video), and/or high-information density are important considerations.
- To effectively use these publication tools, students need to learn design principles. They need to learn to take responsibility for the appearance as

well as the content of the message. Design communicates information just as content does. Effective design is the result of planning before acting, and effective planning involves attention to audience, message, and environment.

- Whereas the visible results of writing are some form of product, writing is best understood as a process. Generally, the writing process can be summarized as the dynamic interaction of four basic processes: prewriting, writing, editing/revising, and publishing.

Databases—Organizing and Analyzing.   A database is a collection of related information or facts stored in a computer. Text-based databases are ones that include only text information—letters and numbers. Hypermedia databases consist of information in nodes such as pages, note cards, or individual objects on a computer screen with access to information made possible through links or buttons. Multimedia databases are databases consisting of information in a variety of media forms—pictures, video clips, text, and sound. They are not, however, primarily structured to make information retrievable using links.

Teachers who wish to use databases as part of their teaching can choose to use student-created, teacher-created, commercial, and online databases. Student-created databases are ones that the students create. Students do the research and then enter their findings into records defined by students. Teacher-created databases are ones in which teachers decide on the type of information necessary, determine the fields needed, locate a source that makes the necessary information available (i.e., an encyclopedia or government document), and type in the information. Commercial databases are ones that a company has created and that teachers or schools can buy for use in classrooms. There are many databases that can be accessed using the Internet.

Intelligently and creatively integrating databases with content curriculum can serve as a significant instructional strategy to promote information-using skills. Databases can engage students in posing and solving problems. Students can sample data, analyze and make predictions, make conjectures, discuss and validate their conclusions, and prepare arguments to convince others of their conclusions. Students using databases can experience problem situations rich in opportunities to formulate and define problems, determine the information required, decide on methods for obtaining this information, and determine the limits of acceptable solutions.

Telecommunications—Communicating beyond the Classroom.   While the most precise definition of telecommunications is "communication at a distance," many people think of it as using a computer to communicate. Telecommunications as a relatively new form of communication has the capacity to support all forms of communication depending on the intent of the sender and the tool or form that is chosen to support communication. E-mail messages may be sent to a particular person. Listservs support distributing a single message to multiple receivers. Bulletin boards allow users to post a public message to a broad range of receivers. Chat rooms promote online conversations with multiple participants, interactively exchanging ideas and interests. E-mail, listservs, bulletin boards, and newsgroups are telecommunications tools that support communication between people without requiring them to be on the computer at the same time.

Synchronous communication refers to electronic interaction that occurs at the same time. This happens when two or more people are interacting with each other at the exact same time. It allows one person to see what the other is writing as they are doing it. This requires both people to be at their computers at the same moment. Synchronous telecommunications tools include Internet relay chats (IRCs), MUDs, MOOs, and MUSEs (interactive virtual worlds that players construct as they go along), and conferencing tools that allow users to interact with people across vast distances and in real time. Chapter 8 explores many forms and uses of telecommunications for telecollaboration.

The Internet—Accessing.   The ability to access information does not guarantee any benefits to those who possess it or can gain access to it. Information is a resource only to the extent that we are able to find it, to use it, and to distribute it. Nevertheless, the first step in making use of information is having access to it. The Internet offers users infinite possibilities for accessing information.

With so much information available, how do students find what they want? Developing search skills is a necessity. Teachers can help students be effective Internet searchers if they help them learn to analyze their topic, choose a search engine, narrow their search, and troubleshoot unsuccessful searches. Although learning to search the Internet for information is an important skill, the ability to make informed judgments about what is found online is even more important. The art of critically evaluating Internet resources should govern how students use what they find online. Forming a balanced assessment of these resources by distinguishing between content and its presentation is the key. Important evaluation skills include separating form from content, attending to the source, and checking for validity.

The Internet can help students master the curriculum in effective and meaningful ways. It can bring the world's libraries to students. It can help them practice important research and writing skills. It can provide in-depth and current resources and information. The challenge is to order and control the information, learn how to ask the right questions, and become aware of the biases of the information provider. Chapter 7 explores the complex process of teaching students to be information users and examines the role of the Internet in support of the process.

Simulations—Experimenting and Structuring.   A simulation is a representation or model of an event, an object, or some phenomenon—a computerized model of a real or imagined system designed to teach how a certain system or a similar one works. Simulations are engaging, gain and hold learners' attention, permit continuation from any stopping point over multiple sessions, allow attainment of meaningful goals within a reasonable time, are realistic, or at least plausible, are appropriately random and unpredictable, and focus on significant content not trivial details. Simulations are unique instructional strategies because they are representations of reality that when used in an instructional context are repeatable, consistent, take less time, cost less than most other instructional strategies, and are always available. As a vehicle for the acquisition of knowledge and skills in an active exploratory learning environment, simulations allow for student interaction by the entering of answers, directions, decisions, or problem solutions. During this process, the learner is actively involved in constructing and reconstructing his or her knowledge base. Learning occurs "by doing."

When teachers choose simulations to be part of students' learning experiences, they are conveying a vision of knowledge different from other forms of instruction. When using simulations, learners do not master a discrete body of knowledge, isolated as a collection of facts. Simulations are complex systems in which programmers have encoded the structures or central concepts that govern a particular knowledge domain and the processes by which those structures interact. They point out to learners the need to understand not a mass of facts or a sequence of events but rather the structures and processes shared by like sets of facts or events.

The market offers many simulations, but it is sometimes difficult to locate one on a desired topic. There are a number of educational software publishers who produce and sell simulations. Many of the home entertainment software publishers sell simulations. Simulations are also available from online sources. Some online simulations are played over the Internet; others are available on the Internet for downloading.

Simulations can be powerful tools for educators. The main advantage in using simulations is that they give students the power to manipulate various aspects of the model. With a computer simulation, students become an active part of the educational environment and can usually see the immediate results of the decisions they make in this environment. In a sense, students are given the power to "play" with a model of the subject being studied and to experience the effects of changing different variables in the model. Simulations are best used when students have mastered a set of concepts and are ready to apply the acquired knowledge. For maximum effectiveness, simulations require careful background preparation of students. In addition, teachers must utilize effective debriefing activities in order to support the learning environment desired. If made an integral part of the ongoing curriculum, simulations have the potential to build student knowledge in different and more elaborate ways. Students learn the implications of new knowledge, how that knowledge can be used for informed decision making and problem solving, and how to build confidence in the power of their knowledge.

Multimedia—Collecting and Presenting.   Multimedia means many mediums. Media are the tools we use to store, process, and communicate information. In a multimedia program, media—of text, graphics, sound, animation, and video—are combined to communicate information. The essential feature of multimedia is the variety of modalities in which information is presented. Multimedia does not suggest "how" that information should be used. The concept of multimedia does *not* include a notion of how information should be organized. Many multimedia programs use a linear system for accessing information—users "flip" through information much as they turn the pages of a book. The power of these presentation tools is to support students as they plan and deliver public representations of their learning.

Hypermedia—Representing and Connecting. Hypermedia is a concept for consulting multimedia information resources. Hypermedia implicitly advocates how to access information elements and how to crisscross information. Hypermedia offers students the opportunity to merge the linearity of print with the nonlinearity of the visual media, adding sound and animation to dazzle us, adding complexity to the information load with which we must deal, and creating a giant web of information. Whether these webs of information are represented as computer programs for the desktop computer or as Web sites on the World Wide Web, choosing hypermedia tools offers students new methods for structured discovery, addresses varied learning styles, motivates and empowers students, and accommodates nonlinear exploration, allowing educators to present information as a web of interconnections rather than a stream of facts. Students learn more when they are the designer and creator of the hypermedia stack as opposed to being the user of someone else's stack because planning a stack requires choosing a topic, identifying the audience, making a storyboard of each screen, and choosing appropriate graphics for the project.

Mathematical Devices—Computing and Modeling. Calculators allow users to perform mathematical operations. All calculators allow users to perform the mathematical operations of addition, subtraction, multiplication, and division. Some calculators also allow users to compute square roots, trigonometric formulas, and percentages. Now, there are even graphing calculators that enable the user to figure out algebraic equations. Graphing calculators allow students to explore mathematical concepts without having to generate graphs and tables. They enable students to see past the routine aspects of a task. Graphing calculators provide a microworld in which students can safely explore, trying out new models and seeing results. With this tool, students are able to take a problem and work out their own approach to solving it. They can experiment with different equations, creating graphs that look quite different from those they have done before. Students can zoom in on interesting features of the graph or zoom out to get a global picture. They can even see what a difference scale makes to the graph.

PROBEWARE Graphing calculators, paired with computer based labs (CBLs), provide students the opportunity to collect and explore real-time data. CBLs, or probeware as they are more commonly referred to, contain a probe or sensor that allows students to measure temperature, humidity, light intensity, distance, acceleration, velocity, force, voltage, motion, heartbeat rate, respiration, and pH levels. The sensor converts the physical quantity being measured into an electronic signal. An interface device tells the sensor what to do and stores the data the sensor is grabbing. This data is stored on the graphing calculator and can be downloaded to a computer. The advantage of using CBLs and graphing calculators together is that students focus changes from measurement and recording to experimentation. Large amounts of data can be collected in one class period, and the effects of several independent variables can be determined quickly. Such activities help students see the relevance of mathematics to their lives and provide students with a better understanding of the world around them and how it functions.

SPREADSHEETS   Spreadsheets are computer programs that allow the user to organize and manipulate numbers. Spreadsheets are able to process calculations faster and more accurately than other tools such as calculators. If a spreadsheet is programmed to add a column of numbers, the sum will automatically change if any of the numbers are altered. Spreadsheet files can be saved and retrieved at a later time. In both of these cases, there is no need to reenter the data as required with most calculators. Spreadsheets allow students to visualize the data. Many spreadsheets include the capacity to create charts and graphs that provide a visual representation of the data.

Spreadsheet programs can be used at all levels of education. Although educators tend to associate spreadsheet use with Math or Business courses, they can also be used in Social Studies, Science, or any subject that requires the manipulation of numerical data. Applications such as spreadsheets allow students to move away from the drill-and-practice software commonly used to teach mathematics and into an environment that allows students to gather, record, manipulate, and display data while seeking reasonable solutions to a problem. Spreadsheet activities emphasize reasoning, problem solving, making connections, and communicating mathematical ideas.

COMPUTER PROGRAMMING   Programming refers to the act of writing a series of instructions that direct the computer to perform a given task. When students write instructions for the computer, they cannot be the same kinds of instructions given to a human being. Computers have limited capacity to understand, and no capacity to compensate for poor communication. Computer programming languages allow students to create models of how the world around them functions.

There are several reasons for including programming in the curriculum. First, programming is the best way to show students that computers are under human control not vice versa. Second, programming offers the opportunity for students to experience success other than in a right/wrong context. Third, programming can be an excellent way for students to collaborate and communicate with each other. Fourth, programming is a viable approach for teaching problem solving.

As we have seen, the tools we use in learning are central to the intellectual activities in which we engage. Tools mediate between our world and our understanding, but they are not neutral. Each tool influences the ways in which experiences are understood. When educators design learning opportunities for students, they must select tools consistent with and supportive of the intellectual challenges presented to learners. Do you want students to understand how plants use water, sunlight, and nutrients? Choose a textbook, a resource book, and/or an electronic library. Do you want students to experiment with the ways in which water, soil, sunlight, and fertilizers interact to produce plants? Choose a computer simulation. Do you want to introduce students to a culture or a social issue of concern? Choose a video or film. Do you want students to research an issue and present their opinion? Choose a combination of library reference material, appropriate Internet sites, paper and pencil, word processors, and presentation software.

What System of Assessment Might a Designer Construct to Appropriately Assess Student Learning?

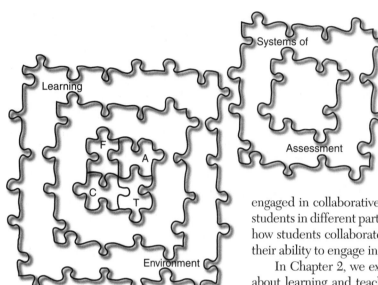

Any design, no matter how well conceived, is not complete without a complementary system of assessment. If students are asked to construct original solutions to the problem of designing a habitat for a desert animal, assessing them only on the name and characteristics of the animal will not help students, teachers, or parents evaluate students' problem-solving abilities. If students are engaged in collaborative data collection on water quality with students in different parts of the world, evaluation must include how students collaborate in electronic communities as well as their ability to engage in scientific data collection and analysis.

In Chapter 2, we explored current and emerging theories about learning and teaching—the multidimensional nature of human potential and constructivist learning. Teachers who view learning from this perspective emphasize different elements for assessment than those used in standardized tests. These teachers notice the knowledge and skills their students bring to class, observe how students interact and solve problems, and then provide multiple ways for students to learn and demonstrate their learning. They often focus on students' in-class work and ask students to tell them how they solved a problem or what their intention is as they write or work on projects.

Designing learning opportunities for students consistent with these perspectives depends, in part, on our ability as educators to embed our designs in appropriate systems of assessment. If, for instance, we design problem-centered learning opportunities for students but hold them accountable for only factual knowledge, students will soon recognize the discrepancy between our actions and our assessments and learn to value their ability to accumulate information over their ability to solve problems. If students are encouraged to become active constructors of knowledge but graded only on memory and recall, students will not learn to value their growth as independent learners. The ways in which foundations, activities, contents, and tools are fit together with assessment influence the overall success of a learning design as well as the overall climate or community of the classroom.

Assessment of student work requires multiple forms of assessment—a system of assessment. A variety of alternative assessment strategies including rubrics, portfolios, peer critiques, exhibitions, and performance assessment, supported by technology applications, can provide designs for assessment compatible with emerging educational goals. Educators must make wise choices from the menu of possibilities and combine them in ways that allow for the assessment of a wide range of student learning. Thus, educators need opportunities to assess development of students' background knowledge. Standardized tests and teacher-made objective tests serve well to learn about the facts, definitions, and content inherent in student learning. Educators need opportunities to assess students' development over time. They also need opportunities to assess how students define and understand their own learning. Portfolio assessment can support both student learning and assessment of student learning over time. Educators need opportunities to assess students' problem-solving abilities, and the ways in which students' problem solving takes on visible form through their productions. Rubrics can support thoughtful and comprehensive assessment of students' individual and collective productions. Learning to make wise choices from this menu of options and combining them into systems that support the outcomes of an overall design are explored in depth in Chapter 9.

How Might Learning Environments Be Constructed to Complement the Overall Learning Design?

Learning environments are instructional strategies. Teachers' choices about the types and organization of learning environments are choices about what and how students will learn. All learning takes place in a context. And, if the decisions teachers make about the learning environment are inconsistent with the designs they create to meet learning goals, the impact of these learning opportunities will be less powerful and important for students than teachers might hope. The arrangement of a learning environment and the presence or absence of materials and tools speak loudly to students about what is expected, what is valued, and how students are to act. It is an important and active part of the teaching/learning process.

Teachers may never have the opportunity to design an entire school building, but they daily make decisions about the organization of their classroom environment. And these decisions are decisions about what and how students will learn. Environmental messages can urge movement, call attention to some learning materials but not others, encourage deep or superficial involvement, and invite children to hurry or move calmly. Environmental arrangements can also promote independence and self-direction, encourage use of skills, and lengthen or shorten attention span. The environment sends messages, and learners respond.

Learning environments are not only physical spaces; they can also be intellectual spaces. Carefully selected intellectual learning environments represent comprehensive systems that promote engagement through student-centered activities including guided presentations, manipulation, and explorations among interrelated learning themes. A learner's interaction with these intellectual environments models, engages, and challenges the user to think in certain ways. These tools create learning environments just as surely as desks, chairs, and chalkboards create learning environments. When learners interact with these environments, they begin to see reality differently simply because these environments structure knowledge and activity in particular ways.

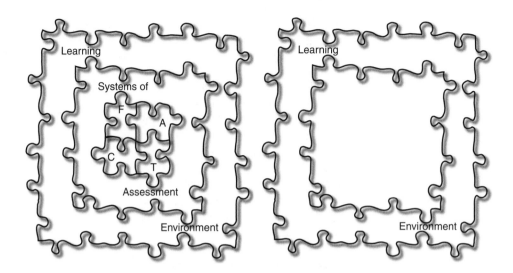

And finally, designers must recognize that in addition to physical and intellectual spaces, learning environments are values spaces. The manner in which learning environments are designed conveys fundamental lessons about the way to learn, about the value of learning, about being a member of one's community, and about who we are as individual learners. These lessons are at least as important, if not more important, than the overt curriculum of orbiting planets, wars fought, or computer programming. Responsibility for establishing a climate of values does not belong to the school alone, however. Values do not start and stop at the classroom door. Any values climate must be consistent with the values of the community. In Chapter 10, we explore criteria for designing physical, intellectual, and values spaces consistent with and complementary to the comprehensive designs for learning.

The FACTS Web-Based Design Tool

The FACTS Web-Based Design Tool is an online interactive environment that supports the transition from the design process presented in this book to designs of action that can be implemented in classrooms. Even though the FACTS design model appears as a linear process when captured by the structure of this book's text, it is, in reality, a dynamic, iterative process.

As mentioned earlier, the process of using the FACTS design model is much like assembling a puzzle. That is, each piece must be identified and created and then fit together with the remaining pieces. You might, for instance, begin with the Content piece by identifying standards and subject matter that you would like to teach. You might then work to analyze that content for its knowledge (one of the Foundations) components, moving next to identify activities and tools. As you work through fitting the pieces together, you may find that you want to return to a previous piece to add, delete, or modify your ideas. Eventually, as you move back and forth between the pieces, a complete learning design emerges. The FACTS Web-Based Design Tool supports and models this process better than a more static paper and pencil environment because an online, linked environment is more flexible and interactive.

You can sign on to the FACTS Web-Based Design Tool, establish a permanent log-in and password, and use the tool anytime you want—even after you are finished reading the book and/or taking a course. The first time you sign on to the Web site you will be prompted to create a user account and password. Be sure you pick a log-in and password that you will remember. It might be wise to record your choices in your textbook, date book, or notebook. The address or URL for the FACTS Web-Based Design Tool is http://www.norton.wadsworth.com.

Using a computer with an Internet connection and a Web browser such as *Internet Explorer* or *Netscape,* enter the aforementioned URL and press return. The opening Web page for the FACTS Web-Based Design Tool will appear (Figure 3.2). On this Web page, there are four puzzle pieces that link to the Design Mentors, the Design Challenges, and the Design Examples, respectively, as well as a puzzle piece that enables you to Create Your Own Design. Using the process of modeling, coaching, and fading, these links support learning to use the FACTS design model. The Design Mentors provide you with the opportunity to observe teachers using the design model. The Design Examples allow you to examine a variety of completed learning designs. The Design Challenges present instructional dilemmas and coach you as you experiment with using the design model. The Create Your Own Design link takes you to the FACTS Web-Based Design Tool environment that you can use to solve your own instructional dilemmas. A more complete description of each of the four links follows.

Design Mentors

Design Mentors are Web-based models that illustrate the thinking processes and design outcomes of Allan Sutton and Brooks White as they use the FACTS Web-Based Design Tool to create a design for learning applicable to their own classroom practice. Mr. Sutton's design, The Timber Lane Detective Agency, invites students to become detectives and learn detecting skills. The unit culminates in students' abilities to solve a crime in their school and make an arrest. Mr. Sutton created the design to teach reading, problem solving, science, and language arts in a multiage fourth- and fifth-grade classroom. Ms. White's design, The Perfect Presidential Candidate, challenges students to join a political action committee and participate in activities that allow them to identify a presidential candidate who will run for office on a platform that promotes solutions to issues identified by high school students. Ms. White created the design for her high school Civics/Government classes.

These Design Mentors allow you to observe the thinking processes of these teachers as they wrestle with an instructional dilemma and illustrate how the content of each chapter informed their design process. They allow you to follow along with Ms. White and Mr. Sutton as they used information in each chapter to add to, delete from, and modify their design. There are two Design Mentors associated with each chapter, beginning with Chapter 4.

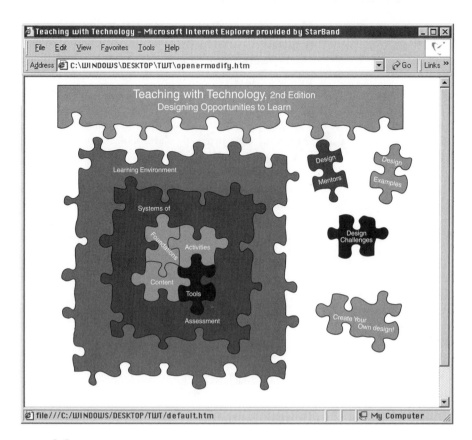

FIGURE **3.2**

THE FACTS WEB-BASED DESIGN TOOL HOMEPAGE

Design Challenges

After you have read each of the remaining chapters in this book, the Design Challenges link takes you to tutorial Web pages that present you with an instructional dilemma and coach you through the process of designing a learning opportunity responsive to the instructional dilemma. The Design Challenges provide links to resources, additional information, and prompts and/or references to sections of this book. These challenges provide text boxes for entering your thinking as you proceed through the Design Challenge. We have found that using these Design Challenges is enhanced if you team up with a classmate or colleague. Planning with others often expands your understanding of the many possible solutions to a single instructional dilemma.

It is important to remember that the ideas you enter in the text boxes will not be saved. When you close this page, your text will be lost. Thus, when you have completed a Design Challenge, you should save your emerging design as a text file. You can open this text file in a word processor and continue to modify it at a later date. You can also print your work, or you can e-mail it to your instructor, classmate, and/or colleague to ask for feedback on the way in which you solved the instructional dilemma.

Design Examples

Design Examples are completed designs created by teachers. They are simply Web pages that demonstrate what the finished product is when you have completed a design using the FACTS Web-Based Design Tool. We have tried to include examples from a number of different grade levels and content and subject matter areas. Perhaps when you have used the tool to complete a design for learning that you are particularly proud of, you will e-mail a copy of it to us for inclusion at this link. Use Priscilla's e-mail address: pnorton@gmu.edu.

Create Your Own Design

This puzzle piece links you directly to the FACTS Web-Based Design Tool where you can create your own design. The Design Challenge for this chapter was created to help you learn about the FACTS Web-Based Design Tool. This might be the time to use the previously mentioned URL http://www.norton.wadsworth.com. Click on the Design Challenges puzzle piece, select Design Challenge Three, and explore the FACTS Web-Based Design Tool.

CHAPTER IDEAS

- There is some controversy and a great deal of discussion these days about the role of the classroom teacher. Some say, in a rather pejorative way, that the role of teachers has traditionally been that of a "sage on the stage." Others would describe the role of a teacher as a "director." In the last 20 years, various alternative descriptors of the educator's role have emerged. A teacher is a facilitator; a teacher is a coach; a teacher is a cognitive mentor. This suggests that as learners what students need is a "guide on the side"— a provocateur and support system.
- Regardless of which of these versions or combination of versions of what a teacher ought to be, there is a much more fundamental but less discussed role. That is, the teacher as designer. The teacher as a designer recognizes the centrality of planning, structuring, provisioning, and orchestrating learning.
- Our design puzzle has five major pieces—Foundations, Activities, Content(s), Tools, and Systems of assessment. As a memory aid, we refer to these as the FACTS of Design. These five pieces form the core considerations for the design of learning opportunities.
- Unfortunately, the design process is not as tidy as it first appears. It is a dynamic, interactive process. To aid teachers in the use of this model, it

occurred to us that an interactive Web-based design tool would be an appropriate design environment.

- *What Foundations of learning do today's students most need to learn?* What is schooling for? What do we hope for all learners as they progress toward the end of their K–12 learning experience? Those who design learning opportunities for today's students must not only think about and design the overt curriculum, they must hold in their minds a set of foundations or habits of mind that they want students to take from their learning experiences. What do we hope for our students? What foundational habits of mind should students be developing over time? What are the fundamentals that transcend topics, projects, assignments, assessments, and grades?

- *What Activities should designers choose to ensure that students become actively engaged in learning through construction?* Educators must design opportunities for students to engage in the kinds of activities that support and shape the ability to think and problem-solve. These activities should help students become competent with at least four categories of cognition: memory, information extending processes, information rearranging processes, and metacognition.

- While it is possible to create designs for developing and refining these heuristic processes, it is likely that their development is better facilitated when anchored in broader learning activities. Anchored instruction creates environments that permit sustained exploration by students and teachers, enabling them to understand the kinds of problems and opportunities experts in various areas encounter and the knowledge that these experts use. One way to plan for anchored instruction is to use problem-based or problem-centered learning.

- Once a design for learning has been anchored in a problem, students must be challenged with appropriate activities that support and direct their ability to solve problems in a robust and comprehensive manner. If student learning is to be contextualized in a culture of practice and anchored with a problem of significance, opportunities for student learning must be bolstered by students' participation in authentic activities, building knowledge activities, constructing activities, and sharing activities—the ABCS of Activity.

- *What Contents, ideas, and/or concepts afford a context for student learning?* When educators design learning opportunities for students, they must select the "something" of learning. This "something" can be selected from the interests and urgencies of students themselves. It can be part of the prescribed curriculum, reflecting the history, literature, science, and values judged by the learning community as fundamental to living in and contributing to that community. It can be drawn from events in the news or from professional standards created by curriculum and disciplinary experts. For most educators today, the source of the "something" around which a design for learning pivots is the standards established by their state.

- While many challenge the adoption of these standards and/or their concomitant systems of assessment (e.g., Ohanian, 1999; Meier, 2000), they are the realities of current educational practice. They are the "something" of education. But only when seen through the lens of the efficiency model do they become a list of objectives to be taught, tested, and retaught. Instead, when viewed as the "something" of learning and placed within a larger design frame they become the content of learning—the vehicle for subsequent deeper understandings about the physical, social, and intellectual world in which we all live.
- *What Tools might a designer choose to best support and enhance student learning?* Making wise choices about the use of technology, then, depends on recognizing the ways in which it facilitates the things humans can do. The tools made available to members of a community provide opportunities for shaping the world in which they live.
- Every technology has properties—affordances—that make some activities easier and some activities more difficult and some activities impossible. Each technology creates a mind-set, a way of thinking about it and the activities to which it is relevant.
- The design of opportunities to learn must include the careful consideration and selection of tools. The kinds of tools offered to students as they interact with content, engage in activities, and develop competence with the foundations of learning determine, to a large extent, the kinds of learning outcomes possible.
- When educators design learning opportunities for students, they must select tools consistent with and supportive of the intellectual challenges presented to learners.
- *What System of assessment might a designer construct to appropriately assess student learning?* Any design, no matter how well conceived, is not complete without a complementary system of assessment. Designing learning opportunities for students depends, in part, on our ability as educators to embed our designs in appropriate systems of assessment.
- Assessment of student work requires multiple forms of assessment—a system of assessment. A variety of alternative assessment strategies including rubrics, portfolios, peer critiques, exhibitions, and performance assessment, supported by technology applications, can provide designs for assessment compatible with emerging educational goals. Educators must make wise choices from the menu of possibilities and combine them in ways that allow for the assessment of a wide range of student learning.
- *How might learning environments be constructed to complement the overall learning design?* Learning environments are instructional strategies. Teachers' choices about the types and organization of learning environments are choices about what and how students will learn.
- Learning environments are not only physical spaces; they can also be intellectual spaces. Carefully selected intellectual learning environments represent comprehensive systems that promote engagement through

student-centered activities including guided presentations, manipulation, and explorations among interrelated learning themes. A learner's interaction with these intellectual environments models, engages, and challenges the user to think in certain ways.

- Designers must recognize that in addition to physical and intellectual spaces, learning environments are values spaces. The manner in which learning environments are designed conveys fundamental lessons about the way to learn, about the value of learning, about being a member of one's community, and about who we are as individual learners.

- The FACTS Web-Based Design Tool is an online interactive environment that supports the transition from the design process presented in this book to designs of action that can be implemented in classrooms. The address or URL for the FACTS Web-Based Design Tool is http://www.norton.wadsworth.com.

DESIGNS FOR KNOWLEDGE

Most important: information is not knowledge. . . . There's a relationship between data, information, knowledge, understanding and wisdom. Our networks are awash in data. A little of it's information. A smidgen of this shows up as knowledge. Combined with ideas, some of that is actually useful. Mix in experience, context, compassion, discipline, humor, tolerance, and humility, and perhaps knowledge becomes wisdom. Minds work with ideas, not information. No amount of data, bandwidth, or processing power can substitute for inspired thought.

Clifford Stoll
Silicon Snake Oil, 1995

The understandings of the disciplines represent the most important cognitive achievements of human beings. It is necessary to come to know these understandings if we are to be fully human, to live in our time, to be able to understand it to the best of our abilities, and to build upon it. The five-year-old knows many things, but he cannot know what disciplinary experts have discovered over the centuries. Perhaps our daily lives might not be that different if we continue to believe that the world is flat, but such a belief makes it impossible for us to appreciate in any rounded way the nature of time, travel, weather, or seasons; the behavior of objects; and the personal and cultural options open to us.

Howard Gardner
The Unschooled Mind,
1991

Education has long been plagued by the need to find an equilibrium between teaching knowledge related to specific skills concerned primarily with one's profession and teaching knowledge that leads to general understandings necessary for dealing with the affairs of life. In the eighteenth century, Benjamin Franklin spoke to the importance of maintaining this delicate balance when he wrote: "It would be well if they [students] could be taught everything that is useful and everything that is ornamental; but art is long and their time is short. It is therefore proposed that they learn those things that are likely to be most useful and most ornamental."

What is most useful for today's and tomorrow's students and what is most ornamental for them in the conduct of their individual and collective lives? Educators must ad-

dress questions like this one as they design opportunities for students to become knowledgeable. They must be prepared to select what is most useful and most ornamental, finding a balance between academic and practical knowledge. They must find ways to teach knowledge that enable students to understand and contribute to their personal, vocational, social, political, technological, and scientific contexts.

This chapter explores (1) teaching disciplinary structures as frameworks for understanding multiple contents; (2) teaching disciplinary habits of mind or processes so that students learn to "do" the disciplines—to act and think as economists, biologists, politicians, and chemists in the conduct of their lives; and (3) using a variety of discourse forms as modes of thinking that support understanding and the development of knowledge.

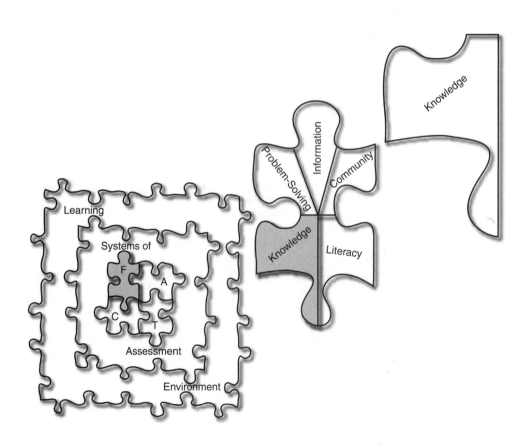

WAYS OF KNOWING

At Stanford University, a young emergency room doctor sits in front of a monitor and watches as a man enters the emergency room, screaming for help and bleeding profusely from a shotgun wound. Attendants lift him onto a stretcher and cut off his T-shirt. A nurse asks, "What are we going to do, Doctor?" On one side of the monitor is a list of possible actions; on the other side, the clock ticks away. A wrong action or a delayed action results in the patient's death. In southern California, a U.S. Border Patrol officer sits in front of a monitor and watches a man carrying a gun run out of a store. "Robbery!" shouts a voice as the man turns and points his gun in the young officer's direction. Sometimes the man with the gun is the store manager, and other times he is the robber. In another scenario, a woman driver reaches into her purse. Sometimes she pulls out her driver's license, and other times she pulls out a revolver. A wrong judgment on the officer's part and an innocent person is dead. Welcome to the new world of "toy universes"!

These toy universes or computer simulations are increasingly replacing textbooks as a means for organizing the essential elements of knowledge (Rogers, 1987). Doctors must know basic content knowledge, but what is important in the practice of medicine is a doctor's ability to put that knowledge to work. Doctors cannot stand outside the world of medicine, observing it objectively. Public safety officers must know the specific laws and policies that govern their work, but what is most important for these officers is the ability to use that knowledge to interpret the ever-changing dilemmas of police work. They must learn that simple actions do not always lead to the same results.

The electronic technologies are creating new and important learning opportunities—not only for training purposes but for research. Scientists at Los Alamos National Laboratory are using simulations to study the immune system, watching as antibodies respond to reproducing viruses created by computer programs. Other scientists are creating toy universes that simulate the Mohave Desert. Is it possible to manipulate these replicas, they ask, to identify ways to preserve species nearing extinction? A third group of scientists is creating simulations of weather patterns. Is it possible to discover more effective strategies for predicting the weather? Students can learn with these toy universes as well.

These "learning environments" point to what is important about knowledge; they serve not only as research and learning tools but as a metaphor for understanding what it is that is important to know. These learning environments are not simple, mechanical, linear systems expressed as collections of facts and events organized by textbooks. They are complex systems in which programmers have embedded understanding of the structures or central concepts that govern a particular knowledge domain and by an expression of the processes by which those structures interact. They point to the need for today's learners to understand not a mass of facts or a sequence of events but the structures and processes shared by like sets of facts or events. It is less important for today's learners to remember the specifics of the Greek, Roman, and Egyptian empires than to understand the various ways in which civilizations come to shape social, political, economic, and cultural realities. It is less important for today's learners to list the human body's bones and organs than to understand how all organisms are comprised of 10 interacting systems. It is less important for students to list a collection of laws than to understand the legislative process and the values and interpretations that underlie both the process and the laws.

Disciplinary learning that incorporates the electronic technologies is not a threat to traditional frameworks for developing knowledge of the disciplines. Instead, the electronic technologies are yet one more tool in the arsenal of the disciplinary thinker. These electronic technologies do not supplant the importance of traditional learning but, rather, highlight the need to extend the habits of thinking that can be used to interpret political, social, economic, biological, chemical, and physical experience. And, it is the combination of these new tools and the traditional tools of the disciplines that equip students with the habits, dispositions, and contents of mind to tackle contemporary problems—the mysteries of evolution, the vagaries of international finance, battling AIDS, designing computers that learn, and charting a course for world peace.

Learning and the Disciplines

Although a somewhat artificial division, disciplinary knowledge may be divided into three broad disciplines: the humanities, the hard sciences, and the social sciences. These categories emerged in the history of Western thought with the fragmentation of philosophy into narrower domains of inquiry and with the birth of the age of science. These general categories serve as useful divisions. They represent the areas in which we have created theories and generalizations about ourselves and the world in which we live. After the first several grades where emphasis is placed on the tools we use to study the disciplines (especially reading, writing, and mathematics), helping students master these ideas and the habits of mind associated with these domains constitutes the main mandate of the educational enterprise.

Today, as in times past, education is being challenged by the media, researchers, and policy makers for its inability to live up to the expectations of this mandate. This is not a new challenge, and the passion for a core of content area knowledge was embraced by such educational notables as Horace Mann in the mid-nineteenth century, Harvard's President Charles Elliot, Chair of the 1893 Committee of Ten, and James Conant who called for providing rigorous academic content in the mid-1950s. The design of an educational response in each instance, including those related to the most current set of challenges, can be characterized as pendular swings between "teacher-centered" and "student-centered" learning and "academic" and "practical" approaches to learning. Yet, these swings have resulted in little more than what Cuban (1990) has called "reform again, again, and again," seldom with substantial consequences for actual classroom practice. Instead, conventional wisdom about design for knowledge has persistently relied on a view of knowledge as an identified, discrete body of essential knowledge and skills. This definition of knowledge has resulted in a "competency-based curricula + direct instruction + standardized tests = measurement-driven teaching and higher test scores" equation that focuses on skills and knowledge that typi-

Swings

cally appear in test items (Cuban, 1986a). It is amazing how enduring this perception is.

It is easy for students and teachers and parents to become confused about the disciplines. All too often, disciplinary learning is reduced to a collection of facts, concepts, or theories to be memorized. Speeding from Plato to NATO in 35 breathless weeks hardly prepares students to appreciate how historians' habits of mind and inquiry might help make sense of the varied claims made about the Vietnam War or the character of Martin Luther King, Jr. "Covering" all that biology has discovered in five hours per week for nine months hardly prepares students to use the intellectual tools of the biologist to avoid the rumors of bio-terrorism or reason through the ethics of bio-engineering. Facts, concepts, and theories are the grist of the disciplinary thinker, but it is the "lens" of the discipline that empowers students to interpret their world. Supporting students as they extract a discipline's characteristic observations and inferences and habits of mind from the grist of facts and concepts and adapt them as their own is the central goal of designs for knowledge.

> Education cannot fit every student with a full set of lenses; indeed, we are doomed to fail if we aim to make each youngster into a historian, a biologist, or a composer of classical music. Our goal should not be to telescope graduate training but rather to give students access to the "intellectual heart" or "experiential soul" of a discipline. (Gardner, 2000, p. 157)

KNOWLEDGE OF STRUCTURE AND PROCESS: CONTENT AS VEHICLE

We know more and more about less and less (Toffler, 1980). Schools can no longer take as their central mandate the goal of ensuring student knowledge about all there is to know in the disciplines. When teachers design opportunities for students to develop knowledge, they must base the study of the disciplines on more than content descriptions of knowledge. That is not to suggest that content is not important, but, rather, that content is not the only aspect of knowledge. Knowledge is more than a collection of one-to-one correspondences to specific objects, events, situations, or interpretations. Educators must design learning opportunities by teaching the structures and processes related to disciplinary knowledge so that students will be able to use their understandings to interpret and influence their world.

Giving primacy to structure and process as central learning goals in the disciplines does not eliminate teaching content. Rather, content can serve as the vehicle by which students learn about structure and process. Particular contents can serve as case studies for extracting the structures and processes that give shape to experience. Content can be used as an illustration of the way in which structure and process shape experience. Careful selection of particular contents can serve to highlight what is seen as central to the values of a particular culture at a particular time.

Learning about Structures

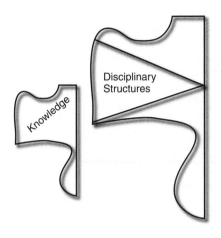

Disciplinary Structures

Knowledge

The role of structure in disciplinary knowledge is not a new concept, just an unrealized concept. The structure of a discipline is defined by the central theories or operations that explain specific cases and form organizing principles for the study of that discipline. It involves actively grasping key principles or concepts. "Grasping the structure of a subject is understanding it in a way that permits many other things to be related to it meaningfully" (Bruner, 1960, p. 43).

If one has children observe an inchworm crossing a piece of graph paper mounted on a flat board, they will soon observe that the inchworm travels in a straight line. If students tilt the board upward 30 degrees, they will observe that the inchworm travels at a 45-degree angle. If they tilt the board to a 60-degree incline, the worm travels at a 67½-degree angle. With teacher assistance, students should be able to infer that the inchworm travels along an incline at 15 degrees. This phenomenon illustrates the structure of tropism, not an isolated fact that applies only to inchworms. Rather, in simple organisms, locomotion is regulated according to a fixed standard. Once students grasp this basic relation between external stimulation and locomotor action, they are well on their way to being able to handle a good deal of seemingly new but, in fact, highly related information because this principle applies not only to an organism's movement along a plane but also to an organism's movement in relation to light, temperature, and salinity (Bruner, 1960).

When students learn about westward expansion using The Oregon Trail 5th Edition (Learning Company), they are learning about more than wagons, oxen, trail masters, food gathering, and Indian battles. They are engaged with a historical case study in the human desire to stretch beyond the familiar. As a case study, this program engages students with the structural concepts inherent in any attempt to move beyond the confines of one's own immediate context—the need for a mode of transportation, the necessity of meeting nutritional needs, the need to deal with medical emergencies, the need for safety, and the need for economic resources. In essence, students are engaged in the manipulation and exploration of the structural elements inherent in all human exploration whether it be taking a summer vacation trip or embarking on a voyage to outer space.

At least three claims can be made for emphasizing the role of structure over content in teaching disciplinary knowledge. First, knowledge about the structures of a discipline makes it more understandable. *understanding* For instance, grasping that any nation must trade to maintain a growing and vibrant economy makes both colonial America's relation to Britain in the 1700s and Japanese–American relations in the 1980s and 1990s more comprehensible. Second, if content knowledge is related in some way to the structural elements of a discipline, it will be more effectively remembered. That is why cramming for a multiple-choice exam so often results in impermanent knowledge. *memory* Third, knowledge organized around the structure of a discipline facilitates transfer of learning. *transfer* To understand a specific case as an example of a more general case is to have learned not only the specific but also a model for making sense of related things (Bruner, 1960).

Mr. McCannon teaches American history to high school juniors. He usually taught about the twentieth century during the last nine-week period of the school year, but he had begun to recognize that his traditional approach to history was boring students. Students had lost interest in videos, lectures, and their text. So, instead of using the sequence of chapters in the text to define his curriculum, Mr. McCannon decided to focus on international relations beginning with World War I. Analyzing international relations, he identified seven structures or central concepts. These included open warfare, guerilla warfare, diplomacy/negotiation, deterrence, imperialism, isolationism, and collaboration. He next reviewed twentieth century conflicts to identify case studies representative of each structure.

[handwritten margin note: structure = central concept]

Although case studies did not always reflect pure examples of each structure, Mr. McCannon was able to identify one twentieth century case study that could serve to demonstrate each of the structures. For open warfare, Mr. McCannon chose World War I. For isolationism, he chose pre–World War II. For deterrence, he chose U.S.–Soviet relations between the end of World War II and the fall of the Berlin Wall. For guerilla warfare, he chose the Vietnam conflict. For diplomacy and negotiation, he chose the U.S. efforts to resolve the Israeli–Arab conflict, emphasizing the Carter and Clinton administrations. For collaboration, he chose the Gulf War and Bush's "new world order." For imperialism, he chose pre-Castro U.S.–Cuban relations.

At the beginning of the last nine-week grading period, Mr. McCannon introduced his classes to Tom Snyder's *The Other Side. The Other Side* presents students with the challenge of earning enough money to purchase bricks used to build a bridge between two imaginary countries. In order to earn money, students must explore and drill for three different kinds of oil. A gallon of one kind of oil is worth $5; mixing a gallon from two kinds of oil is worth $10 a gallon; and mixing a gallon from three kinds of oil is worth $25. The problem is that all three kinds of oil are not available in any one country and must be obtained from the "other side." Before taking their turn at the computer, each team must plan a series of actions and messages to the other side. When students played the game for the first time, Mr. McCannon introduced them to the goal of the simulation, how actions were communicated to the simulation, and how money was earned. He did not talk with students about the possible strategies they might use to accomplish their goal—building a bridge between two countries.

This simulation can be played with one classroom computer, with two classroom computers linked with a cable, and over the Internet. Since Mr. McCannon was able to borrow four computers for his classroom, he chose to use a modified version of the one computer classroom model. When students played *The Other Side*, teams of students took turns going to the computer to enter their planned actions and to receive new information with which to plan their next actions. With four computers, Mr. McCannon was able to divide the class into eight teams of three or four students with two teams sharing a computer, each team role-playing one of the two countries. It was not long before students had lost control of the game, and bombs were launched. The game was soon over.

Bringing the class together for a debriefing, Mr. McCannon asked students about what had seemed to work for them and what had seemed to result in loss of control and bombing. He asked students what their strategy had been. When most teams expressed that they had not developed a clear strategy, Mr. McCannon suggested that the study of examples of international relations during the twentieth century might help them understand how international relations might be better conducted.

Each week, Mr. McCannon provided the teams with a set of materials related to one of the case studies. Appropriate selections from the textbook, fictional and/or informational videos, maps, and reference materials were identified. Students worked in their groups to investigate the case study using the rubric Mr. McCannon provided. Students collaboratively constructed a report summarizing information relevant to each item on the rubric: the history of each of the participants, the sources of the conflict between the two parties, previous attempts at resolution, and an analysis of the strategies used in the resolution of international conflicts. On a designated day, Mr. McCannon led a class discussion related to the rubric, filling in gaps in students' investigation.

Following the discussion day, two days were set aside to play *The Other Side*, using students' new understandings about the structure of international conflict resolution they had been studying. One time they tried guerilla warfare, relying on covert, hit and run actions. Another time they tried isolationism, exploring and drilling for oil only on their side, attempting to amass enough of two kinds of oil to finance their bricks, and ignoring or not sending messages. When students studied U.S.–Cuban relations prior to Castro, teams took turns playing the imperialist. It fascinated Mr. McCannon that the imperialist's demands were at first honored, but, in every case, relations soon dwindled into conflict and aggression. One student even asked Mr. McCannon if he could direct that student to a case study where imperialism had worked well for both sides.

Learning about Processes: Doing the Disciplines

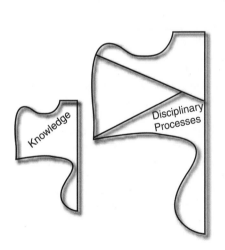

In addition to focusing on structures, teaching in the disciplines must emphasize the processes related to "doing" the disciplines. The disciplines have their greatest relevancy to students' lives as habits of thought and strategies for making sense of experience. Historians examine historical data, compare and contrast accounts of events, refer to additional sources to validate interpretations, and draw connections between events and their impacts. Scientists conduct systematic research projects, draw conclusions from data, and report their findings in scientific journals and at professional conferences. Designing opportunities for developing knowledge that promotes students' abilities to use these processes transcends remembering the outcomes of their use by others.

Teaching the disciplines as "ways to think" about experience has more lasting consequences than only teaching "about" the disciplines. These disciplinary processes

. . . transcend particular goals, particular times, and particular societies. They are transferable from generation to generation almost without being dragged down by semantic details. In a very real sense they are the purest objects we can pass on to our descendants, because they aren't clouded by our own search for advantage.

Our descendants need not have the same search, and will probably not, because of the different circumstances under which they live. But the processes they can use and improve upon. . . . (Perlis quoted in McCorduck, 1985, p. 90)

Teachers who design opportunities for students to develop knowledge by emphasizing the processes involved in "doing" are preparing students to use their understanding of these processes to shape their world. Every discipline has a set of processes its experts use to make sense of experience. Like chemists, biologists, and physicists who use the scientific method, economists, historians, anthropologists, and sociologists use their own processes. They not only study about their discipline, they "do" their discipline.

❋ ❋ ❋ ❋ ❋ ❋ ❋

In Mrs. Suedkamp's fifth-grade classroom, for example, students develop knowledge of economics by acting as economists. They are involved in the invention of marketable products, using division of labor to mass-produce their products, using databases to analyze market surveys, using graphics and video to create advertising campaigns, using spreadsheets to develop accounting systems to keep track of production costs, capital expenditures, and profit, and engaging in salesmanship. For Halloween, students produced, marketed, and sold shrunken heads made of dried apples. For Easter, they produced, marketed, and sold hollowed-out, decorated eggs. For Valentine's Day, they produced, sold, and delivered bouquets of handcrafted flowers and balloons. Students saved the money they made from the sale of each product, using part of their profits as capital for the next product. Their goal was to earn enough money for an end-of-year class camping trip at a nearby national park. They learned economics by "doing" economics. They learned much more than a list of economic concepts and definitions of economic terms presented in their textbook. What they now know about economics prepares them to better understand economic life in a capitalist society as well as to be better, more informed consumers and producers.

❋ ❋ ❋ ❋ ❋ ❋

Don Harvey teaches ninth-grade Biology. In February, 1992, Mr. Harvey read an article in *Discover* magazine by J. Diamond titled "Living Through the Donner Party." It gave him an idea. That year, and as he has done every year since during the first week of school, Mr. Harvey read the story of the Donner Party from the beginning of Diamond's article to his high school biology students. The article describes the Donner Party's journey after they set out for California in late July 1846. As the travelers approached the Sierra Nevada Mountains, they decided to use an untested shortcut, the Hastings Cutoff. Because of delays along the cutoff, it was not until September 30 that a small band of survivors rejoined the Oregon Trail. During the intervening time, the Party had become trapped by snow in the high country of the Sierra Nevadas. Many in the Party died. Survivors had lived by eating stock animals, dogs, hides, and blankets and had eventually resorted to cannibalism.

As always, the story of the Donner Party and the human drama it exemplifies captured the imagination and moral indignation of students. "They what?" queried one student as Mr. Harvey finished reading. "You mean they ate each other?"

blurted a second. "Yuk, I don't believe people would do that," burst forth a third. A lively discussion followed. Students shared their initial reactions and musings. Carefully guided, they soon began to move beyond initial shock and revulsion to confront the central question of survival and what one might be willing to do or not do in order to survive. Diamond (1992) had posed the question this way: "Can you figure out for yourself some general rules about who is most likely to die when the going gets tough?" Grayson (1990) described the Donner Party's tragedy this way:

> When read as sheer historical narrative, the story of the Donner Party provides a powerful look at the dynamics of a small diverse group under conditions that were at best tremendously stressful and at worst catastrophic. When read as biology, the story becomes one of natural selection in action. (p. 241)

Prior to reading the Donner story to the class, Mr. Harvey had created a database using the information provided by the Grayson and Diamond articles. The data on the Donner Party members included age, gender, survivorship, manner of death, and date of death. As the students confronted the questions posed by the episode, Mr. Harvey offered them the use of the database (Figure 4.1). He used a projecting monitor to show them its structure and operating functions. Then, Mr. Harvey divided students into groups of three and set them to work searching for generalizations about which of the Donner Party members had survived and which had perished. They soon discovered that anyone under 5 and over 50 had not survived. "Why?" Mr. Harvey asked. They also discovered that women were more likely to survive than men. "Why?" Mr. Harvey challenged. Men seemed to die from violent causes; women from more natural causes. "Why?" Mr. Harvey pondered aloud. At the beginning of the class two days later, Mr. Harvey offered the groups a second challenge.

"On Monday of next week, the class is going to have a science conference," Mr. Harvey told them. "At the conference, you will be asked to present papers you have written related to what you have learned about survivability and your explanations for these lessons." "Of course," Mr. Harvey explained, "your paper should be backed with supporting data from the database and with accepted scientific theory built from anthropological, geological, evolutionary, and social insights." Students were required to write their papers using a series of subheadings: introduction, statement of the problem, research hypotheses, results with data, conclusions, and discussion. Mr. Harvey offered them a simple desktop publishing tool for publishing their papers. It was not long before students were searching the Internet. They needed answers to many questions. What was the average life span in the mid-1800s? What was the average infant mortality rate in the mid-1800s? Is there any supportive research for the idea that men are more aggressive in their relationships than women? By Monday of the following week, students were ready to present their papers in both written and oral form (Figure 4.2).

The conference was a resounding success, and a lively debate ensued. Students validated each other's conclusions and challenged disparate opinions and interpretations. At the end of the conference, all of the groups were given a copy of Diamond's article and asked to compare and contrast their papers with his. The students rapidly learned that their own powers of interpretation were as effective as that of a professional scientist. Several groups whose hypotheses and interpre-

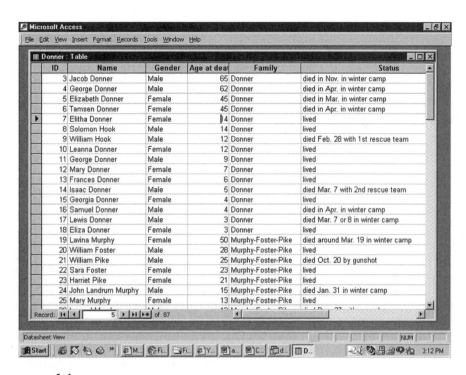

FIGURE 4.1

THE DONNER PARTY MICROSOFT ACCESS DATABASE

Source: Screenshot reprinted with permission from Microsoft Corporation.

tations extended beyond those in the article asked if they might e-mail the author and share their additional conclusions with him. They had invented for themselves the notion of shared dialogue within a scientific community.

This lesson, first reported by Norton and Harvey (1995), illustrates the central difference between design for knowledge that focuses on information retrieval and acquisition of facts and one that focuses on the processes of "doing" science. Science is the process humans have devised to answer questions about their universe. Scientists, in their search for solutions, explanations, and predictive theories, demand evidence, formulate testable hypotheses, use logical reasoning, and value the identification and avoidance of bias. Science can be used to create powerful ideas that cut across political, economic, social, philosophical, technological, and religious boundaries to influence the way the world is viewed and interpreted. Science is, in fact, a knowledge-building process.

mind tools

Much has been said of the importance of "hands-on" science. There is a need to ensure that students have the opportunity to do "minds-on" science as well. Engaging students with sets of data, with using scientific processes to draw and validate conclusions, and to act as professional scientists in publishing and presenting

---

The Tragic Journey

Laura Lerma and Mike Sayle   Volume 947

The Donner Party started their journey from Fort Bridger on July 31st. They intended to reach California before winter set in. The Party ran into many problems on their way—one of which was a lack of water and food. In their attempts to get water, many of their oxen died or wandered off. They stopped at a lake for winter and were stuck in a snow storm. A group set off for help and got caught in the storm. Many people died during this journey. After our exploration of our database, we found that most of the related individuals lived. Therefore those that stuck together were more likely to live.

What we found from the database was that 23 males lived and 24 females lived. 20 males died and 10 females died. In the Donner family, 8 lived and 8 died. In the Murphy-Foster-Pike family, 7 lived and 6 died. In the Graves-Fosdick family 7 lived and 6 died. In the Breen family, all family members lived. In the Reed family, all 6 lived. In the Eddy family, 1 lived and 3 died. In the Keseberg family, 2 lived and 2 died. In the McCutchen family, 2 lived and 1 died. In the Williams family, 1 lived and 1 died. In the Wolfinger family, 1 lived and 1 died. Only 3 out of 16 of the unrelated individuals lived. One generalization we found was that most of the related individuals lived.

Our conclusion is that those who had relatives were more likely to live. We think this is because no less than half of the people in each family died.

The author of the article believed that the reason that certain people lived or died was because of age. The only difference of opinion between us and the author was who was more likely to live. The author's opinion was supported because everyone over the age of 50 died and most everyone under the age of 5 died. Our opinion was supported because no less than half of the people in each family died, but most of the people died who were unrelated.

FIGURE **4.2**

A DONNER PARTY RESEARCH PAPER

opens the door to designing instruction about scientific ways of knowing rather than designing instruction for information about science.

DISCOURSE AND THE DISCIPLINES

Disciplines have particular ways of thinking about "facts." Each discipline has developed its own means for making sense of initial data. "Just as the cobbler and the surgeon perceive the 'man on the street' in quite different lights, so, too, the scientist, the artist, and the historian bring their own lenses and instrumentation to the experiences of every day, and to the phenomena that form the foundation of their work" (Gardner, 2000, p. 157). Marxist scholars interpret the world differently than Royalists. Newtonian physicists interpret the world differently than chaos the-

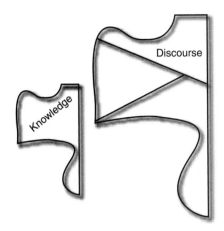

orists. Although used and valued somewhat differently by different disciplines, there are two primary modes of thought shared by most disciplinary thinkers.

Bruner (1986) has identified these two distinctive, yet complementary, modes of thought as the narrative mode of discourse and the expository mode of discourse. Narrative patterns of discourse, writes Bruner, convince one of lifelikeness, present models for the conduct of life, and address how we come to endow experience with meaning.

> It deals in human or human-like intention and action and the vicissitudes and consequences that mark their course. . . . story must construct two landscapes simultaneously. One is the landscape of action, where the constituents are the arguments of action: agent, intention or goal, situation, instrument, something corresponding to a "story grammar." The other is the landscape of consciousness: what those involved in the action know, think, or feel, or do not know, think, or feel. . . . In this sense, psychic reality dominates narrative and any reality that exists beyond the awareness of those involved in the story is put there by the author with the object of creating dramatic effect. (Bruner, 1986, p. 14)

Expository discourse as a mode of thought, on the other hand, leads to a search for universal truth depending on formal or empirical verifiability. It employs categorization or conceptualization as well as operations that establish how general propositions can be extracted from statements or events. It deals in causes and makes use of procedures to assure verifiable references and to test for empirical truth.

> Its domain is defined not only by observables to which its basic statements relate, but also by the set of possible worlds that can be logically generated and tested against observables—that is, it is driven by principled hypotheses. . . . The imaginative application of the paradigmatic mode leads to good theory, tight analysis, logical proof, sound argument, and empirical discovery guided by reasoned hypothesis. (Bruner, 1986, p. 13)

Living within a particular context, an individual comes in contact with a variety of forms through which these two modes of thought may be expressed. Jacob Bronowski (1977) writes, for instance:

> Just after World War II, I became interested in a conflict between the social and personal activity of many people that I knew. . . . This made me very interested in the protesting personality. . . . I began reading a great deal about this; I read a good deal of anthropology, and of psychology, and the history of revolutionary movements. I had it in mind to write a book on this subject. And then quite suddenly, almost overnight, I realized that this was not at all the way to express what I wanted to say. The way to express what I wanted to say was in a perfectly simple drama about what happened to a man in a concentration camp during the war. So I wrote a play called *The Face of Violence*. . . . That seems to me to be a characteristic example of how the mind spends a long time digesting the available material, and then the act of creation is an act of finding the right order to express the whole complexity. (pp. 16–17)

Bronowski perceived his choices within the frame of two alternative discourse forms, each expressed by print. He might just as well have chosen to construct a photo essay or a television drama.

Discourse and the Electronic Technologies

Postman (1982, 1985) has suggested that what is wrong with much of contemporary culture is the result of the breakdown of traditional discourse forms—print-based forms that enhance and promote logical, linear, rational habits of thought. Schools, he suggests, must have as their primary goal the conservation of these traditional modes of thought (Postman, 1979). Yet, the electronic technologies as discourse do not replace traditional discourse but, instead, offer additional patterns of possibility for knowing.

Computers present us with new patterns for organizing narrative discourse and with new patterns for organizing expository discourse. Perhaps the most striking feature of the new forms of computer discourse are the fading lines between traditional forms. It is often difficult to draw lines of distinction between the narrative and the expository in the electronic technologies. Computer simulations, for example, call on the user to step back at certain points and analyze, deduce, and extrapolate. Having done so, the user returns with that knowledge to the story. Computer forms of exposition call on the user to abandon certitude in right and wrong answers, to see worlds of probability, to experiment with a variety of possible scenarios or stories.

As Scollon and Scollon (1984) write:

> We wonder to what extent adults socialized to a literate environment are able to make the next level of insight into the creation of whole possibilities of discourse. . . . [for] it may be that the intrigue children experience with the computer does not lie in the possibility of saying things to the computer or in using the computer as a discourse medium, but in the possibility of creating a new kind of discourse altogether. (p. 140)

Any idea played out in a computer environment is regulated by systems of ideas whose range is bounded only by the limitations of human imagination. The computer presents us with a form of discourse that enables thinkers to test any idea they encounter within the traditions of human knowledge or any idea they can imagine. Anyone using the computer as discourse, whether 5 or 40, can define worlds for which they alone are the lawgivers. Universes of virtually unlimited complexity can be built of disciplinary structures, and a system so formulated and elaborated can be tested according to selected laws and processes. Business executives forecasting profit and loss margins or fifth graders managing a "toy" corporation become participants in a dynamic universe. With the computer as discourse, they can experiment with possibilities, test intuitions, and create and evaluate patterns and connections. Computer-based discourse promotes understanding how complexity and structure derive from observed laws and how we can formulate and test avenues of possible action (Norton, 1985).

If you are role-playing George Washington at Valley Forge, what are your intentions and motivations? What do you know about the world you live in and the enemies you fight? Who is this Benedict Arnold character anyway? Is he a spy? Would he be willing to become a double agent? What shall you, as George Washington, do? In the guerilla-type warfare of the Revolutionaries, where can one hide? Where is there food to be had? If ammunition is short, what alternative weapons are available?

If you are in a shrunken submarine launched into the human body, what do you know about anatomy? What hormones and chemical reactions can you marshal to your ends? Are all drugs bad? Recreational marijuana might not be appropriate. Enter glaucoma. Perhaps marijuana could be useful. Where are the organs in the human body? How are they related? How can you move from one to the other? Can you master the structure of the setting well enough to chase out invading organisms?

Expository Discourse and the Disciplines

As a mode of thought, expository discourse functions as the predominant organizational pattern for explanation and presentation. In contrast to the narrative that attempts to convince one of its lifelikeness, exposition attempts to convince one of truth. Exposition appeals to procedures for establishing formal or empirical proof through well-formed logical arguments. It deals with establishing general causes and makes use of procedures designed to assure verifiable reference. Expository arguments reach maturity when they can be converted into statements defined not only by observable referents but when they create logically constructed explanations driven by principled hypotheses.

The goal of expository discourse is to be able to predict something that is testably right and results in good theory, tight analysis, logical proof, sound argument, and empirical discovery. To do so, exposition uses the language of consistency and non-contradiction. While narratives strive to put timeless themes into the particulars of experience and to locate experience in time and place, expository discourse seeks to transcend the particulars of experience by reaching for higher abstractions and by striving to be conclusive or inconclusive (Bruner, 1986).

When educators choose to use traditional forms of expository discourse to teach disciplinary knowledge, they are also teaching a set of habits or modes of thought. The first is deductive reasoning that starts with statements taken to be true and then tries to see what other more special statements can be logically produced. Second is analytical reasoning that may be described as the ability to identify relevant information, to perceive how concepts are broken into parts, and then comprehend the manner in which the parts are organized to explain the whole. The third is cause-and-effect reasoning that demands differentiating between events or information that coexist without relationship and those that are causally related. In the fourth, sequential reasoning, traditional forms of expository discourse must be negotiated by accumulating information, moving systematically from A to B to C.

Expository discourse associated with the electronic technologies promotes different habits of thinking. One habit of thinking is inductive reasoning that starts with a set of special observations, and, by extrapolation, analogy, or simulation leads to generalizations. Another is what-if reasoning that moves from tidy, coherent, deductive arguments toward patterns for formulating and testing multiple combinations, extending beyond if-then patterns. A third is synthesis thinking that emphasizes searching for important variables and attempting to determine and then apply rules that govern their interactions. This contrasts with more traditional, analytical patterns. A fourth habit of thinking that is promoted by the electronic technologies centers on the need to recognize patterns and connections, which suggests that explanation and argumentation may be organized not by identifying preexisting sequences but by examining relationships and basic principles of interaction and interdependence (Norton, 1985).

Combining Expository Discourse and Teaching Disciplinary Structures

Something had to change. Susan Rudolph had been teaching world history to ninth graders for six years. The one thing she had learned was that ninth graders are not particularly interested in studying world history. As she often says, "The Greeks are Greek to them." Over the summer, she did a great deal of thinking about another way to teach world history. She wanted her students to learn that the problems of today are similar to the problems people in every historical period confront and that there are many different answers to these problems.

Every civilization must find a way to answer the question: Who has the power? Does power reside with a king in a monarchy, a dictator in a dictatorship, or a prime minister in a representative democracy? How does America answer that question and how does that answer influence each of us? How are resources distributed in an economy? Are they distributed by a centralized government in a communist system or through free market enterprise as in capitalism? How does America answer that question and how does that answer influence each of us? What tools are available to a civilization? Are there only sticks, rocks, and animal hides or are there sophisticated electronics? What tools are available to Americans and how do those tools influence each of us? Ms. Rudolph also wanted students to learn that our answer to one of these questions influences how we answer other questions. In short, every civilization can be conceptualized as the complex interactions of at least 10 basic social structures: technology systems, knowledge systems, sustenance systems, belief, values, and religious systems, military/defense systems, political systems, economic systems, leisure/happiness systems, international relations systems, and health systems (Figure 4.3).

"How can I teach these structures in such a way that students come to appreciate their relevance to students' lives and to see the complex interactions of these structures within a multitude of different civilizations," Ms. Rudolph wondered. As she pondered these questions, an instructional design for knowledge began to formulate in her mind. When school opened in the fall, she was ready for the first semester (Figure 4.4).

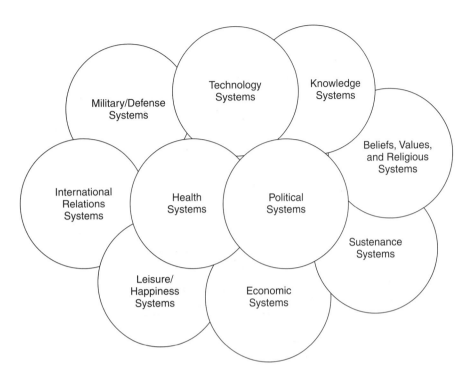

FIGURE **4.3**

A VIEW OF CIVILIZATION AS TEN INTERACTING STRUCTURES

During the first two weeks of school, Ms. Rudolph presented one structure each day and shared a short news clip. For instance, one day she showed an NBC news clip that told of new statistics demonstrating that the number of manufacturing jobs in the United States was continuing a downward trend. The reporter went on to interview two factory managers who said they had many manufacturing jobs available, but they could not find qualified employees. Potential employees did not have appropriate skills to work in factories that used robotic systems as well as a wide range of other electronic technologies. The managers said they were willing to pay as much as $50,000 a year if they could just find qualified people.

Ms. Rudolph and students talked about this news clip. They talked about changes happening within the economic system. Traditional jobs that rely on repetitious labor were being replaced by "smart" skills. Students were impressed by the salary being offered and talked about other changes in the economic system they had observed. One student mentioned how her parents rarely used money anymore, relying mostly on ATM and credit cards. "That means," she reflected, "jobs counting money like bank tellers were being replaced by computer experts." In a burst of insight, Michelle noted that these economic shifts were dependent on shifts in our technologies and that those shifts were, in turn, related to new knowledge. "Yeah," added Jason. "If I had the knowledge, I could get the job and earn a large salary. Then I would have more to spend on leisure activities, would

	Monday	Tuesday	Wednesday	Thursday	Friday
Week 1 and Week 2	A Current Affairs Case Study / Analysis of One Structure Using Students' Lives / Reading Assignment from Text ⟶	A Current Affairs Case Study / Analysis of One Structure Using Students' Lives	A Current Affairs Case Study / Analysis of One Structure Using Students' Lives	A Current Affairs Case Study / Analysis of One Structure Using Students' Lives	A Current Affairs Case Study / Analysis of One Structure Using Students' Lives ⟶
Week 3	Teacher's Day for Whole Group Activities Introducing A Civilization ⟶		Students Assigned to Analysis Group / Students Work Collaboratively to Complete Civilization Analysis ⟶		
Week 4	Continuation of Study Group Analysis / Whole Group Discussion about the Ten Structures and the Case Study	Computer Lab: Work with Civilization II Simulation Group ⟶ / Reading Assignment from Text ⟶			Debriefing of Lessons from Simulation / A Current Affairs Case Study
Week 5 through Week 16	Repeat of Weeks 3 and 4 Which Results in a Total of Six Additional Cycles ⟶				
Week 17 through Week 18	Final Collaborative Project—Invent a Civilization ⟶				

FIGURE **4.4**

Ms. Rudolph's Organizational Strategy

help other people have jobs, and would be much happier." Ms. Rudolph asked students to form small groups and try to write a description of the American economy. As she walked around listening to their conversations, she noticed that students were getting the idea.

As Ms. Rudolph continued the current affairs case studies, she also took part of the class time to introduce students to a simulation called Civilization III, using a projecting monitor to display the computer screen image on the wall (Figure 4.5). She showed students how they could use settlers to explore and reveal the geography of an area and found cities when they thought they had found a good geographical site. She showed them how they could raise and lower taxes and determine what military, social, and economic expenditures would be made. She demonstrated how choices had to be made about what knowledge to seek and how money had to be spent on granaries, libraries, cathedrals, and military barracks. Ms. Rudolph shared with them the game's goal: to manage a civilization's development to the point where it had the resources, the knowledge, the technology, and the security to build and launch a spaceship. In addition, during the second week, Ms. Rudolph assigned the first chapter from the class textbook that introduced the notion of civilization and one chapter that presented information about the Babylonian Civilization. At the end of two weeks, students had a preliminary understanding of the 10 structures and their interactions, a basic understanding about the simulation, and some introductory knowledge about Babylon.

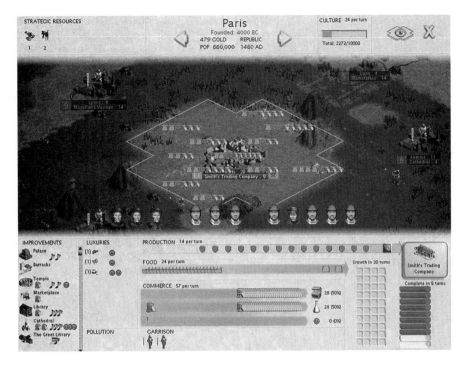

FIGURE 4.5

SID MEIER'S CIVILIZATION III

Source: Civilization III © 2001 Infogrames Interactive, Inc. All rights reserved. Printed with permission.

For the next two weeks, students studied the Babylonian Civilization. Ms. Rudolph used the first two days to present information to the whole class. One day she showed a film on Babylon, and, on the other day, she talked about Hammurabi's Code of Laws and explored with students how that code set the stage for modern law. On the next three days, students were divided into groups of four and asked to analyze the Babylonian Civilization, using the 10 structures and completing an analysis sheet. Monday of the second week was spent in whole-group discussion based on the small groups' analyses with particular attention to the interactions between structures.

The students spent Tuesday, Wednesday, and Thursday in the computer lab playing Civilization III in teams of three. They were able to save the game at the end of each class period and resume play the next day. Several groups were overtaken by other computer-controlled civilizations and ceased to exist. Each time, Ms. Rudolph challenged students to reflect on the reasons for their lack of success. Students soon began to understand that they had to balance their resources between domestic development and military expenditures. They had to carefully plan for libraries and scientists so that knowledge developed and translated into new military technologies, better living conditions for citizens, and advances in government. At the end of the three days, Ms. Rudolph led a discussion about what students had learned from the game about managing a civilization's development and how it related to lessons learned from the Babylonian Civilization.

Ms. Rudolph repeated this two-week process of analysis of historical civilizations and testing of civilization skill through playing the simulation six more times. (During the next six cycles, Ms. Rudolph was able to engage students with the Chinese Civilization, the Ottoman Empire, the Greek Civilization, the Roman Empire, the Egyptian Civilization, and the Mayan Civilization. By combining teacher presentations, textbook readings, small-group analysis, and the computer simulation, students were developing an in-depth knowledge about the 10 civilizational structures—their application to understanding students' own social context, the interactions among the decisions, and choices civilizations make as they seek to fashion human experience. During this time, Ms. Rudolph was forced to provide access to the computer lab before school and during lunch period because many of the simulation teams wanted more time to play the game. By the end of the first semester, all but one team had launched a spaceship at least once, and several teams had become so sophisticated they could do it fairly predictably.

Instead of a final examination, Ms. Rudolph divided the class into groups of four. She charged each group to invent a civilization and·to tell how their civilization would design answers to the challenges inherent in each of the 10 structures and the interactions between structures. During the three days of finals designated for the school, students presented their civilization design. Ms. Rudolph, a parent volunteer, a teacher volunteer, and each student rated the designs on a three-point scale (weak, good, excellent) on five criteria: overall quality of civilizational design, quality of description of structures, quality of description of interactions, creativity, and quality of presentation. Ms. Rudolph totaled all points received from all reviewers, computed a percentage of received versus possible points, and used the percentage to assign a grade that served as the final examination grade. It had been a wonderful semester.

Narrative Discourse and the Disciplines

The narrative as discourse is a primary mode of thought concerned with the conduct of life. As such, it can be rendered in its printed form, its media form, or its computer form. Each form of narrative expression directs our attention to the vagaries of life through its own unique filter and structure. When we collectively share a particular story, told through a particular mode of expression, we create shared, social realities. The models of narrative offered to us by our social context show us how we can play the game of free choice according to a set of rules (Rosen, 1985).

In the struggle for meaning, we all seek to enrich our lives, to stimulate our imaginations, to develop our intellect, to clarify our emotions, to recognize our difficulties and anxieties, and to discover solutions to our problems. We seek to bring meaning to human experience, to understand ourselves and others—to traffic in human possibilities. One way we account for our actions and for the human events that occur around us is through the use of narrative discourse. Our sensitivity to narrative, in fact, provides the major link between our developing sense of self and our sense of others in the social world around us.

We are continually telling ourselves stories about the world and our place in it. Each of us constantly creates our own inner story, our autobiography. The format of narrative is a fundamental way of imposing structure on the sequence of events in life and can thus be seen as an aspect of daily experience (Bruner, 1986). The story is the form through which we discover who we are, the way of our world, motives, values, beginnings, and endings. It is the form through which we create meanings that provide a kind of cohesion to the world of human experience.

Traditionally, the study of the narrative has been restricted to the domain of literature and literary study. Its place in our lives has been perceived as most closely related to our leisure activity. Developing our individual abilities to interpret and use the narratives offered to us by our culture is traditionally the purview of literature classes. We rarely think of the narrative form of discourse as central to other disciplines. We recognize the need to understand historical context to interpret literary and philosophical works. We rarely recognize their role in teaching history. Presidential elections are usually studied as lists of candidates, campaign managers, platforms, issues, debates, and outcomes. Yet, Theodore White (1960, 1964, 1968, 1972) has shown how closely a presidential election resembles a good novel. We read the stories of scientists' lives. We rarely teach students about reproduction as the unfolding story of development—the dance of life.

In fact, much of disciplinary knowledge depends on the story. The economist Robert Heilbroner once remarked, for example, that

> when forecasts based on economic theory fail, he and his colleagues take to telling stories—about Japanese managers, about the Zurich "snake," about the Bank of England's "determination" to keep sterling from falling. There is a curious anomaly here: businessmen and bankers today (like men of affairs of all ages) guide their decisions by just such stories—even when a workable theory is available. These narratives, once acted out, "make" events and "make" history. They contribute to the reality of the participants. For an economist (or an economic historian) to ignore them, even on grounds that "general economic forces" shape the world of economics, would be to don blinders. (in Bruner, 1986, p. 42)

Narrative Discourse and Learning Disciplinary Structures

At Lakes High School, faculty had voted to adopt a block schedule. The particular block schedule they chose had students taking a traditionally year-long course in a semester. Instead of scheduling students to attend six courses an hour a day for a full school year, students were scheduled to take three courses for two hours a day for an 18-week semester. Faculty who supported block scheduling believed that the longer, sustained time period would result in better learning. All faculty understood that this meant changing the way courses were taught. Using a lecture-textbook-worksheet format could not be sustained for two hours a day.

Mrs. Sheldahl, a science teacher, was unsure how she felt about the idea of block scheduling. She taught Anatomy and Physiology and had a hard time visualizing how she could keep students engaged for a two-hour block. Certainly, she could not just do two days of her traditional curriculum every day. When the time finally came to vote, Mrs. Sheldahl decided to vote for the block schedule plan. Maybe it was time to rethink how she taught Anatomy and Physiology. A rumor was circulating at the school that perhaps the school's computer technology might

	Monday	Tuesday	Wednesday	Thursday	Friday
Week 1					Unit Begins with Movie: InnerSpace
Week 2	Academic Program: Experiments, Textbooks, Movies, Attention to System's organization, function, dysfunction, and comparisons to other biological species ——————→		Computer Lab (1 hour) Use graphics program to diagram system and label components	Use InnerBody Works, Sr. database to research connecting points between systems and coding diagram	
Week 3 through Week 10	Repeat of Week 2 for each of the remaining eight systems ——————————→				
Week 11	Computer Lab (1 hour) Use of InnerBody Works, Sr. in the game mode ——————→				
	Classroom: Replay Movie—InnerSpace Students plan solution writing a one page treatment	Classroom: Students design cards for hyper-media stack using guidelines	Computer Lab (1 hour) Create hypermedia stack ——————→		
Week 17 through Week 18	Computer Lab (2 hours) Finish hypermedia stack and Share Solutions ———→		Final Exam Show Remainder of Movie and Compare Solutions		

FIGURE **4.6**

MRS. SHELDAHL'S ORGANIZATIONAL STRATEGY

be part of the solution. As she began investigating this idea, a plan emerged in her mind (see Figure 4.6).

Using her instructional materials budget, Mrs. Sheldahl purchased three lab packs of a program by Tom Snyder Productions titled InnerBody Works, Sr. This purchase allowed her to use the program on 15 computers in the science department computer lab. With students working in teams of two, there were enough programs for 30 students. The program has two formats. One format is a database hypertour for identifying connections between parts of the body and between systems. The other is a game format where students test their knowledge by plotting a course of no more than 16 moves to get from a starting point to four other sites (see Figure 4.7).

When school began, Mrs. Sheldahl used the first four days to present an overview of the course, to set expectations, policies, and procedures for the class, and to review concepts from students' prerequisite biology course. On the fifth day, she showed the first part of *InnerSpace*, a movie starring Dennis Quaid and Martin Short. This funny movie is the story of an errant astronaut, Dennis Quaid, in search of employment. Desperate for a job, Quaid signs on to be the pilot of an experimental vessel that will be miniaturized and injected into the body of a rabbit. Quaid studies rabbit anatomy, prepares for the experiment, and undergoes miniaturization, only to discover (after finding an optic nerve) that he has been injected into a human (Martin Short). He is unable to communicate with

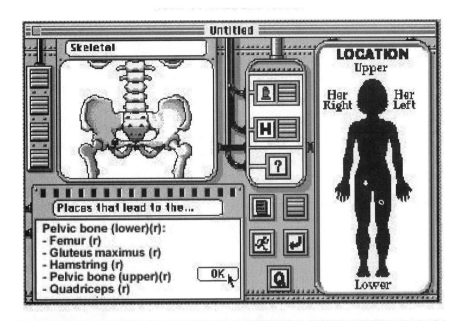

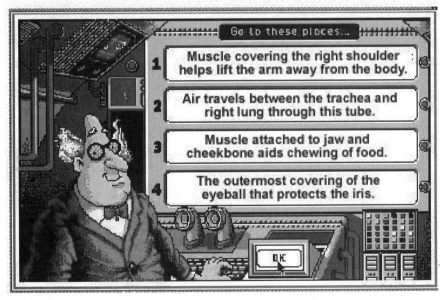

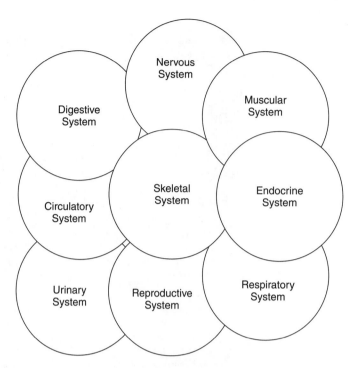

MRS. SHELDAHL'S BIOLOGICAL STRUCTURES

researchers. Mrs. Sheldahl stopped the film at the point when Quaid discovers the mishap and rants, "Now, what am I going to do?" Students groaned.

"Okay, you are the screenwriter. How is Dennis Quaid going to get out of his predicament? What do you need to know in order to create a realistic ending to this story?" A few students had seen the movie, and Mrs. Sheldahl asked them not to tell the ending and challenged them, as the screenwriter, to invent their own ending. Students agreed that in order to save Quaid they needed to know about all the organs, about what precautions they needed to take so that Short is not hurt, about possible dangers along the way, and about safe ways to move around the body. Mrs. Sheldahl tells them that the human body is comprised of nine systems, each with its own set of organs and interactions as well as interactions with other systems. These systems comprise the structures of which most all life forms are comprised (Figure 4.8). Students agree they have a lot to learn.

Mrs. Sheldahl and her students studied one system a week for nine weeks. Each week, Monday, Tuesday, and half of Wednesday, Thursday, and Friday were spent studying the organization, function, dysfunction, and contrasts with other species. They used a combination of textbook readings, movies, and filmstrips as well as participating in experiments. For instance, while studying the circulatory system, students did a series of different exercises and then monitored their pulse rate; they took their blood pressure; they used a resuscitation doll to learn about CPR; and they dissected cow hearts. Mrs. Sheldahl often pondered aloud about possible dilemmas a miniaturized vessel might encounter. Would a foreign object cause a blood clot or possible irregularities in heartbeat?

During the second hour on Wednesday, Thursday, and Friday, students went to the computer lab. They used a graphics program to draw the week's system and label its components. They used the database format of InnerBody Works, Sr. to determine and code each component of the system, identifying possible connections to other systems. For instance, when students were studying the skeletal system, they learned that in addition to moving to other sites within the skeletal system, they could jump from the pelvic bone to the muscular system. They coded the pelvic bone on their diagram with an MS to indicate the muscular system. Diagrams, with completed labels and codes for connecting systems, were stored away for later use.

Once students had completed their study of all nine systems, Mrs. Sheldahl showed students how the game format worked, and students spent one hour a day for a week testing their knowledge and winning trophies for successfully planning appropriate paths throughout the body in response to the game's challenges. They used their diagrams as aids to planning moves. During the second hour on Monday, Mrs. Sheldahl provided a framework for presenting their solutions to Quaid's dilemma. She replayed the first part of *InnerSpace* to refresh students' memory and asked them to write a one-page treatment explaining an overview of their plan to save Quaid. On Tuesday, Mrs. Sheldahl reviewed the program, HyperStudio, and asked students to use the program to present their story endings. She presented them with guidelines for designing their HyperStudio stack. She told them they were to create a sequence of cards that presented their version of the story's resolution. Each card in the sequence had to have a connecting button to a card related to the relevant system's function, a connecting button to a card related to the relevant system's organization, and a connecting button to the next card in the story's sequence (see Figure 4.9). Students spent the remainder of Tuesday planning the cards in their HyperStudio stack. They spent the next seven hours of class completing their stacks. During the eighth hour, students examined each other's stacks and compared story resolutions. The next day they took an exam and watched the remainder of *InnerSpace*. Mrs. Sheldahl had never had such high test scores. The remaining six weeks of the course were spent understanding issues related to health and illness.

In this chapter, we explored designing learning opportunities for students that focus on the development of knowledge. We identified three central concepts as important considerations when designing learning experiences that promote the development of knowledge. First, in an era of proliferating knowledge, students cannot be expected to learn all there is to learn. Instead, designs for knowledge should be built around disciplinary structures that focus students' attention on the underlying concepts of a discipline not the details of a series of cases. Second, students' understanding of the disciplines should be built on their abilities to participate in and use the processes or habits of mind that define the disciplines. Students should learn to "do" the disciplines—to use the habits of thinking associated with the development of disciplinary knowledge. Third, designs for knowledge should capitalize on the discourse forms humans have invented for organizing meaning. The primary forms explored in this chapter were narrative and expository discourse. Examples of teachers' designs were presented to demonstrate how these forms might be used to teach disciplinary structures and processes.

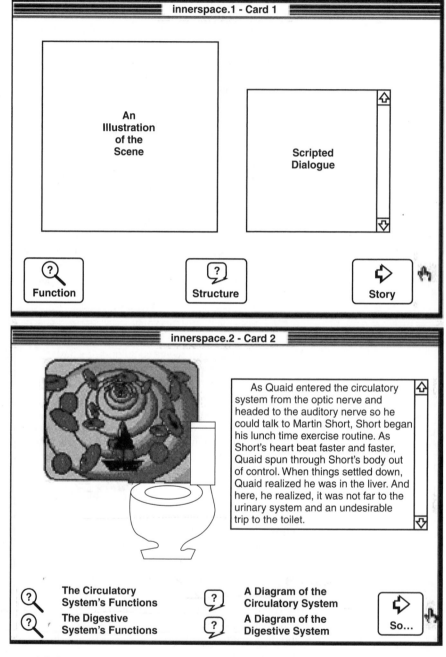

FIGURE 4.9

MODEL OF *HYPERSTUDIO* CARD DESIGN (TOP) AND A STUDENT SAMPLE
JUAN AND GEORGE'S FIRST CARD (BOTTOM)

Source: Cards created with Roger Wagner's HyperStudio.

In addition to modeling the ways in which the three central concepts in this chapter might inform the design of learning opportunities that result in student knowledge, all the designs presented in this chapter incorporated the electronic technologies and used the problem-centered approach. We turn our attention in the next chapter to the question of teaching problem solving and the possibilities inherent in using a problem-centered approach to anchor the ABCS of activity—authentic, building knowledge, constructing, and sharing activities.

Before moving on to Chapter 5, however, we recommend that you go to the FACTS Web-Based Design Tool site. If you click on the Design Mentors puzzle piece, you can access the Design Mentors for this chapter. This chapter's Design Mentors introduce you to Brooks White and Alan Sutton as they begin the design process. You will be able to follow these two teachers as they identify the content/subject matter/standards that will guide their designs. In addition, you will be able to observe their thinking process as they analyze the content/subject matter/standards and identify the knowledge considerations (structures, processes, and discourses) that will be important for their design. After you have studied the Design Mentors, you might find it helpful to return to the opening page of the Web site and complete the Design Challenge associated with this chapter. You can also examine some of the Design Examples and see how they reflect the considerations discussed in this chapter.

[handwritten margin notes: structure content / process methods / discourse forms / purposes]

CHAPTER IDEAS

- Although a somewhat artificial division, human knowledge may be divided into three broad disciplines: the humanities, the hard sciences, and the social sciences.
- After the first several grades, mastering the concepts and methods of the disciplines constitutes the main mandate of content area instruction.
- Education has long been plagued by the need to find an equilibrium between teaching knowledge related to specific skills and teaching knowledge that leads to general understandings.
- Conventional definitions of knowledge learning result in a "competency-based curricula + direct instruction + standardized tests = measurement-driven teaching and higher test scores" model of learning.
- Disciplinary learning that incorporates the electronic technologies is not a threat to traditional frameworks for developing knowledge of the disciplines, but, instead, offers an alternative set of possibilities for knowing.
- We know more and more about less and less, and, as a consequence, schools can no longer take as their central mandate the goal of ensuring student knowledge about all there is to know in the disciplines.
- Educators must design for knowledge by teaching the structures and processes related to disciplinary knowledge.

- Giving primacy to structure and process as central learning goals in the disciplines does not eliminate teaching content—content becomes the vehicle by which structures and processes are learned.
- The structure of a discipline is defined by the central theories or operations that explain specific cases and form organizing principles for the study of that discipline.
- Knowledge about the structures of a discipline makes it more understandable, more effectively remembered, and facilitates transfer of learning.
- Learning in the disciplines must include knowledge of processes related to "doing" the disciplines.
- Teaching the disciplines as "ways to think" about experience has more lasting consequences than teaching "about" the disciplines.
- Discourse is a mode of thought—a pattern of cognitive function.
- Expository discourse as a mode of thought leads to a search for universal truth dependent on formal or empirical verifiability.
- When educators choose to use traditional forms of expository discourse, they are teaching a set of habits or modes of thought that include deductive reasoning, analytical reasoning, cause-and-effect reasoning, and sequential reasoning.
- Expository discourse associated with the electronic technologies promotes different habits of thinking such as inductive reasoning, what-if reasoning, synthesis thinking, and recognizing patterns and connections.
- Narrative patterns of discourse convince one of lifelikeness, present models for the conduct of life, and address how we come to endow experience with meaning.
- Traditionally, the study of the narrative has been restricted to the domain of literature and literary study. In fact, much of disciplinary knowledge depends on the story.
- Perhaps the most striking feature of the new forms of computer discourse are the fading lines between the traditional forms of discourse, often making it difficult to draw lines of distinction between the narrative and the expository.
- Computer-based discourse promotes seeing how complexity and structure derive from observed laws and how we can formulate and test avenues of possible action.

DESIGNS FOR PROBLEM SOLVING

Several weeks ago, I was asked to lead a tour of three major businesses in our community planned for public school teachers who were working with "school to work" programs. The first business we visited was a large law firm, which occupied three floors of a large downtown building. The second was the corporate offices of a major grocery store chain. The third was the main offices of a large bank. I was fascinated to learn that all three of these businesses reported the same dilemmas. In each place, the group heard the same three messages. First, each reported a major emphasis on figuring out how the new technologies could be used to keep their business competitive and about the difficulty of ensuring that their employees were able to use these technologies. Second, each reported a growing awareness that their business depended on their employees' ability to work collaboratively. One even talked about how they had reassigned office and work space in an effort to promote better patterns of cooperation. Third, each reported that they were wrestling with the need to solve a continuous stream of new problems for which they had no previous solutions or precedents.

As the tour ended that day, many of the participating teachers were a bit disappointed. They had hoped the tour would result in locating job opportunities for students as part of the "school to work" program. They had not seen many jobs that were appropriate for their students. As I talked with them, I recognized the urgency of their need to find work opportunities. "But," I told them, "I learned something very important on this tour. If we take what these businesses said to us seriously, it is clear that there will be no job opportunities for our students now or after graduation unless we make sure that they know how to be technology-using problem solvers in social contexts."

**Richard Van Etten,
Director,
School to Work
Programs**

We live in a time of rapidly changing conceptions of what students need to know and be able to do. Learning, once defined in terms of its relationship to observable, reinforceable behavior, is now viewed as the complex interaction of individual cognitive processing, the learner's environment, and his or her historical relationships with culture, language, and media.

Something about current schooling does not match with the demands of an information age. Findings by the National Assessment of Educational Progress (1989) confirm that while students have improved in traditional basic skills, they are doing poorly in problem solving. Business leaders, who have taken much of the lead in the educa-

tional reform movement, are asking schools to produce more students who can think and problem-solve, especially within group contexts.

This chapter explores how teachers can design learning that responds to the growing need for applying these strategies in authentic, situated, community-based problem-solving contexts, for thinking and problem-solving learners. It focuses on (1) general problem-solving strategies—memory, information extending, information rearranging, and metacognition, (2) situated cognition, anchored instruction, and problem-centered learning, and (3) four categories of activity (the ABCS of activity) to include when designing opportunities for learning.

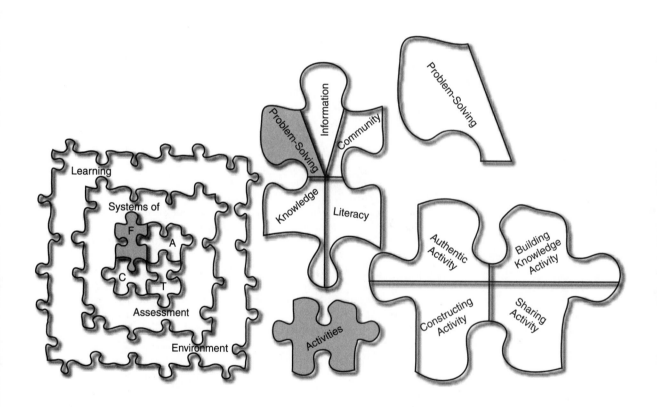

Erica was thinking as she walked into her eighth-grade U.S. history class. She had just returned from a trip with her family, and she was pondering the evidence of many early Native American civilizations she had seen in her home state. She was wondering why her teacher, Mr. Wilson, and the textbook concentrated on the westward movement of Anglo settlers and provided so little information on the long history of the previous inhabitants. She had learned from her father, who studied history as a hobby, that Native Americans had lived in the United States for thousands of years and that the Spanish had occupied parts of the United States as early as 1598, long before any Anglos. She often wondered what it had been like back then.

What had happened to the Native Americans? Why were the Native American pueblos able to revolt and keep out the Spanish from 1598 to 1621, as one of the tour guides at the Acoma Pueblo had explained? Why did the Spanish then take over this part of the world? She had lots of why questions. Whenever she asked Mr. Wilson her why questions, he told her that he would love to talk about it, but they did not have time to explore those questions. They had to move on to the next chapter and finish their U.S. history book by the end of the year. As she thought about it, she realized history was full of whens and whos, but there was little opportunity to think about the whys.

Erica wanted to be a good student so she had studied information about the Gadsden Purchase for her test today. She was still confused, however, about "why" Mexico had been willing to sell so much land to the United States. She knew the date (1854), the price ($15,000,000), and that the Mexican General Santa Anna had sold the land, but she did not really understand the reasons why. She took her seat, confident that she would be able to get a good grade on the test.

Everyone cleared their desks and took out their pencils, getting ready for the test. Erica noticed her friend, Jerry, was especially nervous. He did not like tests and sometimes gave up and did not even try to answer the questions. As a second-language learner, he sometimes was not clear what the teachers meant when the questions contained terms like "compare and contrast." During the last test, he had asked Mr. Wilson what this meant, and the teacher had answered with "You know, just compare and contrast." Well, he did not know, but he was too embarrassed to ask again. After class, Jerry had asked his friend, Erica, what these terms meant. She gave him examples and suggested how he could compare and contrast his after-school work for his father and her after-school work baby-sitting by looking for the things that are the same and the things that are different about their jobs. Then he understood, but, of course, it was too late for the test.

INSIDE THE BLACK BOX

In the early 1600s, a philosopher named René Descartes separated the mind from the body, seemingly for all time. Descartes declared that the body was a machine divisible into parts with elements that could be removed without altering anything fundamental. Conversely, the mind was a unified and decomposable whole—a ghost in the machinery of our bodies, indescribable in physical terms. By positing the mind and body as distinct entities, Descartes created a dualism that still plagues modern thought. The challenge facing educators ever since has been to build bridges that connect the "ghost in the machine" with the overt world of actions, consequences, and behaviors.

Until recently, theorists have sidestepped this dilemma, asserting that it is possible to explain behavior without discussing what goes on in the mind. They stated that it is simply not necessary to know what occurs in the mind. Instead, if one can know what goes into this black box, it is possible to say what will come out. Closely adhering to Descartes' separation of mind and body, Watson (1925), for instance, declared the study of the self as highly suspect. He described the new psychology of 1912 as that of behaviorism, the study of human behaviors or actions. Until the 1960s, educational psychologists, following the theories of Watson, Hull, Tolman, Thorndike, and Skinner, continued to focus on the manipulation and reinforcement of observable behavior. Brown (1994) describes their notion of learning:

> All derived their primary data from rats and pigeons learning arbitrary things in restricted situations. They shared a belief that laws of learning of considerable generality and precision could be found. The principles were intended to be species-age-domain-and context independent. Pure learning was tested in impoverished environments where the skills to be learned had little adaptive value for the species in question. (p. 4)

Today, we know a great deal more about the self, and its study is now far from suspect. It is currently possible, for instance, to look behind human actions to examine living, functioning brains. Technologies such as Positron-Emission Topography (PET) scanning can be used to highlight increased metabolism in brain cells associated with different tasks (Swerdlow, 1995). On a physical level, it is possible to see how generative tasks such as defining words and writing occupy more of the brain than passive tasks such as listening to word lists. Likewise, researchers have come to understand that a child is born with undifferentiated neurons and, that as language develops and the child interacts with the environment, the neurons begin to cluster in distinctive groups. Kandel (1992) discusses learning in terms of how the synoptic connections between neuron cells are strengthened or altered as the person learns through interaction or internal processing.

Slowly supplanting the psychology of behaviorism, the new field of cognitive science reflects diverse perspectives on learning drawn from the fields of linguistics, computer science, anthropology, and psychology. This synergistic study of learning from different disciplines has added greatly to our understanding of human information processing. Metaphors for the mind reflect the input, process, and memory functions of the computer, and research on learning in naturalistic settings provides perspectives more relevant to classroom learning than the results of manipulating single variables in laboratory experiments with rats.

What, then, is inside the black box? Smith (1990) has identified 77 words that Americans use to talk about thinking and suggests that all this new language may obscure the simpler and more understandable aspects of thinking. And, although we are as yet still uncertain about the exact workings of brain and mind, there is much that we do know. The complex mechanisms of brain and mind may not be comprehensively understood, but it is clear that human thinking occurs, that it is shaped by the biology of the brain, the wisdom of culture, and interactions with others, and that tools, activities, and development are important influences in learning to think. Since productive thinking requires a broad range of abilities, educators need to understand thinking and then design opportunities for students to engage in the kinds of activities that support and shape the ability to think and problem-solve. We will turn our attention first to a brief discussion of three important thinking strategies: memory, information extending processes, and information rearranging processes. An example of the ways educators have nurtured each of these strategies is included.

Memory

Human memory is an invisible and intangible phenomenon. No one has ever held memory in their hand nor determined a specific place in the brain where memory is located. In our efforts to understand memory, there have been three predominating metaphors that have helped us understand not what memory is but what memory is like. The first metaphor views memory as a muscle. Although no one has ever claimed that memory is actually a muscle, a popular view holds that like a muscle, memory can be developed and strengthened through regular exercise. This view has led to an emphasis in education on the study of Latin and Greek or mathematics not only for their intrinsic value but as forms of mental gymnastics that increase the power of the mind. The second metaphor views memory as some kind of "writing" on a wax tablet or "brush strokes" on a canvas. In the third metaphor, memory is likened to a reference book or a library. Material stored in memory is classified logically by subject, and its overall structure is hierarchical.

Although each of these metaphors has explained some aspect of memory, none of them serves as an adequate or comprehensive model of memory. In the search for a more accurate metaphor, a model of memory has been adapted from computer science—memory as information processing. This metaphor likens memory to a set of transformations of information—a set of processes. Norman (1982) suggests that learning requires managing three things successfully: the acquisition, retention, and retrieval of information. Failure to remember means failure at managing one of these three components of information processing. In this information-processing notion of memory, information in aural, visual, and symbolic form is perceived by the senses, temporarily stored in short-term memory, operated upon by elaborative processes, and finally stored in long-term memory.

In this model of memory, the elaborative processes form the heart of memory. It seems that some of these processes depend on repetition, but not the kind of repetition suggested by the memory-as-muscle metaphor. Rather, repetition in the information-processing model is repetition in which we look for patterns, chunks, clusters, or associations. For instance, remembering this sequence of numbers—1492181219181941—using repetition is nearly impossible. First, short-term memory is governed by the rule of seven, that is, short-term memory is limited to seven elements. Second, this string of numbers is, at first, seemingly meaningless and difficult to associate with anything. If, however, these numbers are clustered together into chunks reflecting important historical dates (1492, 1812, 1918, and 1941) and associated with the appropriate historical event (Columbus's discovery of the New World, the War of 1812 between the British and the Americans, the end of the First World War, and the beginning of America's involvement in the Second World War), this string of numbers becomes memorable.

Another, more important, elaborative process consists of extracting meanings from concrete or symbolic experiences, classifying those experiences, and then linking this new information to some part of existing memory. Thus, memory is stored as a series of networks between concepts. Whenever one element of the network is activated, a system of interconnecting concepts becomes activated (Schank, 1977). Try remembering this sequence of numbers—9162536496481. Once again, repetition will not likely work. Instead, reclassifying these numbers as the sequence of squares of 3, 4, 5, 6, 7, 8, and 9 activates a network of concepts: numbers in sequence (3 through 9), squares as the number multiplied by itself, and the process of computing squares. Thus, the sequence of numbers is not so much remembered, in the literal sense of memory, but is reconstructed by the network of concepts activated by the effort to remember.

A Network of Concepts: A Memory Case Study.

One strategy for engaging students in the intellectual task of analyzing concepts and constructing a web of connections so that relevant information may be remembered or reconstructed when needed is concept mapping. Concept mapping is a technique for externalizing concepts and propositions by visually representing meaningful relationships between concepts or the component parts of a larger concept (Gowin & Novak, 1984). Concept maps provide a visual road map showing some of the pathways we may take to connect meanings of concepts in propositions. The capacity for visual recall of specific images is a powerful tool in facilitating learning and recall.

Concept maps work to make clear to both students and teachers the small number of key ideas that they must focus on for any specific learning task. As students and teachers construct a concept map, they often recognize new relationships and hence new meanings. Concept maps act as tools for negotiating these meanings and relationships between concepts. Learning the meaning of a piece of knowledge requires dialogue, exchange, sharing, and, sometimes, compromise in the classroom. Teachers and students exchange views on why a particular propositional linkage is good or valid, and they often recognize missing linkages between concepts. After learning a task, concept maps provide a schematic summary of what has been learned.

Once learners come to understand how concept maps are constructed, teachers can use concept maps to help students:

1. Explicitly see the nature and role of concepts and the relationship between concepts as they exist in their minds and as they exist in the world or in printed or spoken instruction;
2. Extract specific concepts (words) from printed or oral material;
3. Visualize concepts and the hierarchical relationships between them;
4. Keep searching their cognitive structures for relevant concepts;

5. Construct propositions between the concepts provided and the concepts they know by helping them to choose good linking words or perhaps to recognize what other, more general concepts fit into the hierarchy; and

6. Discriminate between specific objects or events and the more inclusive concepts those events or objects represent (Clarke, 1990).

Priscilla Norton uses concept mapping as an instructional strategy in her graduate classes often. She finds it particularly helpful to ask students to create concept maps after students have completed a reading assignment. When students are asked to create concept maps of their readings, Dr. Norton is able to combine two important instructional concepts: negotiated meaning and memory as a complex web of interrelated concepts. The software, Inspiration, is a particularly useful tool.

When students arrived for class after reading a draft of this chapter, Dr. Norton asked them to divide into groups of three and create a concept map of the chapter. Students were familiar both with concept mapping and Inspiration. Step 1 of the exercise required students to think about the ideas in the chapter and to negotiate among themselves to separate the important concepts from longer descriptions and examples. Since each reader brings their own past experiences, knowledge, and interests to the reading assignment, it often takes considerable conversation about the ideas to agree on the important ones. In brainstorming mode, each proposed idea is placed on the Inspiration screen, discussed for its importance, accepted or rejected, and combined with similar statements of the same idea.

Once students have agreed on the essential elements of the central idea of the reading selection—designs for problem solving, students begin Step 2. They begin the process of building a web of relationships and connections between the ideas and concepts, creating a kind of hierarchy of ideas. For instance, memory, information-rearranging, and information-extending processes are seen as underneath the concept of general problem-solving strategies or heuristics. Conversely, rote strategies and association strategies might be placed underneath memory. Similarly, logic, sequencing, and cause-and-effect strategies are subconcepts of information-rearranging strategies.

The final step, Step 3, is to begin making connections between the main concept map—designs for problem solving—and previous concepts. So, for instance, students connected building knowledge activities discussed later in this chapter with the concepts of disciplinary structures and processes and narrative and expository discourse from Chapter 4. They also connected situated learning from this chapter with the concept of constructivism presented in Chapter 2.

One of the finished concept maps created by a team of students is presented in Figure 5.1. Students find that the act of collaboratively creating these concept maps helps them grasp the concepts and connections inherent in their reading. It helps cement the ideas in their memory. When it comes time to build their own designs, students find it helpful to use their concept map to remind them of the things they need to consider as they make decisions about the inclusion of problem solving and a range of supporting activities. Most important, students' experiences creating the concept map help them understand both the power and the process of using concept mapping to support their own understanding and memory of concepts. Perhaps the concept map will help you grasp the ideas in this chapter as well.

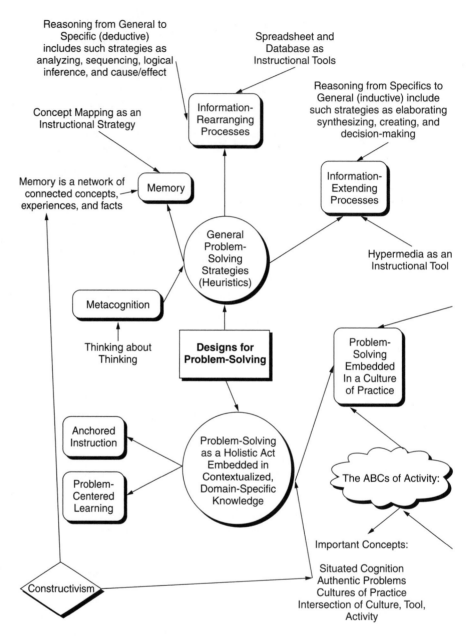

Reasoning from General to Specific (deductive) includes such strategies as analyzing, sequencing, logical inference, and cause/effect

Spreadsheet and Database as Instructional Tools

Concept Mapping as an Instructional Strategy

Information-Rearranging Processes

Reasoning from Specifics to General (inductive) include such strategies as elaborating synthesizing, creating, and decision-making

Memory is a network of connected concepts, experiences, and facts

Memory

Information-Extending Processes

General Problem-Solving Strategies (Heuristics)

Metacognition

Hypermedia as an Instructional Tool

Thinking about Thinking

Designs for Problem-Solving

Problem-Solving Embedded In a Culture of Practice

Anchored Instruction

Problem-Solving as a Holistic Act Embedded in Contextualized, Domain-Specific Knowledge

The ABCs of Activity:

Problem-Centered Learning

Important Concepts:

Constructivism

Situated Cognition
Authentic Problems
Cultures of Practice
Intersection of Culture, Tool, Activity

FIGURE 5.1

A CONCEPT MAP FOR CHAPTER 5—DESIGNS FOR PROBLEM SOLVING

Information-Extending Processes

One of the most pervasive processes humans use to think is the capacity to generalize from specific experiences, concrete or symbolic, and to form new, more abstract concepts. The ability to arrive at such generalizations is critical for thinking about ourselves, each other, and the world around us. How do we do this? Essentially, we engage in a process known as inductive or convergent thinking. *Induction* is defined as the development of general rules, ideas, or concepts from sets of specific instances or examples. By analyzing the similarities and differences between experiences, we extract the general characteristics of objects, events, and situations. We apply these generalizations to new experiences, refine and modify them, and make them a part of our permanent knowledge base by generating or selecting an appropriate continuation of a pattern (Pellegrino & Dillon, 1991). Inductive thinking is an information-extending process that starts with concrete or symbolic information and, by extrapolation or analogy, leads to generalizations or patterns (Hunt, 1982).

Sternberg (1982, 1985) suggests that there are three categories of processes associated with inductive thinking. The first, selective encoding, refers to strategies that permit thinkers to make distinctions between one or more bits of information not immediately obvious. Thinkers learn the importance of being able to sort out relevant from irrelevant information. The second process in inductive thinking is selective combination, that is, to perceive a way of combining unrelated (or at least not obviously related) elements. The third process is selective comparison. This kind of thinking occurs when one discovers a nonobvious relationship between new and old information. It is here that previous experiences held in memory become important. In short, this is the process thinkers use to group similar objects into categories and recognize patterns in events that happen in some regular order.

Jonassen (1996) suggests that information-extending processes include elaborating skills like modifying, extending, and shifting categories, synthesizing skills like summarizing, hypothesizing, and planning, and imagining skills like predicting and speculating. He also identifies skills such as design, problem solving, and decision making. Design skills include those associated with imagining and formulating a goal and inventing, assessing, and revising a product. Problem-solving skills include those associated with sensing and formulating a problem, finding alternatives, and choosing the solution. Decision-making skills include those associated with assessing consequences and making and evaluating choices.

Hypermedia: An Information-Extending Case Study.   The power of today's computers is merging the linearity of print with the nonlinearity of the visual media, adding sound and animation to dazzle us and adding complexity to the information load with which we must deal. The creation of multimedia/hypermedia programs and writing tools has promoted the integration of sound, video, print, and animation into a giant web of information. Whether these webs of information are represented as computer programs for the desktop computer or as Web sites on the World Wide Web, the creation of hypermedia programs and writing tools supports problem solvers in their efforts to integrate information into a giant web of connections—to extend information through its combination and connection to other information. These programs support students as they re-arrange, connect, and build relationships between chunks of information.

The operative concept in hypermedia is *hyper.* Think about a young child described as "hyper." This term refers to a child who moves rapidly between activities, jumping from one thing to another. While it often appears that the child is not attending to anything, most "hyper" children are actually sampling a range of experiences, building their own version of how the world works. So it is in hypermedia. Information is divided or "chunked" into appropriate, fairly small blocks of meaning. Those blocks are then connected or linked in terms of their relationship to each other and to other blocks of information. Information is extended and connected into webs of knowledge.

The idea behind hypermedia is that humans do not always or perhaps even generally think in a linear fashion. We often refer to other ideas in our thinking, jumping from one concept to another related concept and then on to a third. Each of these concepts is related in some fashion. If humans tend to think in this manner, it stands to reason that they can also learn in this manner. Hypermedia programs are designed to emulate the information-extending patterns of human thinking and, when students use these programs to create hypermedia stacks, they are involved in learning through problem solving. Students ponder and decide what connections to make between topics, concepts, content areas, and ideas. Through planning, interpreting, and analyzing information, they combine prior knowledge with remembered and shared information, transforming their own knowledge and understandings (Handler & Dana, 1998).

Catie Angell's students have been studying the process of how a bill becomes a law in the federal government. They have studied the structures associated with the legislative branch—Congress, the Senate, the House of Representatives, the Executive Branch, and the veto. They have participated in a simulation of legislative processes where they researched an issue, drafted a bill, debated proposed bills, voted, and sent a passed bill to the "president." The time has come for students to translate their experiences into an abstraction of the process that has generalizability to all legislative processes.

Ms. Angell has opted to use PowerPoint as a hypermedia environment where students can build a model of the legislative bill-passing process. PowerPoint is often used as a presentation tool. In fact, her students have created several PowerPoint presentations. Most presentations, though, are generally organized using a linear, slide-to-slide format. This format is not appropriate for representing the complexities of the legislative process since the passage of a bill is never linear. It is possible, however, using the hyperlink functions available in PowerPoint, to create an interactive model of the legislative process where the "reader" must make choices at specified decision points in the process. To access the hyperlink function in PowerPoint, click on Slide Show from the main top menu bar. Next select Action Settings and then Hyperlink (Figure 5.2).

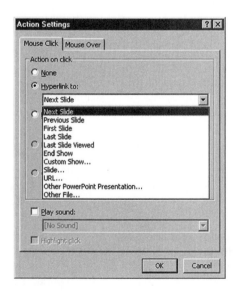

FIGURE 5.2

MICROSOFT POWERPOINT
Source: Screenshot from Microsoft Corporation.

Challenged to make a hypermedia model of the legislative process, students begin by creating a simple representation of the process, chunking the process into discrete steps, and identifying decision points and the alternate paths that emerge at those points. Next, they create a series of PowerPoint slides that capture the discrete steps and embed the decision points as links to appropriate paths. Third, students test their own model, making sure that all links connect to the correct results. Finally, students share their models with other teams and with Ms. Angell to discover if they have captured all the steps, identified all the decision points, and correctly constructed appropriate paths to passage or rejection of legislation. As Ms. Angell observes and assists students, she watches students move beyond their personal experiences from the simulation and their readings to a generalizable model of the legislative process. Using hypermedia has supported her students to extend information.

Information-Rearranging Processes

Try the following syllogism:

> All men are mortal.
> Socrates was a man.
> Therefore, ...

The answer is: Therefore, Socrates was mortal. If you were able to figure out the answer, you were using deductive thinking—an information-rearranging process. You relied on your scripts in memory for "man" and "mortal." Then, from the word "are," you probably identified that mortal is descriptive of man. Also, you most likely understood that Socrates is a subset of the script for man. That ensured that you understood the nature of the problem, but, in order to solve the problem, you had to deduce the relationship between the two general concepts to arrive at the logical relationship between Socrates and mortality.

Deductive thinking is a systematic process of thought that leads from one set of propositions to another based on principles of logic. The purpose of logical principles is to guarantee that a deduction is true, and a deduction is valid only if its premises suffice to ensure the truth of its conclusion. If a conclusion does not follow validly from the premises, then, strictly speaking, the deduction is incorrect, although it may be plausible and may even lead to a correct conclusion (Johnson-Laird, 1985). Deductive thinking allows thinkers to extract implications from what is already given or known. It is an information rearranging process (Hunt, 1982).

For centuries, philosophers and psychologists who studied the human mind believed that thinking takes place according to the laws that govern logic. Such is the tradition that runs unbroken from Aristotle to Piaget. Yet, logical or deductive thinking is not necessarily our usual or natural way of thinking. In fact, thinking that fails to follow the rules of logic, often arrived at inductively, works rather well in everyday situations. When buying a home, for instance, one may logically analyze related issues such as neighborhood, schools, affordability, family needs, and the price in relation to market value. But, all too often, it is the kitchen or the view or even an appealing window that determines which home will be bought.

If the inductive process works so well, why do we need to think deductively? Deductive thinking is the basis of rational thought and is most important when the subject matter is hypothetical or unfamiliar. Deductive thinking is essential for identifying the cause of a mysterious illness, deducing the characteristics of a new subatomic particle, or drafting a piece of innovative legislation. Deductive thinking—information rearranging—is theoretical reasoning, seeing what in principle must be true. Inductive thinking—information extending—is practical reasoning, seeing what in practice can be accomplished (Pagels, 1988).

Of all the thinking processes, deductive thinking is the process most dependent on formal learning. Hunt (1982, p. 79) has written that without education, reasoning is

> . . . limited to inferences based on personal experience and common knowledge. With education, we become capable of thinking in more abstract and general terms—concerning ourselves with the inferential relationships, not the subject matter. Perhaps one value of formal reasoning, as opposed to plausible reasoning, is just this, that it enables us to escape from the confines of personal knowledge and belief.

Included among the information-rearranging or deductive-thinking skills are evaluation skills like assessing information, determining criteria, prioritizing, recognizing fallacies, and verifying. In addition, skills associated with analyzing information include using such problem-solving strategies as recognizing patterns, classifying, identifying assumptions, identifying main ideas, and finding sequences. Finally, deductive problem-solving skills include those associated with connecting information through comparison and contrast strategies, principles of logic, inferential thinking, and identification of causal relationships (Jonassen, 1996).

Spreadsheets: An Information-Rearranging Case Study.   Spreadsheets allow students to drift away from the drill-and-practice software commonly used to teach mathematics and into an environment that allows students to gather, record, manipulate, and display data while seeking reasonable solutions to a problem. Well-planned spreadsheet activities emphasize reasoning, problem solving, making connections, and communicating mathematical ideas (Holmes, 1997). Spreadsheets also support using mathematics to support learning in other content areas. Census data, survey data, and economic data are all familiar data to social scientists. Using spreadsheets in the social studies curriculum allows students to manipulate and problem-solve with social science data. Water quality data, acid rain data, and population growth data are examples of data sets familiar to scientists. Science students can learn to think about and problem-solve with these kinds of data. When students use spreadsheets and embed and/or create formulas to manipulate data, they are rearranging information to solve problems.

> Todd Funkhouser teaches Algebra I. All too often, students see algebra as the abstract manipulation of formula without understanding how those formulas might be used to solve interesting problems. Mr. Funkhouser is determined to make algebra relevant. Toward the end of the period, he has students pack up their books and supplies. When all the students are ready to go, Mr. Funkhouser tells the stu-

dents about a problem he is having. He needs a new car, but he just cannot decide on what kind to buy. Sometimes, he tells students he wants a functional vehicle like a truck or a sports utility vehicle. Other times, he is captured by the fun look of the PT Cruiser and the new VW bug. It would also be nice, he tells them, to have a larger four-door sedan—an "adult" car. Then, of course, it would be really neat to have a super sports car like the Prowler or the new Lexus SC that costs nearly $60,000. In reality, though, he should probably be financially responsible and buy an economy car—maybe a Geo Metro or a Ford Fiesta. Finally, Mr. Funkhouser tells them he thinks he might have a way to solve his problem if they will help him. He has listed 28 cars that he might be interested in purchasing. He asks students to choose one of the cars, search the automobile manufacturer's Web sites, and find five pieces of information for him—the price, torque, rate of acceleration, weight, and horsepower. Students agree to research the car they chose and bring the necessary information to class. Many of them have Internet access at home; others will need to use the school library or a friend's computer.

When students return to class, Mr. Funkhouser has an assignment on the board asking them to solve five equations using their knowledge of equations and exponential numbers. As they work on the equations, he has students come to the computer in the classroom and enter the data about their car in a spreadsheet he has set up. When all the data has been entered into the spreadsheet, Mr. Funkhouser saves the spreadsheet to the school's network so that all students can have access to it. He reviews the assignment students have completed and introduces the day's lesson. As the period comes to an end, Mr. Funkhouser tells students to report to the computer lab for the next class period.

Mr. Funkhouser begins the next class in the computer lab by reading a newspaper clipping he has been carrying in his pocket. The clipping announced the award of the Nobel Prize in Mathematics to a professor who has invented the Fun Factor (Figure 5.3). This mathematical equation can be used to compute a value for determining the relative fun of automobiles. Students groan as they think about having to solve the fun factor equation 28 times. "We don't have to do that," Mr. Funkhouser tells students. "We can use the spreadsheet, but we had better compute the fun factor for three of the cars so we can determine if we have used the spreadsheet correctly." On Mr. Funkhouser's recommendation, students divided into groups of three, opened the spreadsheet, and chose three cars. They computed the fun factor. Then, using the projecting monitor, Mr. Funkhouser shows students how to compute the fun factor using the spreadsheet. Students check the spreadsheet computations against their own computations. When the class is confident that the fun factors are correct, Mr. Funkhouser resaves the spreadsheet to the school server.

"Now," Mr. Funkhouser challenged, "use the database of cars and the calculated fun factors, compare and contrast an economy car, a midrange car, and a luxury or sports car. Make a recommendation to me about what I should buy—what car will be the most fun to own." When students had written their analyses and made their recommendations, they discussed the various interpretations. They talked about how they might change the fun factor. Some students recommended buying larger engine versions of the cars or changing options packages to alter the price. Mr. Funkhouser and students talked about the biases of the fun factor. For instance, safety and miles per gallon were not part of the Fun Factor equation. All in all, students agreed it was a good idea to have criteria for assessing a car before purchasing it, but they also agreed this was probably not the best formula to use.

**News Release
(AP Associated, 2001):**

Professor Franklin Armitage has been awarded the Nobel Prize in Mathematics for his discovery of the "Fun Factor." Professor Armitage—Frank to his friends—was quoted as saying "My fun factor is the ultimate mathematical formula which permits its users to assess the thrill, sheer pleasure, and majesty of almost any phenomenon. Using the Fun Factor, anyone is now able to compute the value for the amount of "fun" associated with a variety of cars and pick the one that is best for them. Professor Armitage's award-winning formula is as follows:

$$\text{FUN FACTOR} = \frac{(\text{horsepower} + \text{torque})^\wedge]\,(1 \times 10^{\wedge}5)}{(\text{price})(\text{weight})(1\text{–}60\text{ time})}$$

FIGURE **5.3**

ANNOUNCING THE FUN FACTOR
Source: Courtesy of Todd Funkhouser.

Thinking about Thinking: Metacognition

"We are to thinking as the Victorians were to sex," writes Papert (1980), "everyone does it, but no one knows how to talk about it." As we create new electronic knowledge environments, they are introducing more structure into our thinking about thinking. Many of the functions of these technologies resemble human cognitive processes, and comparisons between humans and technology are inevitable. Both the mind and these technologies accept information, manipulate symbols, process that information, and then arrive at an output. As researchers experiment with these technologies, trying to make them appear more intelligent, they are learning about the processes the human mind uses to think. Their knowledge can help teachers peer into the black box. When educators use these technologies as part of their designs for thinking, they offer students an intellectual environment that serves as a vehicle for bringing thinking about thinking into the open. This presents students with opportunities to talk about the processes they use to think and to test their ideas by externalizing them (Papert, 1980).

Much has been written about metacognition—the awareness of our own thinking processes. Flavell (1976) states that children gradually acquire metacognitive capacities such as the awareness that they are having more trouble learning one thing or another, the thought that a fact should be checked before taken as true, and the feeling that it would be a good idea to make a note so they will not forget. Metacognition is thus the monitoring and guiding of one's own thought processes; it is mind observing itself and correcting itself (Hunt, 1982).

Learners need to think about their own thinking if they wish to improve it. For instance, research with students at Harvard's Project Zero (Gardner, 1989) found that when students were engaged in metacognitive (thinking about thinking) activities by asking them to explain what it is they were doing while programming, both their programming ability and their problem-solving ability improved. Children were also more able to translate the problem-solving skills gained from programming to other kinds of problem solving when they were explicitly taught to think about thinking. Support for metacognition is, of course, not limited to programming. Educators can ask students to think about their problem solving in all learning situations.

Metacognition: A Thinking About Thinking Case Study.   The first year Mr. Foster was asked to teach four nine-week computer literacy courses to the seventh graders at Wilson Middle School was a disaster, because, as Mr. Foster learned, you cannot learn about computers unless you are using computers for a reason. Mr. Foster used the analogy of a book. Students do not learn to read without reading about something; students do not learn to write without writing about something; students do not learn about computers without using them for some purpose. So, the second year he taught the computer literacy courses he decided that what students would learn was to use computers to solve problems, and, as long as they were solving problems, they could also learn to think about how they solved problems.

> When students arrived for the first day of the nine-week course, there were banners all over the room that read "The Lemmings Are Coming, the Lemmings Are Coming," and Mr. Foster was wearing a green, elflike, felt hat. "Who are the Lemmings?" challenged the students. "When will they be here?" students wanted to know. "Well," replied Mr. Foster. "I can't really tell you who they are, but I can tell you they are beings with BIG problems. And they will be here when you have learned to solve problems."
>
> Mr. Foster divided students into groups of two and introduced them to five workstations around the computer lab. Each workstation consisted of three computers and three manila folders with "Solve This Problem, If You Can" written on the front of each. Mr. Foster told students that the computers at Workstation One had two problem-solving software programs loaded on each of them. One was The Pond and the other one was The Incredible Lab (both produced by Sunburst Communications). The Incredible Lab places the player in the role of a scientist creating monsters in a laboratory. To succeed at predicting which chemicals would result in which monsters, students needed to figure out which monsters were created by which combination of chemicals. Students would have to decide if color or order or body part or number of ingredients were the important variables. Mr. Foster had spent one afternoon solving the problem. The Novice Level was actually solvable in five deductive steps, but much trial-and-error thinking would happen before that discovery. The manila folder contained directions for accessing and operating each of these programs.

Computers at Workstation Two were loaded with the simulation program, Oregon Train III (MECC). "Can you lead a group of people safely to Oregon without death, starvation, or catastrophe?" challenged Mr. Foster. At Workstation Three, students learned about an interactive fiction game called Wishbringer (Infocom) that challenged students to deliver a letter to the Magick Shoppe by "reading" and "writing" a story. Students entered an instruction either indicating a direction to move or questioning a character, received a description of the consequences of their command, and then created the next command. Workstation Four asked students to use a database to solve a series of crimes. The folder contained eight mysteries, each containing a set of clues about the suspects. Students had to identify the clues, enter them into a database appropriately in order to identify the criminal in each case. Next students had to write a mystery of their own that could be solved with the database. Students' mysteries were posted on a bulletin board. Workstation Five required students to use a spreadsheet provided by a fictional store manager to complete the manager's payroll correctly.

Mr. Foster explained the schedule. Students would sign up for three days at each workstation. Six students (three teams of two) could be at a workstation at any one time. They had three days to solve the problem. On the fourth day, students were told they were to use a word processor to write a software evaluation for the workstation they had just completed. Mr. Foster furnished the class with a software evaluation rubric that included the name of the software, a description of the software, and a description of the process(es) students used to solve the problem. It was this last part—describing the processes and strategies they used to solve the problem—that was the most challenging to students. They had difficulty, especially at first, finding words to tell about their problem solving. Mr. Foster noticed that the descriptions of their problem solving, however, steadily improved from their first review to their last.

The first round was the most difficult. Mr. Foster was the only resource in the classroom for helping students figure out how to work the software and how to begin solving problems. As the rounds progressed, however, Mr. Foster encouraged students who had completed a workstation to help students who had just moved to that station. He helped them learn to offer assistance without solving the problem. When students had completed all five workstations and all five software evaluations, the Lemmings came.

The software program, Lemmings (Psygnosis), presents students with 100 levels or problems to solve. Each level releases a stream of Lemmings from a designated source. The Lemmings unfailingly follow the first Lemming in the stream to an exit point. Yet, there are obstacles along the Lemmings' path, and students must assign a series of potential "powers" to various Lemmings in order to create a safe passage for the Lemmings. Each level challenges students to safely get a designated percentage of the Lemmings to the exit point. For instance, one level presents a series of horizontal lines from the entrance point to the exit point. If the Lemmings travel along one of these lines and fall off the edge they "splat" and die. Students must therefore assign some Lemmings the ability to block the path of other Lemmings, placing these blockers at the correct points (Figure 5.4). As the levels progress in difficulty, students must create increasingly complex combinations of powers in order to get the correct percentage of Lemmings to the exit point. Mr. Foster's students were given six days to complete as many levels as they could.

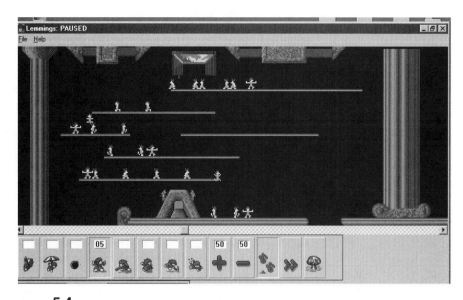

FIGURE 5.4

LEMMINGS

Source: © 1991 Psygnosis. All rights reserved. Printed with permission.

After six days of Lemmings, Mr. Foster demonstrated a graphics program to the class and challenged each pair of students to create a new, original level for Lemmings. Students worked to devise clever obstacles and to use the graphics program to represent the obstacles they invented. As a sort of final test of their problem-solving abilities, students exchanged their graphic Lemmings levels and wrote solutions.

Mr. Foster's course soon developed a schoolwide reputation; students anxiously waited for their turn to take the course. Mr. Foster prided himself on developing a computer literacy course that not only taught the district-prescribed curriculum—students should learn how to operate a computer, learn to use software such as databases, spreadsheets, word processors, graphics programs—but also taught students to use computers to solve problems and to think about their thinking when they were solving problems.

If students are to be problem-solvers, they must be able to use general problem-solving strategies like those taught by Priscilla Norton, Ms. Angell, and Mr. Funkhouser. These heuristics, as general problem-solving strategies are often called, are important in the problem-solving process and can be taught. In addition, students must develop self-monitoring abilities and a conscious awareness of problem-solving strategies. Each of the teachers in previous sections of this chapter not only designed learning opportunities for students to experiment with and develop these heuristics, they also designed opportunities for students to become aware of their own problem-solving processes. Priscilla Norton drew attention to a strategy for interpreting and remembering central concepts. Ms. Angell helped students extend their knowledge of the legislative process by representing connections and patterns in governmental procedures. Mr. Funkhouser assisted students in understanding how algebraic formulas are useful in analyzing data and making comparisons. Mr. Foster's design promoted metacognitive—thinking about thinking—opportunities. His students had to find ways to express the strategies they developed to solve problems—to become self-monitoring problem-solvers. Yet, these general heuristics tell only part of the story of problem solving.

PUTTING THE PROBLEM AT THE CENTER

The Efficiency Model of Learning (see Chapter 2), sometimes referred to as the Transmission Model of Learning, rests on the assumption that learning is the result of a lifetime of accumulating associations between behaviors and their consequences. Consistent with the industrial "assembly line" metaphor, this notion of learning views students as progressing along a moving assembly line picking up specific sets of skills and knowledge along the way. Classroom environments based on the efficiency model usually involve students who adopt the role of receivers of wisdom, which is dispensed by teachers, textbooks, and other media (Means, 1994). The role of the teacher is as deliverer of information and the manager of learning. The role of the student is to engage in "knowledge telling" (Scardamalia & Bereiter, 1991) and demonstrate that what has been transmitted has been retained. Usually, everyone is taught the same thing, although there is some room for "individualization."

Educators' views are shifting from the goal of transmitting skills and knowledge to the goal of helping students develop the confidence, skills, and knowledge necessary to solve problems and become independent thinkers and learners (e.g., Baron & Sternberg, 1987). Instead of knowledge as something to be received, accumulated, and stored, it is viewed as an active construction and reorganization of the learner's mental structures (e.g., Cobb, 1994).

Anchored Instruction

Anchored instruction is a term coined by the Cognition and Technology Group at Vanderbilt (1990) and offers educators a framework for merging problem solving with content-specific instruction. Anchored instruction creates environments that permit sustained exploration by students and teachers, enabling them to understand the kinds of problems and opportunities experts in various areas encounter and the knowledge that these experts use as tools. Anchored instruction derives from insights by theorists such as Dewey (1933) and Hanson (1970), who emphasized that experts in an area have been immersed in phenomena and are familiar with how they have been thinking about them. When introduced to new theories, concepts, and principles, experts experience changes in their own thinking that these ideas afford. For novices, however, the introduction of concepts and theories often seem like new facts or mechanical procedures. Because novices have not been immersed in the phenomena being investigated, they are unable to experience the effects of new information on their own understanding. Anchored instruction suggests a way to structure the design of opportunities for learning that help novices adopt expert ways of using tools as reflected in the ways practitioners use these tools to solve problems.

One way to anchor instruction is to embed it in minicases that serve as microcontexts to focus attention on specific subsets of a larger problem of domain. For example, many law school courses on tort law use separate real-world cases to explain new dimensions of law. Another way to anchor instruction is to select complex problem spaces referred to as macrocontexts. Macrocontexts enable the exploration of a problem space for extended periods of time and from many perspectives. For example, the Cognition and Technology Group at Vanderbilt (1990) used the feature-length film *Young Sherlock Holmes* to anchor instruction for a semester-long investigation of Victorian era history, scientific concepts (weather, geography, and inventions), and aspects of literature. The use of a single film for an entire semester might invoke images of students bored to tears when viewing the film for the tenth or thirtieth time. But viewing the film from new perspectives that resulted from new learnings proved challenging and motivating to students.

At the heart of anchored instruction is an emphasis on the importance of creating an anchor or focus that generates interest and enables students to identify and define problems and to pay attention to their own perception and comprehension of these problems. Students can be introduced to information that is relevant to their anchored perceptions. The major goal of anchored instruction is to enable students to notice critical features of problem situations and to experience the changes in their understanding of the anchor as they view the situation from new points of view (Bransford, et al., 1990).

Perhaps the strongest and most obvious advantage of anchored instruction is the use of complex, realistic contexts to provide meaning and reasons for why information is useful. For example, if one wanted students to learn to use a band saw, instruction might be anchored in the problem of building a building. While students might possess a band saw, they do not necessarily have knowledge of how to use the tool. In anchored instruction, it is the building that provides the meaning and motivation for learning about the band saw. At any point, a student could meaningfully respond to the question of why they are working so hard, by appealing to the importance of building the building—the meaning and reasons for why information is useful. "It is unlikely," write Young and Kulikowich (1992, p. 4), "that an equally meaningful explanation would be given by a student learning logarithms in a traditional Algebra classroom."

Van Haneghan, et al. (1992) showed that students who solve mathematics problems "anchored" in a complex context acquired problem-solving skills, such as problem formulation and relevant information detection, to a greater degree than did students who solved isolated, decontextualized word problems. These data provide evidence that anchored instruction affords acquisition of all the knowledge and skills typically taught in the abstract by traditional mathematics texts. In addition to affording traditional learning outcomes, using anchored instruction provided teachers an opportunity to direct students' attention to general approaches to problem solving.

Ideally, an instructional anchor will be intrinsically interesting and will enable students to deal with a general goal that involves a variety of related subproblems and subgoals. Effective anchors should also help students focus on the relevant features of the problems they are trying to solve (Bransford, et al., 1990). Anchors should engage students in authentic activity (Cognition and Technology Group at Vanderbilt, 1990). Authenticity should include a factual level of authenticity—the objects and data in the setting should be real. Another level of authenticity involves the degree to which the tasks students are asked to perform reflect the actual tasks of practitioners. For example, students might be presented with a realistic problem, yet be asked to complete tasks that are contrived. Last, designers must think about authenticity in terms of for whom the tasks are authentic. Should tasks be authentic for the professional mathematician or for a well-informed parent who helps his or her children reflect on the types of skills and concepts necessary to deal with problems that can occur in everyday life?

Problem-Based Learning

One way to plan for anchored instruction is to use problem-based or problem-centered learning. The traditional debate between a "student-centered" and "teacher-centered" curriculum, writes Norton (1997), is likely asking the wrong question. Rather, an effective strategy for creating a curriculum is to place a "problem" at the center. A problem-centered curriculum is one that is built around the solution to a real-world problem of interest. The phrase "at the center" means that a theme, a unit, or mastery of specific content is replaced as the main focus of the curriculum. Instead, students' abilities to solve the problem, to present their solution, and to revise their solutions in light of additional information become the goals. Placing the problem at the center emphasizes students' doing rather than their mastery of discrete pieces of information or skills.

In selecting appropriate problems, Norton continues, educators should pick problems that are contemporary, nontrivial, and real (not realistic)—complex enough to engage students, and amenable to concrete outcomes. In the selection of appropriate problems, one should keep in mind John Dewey's creed, part of which reads, "Education is a process of living and not a preparation for future living." Traditional curricular goals are thus recast in a "problem-centered" curriculum. Curriculum designers select content to be taught not because a textbook, tradition, or curriculum guide specifies its teaching but because it is necessary and related to the problem's solution.

Students working on problems practice important "life skills" (Drinan, 1990) in the patterns that will be most common when they take on adult responsibility in family and work. Among the life skills they practice are developing the ability to make decisions, raising awareness of the complexity of real-world issues, acquiring a body of knowledge, developing the capacity for self-directed learning, and generating the desire and ability to think deeply and holistically. "They may come to respect knowledge as an aim of learning, but students also recognize how managing the processes of their own minds makes knowledge valuable" (Clarke & Agne, 1997, p. 222). The more authentic the problem—the more closely the problem resembles real life—the more learners respond. "We are hardwired to respond to a challenging environment" (Stepien, 1997, p. 209).

Good problem-solving situations share common characteristics. Greenberg (1990, p. 147) defines a good problem-solving situation as one which:

1. Demands that students make a testable prediction (one preferably testable by the students);
2. Makes use of relatively inexpensive equipment. Fancier equipment might be used to obtain higher precisions, but the problem should work well at the low-tech end of the spectrum;
3. Is complex enough to elicit multiple problem-solving approaches from students; and
4. Benefits from (as opposed to being hindered by) group efforts.

Brooks and Brooks (1999) add a fifth requirement to this list. For a situation to be considered a good problem-solving situation, the problem-solvers must view the problem as relevant. Problems with little or no initial relevance to students can be made relevant, they write, through teacher mediation before or after the problem is posed. For instance, high school freshmen rarely ask spontaneous questions about ethical issues related to technology or about federal processes of legislation writing and passing. Yet, as we will see later in this chapter, this can, through effective introduction of the process and teacher mediation strategies, become a quite relevant problem.

Effective problems at the center of the curriculum are ill-defined problems. Stepien, Gallagher, and Workman (1993) describe ill-defined problems as ones that require more knowledge than is initially available in order for understanding and decisions about actions for resolution to occur. Ill-defined problems are problems where there is no absolutely right way or fixed formula for conducting an investigation. As new information is obtained, ill-defined problems change. When students solve ill-defined problems, they are never sure they have made the right decision because important information might be lacking or data or values may be in conflict. Nevertheless, decisions have to be made. Students working through an ill-defined problem gain respect for the volume of knowledge related to any problem situation and also recognize the element of risk that accompanies any solution. The "real" character of the problem, however, forces students to propose solutions, recognizing the level of risk embedded in the whole process. Good problems engage students in proposing solutions to problems that are as real for them as they are for the adult community.

Teachers who employ problem-based learning continue to be content experts but, instead of passing their expertise through presentation, they use their expertise to facilitate and guide; they craft problems, specifying content and process goals clearly in advance. They set up criteria by which they and their students will measure success (Marshall, 1993). Teachers can design problem-based learning that covers virtually all the material in some part of the curriculum or they may embed problem situations at points in the curriculum where they want students to synthesize information and concepts they have learned from more conventional methods.

Although it is possible for students to work independently on a problem, the size and complexity of good problem-based learning make group work a practical necessity. If teachers choose to pose one problem to a whole class, cooperative groups might take on different aspects of the investigation. On the other hand, students might join competing teams of investigators who work together to propose a solution that will win the vote of a panel of experts at the end of the unit. In problem-based learning, learning has a clear purpose. It is a public event in which errors of process or fact may receive instant recognition and clarification. Problem-based learning gives students control over the process of learning new material and representing what they know (Glaser, 1986).

How do teachers identify problems to place at the center of their instructional designs? One way is to monitor your experiences and resources to identify "inspiration" pieces. A film, a news story, a favorite story, or a personal experience might all serve to inspire a problem. Another way is to pay careful attention to events in the current social context. Ethical issues in the news present challenging problems. World events, local community activities, and local, national, and international controversies offer numerous problems. A third way to identify appropriate problems is to think about the kinds of challenges various occupations confront. A real estate agent is challenged to find a new home for a client. Electricians wire houses; architects and engineers design structures. School cafeteria workers plan healthy menus and alter recipes. A fourth source of relevant problems derives from students' lives. Students' lives are often filled with interesting problems or dilemmas. What is of concern to them? What issues are they wrestling with? What things are they interested in that you would like to encourage? What things are they interested in that you would like to discourage? What issues, problems, or activities might be worth studying, considering, or perhaps reconsidering? What experiences are they having that might be better understood if more carefully examined?

°°°°°°

Becky Davidson's fifth-grade class was excited about their upcoming week at Outdoor School, a planned week at an outdoor school mandated for all fifth-grade California students. The six-week countdown had begun when Ms. Davidson received a letter from the Outdoor School staff confirming the dates for her class's attendance, expressing their excitement at the class's impending arrival, and listing five areas her students should know about. Reading the letter, Ms. Davidson gasped in dismay. How could she teach fifth graders about the required aspects of astronomy, plants, animals, geology, and ecology requested by the school staff in the next six weeks? After several late nights of planning, Ms. Davidson called her class together and read them the letter. "According to this letter, we can't go to Outdoor School until we have learned about all these things," she told her class. "How do you think we can do that?" The class sighed in disappointment but soon began brainstorming how they might learn everything. With some subtle, but expert guidance from Ms. Davidson, they soon hit upon the idea of dividing into groups with each group accepting responsibility for teaching the rest of the class about one of the topics. "We will become the teacher," they assured Ms. Davidson. Activity during the remaining five weeks was fast and furious.

✿✿✿✿✿✿

It was spring semester at Highland High School. Hormones were raging in Ms. Angell's semester-long government class required of all ninth graders. The last thing on students' agenda was a concern with the ways in which federal law is written and legislated. It was going to be a long semester unless students could somehow be engaged with the way in which legal responses to urgent social issues were created. Ms. Angell knew she needed an appropriate and evocative anchoring problem if students were to become engaged in learning. She had an idea.

Ms. Angell entered the classroom clutching a collection of Ray Bradbury stories. She told the class that while reading some of the stories in the collection she had read one that made her think. She asked to share it with the class and began reading. It was the Bradbury story titled, *There Will Come Soft Rains*, which told of the automated routine of a suburban house. Soon, the author revealed five burned shadows on the side of the house—a man, a woman, two children, and a ball. Slowly, the computer programs running the house went awry; the house burst into flames. As the story ended, no evidence of humanity existed, not even its artifacts.

The class sat in stunned silence. Allowing a moment of silence, Ms. Angell began inquiring about the theme of the story (the threat of nuclear annihilation), about what other similar issues were confronting humankind today, and about the ways students could influence possible resolutions. As the discussion progressed, students added computer issues such as piracy and privacy, issues associated with robots replacing workers, and issues of bioengineering as well as the threat of nuclear annihilation, nuclear waste, and nuclear energy. Students discussed these issues. They had lots of concerns about these issues but little real understanding of the complexities of how a culture might come to cope with these developments. Finally, one student recognized the need for new laws to deal with these problems. "How is that done?" queried Ms. Angell. Students were ready to engage the problem.

SOLVING CONTENT-SPECIFIC PROBLEMS: THE ABCS OF ACTIVITY

Writers, scientists, and mathematicians learn through continuous interaction with knowledge, skills, tools, and other people in their field. They are not required to take tests on isolated facts. Instead, they must solve real problems whose solutions have consequences. Often, the problems they attempt to solve are messy and require an understanding of many different disciplines and their interaction. City planners, for example, need to know not only how buildings, streets, and parks are constructed and which types of construction are safe in which kinds of environment but also how background

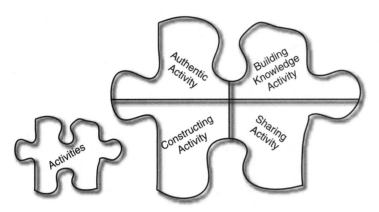

or disciplinary knowledge can be applied to resolving a new city planning problem. As this example demonstrates, authentic problem solving is significantly different from typical school "problems" that are well-defined, have clearly defined boundaries, and "right" answers.

Once a design for learning has been anchored in a problem as Ms. Davidson and Ms. Angell did, students must be challenged with a series of appropriate activities that support and direct their ability to solve the problem in a robust and comprehensive manner. A design must present opportunities for students to enter the community and culture of practitioners who solve similar problems and engage in a range of activities that mirror the activities used by problem-solvers. Much of classroom activity, however, takes place within the culture of schools, although it is often attributed to the culture of readers, writers, mathematicians, historians, economists, geographers, and so forth. Many activities students undertake are not the activities of practitioners but the activities of school—test taking, question answering, memorization, and answering isolated problems. Classroom tasks, therefore, often fail to provide the contextual features that allow students to understand how and for what purposes acquired knowledge is useful. Knowledge that is separated from situations where it is useful is less robust and less fully understood. Teachers can help students learn by designing opportunities for them to encounter contents and knowledge through a variety of activities, carefully selected and organized. If student learning is to be contextualized in a culture of practice and anchored with a problem of significance, opportunities for student learning must be bolstered by students' participation in authentic activities, building knowledge activities, constructing activities, and sharing activities—the ABCS of activity.

A Is for Authentic Activities

Methods of education like those associated with the efficiency model (Chapter 2) separate knowing and doing and treat knowledge as independent from the situations in which it is learned and used. Learning activities and contexts are viewed as distinct and even neutral with respect to what is learned. Recent investigations of learning, however, challenge separating what is learned from how it is learned and how it is used (Lave, 1988). The activities through which knowledge is developed and deployed cannot be separated from what is learned. Rather, activity is integral to what and how knowledge is learned.

Learning and knowledge are fundamentally situated (Brown, Collins, & Duguid, 1989). They are not embedded in the mind of the individual or self-sufficient. They are embedded in the activities and practices of the culture in which they are situated. Knowledge that is separated from activities and a culture of practice is

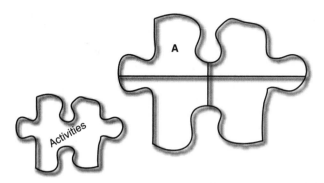

"inert." Inert knowledge (Whitehead, 1929) is knowledge that can usually be recalled when people are explicitly asked to do so but is not used spontaneously in problem solving even though it is relevant. Knowledge, if it is to be useful, must be inextricably linked with activities and situations. It must evolve in contexts of new use, new situations, and new activities; it must be in continual construction. "Activity, concept, and culture are interdependent" (Brown, Collins, & Duguid, 1989, p. 33).

Authentic activity is defined as the ordinary practices of a culture. Authentic activity is important for learners because it is the only way they gain access to the standpoint that enables practitioners to act meaningfully and purposefully in solving problems related to their practice. It is activity that shapes and hones their emerging knowledge. Authentic activity provides experience for subsequent activity. Authentic activity provides the bridge from "inert" knowledge to entrance into the culture of practice. Well-designed opportunities for student learning help students understand what a culture of practitioners does and how that culture uses knowledge to solve problems and inform the conduct of their lives. A by-product of participating in and practicing those activities is a richer and deeper understanding of the knowledge and skills.

It is unrealistic to expect young, novice learners to replicate the complexity of expert activity. It is not, however, unrealistic to expect young, novice learners to approximate and come to appreciate the activities of experts. Identifying authentic activities for student learning depends on a careful analysis of the kinds of things practitioners "do" when solving problems. These activities include both the types of thinking practitioners engage in as well as producing the kinds of products practitioners create. Thus, detectives use knowledge of forensic science to collect evidence. They interview suspects to identify clues. They use analytical skills to solve crimes. They make arrests. Travel agents research destinations, identify travel arrangements, create travel itineraries, locate hotel accommodations, create budgets, and prepare travel materials for prospective clients. Selection of relevant authentic activities depends on asking and answering such questions as: What kinds of practitioners use the content knowledge I want students to master? What do they use the content knowledge for? What do they "do" to solve the problems they encounter? What products do they produce to support and communicate the solutions they devise?

B Is for Building Knowledge Activities

Over the past 30 years, considerable research and controversy have surrounded the relationship of general problem-solving strategies to success at problem solving. Psychologists have asked: Is skillful, thought-demanding performance context-bound, or does it principally reflect use of general problem-solving abilities? Are the problem-solving successes of physicists, mathematicians, or "just plain folk"

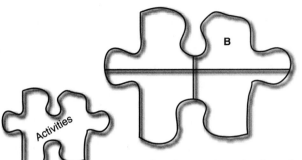

(Lave, 1988) dependent on their general problem-solving abilities or their deep understanding of their subject matter? What are the roles of general knowledge about problem-solving heuristics and of context-specific knowledge?

Clearly, knowledge counts in problem solving. The question is, Which kind of knowledge counts most—general knowledge of how to think well or specific knowledge about the detailed ins and outs of a field (content knowledge)? Perkins and Salomon (1989) ask, "Should we teach entirely for richly developed local knowledge, subject matter by subject matter? Or should we invest a significant portion of educational resources in developing general skills of problem-solving, self-management, and so on?" (p. 17).

Thirty years ago, it was widely thought that good problem solving and other intellectual performances reflected general strategies. True ability resided in general strategies with subject matter knowledge an incidental necessity. Polya (1957), for instance, argued that the formalities of mathematical proof had little to do with the real work of problem solving in mathematics. Success in finding solutions, he stated, depended on a repertoire of heuristics. Researchers in artificial intelligence further support the importance of general problem-solving strategies (e.g., Newell & Simon, 1972). As these researchers attempted to create general problem-solving computer programs by embedding heuristic strategies in a computer's code, their early successes supported the notion that problem-solving power lies in general principles. The combined positions supported the notion that good thinking depended in considerable part on a repertoire of general heuristic knowledge. These researchers helped to identify such heuristics as memorizing, inventive thinking, decision making, inductive and deductive processes, and general mental management (Nickerson, Perkins, & Smith, 1985).

In the years that followed, however, some findings cast doubt on the centrality of general ability. Research on expertise—studies of expert problem-solvers in such fields as physics (Larkin, McDermott, Simon, & Simon, 1980), mathematics (Schoenfeld & Herrmann, 1982), computer programming (Erlich & Soloway, 1984), and medicine (Patel & Groen, 1986)—revealed the naiveté inherent in discarding the role of context-specific knowledge in problem solving. They revealed that experts depend on a rich database of knowledge about their content domain. In fact, the broad heuristic structure of the expert problem-solver as compared with the novice problem-solver could be attributed not to sophistication with general problem-solving heuristics but to the expert's rich database of knowledge.

Continuing work in artificial intelligence also began to undermine the centrality of general problem-solving skills. General problem-solving programs continued to do well on simple, formal problems but seemed quite helpless in complex problem-solving domains such as chess, medical diagnosis, and mathematics. Instead, programs designed specifically for a knowledge domain were more successful (Rich, 1983).

Recently, researchers have begun to recognize that treating general problem-solving strategies and contextualized, domain-specific knowledge as exclusive of each other creates an artificial distinction between the two. Instead, they are recognizing that there are general heuristics, but these strategies always function in contextualized ways (Perkins, Schwartz, & Simmons, 1991). Early advocacy of general problem-solving ability overlooked the importance of a rich knowledge base; later advocacy of contextualized knowledge neglected the ways in which general heuristics contributed to problem solving in specific domains of knowledge. A synthesis has become necessary.

General problem-solving abilities do not take the place of domain-specific knowledge. Rather, they are general tools in much the way the human hand is. Your hands alone are not enough; you need objects to grasp. Moreover, as you reach for an object, whether a pen or a ball, you shape your hand to assure a good grip. And you need to learn to handle different objects appropriately—you do not pick up a baby in the same way you pick up a basket of laundry. Likewise, general problem-solving abilities can be thought of as general gripping devices for retrieving and wielding domain-specific knowledge, as hands that need pieces of knowledge to grip and wield and that need to configure to the kind of knowledge in question. "To be sure, general heuristics that fail to make contact with a rich domain-specific knowledge base are weak. But when a domain-specific knowledge base operates without general heuristics, it is brittle—it serves mostly in handling formulaic problems" (Perkins & Salomon, 1989, p. 23). The approach that now seems warranted calls for the intermingling of general problem-solving strategies with context-specific background knowledge.

Research has demonstrated that the teaching of a generous number of carefully chosen exemplary facts within a meaningful explanatory context is the most appropriate method for supporting the ability to engage in insightful thinking and problem solving (Hirsch, 1996). There is an unavoidable interdependence between relational and factual knowledge, and teaching a broad range of factual knowledge is essential for effective thinking both within domains of knowledge and among domains. It is imperative that learners gain essential background knowledge.

Learners need to master facts. They are important for thinking and problem solving. Research on expertise in areas such as chess, history, science, and mathematics demonstrates that thinking and problem solving depend on a rich body of knowledge about subject matter (e.g., Chi, Glaser, & Rees, 1981). However, research also shows clearly that "usable knowledge" is not the same as a list of facts. Experts' knowledge is connected and organized around important concepts. It is specifically tied to the contexts in which it is applicable. It supports understanding and application to other contexts rather than only the ability to remember.

If students are to be successful problem-solvers, educators must include rigorous knowledge-building activities in their designs for learning. Knowledge-building activities include reading and discussing ideas, watching demonstrations, viewing films, responding to questions, completing structured experiments, exploring concepts and testing their application, examining well-formed models and productions, analyzing case studies, listening to presentations or lectures, interviewing experts, mastering definitions, and attempting and completing sample problems. Building knowledge does not mean avoiding facts, but primacy is given to the kinds of activities that connect these facts into webs of meaning.

Each of the scenarios presented in the general problem-solving part of this chapter represents an activity designed to help students build knowledge. Priscilla Norton's concept-mapping activity encouraged students to identify, organize, and connect concepts. Building hypermedia models of the legislative process helped Ms. Angell's students to connect their experiences of the legislative process gained during the bill writing and passing simulation with their textbook knowledge of governmental structures (e.g., the Senate, the House of Representatives, veto, law, public opinion) and processes (voting, researching, drafting legislation, compromising, debating) and their building of a generalizable model of the legislative process. When selecting activities to support knowledge building, educators should ask: What learning environments will provide students with the opportunities to confront facts, ideas, and concepts—reference material, Internet resources, videos, textbooks, discussions, lectures or presentations, simulations, databases, or illustrations? What kinds of things can students "do" with these materials to help them extract and interpret facts, ideas, and concepts—making concept maps, outlines, and flowcharts, asking and answering questions, explaining and reporting, completing experiments, researching, or applying knowledge to interpret new instances?

C Is for Constructing Activities

Berliner and Biddle (1995, p. 302) write:

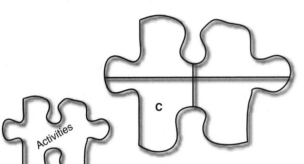

Let there be no mistake. We are *not* arguing here that students should be ignorant of the knowledge base that constitutes our cultural heritage. On the contrary, our country badly needs a citizenry that shares such a heritage, but those who cannot think beyond the traditional image . . . confuse the necessary with the sufficient. It is *necessary* that students have an appropriate knowledge base, but such a base is far from *sufficient* if students are to be well-educated.

" 'Applying what one knows requires knowing something' but application is of equal importance . . ." (Tucker & Codding, 1998, p. 77). Students need opportunities to test their knowledge with nonroutine problems, problems that may have many right answers, and problems that have no predetermined path for their solution. Learners really understand when they test what they have come to know against what they want to do. No one knows whether they understand what they know about carpentry, for instance, until they attempt to build something.

Constructing activities push students beyond building knowledge to using emerging knowledge to make or form something that represents their deepening understanding. Moving from knowledge to understanding involves a set of performances (Perkins, 1995) or "performances of understanding" (Gardner, 2000). Performances of understanding are structured by engagement in a unique kind of activity—activity that gives learners opportunities to apply knowledge to solve a range of problems related to a diversity of situations.

Blythe and Associates (1998) list three key features of performances of understanding. First, performances of understanding are activities that require students to use what they know in new ways or new situations to build their understanding of unit topics. In performances of understanding students reshape, expand on, extrapolate from, and apply what they already know. Second, performances of understanding are activities that help students build *and* demonstrate their understanding. They give both learners and teachers a chance to see understanding develop over time in new and challenging situations. Third, performances of understanding require students to show their understanding in an observable way. They make students' thinking visible. It is not enough for students to reshape, expand, extrapolate from, and apply their knowledge in the privacy of their own thoughts. While it is conceivable that a student could understand without performing, such an understanding would be untried, possibly fragile, and virtually impossible to assess. So performances of understanding involve students in publicly demonstrating their understanding.

Constructing activities are performance activities that ask students to expand, reform, apply, or extend their knowledge by making something, producing something, building something, or creating something. The outcomes of constructing activities serve as observable performances of understanding. What learners make, produce, build, or create demonstrate what they are able to "do" with their knowledge. Thus, to Perkins's (1995), Gardner's (2000), and Blythe and Associates' (1998) descriptions of performance activities as observable, we add to our definition of constructing activities the need for such activities to culminate in concrete and tangible products. We believe that the act and art of embedding understanding in visible products helps learners to structure, communicate, and judge the impacts of their understanding. Thus, constructing activities are those that result in the construction of essays, videos, computer programs, research papers, songs, dances, plays, Web pages, displays, and presentations as well as an unlimited array of similar concrete outcomes.

Choosing constructing activities should flow logically from authentic and building knowledge activities. In a business class it makes little sense to situate activities in the culture of real estate agents, support students as they build knowledge about marketing and advertising activities, and then ask them to write an essay. Instead, it would be more appropriate to ask students to construct a market analysis for a customer interested in selling and/or purchasing a home. In an upper elementary classroom, it makes little sense to situate activities in the culture of a school cafeteria manager, build knowledge about good nutritional principles and the mathematics of fractions, and then ask them to produce a video. Instead, it would make more sense to ask them to plan nutritional lunch menus and convert recipes designed to serve eight into recipes to serve eight hundred. Thus, determining what kinds of constructing activities ought to be part of an instructional design rests with an identification of what products would be authentically produced by practitioners.

S Is for Sharing Activities

"Not all meaning is created equally," writes Jonassen, Peck, and Wilson (1999). The litmus test for knowledge is its viability (Duffy and Cunningham, 1996). Jonassen,

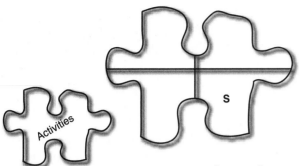

et al. (1999, p. 6) state: "Within any knowledge-building community, shared ideas are accepted and agreed upon. That is, meaning is reflected in the social beliefs that exist at any point in time. If individual ideas are discrepant from community standards, they are not regarded as viable unless new evidence supporting their viability is provided." When students build knowledge and construct products that reflect their understanding in situations that mirror the authentic activities of practitioners, they need opportunities to test their knowledge and judge their products through sharing activities.

Sharing activities allow students to test their understanding in public arenas, to receive feedback that supports their successes, or to be challenged with new evidence or missing evidence or faulty connections and applications. Students need opportunities to compare the meanings they have built about knowledge domains with those of others. How are the things they produce the same or different? How might they need to revise their work? How closely does their understanding and ability to model the behaviors of practitioners mirror the real thing? Designers must provide opportunities for students to make these comparisons and to validate and/or revise their work.

When making decisions about the kinds of sharing activities appropriate for a learning design, educators should ask: What is an appropriate audience for students' work (e.g., peers, older or younger students, practitioners from the culture in which students' experiences have been embedded, parents, community members, or a combination of audiences)? What publication opportunities are available to students and consistent with the products students have produced? What kinds of feedback are appropriate and how should that feedback be structured? What sharing formats are appropriate (e.g., presentations, publications, letters, conversations with experts, conferences, museums, or community service projects)?

In this chapter, we have explored problem solving as a general set of heuristics—memory, information-extending processes, and information-rearranging processes. Yet, these heuristics are insufficient. They must be linked with content-specific knowledge. This chapter suggested that designing opportunities for learning that link general heuristics and content-specific instruction are best created using an anchor for instruction. This is well accomplished by using a problem-centered approach. Once instruction has been anchored by an authentic problem, educators should carefully select four kinds of activities: authentic activities, building knowledge activities, constructing activities, and sharing activities. In Chapter 6, we turn our attention to how educators can design literacy learning opportunities.

But first, we recommend that you go to the FACTS Web-Based Design Tool site (http://www.norton.wadsworth.com) and click on the Design Mentors puzzle piece. This chapter's Design Mentors follow Brooks White and Alan Sutton as they add to the designs they began in the Chapter 4 Design Mentors. You will be able to follow these two teachers as they build on content and knowledge by creating an authentic problem to anchor instruction and begin the process of selecting appropriate authentic, background knowledge, constructing, and sharing activities. After you have studied the Design Mentors, you might find it helpful to return to the opening page of the Web site and complete Design Challenge Five. You can return to some of the Design Examples and see how they reflect the considerations discussed in this chapter.

CHAPTER IDEAS

- The complex mechanisms of brain and mind may not be comprehensively understood, but it is clear that human thinking occurs, that it is shaped by the biology of the brain, the wisdom of culture, and interactions with others, and that tools, activities, and development are important influences in learning to think.
- Human memory is an invisible and intangible phenomenon. No one has ever held memory in their hand nor determined a specific place in the brain where memory is located. In our efforts to understand memory, there have been three predominating metaphors that have helped us understand not what memory is but what memory is like— memory as a muscle, memory as some kind of "writing" on a wax tablet or "brush strokes" on a canvas, and memory as a reference book or a library.
- In the search for a more accurate metaphor, a model of memory has been adapted from computer science—memory as information processing. This metaphor likens memory to a set of transformations of information—a set of processes that organize and abstract things to be remembered as a network of concepts activated by the effort to remember.
- Concept mapping is a technique for externalizing concepts and propositions by visually representing meaningful relationships between concepts or the component parts of a larger concept.
- One of the most pervasive processes humans use to think is the capacity to generalize from specific experiences, concrete or symbolic, and to form new, more abstract concepts. The ability to arrive at such generalizations is critical for thinking about ourselves, each other, and the world around us.
- The creation of hypermedia programs and writing tools supports problem-solvers in their efforts to integrate information into a giant web of connections—to extend information through its combination and connection to other information. These programs support students as they rearrange, connect, and build relationships between chunks of information.
- The idea behind hypermedia is that humans do not always or perhaps even generally think in a linear fashion. Hypermedia programs are

designed to emulate the information-extending patterns of human thinking and, when students use these programs to create hypermedia stacks, they are involved in learning through problem solving.

- An information-rearranging process or deductive thinking is a systematic process of thought that leads from one set of propositions to another based on principles of logic. The purpose of logical principles is to guarantee that a deduction is true, and a deduction is valid only if its premises suffice to ensure the truth of its conclusion. Deductive thinking allows thinkers to extract implications from what is already given or known.

- Logical or deductive thinking is not necessarily our usual or natural way of thinking. Yet, deductive thinking is the basis of rational thought and is most important when the subject matter is hypothetical or unfamiliar. Deductive thinking—information rearranging—is theoretical reasoning, seeing what in principle must be true. Of all the thinking processes, deductive thinking is the process most dependent on formal learning.

- Well-planned spreadsheet activities emphasize reasoning, problem solving, making connections, and communicating mathematical ideas. When students use spreadsheets and embed and/or create formulas to manipulate data, they are rearranging information to solve problems.

- Metacognition is the monitoring and guiding of one's own thought processes; it is mind observing itself and correcting itself. Learners need to think about their own thinking if they wish to improve it.

- If students are to be problem-solvers, they must be able to use general problem-solving strategies. These heuristics, as general problem-solving strategies are often called, are important in the problem-solving process and can be taught. In addition, students must develop self-monitoring abilities and a conscious awareness of problem-solving strategies. Yet, these general heuristics tell only part of the story of problem solving.

- Anchored instruction offers educators a framework for merging problem solving with content-specific instruction. Anchored instruction creates environments that permit sustained exploration by students and teachers, enabling them to understand the kinds of problems and opportunities experts in various areas encounter and the knowledge that these experts use as tools.

- At the heart of anchored instruction is an emphasis on the importance of creating an anchor or focus that generates interest and enables students to identify and define problems and to pay attention to their own perception and comprehension of these problems. Students can be introduced to information that is relevant to their anchored perceptions.

- One way to plan for anchored instruction is to use problem-based or problem-centered learning. A problem-centered curriculum is one that is built around the solution to a real-world problem of interest. Placing the problem at the center emphasizes students' doing rather than their mastery of discrete pieces of information or skills.

- One way to identify problems to place at the center of instruction is to monitor your experiences and resources to identify "inspiration" pieces. Another way is to pay careful attention to events in the current social context. A third way to identify appropriate problems is to think about the kinds of challenges various occupations confront. A fourth source of relevant problems derives from students' lives.

- Once a design for learning has been anchored in a problem, students must be challenged with a series of appropriate activities that support and direct their ability to solve the problem in a robust and comprehensive manner. Opportunities for student learning must be bolstered by students' participation in authentic activities, building knowledge activities, constructing activities, and sharing activities—the ABCS of Activity.

- Learning and knowledge are fundamentally situated. Knowledge, if it is to be useful, must be inextricably linked with activities and situations. It must evolve in contexts of new use, new situations, and new activities; it must be in continual construction. "Activity, concept, and culture are interdependent" (Brown, Collins, & Duguid, 1989, p. 33).

- *Authentic activity* is defined as the ordinary practices of a culture. Authentic activity is important for learners because it is the only way they gain access to the standpoint that enables practitioners to act meaningfully and purposefully in solving problems related to their practice.

- It is unrealistic to expect young, novice learners to replicate the complexity of expert activity. It is not, however, unrealistic to expect young, novice learners to approximate and come to appreciate the activities of experts. Identifying authentic activities for student learning depends on a careful analysis of the kinds of things practitioners "do" when solving problems.

- Selection of relevant authentic activities depends on asking and answering such questions as: What kinds of practitioners use the content knowledge I want students to master? What do they use the content knowledge for? What do they "do" to solve the problems they encounter? What products do they produce to support and communicate the solutions they devise?

- Over the past 30 years, considerable research and controversy have surrounded the relationship of general problem-solving strategies to success at problem solving. Recently, researchers have begun to recognize that there are general heuristics, but these strategies always function in contextualized ways.

- General problem-solving abilities do not take the place of domain-specific knowledge. The approach that now seems warranted calls for the intermingling of general problem-solving strategies with context-specific background knowledge.

- Research has demonstrated that the teaching of a generous number of carefully chosen exemplary facts within a meaningful explanatory context is the most appropriate method for supporting the ability to engage in insightful thinking and problem solving. Teaching a broad range of factual knowledge is essential for effective thinking both within domains of knowledge and among domains.

- Research also shows clearly that "usable knowledge" is not the same as a list of facts. Experts' knowledge is connected and organized around important concepts. It is specifically tied to the contexts in which it is applicable. It supports understanding and application to other contexts rather than only the ability to remember.

- If students are to be successful problem-solvers, educators must include rigorous knowledge-building activities in their designs for learning. Building knowledge does not mean avoiding facts, but primacy is given to the kinds of activities that connect these facts into webs of meaning.

- When selecting activities to support knowledge building, educators should ask: What learning environments will provide students with the opportunities to confront facts, ideas, and concepts? What kinds of things can students "do" with these materials to help them extract and interpret facts, ideas, and concepts?

- Applying what one knows requires knowing something, but application is of equal importance. Students need opportunities to test their knowledge with nonroutine problems, problems that may have many right answers, and problems that have no predetermined path for their solution. Learners really understand when they test what they have come to know against what they want to do.

- Constructing activities push students beyond building knowledge to using emerging knowledge to make or form something that represents their deepening understanding. Constructing activities are performance activities that ask students to expand, reform, apply, or extend their knowledge by making something, producing something, building something, or creating something. Constructing activities need to culminate in concrete and tangible products.

- Choosing constructing activities should flow logically from authentic and building knowledge activities. Determining what kinds of constructing activities ought to be part of an instructional design rests with an identification of what products would be authentically produced by practitioners.

- Not all meaning is created equally. The litmus test for knowledge is its viability (Duffy and Cunningham, 1996). When students build knowledge and construct products that reflect their understanding in situations that mirror the authentic activities of practitioners, they need opportunities to test their knowledge and judge their products through sharing activities.

- Sharing activities allow students to test their understanding in public arenas, to receive feedback that supports their successes, or to be challenged with new evidence or missing evidence or faulty connections and applications. Students need opportunities to compare the meanings they have built about knowledge domains with those of others.
- When making decisions about the kinds of sharing activities appropriate for a learning design, educators should ask: What is an appropriate audience for students' work? What publication opportunities are available to students and consistent with the products students have produced? What kinds of feedback are appropriate and how should that feedback be structured? What sharing formats are appropriate?

DESIGNS FOR LITERACY

Whenever I am creating my lesson plans, helping my students become literate is always on my mind. I want my students to be effective senders and receivers of messages. I want them to be able to understand and profit from all the ideas and passions captured in print. When they read a story or a nonfiction book, I am delighted when they say things like "That reminds me of something" or "That makes me wonder about something" or "That gives me an idea."

I try daily to create experiences for students to unravel the mysteries of print and to capture their own experiences or thoughts in printed form. When students have polished one of their writings, I have a special place in the room where they can leave it for others to read.

I have noticed in the last four or five years though that students are not satisfied with just reading or writing stories or reports. They want to include pictures; they want to leave messages for each other on the classroom tape recorder; they want to make phone calls from the office. Sometimes they talk about their Segas or Nintendos. One student even asked me a question about their Super Mario game. I couldn't help, but one of the other students jumped in with advice. I felt left out.

I went to an in-service not long ago where the speaker said children today "read" and "write" in lots of symbolic environments. You know, it's true. My students do "read" television and computer programs. And they sure would like to be able to "write" with video cameras and computer programs like HyperStudio. I'm just not sure that these technologies belong in my classroom.

Jenny Havlick,
Elementary Teacher

As one of the foundations of learning, literacy may be the most essential. Without literacy, students do not have the power to take meaning from the vast and complex array of symbolic environments available to them. Literacy occupies a prominent place in the learning of students in the early grades. It is, perhaps, the most important tool they have for encountering new ideas and concepts. Traditionally, literacy, at the denotative level, is the ability to use letters. At the connotative level, it is traditionally defined as the ability to read and write to learn. Although designing opportunities for literacy learning has traditionally been firmly entrenched in the technology of print, today's students must navigate a "supersymbolic" world created by the electronic technologies—one far less dependent on print symbols alone. This supersymbolic world uses the full variety of symbol systems invented by humans—numeric,

alphabetic, visual/graphical, musical, verbal, and gestural. Getting meaning from or acquiring knowledge about the complex and rich information environment of the twenty-first century rests on students' ability to fully use all of these symbolic forms. To do so, students must master the workings of these symbol systems, be able to comprehend how meaning is captured by these symbolic forms, and understand how the rules of discourse structure messages.

This chapter examines how teachers can promote a broader conception of literacy by designing instruction that (1) presents students with representative models of how others have created patterns of communication in a variety of symbolic mediums, (2) provides students with opportunities to learn from and interpret these models, and (3) encourages students to use these media to capture their own thoughts and experiences.

DEFINING LITERACY

Jason was born in August of 1986. Beginning in his sixth week, he spent his days with his grandmother while his mother and father went to work. Jason's grandmother was a very special day-care provider. Jason's "Ama" summoned up her philosophy of grandmothering and day care in two short principles. "First," she always

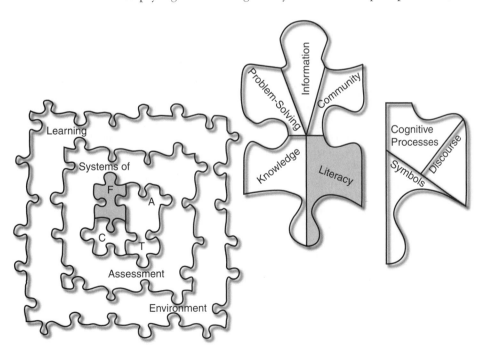

said, "my job is to provide Jason a safe, rich playroom. Second, I have to be his playmate." So, for Jason's first seven or eight months, Ama defined his playroom as a quilt on the floor scattered with toys. By the time Jason was crawling and experimenting with walking, Ama had blocked off the living room. Jason's playroom was restricted to the "front room." As he approached his third birthday, Ama had extended Jason's playroom to include the kitchen, a patio off the living room, and her study. At five, the entire house and the backyard had become Jason's playroom.

Jason's playroom expanded as he grew. The most interesting thing about Jason's playroom was what he did in that playroom. From his first birthday to his second, Jason discovered language and struggled to understand how to communicate with others. His grandmother read to him constantly and marveled at his labeling of the pictures, his early attempts at answering her questions, and his simple retellings of the story. His love of reading books with his grandmother continued, but between two and three Jason extended his interests to the television in the "front room" and later to the computer in his grandmother's study.

Whenever a television commercial came on, Jason would stop what he was doing, run to the television and watch, occasionally even dancing to the jingles. Soon, on trips around town and to the grocery store, Jason would recognize signs and brand names. He learned to sing the *Sesame Street* song. From *Sesame Street,* Jason began to develop an interest in letters and numbers. To capitalize on this interest, a friend of his Ama's gave Jason several computer software programs for preschoolers for his third birthday. Soon, Jason would ask to use the computer in Ama's study several times each day, playing with colors, shapes, letters, and numbers. The afternoon Jason showed a forked twig from the patio to his grandmother and called it a "brown Y," she knew his computer play was not random play.

For his fourth Christmas, Jason received a Touch and Tell. This was a computerized toy with multiple circuit boards and overlays. When Jason pressed his finger on a picture or letter, a voice would name the item or letter. More sophisticated circuits and overlays resulted in questions asking him to touch certain letters or pictures and offering "That is right" whenever he pushed the right picture. Now, Jason was "playing" with computerized toys, with his grandmother's computer, with the television, and with his books.

For his fourth birthday, Jason received a set of rubberized letter stamps and some ink pads. "His fine motor coordination is still rough," his grandmother informed onlookers. "So, I figured he could write with the stamps." One afternoon while Jason was playing with his letter stamps, he stamped out his name. He then asked his grandmother to help him sound out words he wanted to print. Then, he announced he was going to write "football." As Ama watched, he carefully stamped out the letters *NFL.* "There," he said with pride, "I wrote football." His grandmother simply affirmed his success.

At five, Jason's favorite area in his playroom was a private corner in his grandmother's study. He would often go into that room where he had a desk with crayons, markers, paper, a television, a bookshelf of books and computerized toys, and a transistor radio. Occasionally, he would emerge to show her something he had written or drawn or to tell her about something he had seen on television or heard on the radio. Each day, he would emerge to retrieve the cordless phone. "I am going to call my mother at work," he would announce, using up his one allotted phone call to his mother's office. Selecting the precoded number (1), he would jump on his Super Big Wheel and depart for the cemented strip around the backyard pool. His grandmother would watch out the patio window as he rode around and around the pool, summarizing his day for his mother.

When he turned six, Jason started first grade. And Jason's playroom began to shrink. True, there were many familiar things like books, paper, pencils, crayons, scissors, and markers. There was, however, no television, no radio, no computer, no telephone. Jason's day at school was defined by the four walls of his classroom, by his classmates, his teacher, and by the materials placed in his classroom. Jason's neighborhood friends next door told him he was going to school because he had to learn to read. "But," Jason wondered, "I can already read. I know how to use books, letters, phones, radios, and television."

As we write this second edition, Jason has turned 16. He is a handsome, athletic, academically successful high school student. He is a skilled user of texts. He has been relatively successful at mastering the symbols and meanings captured by linguistic, printed, and numeric symbol systems. When he stops long enough to talk with adults about his school experiences, he often expresses regret that he has not had as many opportunities as he thinks he might have liked studying film, a range of computer applications, or about art and music. He still feels a bit frustrated that he had to choose between band and football and between art, film, and computer "electives" and "real" college prep classes.

In a simple and rather sad way, Jason's friends were right. School success does depend on learning to read, but his teachers, his parents, and the district curriculum goals would not have defined the goal quite so narrowly. They would, more likely, have defined educational goals for Jason more broadly as the need to become literate. Few would question that one of the central goals of schooling is literacy development. America today is much concerned with literacy. Public dialogue is laced with discussions of functional literacy, workplace literacy, cultural literacy, the Great Books curriculum, and the high costs associated with illiteracy. The literacy debate is equally full of arguments about phonics versus whole-word approaches, the potentials of a whole-language approach or a literature-based approach for literacy instruction, the reading/writing connection, the role of skills in literacy development, and the need to promote comprehension and critical reading. In addition, we often hear about the need to teach cultural literacy, computer literacy, scientific literacy, and numeracy.

What is literacy? Gray and Reese (1957) proposed the following omnibus definition: "A person is functionally literate when he has acquired the knowledge and skills in reading and writing which enable him to engage effectively in all those activities in which literacy is normally assumed in his cultural group." To be a literate person, says the dictionary, is to be a "man of letters." These definitions are representative of most definitions of literacy. They carry both a denotative and a connotative meaning. Both meanings shape how literacy instruction is designed in today's classrooms.

Literacy at the Denotative Level

At the denotative (literal) level, literacy is the ability to use letters—to have and be able to use the skills necessary to read and write print. At this level, literacy instruction centers on mastering word-attack skills (the ability to identify unknown words), vocabulary development (associating strings of spoken and printed symbols with meaning using skills such as phonetic analysis or visual cueing), and comprehension (the ability to take both literal and inferential meaning from printed symbols as well as to judge the validity and consequences of that meaning).

Traditional learning experiences designed to help students learn how to read and write are familiar to most of us. Workbooks, basal reading series, skill packets, and reading groups are time-honored practices. Lessons designed to teach capitalization, sentence and paragraph structure, and spelling frame writing instruction. More recently, the literature-based approach (Harris, 1996; McGee & Tompkins, 1995) and the whole-language approach (Goodman, 1984) have challenged the more traditional design of literacy instruction. Opposing the segmented, skill-oriented learning activities, these approaches suggest avoiding a parts-to-whole approach in favor of challenging learners to approach intact, meaningful texts. Acquisition of skills, from this more holistically oriented approach, should be embedded in engagement with text and attended to as the learner's needs arise. Learning to write is framed by frequent writing experiences such as stories, journals, and book publication. Again, particular skills are addressed as they arise in the context of the learner's attempt to communicate effectively in writing.

Literacy at the Connotative Level

Literacy is, however, more than a cluster of skills taught either separately or embedded in learning to read larger units. Literacy is more than simply learning how to read and write. At the connotative (inferential) level, a literate person—a "man of letters"—not only knows how to use letters but how to share in the fruits of a literate culture. Literate people read and write to learn. They use their abilities to read and write to explore ideas, gather information, and reflect on and profit from the debates, histories, wisdom, and theories collected in printed material. In a report prepared for the Ford Foundation, Hunter and Harmon (1979) captured the spirit of literacy as:

> The possession of skills perceived as necessary by particular persons and groups to fulfill their own self-determined objectives as family and community members, citizens, consumers, job-holders, and members of social, religious, or other associations of their choosing. This includes the ability to read and write adequately to satisfy the requirements they set for themselves as being important for their own lives; the ability to deal positively with demands made on them by society; and the ability to solve the problems they face in their daily lives. (pp. 7–8)

Learning opportunities designed to help students read and write to learn becomes increasingly important during the late elementary grades and is a major preoccupation of instruction during the middle school and high school years. Students read to explore ideas in the sciences, the social sciences, and literature. They read to learn about history, geography, biology, physics, and chemistry, and they explore the human drama as they read Judy Blume and Shakespeare. As their abilities become more sophisticated, students are encouraged to distinguish fact from fiction, fact from opinion, and to judge and criticize ideas embedded in print. Students

write to communicate messages that express their reflections a
learn to write essays to convince, reports to support a researc
stories and poems to reflect their ideas and feelings about expe
literacy instruction encourages students to participate in the dy͏͏͏͏ ͏͏ ͏͏͏͏ ͏͏͏͏ ͏͏͏
and-take inherent in using writing to develop and share ideas in academic as well
as practical situations.

An Expanded Definition of Literacy

Whether at the denotative or the connotative level, designing opportunities for literacy learning is squarely entrenched in the technology of print. The primacy of print in education is nearly indisputable, but not unchallenged. The modern electronic technologies—the telephone, the television, the computer—have become prominent technologies outside of school. If Jason's classroom is not to shrink into obsolescence, the electronic technologies must become part of the experiences designed for students to promote literacy learning. It is important that educators use the lessons of literacy taken from years of helping learners become literate in print environments and apply them to helping learners become literate in multiple symbolic environments.

A literate person, then, must be understood as more than a "man of letters," and literacy must be defined as more than the ability to use letters and understand the meanings captured by letters. We find Eisner's (1994) definition of literacy to be the most useful. He defines *literacy* as "the power to encode and decode meaning through any of the forms that humans use to represent what they have come to know" (p. xii). Forms for representing meaning include a range of notational systems including spoken language systems, alphabetic systems, musical notation systems, visual or graphic systems, and mathematical systems. Encoding is the process of moving from insight, understanding, or experience to representation using one or a combination of these systems. Decoding is the process of changing symbolic representations into insight, understanding, or experience. Encoding and decoding in print environments are referred to as writing and reading. In spoken environments, we talk of speaking and listening. In television and film environments, we talk of viewing and filming. Thus, literacy is the ability to capture the things we think and feel in symbolic form and to profit from and take meaning from the symbolic products others create—to send and receive messages using all of the communication forms valued and available in our culture.

DESIGNING OPPORTUNITIES TO LEARN LITERACY

Each of us is constantly bombarded by printed information in books, newspapers, billboards, and mail. Design for literacy that focuses on these symbolic environments enables students to use this information. Additionally, students are bombarded by information that has been processed by television, film, radio, and a variety of computer programs. Adults and children alike live in a world where symbols represent little more than other symbols (e.g., credit cards stand for money and money stands for purchasing power). The art of being literate—that is, to be able to derive knowledge from and participate fully in this symbolic environment—requires capabilities and activities beyond those that frame a predominantly print-oriented environment.

Must educators abandon all their existing understandings in order to embrace the electronic technologies within the design of literacy instruction? Certainly not. Just because we invented print does not mean we stopped talking. Just because we have invented an array of electronic information environments does not mean we will stop reading. Instead, literacy is

> . . . a concept that assumes different definitions in different places, at different times, as conditions warrant. Consequently, different contexts and groups evolve definitions of literacy that have a diversity of content and strive to inculcate those definitions among their members. (Harmon, 1987, p. 96)

Much of what educators have learned in the long years of designing literacy instruction suggests a framework for conceptualizing literacy in the "supersymbolic" age of the electronic technologies. This framework centers on an understanding of how a variety of technologies including books use symbols to represent ideas, what cognitive strategies are necessary to interpret the messages embedded in these diverse symbolic forms, and how patterns of discourse forms organize information.

Literacy as Symbolic Competence

Humans have developed and use a variety of symbol systems including:

- graphics in charts and graphs and oscillating computer images that clutter our lives,
- visual representation in the form of television, advertising, training videos, and films,
- mathematical symbols embedded in computer modeling, spreadsheets, databases, and tables and charts,
- musical symbols that shape the mood and background atmosphere whether alone or in combination with the visual symbols, such as television, film, and radio, and
- printed and spoken language symbol systems which, far from disappearing, are being integrated into a larger array of symbolic environments.

Each of these symbol systems functions as a means for both the conceptualization of ideas about aspects of reality and as a means for conveying what one knows to others. Each symbol system has unique capabilities and sets parameters upon what can be conceived and what can be expressed. Together, all of the symbol systems form the basis for grasping the content and structure of physical and theoretical systems and lead to the ability to construct meaning. Getting meaning from or acquiring knowledge about the complex and rich information environment of the twenty-first century rests on the ability to fully use all of these symbolic forms. The ability to use these symbol systems marshals human cognitive potential and paves "the royal route from raw intelligence to finished cultures" (Gardner, 1983, p. 300).

Human thought is marshaled by cultural symbol systems. Conversely, it may be that symbol systems evolve when there exists a human cognitive capacity ready to be harnessed. Although it may be possible for some aspects of intelligence to proceed independent of a symbol system, "a primary characteristic of human intelligence may be its natural gravitation toward embodiment in a symbol system" (Gardner, 1983, p. 66). Meaning and knowledge, then, depend on the symbolic representation of experience, either the kind of experience that comes from direct contact with qualities of the environment or from experience born of imagination and conceptualization. And, "the choice of a form of representation is a choice in the way the world will be conceived, as well as a choice in the way it will be publicly represented" (Eisner, 1994a).

Beginning in the early grades, teachers design instruction that permits students to explore how printed letters represent sounds and the rules that govern how those letters might be combined to form larger sound units or words. In the conventional literature on literacy, this is called *phonics* or *decoding* and has long been considered the cornerstone of literacy development. Progress at first is rather slow, but as the logic of the system is revealed, students begin to grasp the rules that organize printed symbols and soon generalize those rules to an increasingly larger array of words. Knowledge, both intuitive and explicit, about how the printed symbol system works is a necessary foundation for literacy development. Increasingly, as the electronic technologies play a larger role in shaping the contemporary knowledge environment, printed symbols are joined by other systems of symbolic representation. Any comprehensive design for teaching literacy must include designing opportunities for students to learn about all the symbol systems humans use to represent what they have come to know.

> In her third-grade classroom, Mrs. Festa designs the part of her day that she devotes explicitly to literacy instruction around a theme and creates a series of learning centers that engage students in developing their literacy abilities while exploring the selected theme. This week she has picked the theme of time, and focused her literacy instruction on how a variety of symbol systems convey time. One center focuses on the numeric symbol system and challenges students to "read" clocks and record how long it takes them to complete simple tasks like coloring a picture or hopping on one foot 30 times. Another center asks students to participate with her in the reading of a story selected from their basal text. She uses this text to challenge students to identify how a variety of words and phrases have been scattered throughout the story to alert the reader that time has passed.
>
> A third center focuses on how color and shadow are used in photographs to convey time. In small groups, students work to determine how different times of the year are expressed by color. Using another collection of pictures, students are asked to sequence the pictures by interpreting the way in which shadow is used to

reflect time. In a last center, students experiment with musical symbols organized in 4/4 time and 3/4 time, beating out tunes on rubberized drum pads.

As they progress through these centers, students are learning to "read" clocks and numbers, to "read" pictures, to "read" music, and to "read" print. During the students' studies of science, they will use their emerging symbolic competencies to "clock" chemical reactions and changes in the states of matter; during social studies, they will use these symbolic competencies to become historians, fixing time periods associated with pictures taken around their community.

✿ ✿ ✿ ✿ ✿

In Mr. Holcomb's eleventh-grade English class, students are learning to identify themes embedded in the short story form. Mr. Holcomb has selected a television version of Ray Bradbury's story, *I Sing the Body Electric*, titled *The Electronic Grandmother*. He and his students have watched the half-hour video twice as they attempt to catch the story's theme. As Mr. Holcomb had hoped, students have decided that the story actually has two themes: one that explores the relationships between machines and humans and a second that explores how we learn to trust even after we have been disappointed. The class discusses how these themes are never explicitly stated by the video's director and cast.

"How then could you identify these themes?" queries Mr. Holcomb. "Why," respond students, "the director uses a series of symbolic images to subtly alert you to these meanings." Mr. Holcomb divides the class into groups of five, provides each group with a VCR and a copy of the video, and challenges them to assess the ways in which the video's director used visual symbols to convey the tensions that portray the story's themes.

"The first theme," states one student after a long debate with peers, "is embedded in a series of contrasting images. First, the grandmother hugs the children; then she pours orange juice out of a spigot in her finger. Next, she is seen cooking meals; then she is seen hanging laundry from a kite string coming from her finger. The first images—hugs and cooking meals—make you think of a nurturing human. But these nurturing images are immediately countered by images of her pouring juice from her finger and hanging laundry from a kite string. You are reminded of her machine qualities. At another point in the video, the electric grandmother is tucking children into bed and singing them lullabies. In the next scene, she is plugging herself into a wall socket and shutting down for the evening. The director uses a series of symbolic images, none of which, if left standing alone, convey the theme. But organizing the images to shift back and forth between human and machine, the symbols combine to draw attention to the theme."

When students have completed their analysis and shared their new knowledge of how visual symbols encode meanings, Mr. Holcomb provides students with a printed version of the story. He challenges them to compare the ways in which printed symbols and visual symbols convey theme.

These examples demonstrate how both Mrs. Festa and Mr. Holcomb have designed instruction in which students learn how symbol systems express meaning. Mrs. Festa has made learning about a variety of symbol systems part of her explicit literacy curriculum by designing centers that engage students with the ways in which four different symbol systems encode meaning about time. She then implicitly reinforces her students' emerging knowledge by creating opportunities for students to experiment with this knowledge within the design of her content instruction.

Mr. Holcomb, on the other hand, has focused the design of opportunities for his students to learn not on the individual elements of symbolization but on the dynamic interactions between meaning and symbolization. He focuses his students' attention on the symbol system users' intentions. What were the video's authors attempting to communicate? How did they use the representational systems available to them to capture their message with artistry and subtlety? What must a "reader" look for in the structure of symbolic information that might enhance their understanding of the author's or authors' message? In their own way, both Mrs. Festa and Mr. Holcomb have designed literacy instruction that promotes student mastery of symbolic forms.

Literacy as Cognitive Strategies

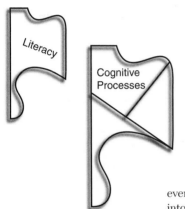

Learning to comprehend the message embedded in symbolic information is the second cornerstone of literacy instruction. Comprehension derives from the complex transactions between information that is received and higher cognitive strategies that mediate downward to evaluate information. The following example, observed by one of the authors, may help to illustrate the transaction process.

Franklin was 19 months old when he went to visit his Aunt Becky for the Thanksgiving holiday. Knowing that toddlers like to get into kitchen cupboards, Franklin's aunt had prepared a drawer especially for him. This drawer was filled with measuring cups, small toys, and a few books. After Thanksgiving dinner, Aunt Becky placed the long plastic baster she had used for the turkey in Franklin's drawer with the other things. Later that evening when Franklin went to his drawer, he discovered the baster. He reached into the drawer, withdrew the baster, and examined it intently (action). He had never seen such a strange implement, and after looking it over, he could attach no meaning to it. So Franklin put it back, closed the drawer tightly, and went to pester the dog (reaction).

The next morning Franklin went to the kitchen to help with breakfast. He opened his drawer only to be confronted with the baster once again. Still perplexed, he withdrew it and held it up to his aunt. Aunt Becky took the baster, told Franklin it was called a "baster," and then squeezed the bulb at the end blowing small spurts of air at Franklin's face (interaction). However, Franklin still did not know what the baster was; so, he examined it once more. Then, with a burst of comprehension, he put the baster to his nose—first one side and then the other—and then clapped his hands in excitement (transaction). He had a meaning for that strange implement and understood its purpose. It was merely a gigantic aspirator like the one his mother used when he had a cold. Franklin had comprehended.

As each of us develops past the toddler stage, transaction remains at the core of our ability to comprehend. Unlike Franklin, we move beyond information gathered from our direct experiences of concrete objects to information represented by symbols. Instead of learning by manipulating our environment, we learn by manipulating symbols. Information is presented in symbolic form and, through the transaction process, we transform it using cognitive strategies we have learned.

Cognitive strategies commonly associated with literacy in a print environment include identifying the main idea, locating supporting detail, detecting sequence, following printed direction, identifying cause-and-effect relations, and remembering what one has read. In addition, comprehending print requires linear, sequential, propositional, analytical, objective, hierarchical, and rational strategies—the information-rearranging strategies identified in Chapter 5. When transforming print symbols into meaning, we must analyze information, break it down into pieces, identify constituent parts, and then arrange them in logical order. Thus, the act of becoming literate in a print world requires not only learning how printed symbols work but also learning how to use these cognitive strategies.

The electronic technologies (film, television, photography, and computer imaging), which depend on visual/graphical systems of symbolization, structure information about our experience of the world in a manner quite different from print—requiring students to develop a different set of cognitive strategies. Understanding in a visual/graphical environment bypasses to a large extent language-and-print dominated strategies and substitutes a different set. Visual/graphical information is not structured in a hierarchical manner but in a horizontal manner. Images do not lead the observer's thinking from A to B to C, with an objective conclusion as in print. Thinking is not directed to objective abstractions but to subjective feelings. Visual/graphical information presents us with a vision of how to think that is nondiscursive, presentational, impressionistic, subjective, emotive, and nonrational (Postman, 1982, 1986). Recognition of the whole is more important than identifying and chaining together the parts. Full access to and command of these strategies are as subject to learning as those associated with print.

Computer technologies also restructure the cognitive strategies we use to encode and decode experience. Working within a computer environment demands thinking even more abstract than print with concepts even more transitory and fleeting than images. A computer environment does not create certainties that can be extracted by following cause-and-effect, right/wrong, linear, or logical sequences. Instead, a computer environment depends on a complex system of interacting variables ruled by the grammar of mathematics. Elements of experience are coded using mathematical relationships, and output must be organized and interpreted by searching for connections and patterns. Knowledge gleaned within a computer environment is tentative, flexible, relational, probabilistic, and interactive. Learning within the environments created by computers allows students to explore options and possible outcomes. Only when computers are used for drill and practice do they suggest right and wrong answers. Students cannot depend on strategies of analysis they have learned to comprehend books but must use strategies for synthesis if they are to comprehend the message embedded within the structure of computer programs (Norton, 1985).

On Monday morning of the third week of summer school, Ms. Angell arrived at school to find Johnny Doranes and his father waiting for her. As she greeted Johnny, Mr. Doranes stepped forward saying, in a not-so-friendly voice, "I took three days off this week to take Johnny fishing. However, he refuses to go with me because he does not want to miss your class. I just can't see how all this playing with computers can be that important. I figured I had better come to school and find out what is happening." As Ms. Angell opened the door and invited Mr. Doranes in she reflected, "Something is certainly going on here, and it is truly exciting not only for the children but for me as well."

That summer, Ms. Angell and three other teachers were helping with a research project designed to evaluate the use of problem-solving software to support the reading curriculum. Johnny was one of the 98 students enrolled in the experimental program—49 students were in the experimental group and 49 students were in the control group. Like all the students, Johnny came to school that summer for one hour of reading instruction as part of his district's Chapter 1 summer school program. All the students spent half of their time completing exercises presented by an Integrated Learning System designed to teach reading skills like phonics and main ideas. This system was similar to the one that was described in Chapter 2.

Johnny considered that part of the class boring. Those, like Johnny, who were in the experimental group were then also able to select from nine different computer programs created to teach problem-solving skills and to play them during the second half hour of their summer class. That was Johnny's favorite part of summer school. Those in the control group participated in traditional reading instruction for the remaining half-hour. They listened to the teacher read stories out loud, completed worksheets, and participated in silent sustained reading and writing.

The researchers who had designed this summer project were familiar with Eiser's (1986) and Miller's (1985) work. Eiser had stated that if one looked beyond the "problem-solving" label, these programs teach a surprisingly diverse assortment of thinking skills or cognitive strategies. She had suggested that these programs engage students with logic, memory and recall, noting patterns, trial-and-error experimentation, and breaking a task into parts as well as other thinking skills. Miller had established in an earlier study that if students were permitted to play with these software programs their reading comprehension and their problem-solving abilities improved significantly more than students who were taught reading using a skills approach. This seemed an incredible finding to the researchers. How was it possible that computer programs unrelated to reading instruction, or at least seemingly unrelated, could lead to improvements in reading comprehension?

At the end of summer school, Johnny and the other students were posttested and their final scores statistically analyzed. Like the students in Miller's study, the students who had been able to play with the problem-solving software scored significantly higher in both problem-solving ability and reading comprehension (Norton & Resta, 1986). Two similar studies—one with middle school learning disabled students (Shinn, 1986) and one with elementary students with communication disorders (Norton & Heiman, 1988)—were later conducted. In both studies, those using the problem-solving software scored significantly higher in reading comprehension.

These studies reinforce the notion that the distinction between comprehending as a process and comprehension as a product is important and useful (Goodman, 1984). If opportunities designed for literacy learning are aimed at comprehension as a product and identified as a series of skills or as correct answers to reading comprehension questions, it is difficult to understand how problem-solving software can result in literacy gains. However, if opportunities for literacy learning are directed toward facilitating the development of cognitive strategies related to interpreting symbolic information, it is possible to understand how problem-solving software might lead to improved literacy and why Johnny did not want to miss school.

Ms. Forsyth's middle school students are beginning to develop habits of thinking that Piaget might characterize as formal operations. Yet, Ms. Forsyth is familiar with the literature that suggests that success in developing these cognitive strategies is far from guaranteed. But how can a literature teacher promote the development of formal, logical operations?

As the germs of an idea formulate in her mind, Ms. Forsyth locates a series of robot stories. She selects several stories from Asimov's *I, Robot* short-story collection. She selects two episodes from *Star Trek: The Next Generation* that feature Mr. Data as the central character. Using these short stories, Ms. Forsyth creates a science fiction, short-story unit. As they "read" these stories, Ms. Forsyth helps students with character analysis, with describing settings, and with identifying plots. As the students progress through the unit, Ms. Forsyth notices a growing interest in logical thought. Sometimes students parody overemphasis on logic; other times students seem stumped by their inability to understand a logical conclusion on which the story ending depends. When this happens, Ms. Forsyth helps students figure out the logic, often drawing diagrams on the board.

Near the end of the unit, Ms. Forsyth asks students to reflect in their journals on exactly what they think logic is and what the rules governing logic might be. When they share their journal entries, students agree that they really want to learn more about the rules of logic. Ms. Forsyth suggests that they might be able to learn some of the rules of logic using a program called Yoiks! published by TercWorks (Figure 6.1). Students seem interested so she schedules a week's worth of class time in the school's computer lab. Students spend three days trying to complete as many of the 30 levels as possible. As they work in groups of two or three, Ms. Forsyth talks with students about what strategies are working and which are not. She helps them formalize their trial-and-error efforts as "and," "or," "not," and "nor" statements. Each day before students move on to their next class, Ms. Forsyth discusses one of the rules of logic with students.

During the last two days of their time in the school lab, Ms. Forsyth challenges students' ability to construct logical statements to search the Internet for information. Using prepared requests for information, Ms. Forsyth challenges students to use their emerging knowledge of these logic rules to develop sophisticated search strategies to locate information using search engines like Yahoo (http://www.yahoo.com) and Google (http://www.google.com).

When their week in the computer lab is over and students return to their classroom, Ms. Forsyth tells the class about Lewis Carroll, the author of *Alice in Wonderland*. She tells students how Mr. Carroll wrote the story to teach two young friends the rules of logic. She challenges the class to read each chapter in the book and determine which principle of logic Mr. Carroll is trying to teach the reader. As students near the end of their reading, Ms. Forsyth notices that students are becoming quite proficient at identifying logical relationships and notes that they often identify the rules in a variety of other contexts.

Teachers know that students do not succeed at literacy events until they develop the cognitive strategies necessary for interpreting symbolic information. Young children will not remember more than two or three steps in written in-

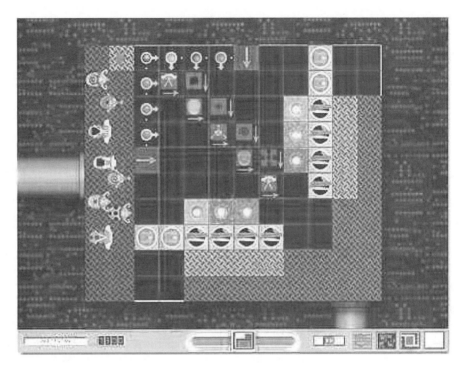

FIGURE **6.1**

TERC WORKS' YOIKS! WHICH BUG SHOULD ENTER THE GRID FIRST? WHICH ONE THE SECOND?
Source: Reprinted with permission of TERC.

structions until their memory strategies mature. Older students will not grasp sequences of events or relationships of time captured by symbolic information until they have also developed appropriate cognitive strategies. Students in science classes will not grasp the life cycle of plants or the changing of the seasons until they have learned the cognitive strategies prerequisite to recognizing patterns. The descriptions of the range of tools available to educators presented in Chapter 3 included references to the kinds of cognitive strategies that are most closely associated with each category of tool.

Literacy both promotes and requires a range of cognitive strategies in order to make sense of meanings inherent in symbolic information. Rather than waiting for these strategies to evolve through experience with interpreting information, literacy instruction designed to guide students in the development of these strategies explicitly brings them within the purview of students' command. Teachers like Ms. Forsyth thoughtfully design literacy instruction that helps students develop intentional command of these strategies. Their students learn to determine which strategies are appropriate in which information contexts. These teachers are enhancing student literacy.

Literacy and Discourse Forms

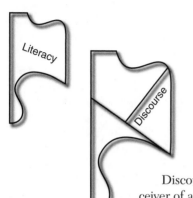

In Chapter 4, we explored the concept of discourse as a primary mode of thought. Foucault (1976) further refines the concept of discourse when he describes discourse as a "system of possibilities" ordered by rules. Using these rules to structure communication permits certain statements to be made, imposes order upon these statements, allows statements to be identified as either true or false, and structures the ways in which maps, models, and classificatory systems are constructed. The universe of discourse that results from the application of these rules creates a unity wherein somebody has constructed a message intended for somebody about something. This unity becomes a map from which actions and thoughts emerge.

Discourse specifies a set of relations between the sender of a message, the receiver of a message, and the topic (Moffett, 1968). Senders must choose the form of discourse most suitable for the message they wish to convey. They must decide whether or not they will interpret experience by focusing on what is happening (the drama), what happened (the narrative), what happens (the exposition), or what may happen (logical argumentation). Understanding the message depends on the receiver's ability to recognize and reapply the patterns that govern the discourse.

Living within a particular context, individuals come in contact with a variety of agreed-upon discourse forms. Being able to recognize and understand how these discourse forms organize information empowers individuals to contribute to their cultural context. Patrick Henry's call to battle delivered as oration is rousing, pushing the listener to interpret Colonial experience through the lens of passion. The same call in printed form seems unnecessarily redundant and devoid of rational analysis. An historian's textbook chapter on Civil War battles with an analysis of lives lost and battle strategies gone awry presents a different interpretation of experiences than Kenneth Burns's Civil War documentary with successive images of soldiers, battlefields, and generals overlaying the reading of a soldier's letter to his wife.

As students progress through the grades, mastering symbol systems and a variety of cognitive strategies, they also need to learn the larger patterns used within their cultural context to structure messages. In the later grades, students learn the structure of an essay; they learn the elements necessary to formulate a story; they learn how information is structured in textbooks, learning to attend to subheadings, glossaries, indexes, and tables of contents. Just as printed environments reflect unique organizational patterns or discourse forms, the electronic technologies have their own unique information patterns. To be literate, to profit from these electronic environments, one must understand their organization and learn how to navigate each form, understanding where information can be found, how information is connected, and the unique potentials inherent in a diversity of discourse forms.

Take, for instance, the nightly news programs. Ask yourself, what is the most important news story covered? How do you determine which story is the important one? Most answer, "the first or opening story." The first program's placement at the program's opening signifies to the viewer that it is the central, or most important, news item. Here is the problem. The NBC nightly news program and the ABC nightly news program often open with different stories. If you attend to this discrepancy closely, you might finally determine that if two stories of import need to be reported, NBC will open with the international story and ABC will open with the national story. NBC's basic news bias favors international relations as more important for understanding your world; ABC's basic news bias favors national events as more important for understanding your world.

Researchers report that knowing where information is placed within the structure of a discourse form is not the literate individual's only challenge. Those seeking information must also learn which form is most likely to provide the information they seek (Neuman, Just, & Crigler, 1992). For instance, those who want an overview and introduction to the day's current events will find television a useful discourse form. On the other hand, those who want an in-depth analysis of a particular event might find one of the weekly news magazines (e.g., *Time* or *Newsweek*) or the Sunday morning news programs (e.g., *Meet the Press, Face the Nation,* and *This Week*) to be most helpful. Those who seek a variety of interpretations of a news event might consult the editorial page of their newspaper or a search of the Internet might be useful.

Television is not a passive, benign medium any more than books are. Television programming is a collection of diverse organizational patterns—the news documentary, the situation comedy, the talk show, the prime-time drama, and the soap opera. When you understand television as discourse, you understand that literacy education must be designed to include the workings of these forms just as you attend to the organizational patterns of the textbook, the manual, and the novel. Educators and scholars who are interested in teaching students about the ways in which television and film shape our understanding and our culture as well as helping students develop their abilities to interpret the media refer to the process as "media literacy."

Particular categories of computer programs also create discourse forms. Word processors, for instance, structure the writing environment in a similar way. Database programs structure information in predictable patterns and require the mastery of a particular set of search strategies to access information. Strategies for searching for information in a database are different from strategies for locating information in a library, but they are both learned through well-designed instruction. Spreadsheets, simulations, and hypermedia programs also share unique sets of organizational patterns just as all textbooks and all novels share organizational characteristics. Whether students are learning from video and television forms of discourse, printed forms of discourse, or computer forms of discourse, capitalizing on the potentials of the information in that environment depends on the ability to understand how the discourse form structures the message.

In today's information age where information pervades contemporary culture and where the new tools of word processors, desktop publishers, and Web-based editors make it easier to construct, publish, and disseminate written messages, there is the chance that we are creating an "anything goes" information environment. The act of publishing has, in many instances, become more important than the merit of the publication. To avoid this "publish regardless of quality" mentality, educators need to help students study examples of excellence so that they learn to formulate messages of quality. Studying the masters helps students become masters. Students need opportunities to read and discuss models before and as they write themselves. And when they read selected models, they need to discuss not only the ideas embedded in those examples but also the ways in which the ideas have been structured and communicated. Students need to be encouraged to examine not only what other writers are saying but how those writers are saying it. They need to ask how the organizational pattern the author used affected the message, what the elements of the pattern are, and why a particular piece is a good or bad example of the discourse.

These patterns are not learned as abstractions alone or even primarily. Knowing that an essay should state a thesis, present three arguments or evidences, and conclude with a restatement of thesis or position is not the same as studying the expert examples of Norman Cousins or Ralph Waldo Emerson. Students also need opportunities to use the patterns to structure their own messages. Good literacy designs give students ample opportunities and support to use these discourse forms as patterns for communicating their own ideas and understandings.

Mrs. Foster's sixth graders have been studying the structure of well-formulated stories. For several weeks, Mrs. Foster helped students focus on how authors develop characters as they examined short stories in their basal readers, watched half-hour video stories, and listened to old radio broadcasts. For another week, students examined settings in these stories, exploring not only how settings are presented but how settings influence characters. Similar activities encouraged students to analyze plot, theme, problem, climax, and resolution in stories. Mrs. Foster feels confident that students are becoming quite sophisticated at recognizing story elements.

It is time, Mrs. Foster thinks, to challenge students to investigate the ways in which story elements influence stories in different ways when they are told with different discourse forms. She selects Rosemary Sutcliff's (1994) version of the King Arthur tale *The Sword and the Circle* available as a paperback set through her school library. She adds to the paperback set an Arts and Entertainment Biography episode called *King Arthur: His Life and Legend* as well as multiple copies of the computer program Arthur: The Quest for Excalibur. This interactive fiction program presents the "reader" with situations and asks the "writer" to construct appropriate actions (See Figure 6.2). For example, students are presented with a setting in which they find themselves in an ancient churchyard with a stone wall, an ironwork gate, and gravestones. A prompt and flashing cursor awaits students' input. Students might attempt to manipulate the setting by opening the gate and entering the churchyard. Soon, the program tells students that voices are heard in the distance and that strangers are approaching. Should students find a place to hide or should they await the strangers and ask them questions? Navigating the story depends on the decisions students make.

Mrs. Foster introduces the three versions of King Arthur to her class. She divides them into groups of four and provides them with a contract directing them to "read" each of these versions during the next two weeks and to work collaboratively to analyze each story for its elements as well as for how each element is conveyed. She observes groups working on their analysis. One group is comparing the presentation of characters in each version. "Look," says Martha. "In the first chapter of the book, each character is introduced and described. We have to create an

```
Churchyard                                    St Anne's Day, Compline
>look
You are standing in the bright moonlight of a mid-winter's night in a
deserted English churchyard. At the foot of the church steps is a large
stone with a jewelled sword protruding from it. The church entrance lies
to the east, and just west of you is a large gravestone. A stone wall
encircles the churchyard, but there is an ironwork gate in the wall to
your south.

>go south
The gate isn't open.

>open gate█
```

FIGURE **6.2**

INFOCOM'S ARTHUR: THE QUEST FOR EXCALIBUR

Source: Courtesy of Activision Publishing, Inc. Used by Permission. © 2002 Activision, Inc. and its affiliates. Activision and ARTHUR: THE QUEST FOR EXCALIBUR are registered trademarks of Activision, Inc. and its affiliates. All rights reserved.

image of each character from the descriptive words. In the movie, we learn about the characters by watching their facial expressions and by paying attention to their body language. But in the software program, the author does not give us much of a description of the characters. We have to learn about each one along the way. What we discover about a character depends on what we ask them. We have to look for information about the characters in different ways in each story. It's also interesting that some characters in the book are missing from the video, and other characters have been added to the movie. I wonder why?"

As Mrs. Foster moves on, she overhears another group comparing the presentation of setting in each story. "In the book," reflects one student, "the description of the setting goes on and on, and we have to fill in a lot of information ourselves. On the video, everything is there, but it moves so fast you do not really notice it. Sometimes it helps to rewind the video and look more closely. And in the book and the video, the author lets us know what we need to know about the setting. The software program is different. You can't tell what is important and what isn't. If you don't think about each setting element or test its function, you might miss an important clue."

Students are making real progress, observes Mrs. Foster. They will soon be ready to attempt to write their own story. Beginning next week, Mrs. Foster's class is going to define all the story elements for a space adventure together. They will decide on characters, do some research to describe the setting on their selected planet, create a problem, and suggest several solutions. Then, in groups of four or five, students will choose a discourse form to use to develop their story. Some will create a radio broadcast; others will word-process stories, film videos, or design interactive stories using a hypermedia program. It will be interesting to see how they use their knowledge of the discourse forms they studied to shape the ways in which they tell their space adventure.

Similar literacy instruction is being designed throughout Mrs. Foster's school district. In the eighth-grade science class at the nearby junior high school, Mr. Mulder's students are studying environmental issues. His students have studied the chapter on environmental issues in their text for background understanding. Now, they are watching PBS documentaries on a variety of environmental issues. They are reading selected articles from *Scientific American* and a variety of Internet sites. They spent one week playing Tom Snyder's computer classroom simulation The Environment. The Environment is a simulation in which teams of four or five students attempt to make a series of decisions that lead to the resolution of a pollution problem in the town of Malaco (Figure 6.3). Mr. Mulder's primary goal is for students to learn about a number of environmental concerns. Yet, throughout, he

FIGURE **6.3**

DECISIONS, DECISIONS® 5.0: THE ENVIRONMENT.
Source: Reprinted with permission of Tom Snyder Productions.

has drawn students' attention to the ways in which each discourse form structured information about environmental issues. Next, Mr. Mulder will assign a variety of local environmental dilemmas to be researched by small groups of students. They will be assigned the job of creating a literacy set—a news documentary, a journal article, and a hypermedia database—using their research.

In Mrs. Sherman's senior honors English class, students are studying the mystery. They are comparing taped versions of original *Perry Mason* episodes, copies of Shakespeare's *Hamlet*, and an interactive fiction mystery by Ubi Soft titled *Myst III: Exile* (Figure 6.4). The interactive fiction program is a complex mystery that relies heavily on a visual world. Students must carefully analyze the visual environment, manipulate objects, and confront characters. It is much like Arthur: The Quest for Excalibur only instead of manipulating print students manipulate images. In each discourse form, they encounter clues and witnesses and confront the need to resolve a mystery. Their final project will be to write individual essays, taking a position on which form is most effective for conveying aspects inherent in a mystery. Mrs. Sherman knows, and her students remind her, that there is no "best" medium. Nevertheless, Mrs. Sherman believes it will be an interesting challenge for students to take and defend a position and to use the essay as a discourse form to convince others of a position, whether or not they "believe" that position.

FIGURE 6.4

MYST III: EXILE
Source: Reprinted with permission of Ubi Soft Entertainment.

Communicating with Symbols

The final design consideration for effective literacy instruction needs no further examples for it is a design consideration embedded in the examples already presented. As Eisner (1994a) has written, literacy pivots on an individual's ability to encode and decode content embodied in different forms of representation. By decoding, he is referring to the process of translating symbolized information into experience and thought. By encoding, he is referring to the process of translating experience and thought into symbolized form. When you observe a painting, you are decoding the symbolized version of the painting's content into a set of impressions of its content. When you draw, you are transferring your own experiences and impressions of something into a symbolized rendition. When you read about an international crisis or watch a news report about that crisis, you are decoding, turning symbols into insight. When you write an essay about that event, you are turning your own insights and interpretations into symbolized form.

Encoding and decoding are different aspects of the same process. Instruction designed to promote literacy incorporates both aspects in a balanced dynamic of experiencing and symbolizing, symbolizing and experiencing. Teachers who promote literacy development design instruction that presents students with representative models of how others have combined symbols and cognitive strategies into culturally recognized and valued organizational patterns to communicate. Teachers who promote literacy development recognize the importance of providing students equal opportunities to emulate this process, moving from their own experiences and interpretations to symbolized representations of their thoughts. Students learn about thoughts and feelings through others' communications. Students learn to communicate their own thoughts and feelings by emulating how others communicate.

Mr. Mulder's students examined how others have communicated their understanding about a number of environmental issues; they created literacy sets to communicate the sense they made of environmental issues in their own community. Mrs. Sherman's students learned how others have told mysteries; they became media critics when they learned to use essays to critique mysteries and convince others of their opinions. Mrs. Foster's students examined how others formulated and shared adventure stories; they learned to share adventure stories they imagined with others in a variety of formats. These teachers recognize the ways in which learning to decode and learning to encode complement and extend each other.

> Lita awoke early as the sun filtered through the window coverings. She dressed quickly and stepped outside to greet the morning. Her mother was already at work setting the fire to heat the stones for making piki bread. It had snowed lightly, and the snow sparkled as the early morning sun danced across its surface. Lita spoke briefly with her mother and returned to finish getting ready for school. She was anxious to catch the bus. Today, the long-awaited videotapes should be arriving.
>
> Nearly two months had passed since Lita and her classmates began their joint project with Jamal in Atlanta, Georgia, and Mike in Madison, Wisconsin. It all began in her American history class when Mr. Benally assigned students a project related to the unit on World War II. He talked with the class about the resources

available to them to complete the research for their projects. He had made the long drive into the neighboring town to check out reference material from the library to offer as support to the school's existing resources. He also reminded students that they could use the school's Internet resources to tap the wide array of databases available. Mr. Benally had been helping students develop search strategies for online research.

Mr. Benally met with students to discuss what topic they might choose for their project and what discourse form they might use for their final project. Students could select to write research reports. Word processors were available. They could choose to create newspapers. Desktop publishing programs and image scanning could be used to create professional-looking products. For those with programming skills, Mr. Benally suggested the design of a simulation to teach others about an aspect of World War II. Others, he suggested, might want to use video cameras to produce documentaries.

When it was Lita's turn to meet with Mr. Benally, she talked with him about her grandfather. Her grandfather, Jimmy Platero, had been a code talker during the war. What about making a documentary about the contributions of the Navajo Nation during the war using video interviews with her grandfather as the unifying theme? Mr. Benally thought that a splendid idea but wondered if there might not be a way to extend the project to include contributions of other groups as well. Together, they struck upon the idea of using one of the educational bulletin boards on the telecommunications network.

Lita had composed a message outlining her project with her grandfather and asked if anyone else might have relatives who had made unique contributions. If so, would they like to join her in her project? Lita was delighted when she received replies. Jamal in Atlanta wrote her that his grandfather had served with the 761st Tank Battalion, an all-Black battalion. Mike in Madison asked to join the two several days later. His grandfather had served with a group of 20 other men assigned to a special battalion of Wisconsinites. The three switched to e-mail and exchanged messages over the next two weeks as they planned a common approach. They watched several Bill Moyer interviews to explore how best to videotape and organize interviews. They watched several of Kenneth Burns's tapes on the Civil War to explore how other images and narrations might be integrated with the interviews. Eventually, the three were able to design a plan so that their videotapes would share a common production format.

As Lita began her research, she realized that the project was too big to complete alone and enlisted the help of three other classmates who had not selected their own project. Jamal and Mike did likewise. Lita's team participated in the e-mail discussions with Jamal's and Mike's teams, in the library and online research, in the planning and taping of interviews with her grandfather, and in the final editing and narration of the videotape. The group made copies of the tape for Jamal's and Mike's teams and sent them. Jamal's and Mike's teams sent a message that copies of their tapes were in the mail also.

As the school bus pulled up in front of the school, Lita grabbed her books and dashed to Mr. Benally's room. The tapes had arrived. Class was given over to viewing the tapes. Lita's entire class joined in the viewing. Lita and her team had shared their own tape with the class the previous week. Skillfully guided by Mr. Benally, the class discussed the three tapes. Everyone was amazed at the number of similarities among the experiences of all three grandfathers. Each spoke of their pride in the contributions they had made to their country. Jamal's grandfather and Lita's grandfather had even been in France at the same time. Students also noted that Mike's group had used some very interesting camera tricks during the interview. They had actually filmed with two cameras, one set for close-ups and one for a wider angle. When they edited the video, they juxtaposed the two angles. It proved an effective technique, allowing the integration of emotional appeal and analytical reflection.

As the discussion neared its end, another student, Johnson, reflected on the three tapes. "You know," he commented, "there ought to be a way to combine all three tapes so that the commonalties emerge. That would create a second message—not one about different cultures but one about human culture." George, whose group had created an interactive, hypermedia program using old newsreel clips to explore the role of technological innovations in the conduct of the war, suggested that a similar format might accomplish Johnson's vision for merging the three tapes. "What a good idea," chorused the class. Lita's and George's teams agreed to join forces. That would take care of the next two weeks.

When the lunch bell rang and the students filed out, Mr. Benally sat back to reflect. The educational process had certainly changed since he had begun teaching. Yes, he was a social studies teacher, and his students were learning the story of America and the role of their community as part of the larger tapestry. As important, however, they were learning the lifelong literacy skills they would need to contribute to the human story as it would be created in the future. The technologies of the school had changed from books and paper and pencil as the primary modes of communication to a multiplicity of tools. The literacy curriculum embedded in the design of Mr. Benally's class would serve students beyond the walls of the school.

It had taken a while for Lita's teachers to learn that "literacy" could not be defined only as the "ability to read and write—to be able to use print." Learning had to be designed that taught students not only how to use books—to learn to read and write and to read and write to learn—but to use all the tools of communication—to learn about and to learn with these tools.

In this chapter, we explored ways in which teachers can design opportunities for students to develop literacy. We defined literacy as the ability to encode and decode meaning using all of the symbolic forms of representation available to a culture to communicate and create meaning. Considerations for designing opportunities to support literacy were described as (1) providing opportunities for students to develop the ability to understand and use a variety of symbolic systems, (2) providing opportunities for students to master a series of cognitive strategies for getting meaning from symbolic forms, and (3) providing opportunities for students to understand and interpret the patterns used by a culture to organize symbols into larger texts—discourse forms. In the next chapter, we will explore ways in which educators can design opportunities for students to become competent users of information.

However, before you move on to Chapter 7, we recommend that you go to the FACTS Web-Based Design Tool site and click on the Design Mentors puzzle piece. This chapter's Design Mentors follow Brooks White and Alan Sutton as they add to their designs. You will be able to follow these two teachers as they continue the design process. Pay particular attention to the ways in which the activities change and grow as they consider how to make literacy part of students' learning opportunities.

You will also notice how the range of tools Ms. White and Mr. Sutton select changes as their design becomes more robust. After you have studied the Design Mentors, you might find it helpful to return to the opening page of the Web site and complete Design Challenge Six. You can also examine some of the Design Examples and see how they reflect the considerations discussed in this chapter.

Chapter Ideas

- Traditionally, literacy, at the denotative level, is the ability to use letters—possession of the skills inherent in reading and writing print. At this level, the educational goal is to help students learn how to read and write.
- Literacy, at the connotative level, is traditionally defined as the ability to read and write to learn—to explore ideas, gather information, reflect on and profit from the debates, histories, wisdom, and theories collected in printed material.
- Traditional design for literacy is squarely entrenched in the technology of print.
- A redefined notion of literacy and literacy instruction is necessary if today's students are to navigate the "supersymbolic" world created by the electronic technologies.
- Understanding literacy as more than the printed word permits teachers to see that the electronic technologies can be positive additions to design for literacy.
- To design literacy instruction, educators should choose relevant contents taken from student interests and the larger social context, identify representative sets of symbolic examples, and provide opportunities for students to interpret and reflect on those examples.
- Humans have developed and use a variety of symbol systems—numeric, alphabetic, visual, musical, verbal, and gestural. Each of these symbol systems functions as a means for both the conceptualization of ideas about aspects of reality and as a means for conveying what one knows to others.
- Getting meaning from or acquiring knowledge about the complex and rich information environment of the twenty-first century rests on the ability to fully use all of these symbolic forms. Any comprehensive design for learning literacy must include designing opportunities for students to master all the symbol systems.
- Learning to comprehend the message embedded in symbolic information is the second cornerstone of literacy instruction.
- Comprehension derives from the complex transactions between information that is received and higher cognitive strategies that mediate to evaluate information. Research has demonstrated that teaching cognitive strategies leads to significant improvement in comprehension.

- Discourse specifies a set of relations between the sender of a message, the receiver of a message, and the topic.
- Discourse is ordered by rules that permit certain statements to be made, impose order upon statements, allow statements to be identified as either true or false, and structure the ways in which maps, models, and classificatory systems are constructed.
- To be literate, one must understand how various discourse forms are organized, understanding where information can be found, how information is connected, and the unique potentials inherent in a diversity of discourse forms. Whether one is learning from printed, video, television, or computer forms of discourse, literacy depends on one's ability to work within the frame of that discourse form.
- Teachers who promote literacy development design instruction that presents students with representative models of how others have combined symbols and cognitive strategies into culturally recognized and valued organizational patterns to communicate.
- Teachers who promote literacy development provide students with opportunities to learn from representative models and encourage students to move from their own experiences and interpretations to symbolized representations of their own thoughts.

DESIGNS FOR USING INFORMATION

Several years ago, I was asked to lead bimonthly Wednesday afternoon workshops focusing on integrating technology with the curriculum at an elementary school in Albuquerque. Before one of those workshops, I stopped by the school's media center to use one of the computers to write a short memo. Sitting next to me was a fifth-grade student. He was attempting to use the school's electronic reference system, Athena, to locate some information. He seemed quite competent with the system so I kept working on my memo.

After fifteen minutes of searching, the young man turned to me for help. He told me he was looking for information on the Grand Teton National Park but was not finding anything. I asked him to explain what he had tried so far. As he talked, it dawned on me that he was using the wrong information source. The Athena system was an online database of library books organized by subject, author, or title. Yet, the school's library probably did not have any resources specifically on the Grand Teton National Park. I explained to him the limitations of the resource he was using and suggested that perhaps an encyclopedia might be more appropriate.

Together, we walked to the reference section and selected the appropriate volume of the World Book Encyclopedia. *Quickly, we located a long paragraph on the Grand Teton National Park. He was delighted with his find. With all my technological wisdom, I asked him if he would like to connect to the Internet and search for more information. "No," he responded. "But", I explained, "on the Internet we would be able to find a lot more information and probably pictures of the national park as well." "No thanks," he assured me. "This is all I need." Even though I tried to convince him of the exciting things he might find on the Internet, that short paragraph was all it took to meet his information needs.*

I learned an important lesson that day. Students need to learn to use a range of information sources to meet their information needs. They need to learn which resource is likely to result in what kinds of information, that more is not necessarily better, and that the available array of technological information resources is not nearly as important as knowing what information you need. I changed the topic of that day's workshop.

Priscilla Norton

We are surrounded by information. It comes to us in the form of television, video, movies, books, magazines, and newspapers. We encounter information as Silent Radios scroll the latest news across their screens as we stand in line to return rental cars. Friends, associates, and even casual acquaintances tell us about what they heard or believe or even speculate. Recently, we have added the power and the confusion of the Internet. Although the Internet is a wonderful communication tool, its equalitarian nature also permits the spouting of rumors and misinformation. The Internet contains thousands of theories about thousands of ideas. We are in the midst of an information explosion and at risk of collapsing under information overload. Francis Bacon once wrote, "Information is power." Yet, what we need in today's fast-paced, information-riddled world is not more power, but the power to manage the information we have.

Today's students must learn to function in this information environment. They must be able to search for in-formation that is relevant to their needs and interests while learning to wisely put aside that information which threatens to drown them. They must learn to sort through this information, judging it for its reliability, validity, and relevance. They must be able to use appropriate information for creating and communicating viable conclusions and plans of action to inform the conduct of their lives. This chapter looks at how educators can design learning opportunities that assist today's students to become effective information users. This chapter explores (1) today's information environment, (2) the role of an integrated approach and a process approach to design information using learning opportunities, (3) a process model of information use built around the skills of searching, sorting and judging, and creating and communicating (SSCC), and (4) six virtual instructional strategies for engaging students with the process of information use.

THE ELECTRONIC STUDY

Bob Foard had spent a large part of his day at Del Norte High School with his chemistry students. He had then met several colleagues to review science texts for possible adoption. Next, he joined his family at a local restaurant for a quick dinner before going on to his daughter's school concert. Now, as his day began to draw to a close, he stepped resolutely into his "electronic study." He had often thought about how, without leaving this room, he had the ability to access information about anything that happened in the world.

Sitting in his recliner, Bob pressed the "play" button on the telephone answering machine. The first message was from a friend of his son's requesting a ride to school. He jotted a quick note to pass on to Frank. The second message reminded him to come in a little early the next day in order to attend a meeting on the upcoming Science Fair. The remaining two calls were hang-ups. Having dispensed with the telephone, Bob watched the national and local news programs he had recorded during his absence. In many ways, he preferred watching the news this way rather than at its scheduled time. He could use the fast-forward option whenever he wanted to skip an advertisement or a news story that did not interest him. In fact, it took him only about 35 minutes to review an hour's worth of news.

Tonight, two stories captured his attention. The first concerned an apparent rift between the President of the United States and the Secretary of the Navy. Bob jotted down a reminder to himself to get more specific details on this. The second story concerned a statement by the Governor asking the State Legislature to hold down spending, recommending that the proposed 6 percent raise for teachers be reduced to a more modest 1.6 percent. Before turning his attention to these news items, Bob replaced the news cassette with another one he had used previously to

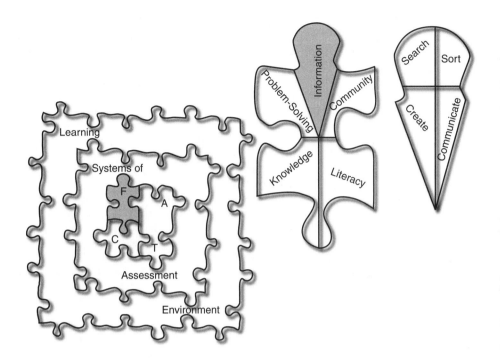

record an episode of *NOVA* on atomic reactors, atomic submarines, and atomic power plants. He planned to show it to his chemistry classes the following day and hoped the combination of readings from the text and the more visual representations in the *NOVA* episode would result in a lively discussion about the application of scientific theories to real-world problems.

About halfway through the tape, Bob decided it was exactly what he needed for class. He turned off the VCR and turned his attention to his computer. He connected to the district's computer network and began reading his e-mail messages. One of the messages was a reminder to attend the textbook adoption meeting. He had done that. He replied briefly to two other messages, quit e-mail, and accessed the teachers' Bulletin Board. The Bulletin Board intrigued Bob. Here anyone could leave a message for all the system's users. A lot of the messages tonight were general requests for assistance. One request from a science teacher at another school asked if anyone had extra beakers. Bob had a few and would send them through the district mail tomorrow.

Bob turned his attention next to the news report about the Governor's suggestion lowering teacher pay raises. This news report was not just a trivial blip of information to be stored away or ignored. Perhaps he could start a discussion using the Bulletin Board to mobilize district teachers to create a response to the Governor's recommendation. He posted a brief summary of the news report to the Bulletin Board and ended by suggesting a letter-writing campaign. He concluded his message by stating that he had drafted a possible letter and that anyone who would like a copy should send him an e-mail message, and he would forward a copy of the letter.

Bob closed his e-mail program and connected to the Internet. Using a search engine called Yahoo (http://www.yahoo.com), Bob searched for information related to the dispute between the President and the Secretary of the Navy. He was able to locate the text of the Secretary's resignation speech. Apparently, the Secretary had resigned because of cuts in the nuclear submarine force proposed by the President. The Secretary had stated firmly that he felt such reductions would seriously jeopardize national security. Searching again, Bob located the text of the President's speech published several days earlier.

Bob downloaded the text of both speeches, saving them to read to his classes the next day. He was not sure whether he agreed with the President or the Secretary, but he was certain that the debate would lead to an interesting class discussion. It seemed a good strategy for engaging his students in thinking about nuclear technology and would build a bridge between contemporary issues and the students' study of atomic structure. The study of science, Bob believed, was not just mastery of abstract, unrelated information and theories but should help in interpreting real-world dilemmas. These articles would help him demonstrate this to his students. As Bob shut down his electronic study for the night, he pondered on the complex world of concepts and information he and his students confronted daily.

TODAY'S INFORMATION ENVIRONMENT

In today's information age, attention has been shifted away from the physical extensions of man and become focused on the electronic technologies as extensions of the human mind. As Gilder (1989, p. 17) writes:

> The central event of the twentieth century is the overthrow of matter. In technology, economics, and the politics of nations, wealth in the form of physical resources is steadily declining in value and significance. The powers of mind are everywhere ascendant over the brute force of things.

What is unique about these powers of mind is that they do not process and produce goods so much as they process and produce information. As they do so, they create an increasingly abstract world. Information about the world we live in is symbolic information, increasingly removed from our direct experience. For example, we are often asked by politicians to make decisions about a trillion-dollar deficit. What is a trillion-dollar deficit? Have you ever seen a trillion dollars or counted a trillion dollars? A trillion dollars is, in fact, little more than an overwhelming abstraction for most of us. Or take, for example, the international money market. Gold is not shifted from bank to bank; bank notes are no longer sent from country to country. Instead, symbols representing some abstract system of value are sent along electric cables. How do we learn to cope with an instantaneous world economy? As a last example, consider the checks and credit cards children watch us use daily. Single pieces of paper or plastic seem to them to represent an infinite array of abstract values. A single credit card buys a carton of milk or a bicycle. How do children learn the relative value of these things?

Even traditional job categories are being shaped by the information technologies. The mechanic no longer lifts the hood of your car, listens to the pings and whirs, and then tells you the problem. Instead, the mechanic connects your car to computerized instruments and watches as graphs and lines move across a monitor. Interpreting these symbols, the mechanic soon knows to replace a malfunctioning computerized part. Those in the medical profession increasingly use computerized heart monitors or CAT scans, examining computer readouts to diagnose disease. Long gone is the nurse whose primary responsibility was bedside care. Instead, a nurse often sits in front of a row of monitors checking for irregular graphs that signal an irregular heartbeat.

The Information Explosion and Information Overload

Many talk about the information explosion, but what specifically does it mean? Large (1984, p. 46) states that more information has been produced in the last 30 years than in the previous 5,000 years, that about 1,000 new book titles are published each day throughout the world, and that the total of all printed knowledge is doubling every eight years. Naisbitt (1982) states that information in the sciences doubles approximately every 5.5 years. This means that today's high school biology students have to cope with five times more information than their parents did when they were in high school. The number of books published per year in the United States increased from 8,422 in 1920 to 42,377 in 1980. Likewise, the number of periodicals published per year rose from 4,496 in 1925 to 11,090 in 1985. Electronically stored information available online has grown an astonishing 700 percent between 1980 and 1990: from approximately 600 online databases provided by 93 vendors to 4,615 databases provided by 654 vendors (Eisenberg & Spitzer, 1991). In 1971, the average American was targeted by at least 560 daily advertising messages. In 1991, that figure rose sixfold to 3,000 messages per day. An average of 60 percent of each person's time at the office is spent processing documents, and the typical business manager is said to read 1 million words per week (Shenk, 1997).

The information age forces us to face massive amounts of information transmitted at accelerating speeds. In fact, information is everywhere—on television, in books, on billboards, in magazines and newspapers, on the Internet. The result is often information overload. In an April 18, 1997 report on information overload, *CNN Headline News* reported that psychologists now have a term for information overload—information fatigue syndrome. In the news item, David Lewis described symptoms of information fatigue syndrome as failure to concentrate, loss of motivation and morale, and greater irritability. Physical symptoms associated with information fatigue syndrome include digestive and heart problems, hypertension, high blood pressure, and sleep disorders. In the same news item, Paul Waddington of the Reuters News Organization reported results of a survey of 1,300 managers worldwide in which 50 percent of those surveyed report the Internet as the prime cause of information overload. One-third of those surveyed reported stress-related health problems due to excess information, and 43 percent stated they had trouble making important decisions because of too much information. Two-thirds of respondents reported that their personal relationships suffered as a result of information overload. Paraphrasing Francis Bacon's notion that information is power, Kathy Nellis, the CNN reporter, concluded "what is most needed now is not more information but the power to manage the information we already have."

Clearly, we can no longer expect students to "learn it all," since we cannot significantly increase the human capacity to absorb content (Eisenberg & Spitzer, 1991). Yet, the reaction in many situations is to constantly expand the amount of content material and to teach it earlier and earlier. This is a losing battle. If scientific information is doubling every five or six years, it is unrealistic to expect that we can double the amount of information to be covered in science courses every five or six years. Writes Postman (1993, p. 26): "Information has become a form of garbage. It comes indiscriminately, directed at no one in particular, disconnected from usefulness. We are swamped by it, have no control over it, and don't know what to do with it."

In 1982, Naisbitt cautioned that we might all be in jeopardy of "drowning in information while remaining starved for knowledge." Fifteen years later, Shenk (1997) recognized the continuing dilemma posed by the information age when he wrote:

> When it comes to information, it turns out that one can have too much of a good thing. At a certain level of input, the law of diminishing returns takes effect; the glut of information no longer adds to our quality of life, but instead begins to cultivate stress, confusion, and even ignorance. Information overload threatens our ability to educate ourselves, and leaves us more vulnerable as consumers and less cohesive as a society. (p. 15)

While the notion of too much information as bad might at first appear odd, it seems to some that we are approaching an important milestone in the human experience—we have begun to produce information faster than we can process it. For centuries, the three stages of the communication process—production, distribution, and processing—were more or less in sync with each other. People have historically been able to examine and consider information about as quickly as it could be created and circulated. But since the mid-twentieth century this equilibrium has been disrupted by the introduction of computers, television, and satellites, creating a discrepancy between the production and availability of information and our ability to interpret and use it. This discrepancy, writes Shenk (1997), has resulted in a dichotomy between "data and knowledge, between publicly available information and public understanding."

How do we cope with information discrepancy and learn to live with information overload? In his book, *Data Smog*, Shenk recommends five anecdotes. One, be your own filter—identify the clutter and begin sweeping it away. Turn off the television, throw away your pager and cell phone, and limit your e-mail. Two, give a hoot, don't info-pollute. Learn to be economical about what you say, write, publish, broadcast, and post online. Three, embrace simplicity. This means returning to more fundamental technologies. Instead of attending to technologies that provide swift access to information, seek ordered knowledge. Instead of searching for vast amounts of information form associations with those who can explain what is worth knowing and why. Four, de-nichify. To de-nichify means to avoid overly specialized, exclusive jargon and to cross boundaries by seeking the company of generalists seeking a less fragmented world. Those who seek to de-nichify avoid becoming overly specialized. While specialization might be empowering and rejuvenating, it is inherently limiting. Last, demand that government—local, state, and national—begin a dialogue that moves toward an informed public policy that shapes the use of the information technologies in a manner that protects basic freedoms and restricts inappropriate information excesses.

These five anecdotes for coping with the information glut might inform personal choices and actions. They do little, however, to help educators devise learning opportunities for students growing up in an information age. While it is true that today's students will never be able to or need to make sense of *all* the information that might be available, it is also true that they need to be able to (1) sample the available information resources, (2) choose information that might serve their purposes, and (3) construct and communicate useful insights and implications that result from using information.

Among educators, there is a growing recognition of the need for today's students to have the ability to use information to acquire both core and advanced knowledge and to become independent, lifelong learners who can contribute responsibly and productively to the learning community (American Association of School Librarians, 1998). This means teaching information literacy—a set of competencies, an information problem-solving process, and a set of skills that provide a strategy for effectively and efficiently meeting information needs (Valenza, 1996). Among the skills identified by Doyle (1992) as part of information literacy are the ability to:

- Recognize that accurate and complete information is the basis for intelligent decision making;
- Formulate questions based on information needs;
- Evaluate information;
- Organize information for practical application; and
- Use information in critical thinking and problem solving.

Educators' Challenge

Two million years ago, an assortment of fossils and vegetation were pressed tightly between massive blocks of shale and transformed into oil. It was not until the 1800s, however, that man was able to systematically search for oil, to recover and refine it, to invent and implement viable uses for it, to distribute it, and to obtain a return on its production. This, in turn, provided an economic base to look for more oil and, when oil supplies appeared to be running short, to begin looking for alternative sources of fuel. It was not the oil itself that transformed human society, but the ways in which oil was used that reshaped many aspects of our lives.

And so it is with information. For better or worse, symbols capable of informing have come to permeate the environments in which we live. Information, the ideas and concepts encoded in symbols, is challenging the fiber of our social, political, economic, and intellectual lives. However, information alone does not guarantee any benefits to those who possess it or can gain access to it. It is the human ability to add structure and meaning to random and unstructured information that is central to its value. Like oil, information is a resource only to the extent that we are able to find it, to use it, and to distribute it. In a society where information is becoming our most important resource, educators are faced with the problem of designing learning opportunities for students that assist them to make sense of the complex information environments they encounter. Specifically, today's educators are challenged by four central questions:

- How can learning opportunities be designed that help students search for and locate the information that might be important to them?
- How can learning opportunities be designed that help students learn to sort through, interpret, and judge the information to which they gain access?
- How can learning opportunities be designed that help students learn to use information to make decisions, to create order of their experiences, and to arrive at new understandings?
- How can learning opportunities be designed that help students communicate the understandings they have shaped from their interactions with information?

Meeting the Challenge: Two Considerations

Few in the educational community challenge the importance of teaching information skills to today's students. Support can be found, for instance, in the mission statement of *Information Power* (American Library Association, 1988) that recognizes the need "to ensure that students and staff are effective users of ideas and information." *Information Power* articulates the goal of providing "intellectual access to information through systematic learning activities which develop cognitive strategies for selecting, retrieving, analyzing, evaluating, synthesizing, and creating information at all age levels and in all curriculum content areas." Trends in thinking about the challenges of teaching students to live in an information age include:

- A shift in curriculum design from a focus on knowledge and skills to problem solving and critical thinking within an authentic assessment model;
- A change in the teacher role from one who imparts knowledge and skills to that of coach and manager of a learning environment;
- A transformation of the learner from a passive receptacle of information to one who is actively engaged in the process of constructing knowledge and personal meaning; and
- A reconstruction of educational institutions from closed environments where knowledge was guarded in a sacred manner to a perspective that fosters real-world learning based on an open flow of information through local networks and global access (Ames, et al., 1995).

Given these changes and a recognition of the value of information skills, two important themes are emerging as considerations for the design of learning opportunities for information use. First, information skills should not be taught in isolation. The skills program must be fully integrated with the school's curriculum. Second, essential information skills encompass more than just location of and access to sources. The skills curriculum should emphasize general information problem-solving and research processes and the specific skills within these general processes.

The Integrated Approach.   Using an integrated approach to teaching information skills refers to the teaching of such skills in the context of subject area curriculum and classroom learning. This approach requires that instruction be tied to real needs. This is a major change from traditional, often isolated, bibliographic instruction, which frequently takes place independent of any classroom activities or assignments. Integrated instruction gives students skills for coping with topics of study and life situations. Students learn information problem solving by using real information related to real needs. Because the skills are transferable, such integration may occur across all settings and subjects, and it does not require the creation of new courses or instructional units (Eisenberg & Spitzer, 1991).

Teaching information skills independent from subject area curricula is like teaching auto-mechanics students how to use certain tools one at a time and then expecting them to be able to use the appropriate tool in a specific situation (e.g., fixing a car). The integrated approach would be, "Here is a car, and I'll show you how to fix it by using certain tools." An integrated approach moves the focus away from the tools and toward accomplishing the task at hand. "It is meaningless to teach locating, organizing, and synthesizing of information without practice. Practice involves using information-management skills with content or subject matter: the existing curriculum" (Bureau of State Library, Pennsylvania Department of Education, 1988, p. 4).

The Process Approach.   Traditionally, teaching students to cope with information focused on skills related to sources: locating, accessing, and using a variety of information sources. These isolated, library-dependent skills were frequently taught out of subject context, without any formal, articulated curricular framework. Later, specialists developed scope-and-sequences of skills, although most still emphasized a source approach. In recent years, a newer approach to skills instruction has emerged, one that centers on a process approach to information skills (Eisenberg, 1992).

A process approach does not depend on any particular source or library. Instead, the emphasis is on developing transferable cognitive skills that should increase students' effective use of information in general as well as their use of specific libraries, reference materials, online databases, and Internet sources. Although there is a lack of research related to the appropriateness of a process approach to information skill, there is evidence that a process approach is more effective than traditional resource-based approaches. Dewees (1987), for instance, tested two average-level, fourth-grade classes on seven reference skill areas: table of contents, encyclopedia, card catalog, dictionary, table interpretation, index use, and map reading. The group that was taught using the "Pooh Step-by-Step Guide for Writing the Research Paper" scored significantly higher on overall performance and higher on each skill area tested than the group taught information skills using a traditional method (i.e., instruction on individual research skills as separate entities). The findings of the Dewees study suggest that a process-oriented approach can be more effective than an approach that focuses on use of individual sources. Further support for the process approach can be found in the work of Kuhlthau (1985).

Recent examples of the process approach include Kuhlthau's (1985) process model for library research; the "Big Six Skills" information problem-solving framework of Eisenberg and Berkowitz (1988); Irving's (1985) use of information and study skills to deal with assignments and other student information needs; and Stripling and Pitts's (1988) description of library research as a thinking process with 10 steps. These models are summarized in Table 7.1. All these works share the belief that specific information skills should be taught within the context of an overall process.

BECOMING INFORMATION USERS—SSCC

In order to successfully design learning opportunities that support students to become users of information, one or more of these process approaches needs to be integrated into content curriculum. The question remains, however, which process approach to use. Are there relationships—commonalities and differences—among the models? Does each model simply use different terms to describe the same thing, or are there substantive differences? Eisenberg (1991), after reviewing each of the models, found that a common process model did appear to be emerging. Whereas each model explains the process with different terms, divides the various actions at different levels of specificity, and/or emphasizes different phases of the process, all seem to agree on the overall scope and general breakdown of the process.

Although the similarities among the models are clear, we have two concerns. First, the process of being an information user is not as linear as these models suggest. Problems are defined not as first steps in the information-using process, but within the frame of disciplinary and interdisciplinary inquiry. Problem definition is not the first step in the process of using information, but the reason one seeks to use information. As problems provide the impetus for seeking and using information, they are often later redefined as new information is located. Missing information is identified as the synthesis, interpretation, and analysis phases are begun. More information must be collected as final products are created and presented. Second, not all aspects of a process can be mastered or learned within one curricular unit. There may be times when a design for learning to be an information user is best focused on identification of appropriate sources. Other times, instruction might best be focused on particular search strategies for locating information. In still other instances, instructional attention might best be focused on assessing the validity and reliability of information.

TABLE 7.1	**FOUR PROCESS MODELS FOR INFORMATION USE**		
Kuhlthau's (1985) Information-Seeking Model	**Eisenberg and Berkowitz's (1988) Information Problem-Solving Model**	**Irving's (1985) Information Skills Model**	**Stripling and Pitts's (1988) Research Process Model**
1. Initiation	1. Task Definition	1. Formulation and Analysis of Information Need	1. Choose a Broad Topic
2. Selection	1.1 Define the Problem	2. Identification and Appraisal	2. Get an Overview of the Topic
3. Exploration (investigation of likely sources of information on general topic)	1.2 Identify Information Requirements	3. Location and Access	3. Narrow the Topic Statement
4. Formulation of Focus	2. Information-Seeking Strategies	4. Information Use	4. Develop a Thesis/Purpose
5. Collection (gathering of information on the focused topic)	2.1 Determine Range of Sources	5. Synthesis	5. Formulate Questions to Guide Research
6. Presentation	2.2 Prioritize Sources	6. Evaluation	6. Plan for Research and Production
7. Assessment of Outcome	3. Tracing and Locating Individual Resources	7. Interpretation, Analysis, Synthesis, and Evaluation of Information	7. Find, Analyze, and Evaluate Sources
	3.1 Locate Sources	8. Shape, Presentation, and Communication of Information	8. Evaluate Evidence, Take Notes, and Compile Bibliography
	3.2 Find Information	9. Evaluation of Assignment	9. Establish Conclusions and Organize Information in an Outline
	4. Examining, Selecting, and Rejecting Individual Resources		10. Create and Present Final Product (Reflection Point—Is the Paper/Product Satisfactory?)
	4.1 Engage (read, view, etc.) and Process Information		
	4.2 Extract Information		
	5. Interrogating and Using Individual Resources		
	5.1 Organize		
	5.2 Present		
	6. Recording and Storing		
	6.1 Judge the Product		
	6.2 Judge the Process		

Thus, to guide the design of opportunities for students to become information users, we believe effective instruction should help students learn to *search* for information, *sort* and *judge* information, and *create* and *communicate* ideas and concepts as the result of information use (SSCC). Each of these activities can be supported by a range of tools, related to a particular problem arising within the domain of particular content areas, and woven together with knowledge, problem-solving, and literacy abilities.

Searching for Information

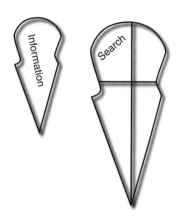

Until the thirteenth century, there was, for most people, only one source of information and that was the spoken word. Most of what people needed to know depended on information passed from generation to generation. Most jobs were learned by apprenticeship, and values and history were learned from the stories told by parents, grandparents, and village storytellers. For the vast majority of people, printed material provided little if anything in the way of an information resource. Searching for information consisted primarily in seeking out elders or recognized practitioners or waiting for roaming bards or travelers to bring information. In the fifteenth century with the invention of the printing press, books became an additional resource and repository of human knowledge. As people's information needs changed, they began to rely on books, pamphlets, newspapers, and increasingly on libraries. It was only logical that schools began teaching skills associated with the ability to search for information in printed material—skills such as using tables of contents, indexes, and organizational schemes like the Dewey Decimal System. Today, information may be found in an ever-expanding variety of sources—videos, magazines, television news and documentary programs, books in libraries or bookstores, and electronic forms like CD-ROM libraries and the Internet. Searching skills have broadened once again.

Ames et al. (1995) define skills associated with effective searching as the ability to develop a broad overview of the topic, to integrate broad concepts by developing a basic understanding of words and related concepts that expand the topic, to locate information providers, to identify information resources and tools, and to search for relevant information. These skills are elaborated and extended by the development of the ability to narrow the topic, to develop specific questions and a thesis, and to plan a search strategy. Effective searchers learn to identify the location and function of information resource facilities: home computer resources, classroom information and technology resources, library media centers, public libraries, museums, academic libraries, special libraries, and community resources.

The development of an appropriate search strategy lies at the core of effective searching. Search strategies may be browsing searches that allow information users to casually inspect information sources. Searches can be hypertext searches that depend on moving electronically from a word/phrase to related information. They can be hierarchical searches that examine a body of knowledge beginning with broad topics. Last, searches can be analytical searches that use Boolean (and, or, not), truncation, wild card, or proximity. To structure an effective information search, students must learn to clearly define the kind of information they need, the most likely sources for such information, and an appropriate search strategy.

If one seeks general information about a broad topic, it would not make sense to search the Internet. Instead, a general encyclopedia or a specific encyclopedia like the *Encyclopedia of the Social Sciences* might contain the kind of overview information one seeks (a hierarchical search). Encyclopedias can be found electronically on the Internet, on purchased CD-ROMs, or in libraries. If one's information needs are more specific, the Internet might be an appropriate resource. For example, if you are interested in "education" and are connected to a variety of electronic databases, searching for information on education might lead to 20,000 or more possible sources. It would be impossible to scan all of these. One would need, therefore, to be more specific about their information need. Perhaps a search strategy that asked for only those articles that included education *and* elementary *and* spelling would result in a manageable set of sources (an analytical search). If it is not possible to narrow a search that specifically, a different resource such as a trade book on the subject located with a card catalog—electronic or manual—might be a useful place to start or a kind of experimental Web surfing might work as well (browse search).

> In Mrs. Williams's fifth-grade classroom, students were required to prepare a presentation for the class on an interesting topic of their choice each nine-week period. This quarterly project was designed to promote students' ability to pursue a topic on their own, to improve their information skills, and to help them develop their presentation skills. They were encouraged to support their presentation using a variety of forms. Students could elect to create a video or a written report or a graphic slide show or a hypermedia stack or a newspaper. The only requirement was that each nine-week period they choose a different format to use for their presentation. In preparation for this presentation, Mrs. Williams encouraged students to keep an idea log. Students recorded interesting things they encountered during their studies or their reading. When it came time to prepare their presentation, students reviewed the interesting ideas and topics recorded in their logs. As each student began to prepare for their presentation, students designed a search strategy using a procedure posted on a wall chart and discussed their strategy with Mrs. Williams before beginning their research.
>
> During the third quarter of the year, Allison had read an old Indian legend about a huge fire in the sky. A small paragraph at the end of the legend stated that it was thought the legend originated with a supernova explosion, the violent death of a star in 1054 that may have been as much as 10 times more massive than our sun and resulted in the Crab Nebula. Allison was very interested in the nebula of the Indian legend. She constructed a search strategy by first creating a web of topics she wanted to include in her presentation and questions she wanted to answer. She placed things like defining a supernova and a nebula, understanding why stars explode, learning about the history of the Crab Nebula, and learning more about the Indians who had created the legend on her web. Next, she listed possible resources for locating the information she desired. She included dictionaries and astronomy books to help with definitions, science texts and possible interviews with scientists (using telephone, e-mail, and personal interviews) as resources for learning about why stars explode. Among the possible resources she listed for learning about the history of the Crab Nebula were history texts and encyclopedias. Last, Allison's plan included an Internet search to locate information about the Indians in the legend. She had carefully constructed several analytical search strategies using *and, or,* and *not* statements that she planned to use to identify the information she desired.
>
> When Allison had completed her research and prepared a slide show using AppleWorks to support her presentation, her presentation was nearly complete. Yet, one of the things Allison had learned while doing her research was that the American

Indians living in northern Arizona at the time of the Crab Nebula's formation had been so inspired by the event that they drew pictures of it. Two pictographs had been found, one in a cave at White Mesa and the other on a wall of Navajo Canyon. Both pictographs showed a crescent moon with a large star nearby. Scientists had calculated that on the morning of July 5, 1054, the Moon was located just 2 degrees north of the Crab Nebula's current position just as the pictographs showed. Allison thought that a copy of one of the pictographs as her last slide would make a perfect ending to her presentation, but she had no idea how she might find a copy of the pictograph.

Allison consulted with Mrs. Williams who suggested that she use the Internet. Choosing the search engine, Excite (http://www.excite.com), Allison entered crab nebula and selected the search button. At the completion of the search, the engine reported 43,334 references. There was no way Allison could examine each of those to see if they contained a copy of one of the pictographs. With Mrs. Williams's assistance, Allison reconstructed her query as crab + nebula. This resulted in 1,250 references. So, Allison next tried crab + nebula + pictograph, and the search engine returned only 4 references. Allison looked at each of the possible references. The third one yielded a picture of one of the pictographs, and Allison was able to save it as an electronic file and load it into her slide show presentation. You can see the pictograph Allison found at http://physics.carleton.edu/Faculty/Joel/picto.html.

Sorting and Judging Information

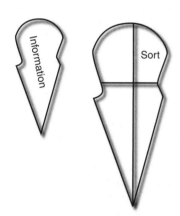

Not all information must be searched for. We are bombarded by countless bits of information that invade our lives without our direct search for them. As we stand in line to return rental cars, for instance, the Silent Radio, a longish rectangular black box with red, scrolling, electronic letters, tells us of the latest terrorist bombings and current stock market fluctuations. When we turn on our televisions to watch our favorite detective show, we are occasionally interrupted by news bulletins or a thin line of letters running along the bottom of the screen warning of flash floods or tornadoes. Access to all this information requires no locating skills. Instead, it demands interpretation and sometimes the design of an appropriate response—sell those stocks or do not drive to a neighboring town. Knowing how to sort through and structure the unstructured jumble of information sometimes seems a more pressing concern for today's and tomorrow's students than locating information.

To be an effective sorter, students must be prepared to judge the validity of the information they have gathered or encountered in the conduct of their lives. It is rarely possible to personally verify the validity of information, particularly since most information refers not to a direct or concrete experience but to already interpreted phenomena. Is *Time Magazine* or the *National Enquirer* a more reliable source? What is the bias that underlies the information? Students must learn to both question and check on the validity of information resources. Some information can be checked interpersonally. In most situations, however, students are dependent on symbolized sources of information that they must learn to verify by turning to other symbolized sources. Cross-media checking (same medium, but different source) and intermedia confirmation (different medium) become our most reliable strategies for verification (Gumperts, 1987). Thus, sorters must learn to cross-reference—to compare television news with newspaper accounts or to compare different authors writing on the same topic.

Once information has been sorted based on its reliability and validity, effective sorters must be able to determine what of the remaining information is important and what is superfluous. In a world producing information faster than it can be sorted, deciding what not to attend to becomes as important as deciding what to attend to. Students must learn to determine what information is truly related to their needs and interests and what information is unimportant. Last, they must learn to pose questions that help them sort through information in a manner that reveals relationships and connections between individual and disparate bits of information. In short, good information sorters assess information for its reliability, validity, and usefulness as well as use information to develop personal meaning.

One Sunday evening as Larry Jeffryes was watching *60 Minutes,* Leslie Stahl presented a story titled "The Rumor Mill" (1997). In her story, she addressed the cacophony of rumors and misinformation that can so easily be found on the Internet. Interviewing Andrew Canter, Senior Editor of *Internet World Magazine,* Stahl showed the viewing audience how easily anyone can get their opinion or their story on the Internet and how easily it can be accessed by others. Using a search engine, Canter typed in "TWA 800" and showed Stahl the list of articles to be found. Some of those articles were associated with mainstream government and media sources. Other articles had been posted by private individuals or organizations with claims of media cover-ups and bizarre theories. This demonstrates how the Internet contains thousands of wild theories on thousands of topics, she told the audience. And, "while the Internet can be a wonderful communication tool full of valuable information, it has also turned out to be the most powerful system for spouting off and spreading rumors and scams. Good luck trying to tell the truth from the lies."

As Mr. Jeffryes watched Stahl's report, he began thinking about his high school biology students. How could he help students learn to distinguish between credible and noncredible information? Over the next week, Mr. Jeffryes used his school's Internet access to identify a series of Internet sites that presented information about the TWA 800 crash and recorded the address for each site. He then began exploring the Internet to locate a list of sites that might provide his students with information about how to critically evaluate information on the World Wide Web. He recorded the addresses for these sites as well.

When he was ready to begin the lesson, Mr. Jeffryes read three short articles from the Associated Press to students. The first identified for students the existence of three possible crash theories—a bomb, a missile, or mechanical failure. The second reported the release of a 69-page document and set of radar images by Pierre Salinger supporting his theory that the crash was the result of a Navy missile shot. The third article quoted FBI Assistant Director James Kallstrom stating that the Salinger claims were just plain false information. Mr. Jeffryes led a class discussion about how one might find more information about the two positions and about how one might begin to establish whose position was most credible. Mr. Jeffryes's classes agreed to meet in the school's computer lab where Internet access was available for the next four class periods.

As the class members gathered in teams of two at the computers, Mr. Jeffryes distributed the list of sites he had identified to help students establish criteria for evaluating information on the World Wide Web. He challenged students to use information at these sites to create a rubric that they could use to judge information about the crash of TWA Flight 800. The six Web site addresses provided to Mr. Jeffryes's students are listed in Table 7.2. As students examined these and similar sources, they began to compile a list of criteria for evaluating information. Students soon began constructing a rubric of questions and considerations they thought were important criteria for evaluating information. Their rubrics began to list questions related to content, source, date, and structure. Roger and Barbara were impressed by the checklist created by Alexander and Tate that included questions related to five criteria: authority, accuracy, objectivity, currency, and coverage. Barbara was particularly interested in the question "Is there a way of verifying the legitimacy of the page's sponsor? That is, is there a phone number or postal address to contact for more information?" She asked Mr. Jeffryes if they would be able to follow through on this question if it was included on their rubric. He assured them he would be willing to help.

When all the rubrics were completed and shared among classmates, Mr. Jeffryes introduced the next task. He distributed the addresses to a number of sites that contained information about the TWA 800 crash. He had carefully constructed the list to include sites that represented a range of opinions and contrasting claims. He challenged the class to write an essay not about what happened to the TWA 800 flight but about which set of opinions (Salinger's or the government's) seemed most credible. Students used their rubrics to judge the information sites on Mr. Jeffryes's list. With his guidance, they created a grid that listed their rubric down the side and the Internet sites across the top. Each site was evaluated on each criteria. If a site met the criteria a $(+)$ was marked on the grid. If a site did not meet the criteria a $(-)$ was marked on the grid. When students had evaluated each of the sites, they disconnected from the Internet and used a word processor, their notes, and their grids to create a convincing argument about the credibility or noncredibility of each position. When the essays

---

TABLE 7.2   **SITES FOR EXAMINING CRITERIA TO JUDGE WEB PAGES**

1. Evaluation of Information
   http://alexia.lis.uiuc.edu/~janicke/Eval.html

2. Internet Source Validation Project
   http://www.stemnet.nf.ca/Curriculum/Validate/valid.html

3. Checklist for an Informational Web Page
   http://www2.widener.edu/Wolfgram-Memorial-Library/webevaluation/inform.htm

4. CyberGuides
   http://www.cyberbee.com/guides.html

5. Kathy Schrock's Critical Evaluation Surveys
   http://school.discovery.com/schrockguide/eval.html

6. Thinking Critically about World Wide Web Resources
   http://www.library.ucla.edu/libraries/college/instruct/web/critical.htm

were complete, Mr. Jeffryes led a very animated and exciting discussion. He was confident that students had learned a great deal about sorting through and judging information.

◦ ◦ ◦ ◦ ◦ ◦ ◦

Kevin is seven and in second grade. He and his father often spend time in the evening at the family computer exploring the Internet. Sometimes they search for information related to a question that Kevin has asked. Sometimes they look for information related to something Kevin is studying in school. Sometimes they just explore all the information sources on the Internet just to see what they can find. One night, Kevin and his Dad stumbled across an address for the Mighty Morphin Power Rangers. They sent the White Ranger an e-mail message.

The next night when they checked their e-mail they found a message from Tommy, the White Ranger. Kevin and his Dad read the message. "I wonder," asked Kevin's Dad, "if this is a message just to us or if all kids who send a message get the same thing." At first, Kevin thought perhaps Tommy had written just to him, but Kevin's Dad helped him figure out that there were probably many children writing messages so Tommy probably sent the same message to all children. Then Kevin's Dad asked him why he thought Tommy had written so much about the new, upcoming Mighty Morphin movie. At first, Kevin thought it was really "cool" to learn all about the movie. But as he and his Dad talked, Kevin realized that Tommy's message was an advertisement. It was not bad, Kevin concluded, to advertise on the Internet, but it was important for him to recognize that Tommy was trying to persuade him to go to the movie.

The part of Tommy's message that Kevin's Dad liked best was the advice on how to be safe on the Internet. He and Kevin talked for a long time about dealing with strangers, both in real life and in "cyberspace." They talked about how to tell the difference between a safe question and an unsafe question. Kevin and his Dad agreed that whenever Kevin was unsure, he would consult with one of his parents before responding.

Kevin now sends a message to one of the Power Rangers every week. Each week he receives a message back. Every message tells him about Mighty Morphin movies or books or toys. It also includes an Internet tip. One time, the Pink Ranger wrote:

> It's easy to get completely hooked on the Internet! But remember to use the Net responsibly, you need to keep track of your time, and make sure that your parents know what you're doing. There are a lot of places to explore. The best way to find the best places is to let your parents help guide you. Who knows? They might even learn something!

Another time, the Yellow Ranger wrote:

> The Internet and Web are big—and sometimes, you might find something that you don't understand, or be asked questions by somebody you don't know. Remember, you can think for yourself on the Net. If somebody asks you to do something that bothers you, tell a parent or a teacher.

Kevin and his Dad discussed each tip. Kevin, with the expert guidance of his Dad, is learning important lessons about consumerism, about thinking critically about all the information that surrounds him, and about the ethics and etiquette of this new medium of communication.

Creating and Communicating

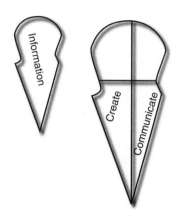

It is not enough to have information or to access information. Neither is it enough to sort through and judge information for its reliability, validity, and relevance. Students must learn processes for using information that lead to the creation and communication of ideas. To use information to create, students must be fluent at combining disparate information in order to generate knowledge, to find solutions, and to make decisions. As creators, students need to be able to hypothesize, asking why, what if, what is similar, what is different, and what inferences can be drawn. They need to draw on their powers of induction and deduction, to move from generalizations to specifics and from specifics to generalizations. They must have experiences that empower them with abilities to use sought-for and sorted information to build structure from variables, to see how complexity derives from interactions, to generate patterns and probabilities, and to be willing to subject perceived connections to careful scrutiny.

The process skills associated with using information to effectively create concepts, ideas, and knowledge are integrally linked to the communication process. In the process of structuring communication in ways that permit others to understand and interact with emerging ideas, students must bring order to the disorder of isolated pieces of information. In the process of structuring information using patterns of discourse, students begin to see the connections and relationships that lead to creative interpretation and use of information.

To be an effective communicator, students must learn to share both raw information and the results of their creating. They must be presented with opportunities that lead to proficiency with the kinds of communication skills required by the social dialogue. Nurses must be able to communicate information to doctors, mechanics to car owners, accountants to managers, scientists to colleagues, parents to children, and friends to friends. In the act of using information to design effective communication, students need to learn to choose an appropriate style, format, and medium.

The act of communicating engages students in the symbolization of understandings gleaned from information. They must learn to choose an effective form for presenting information. Are information and interpretations best represented with pictures, with text, with an oral presentation, with graphs, or with a combination of forms? Are insights best presented using an expository, narrative, oratory, or essay format? Students must learn strategies for showing connections and relationships for personal and public scrutiny and sharing. They must master techniques for choosing what information is necessary to support their insights and what information is irrelevant or unnecessary. They need to learn to provide enough information to make their point without providing so much information that their message becomes obscured.

Ames et al. (1995) summarize the processes of creating and communicating with information as interpretation of information, organization and formatting of information, and sharing new knowledge. They identify subskills of the creating process as drawing conclusions, evaluating information to support or refute a thesis, understanding cause and effect, connecting concepts, and determining trends, patterns, similarities, and differences. Subskills of the communicating process include determining effective methods of communication, organizing information, speaking, listening, writing, demonstrating, designing, composing, and presenting.

Just as the overall information-using process can be represented by the acronym SSCC, the creating and communicating part of that process can be represented by the acronym DEAPR. When teachers seek to provide a framework for the design of opportunities for students to learn to become effective creators and communicators, they should provide opportunities for students to *design, encode, assemble, publish,* and *revise* their ideas and the products they design to communicate those ideas—to go DEAPR.

Skills associated with design allow students to bring order to information. In the process of design, students begin to impose order to information by classifying, grouping, sequencing, connecting, or relating information. As they do so, concepts, patterns, generalizations, and insights emerge, leading to reflection and critique. These emerging ideas are assessed in light of information and can be elaborated with additional information or discarded because of conflicting information. Once ordered, students can reorder into more elegant and appropriate patterns and concepts. Strategies educators can teach students that support the design process include creating outlines, flowcharts, mind maps, webs, graphical organizers, and combinations of these strategies. Design is a necessary first step and returning to redesign a design as students progress through the DEAPR process should be encouraged. Students should be asked to review their designs with fellow students and teachers.

Once a preliminary design has been crafted, students begin the process of encoding. As we saw in Chapter 6, encoding is the process of turning thoughts and experiences into symbolic form. A first phase in the encoding process is the selection of an appropriate symbolic form. Is information best captured in graphic, numeric, text, sound, or a combination? The second phase of the encoding process centers on choosing an expressive format. What format is appropriate for expressing one's thoughts and experiences? Is the story form, research report, essay, documentary, news report, or comic book format best? Next, students must choose a medium. Are ideas best captured by video, by text, by hypermedia, by a desktop publisher, by a spreadsheet, or by a combination of mediums? Last, what procedure will be used to encode? In some mediums, a strict linear process must be adhered to as when creating videos using in-camera editing. Yet, often the component parts of a communication can be crafted in modules. For instance, when video editing capabilities are available, it makes sense to shoot all scenes related to a particular setting and then move on to the next setting. When writing with a word processor, paragraphs can be written and then later moved. When creating hypermedia stacks, all scanned images can be compiled when access is available to a scanner. Then, all graphic images can be created using a graphics program. Individual cards in the stack can be created and stored.

When all elements deemed necessary by the design have been encoded and stored, the process of assembling the parts into a cohesive communication begins. Oftentimes in the process of assembly, missing components are identified and must be encoded, or parts previously encoded become superfluous or redundant and must be discarded. Sometimes, designs must be revised or reconstructed. In the process of editing and assembling a video, various scenes can be sequenced, eliminated, or cut. Rarely does a finished video include all footage that has been shot. When assembling a desktop-published newsletter or pamphlet, some pictures are not included. Some text is modified to fit space requirements. Additional stories or items must be created. The parts of a research paper produced in a word processing environment are often moved up and down within the document to better present an argument. Sometimes, new paragraphs must be written to express bridges between ideas. Prepared tables or illustrations may be inserted or may need to be created to reinforce an idea. It may be necessary to return to the searching and sorting process in order to supplement existing information with additional sources. Or, in the process of assembling the communication, certain ideas or information may be contradictory, and new information is needed.

The publishing and revising processes represent an important dynamic. As a communicator or group of communicators begin crafting their product, they become the first audience. As a communication begins to emerge, the creators can see and assess their product. In reviewing their publication, they are able to take a small step back and reflect on the cohesiveness, expressiveness, and appropriateness of their ideas. At this point, revisions are made. Once a communication passes the scrutiny of its creators, it must be shared with peers, experts, and other interested people for feedback. Communicators publish their work to receive confirmation of their insights, to judge the effectiveness of their communication, and to receive additional ideas and insights that confirm and strengthen or challenge and cause reconsideration. Communicators need to know if they have achieved their goals. Some say no communication is ever truly finished; all work is part of a continuing process. That is why many authors return to the same theme repeatedly in their works and why scientists design varied experiments that elaborate theories. Nevertheless, students must learn when a particular communication has met the goals they established for that product and to draw lessons from what they have learned that might influence their next product. They must learn to declare a product finished—at least for the time being.

In Kim Chase's ninth-grade literature class, one of the year's themes is tolerance. Students had read several books that emphasized this theme. Ms. Chase felt it was time students explored tolerance from a different point of view—the consequences of intolerance. However, she did not want to explore intolerance with her students as an abstract concept. Instead, she wanted them to see the impacts of intolerance on the lives of real people. It seemed that the Holocaust experience might be one of the most powerful ways in which to engage students with intolerance. She began her design by asking students to read *The Diary of Anne Frank*. When Ms. Chase introduced the assignment, students groaned. Some had read the book before, and many of the boys felt it was dumb to read a girl's diary. In introducing the book to her classes, Ms. Chase asked them what they knew about the Holocaust and about Anne Frank. She was amazed that many of the students knew about Anne Frank, but few seemed to know much about the Holocaust. One student explained that she thought Anne Frank was on a vacation while in the attic, and she could not figure out why one would choose an attic for a vacation and why the family did not leave after two weeks.

It seemed that students were simply not going to appreciate Anne Frank's experience and connect it to the theme of intolerance unless Ms. Chase found a way to personalize their experience of the Holocaust. Ms. Chase had attended a conference for educators at the United States Holocaust Memorial Museum in Washington, D.C. One theme during the conference had stressed again and again the need to personalize the Holocaust experience. She remembered clearly the museum's message: We must remind ourselves that the Holocaust was not six million; it was one, plus one, plus one. She wanted her students to do research about the Holocaust and to realize that the victims were true people, who had real lives and family members who cared about them. They were not people from far away and long ago. She remembered that when one tours the museum, they are given a small identification booklet that traces one person's journey through the Holocaust. The card is divided into four sections roughly representing life before the war, life in the ghetto, life in the concentration camp, and life after the war if the victim survived. Ms. Chase e-mailed the museum, and they sent her enough recycled identification cards to allow each of her students to have one.

Using these cards to structure student activities, Ms. Chase combined the diary technique with her knowledge of the information-using process to design a plan. She wanted to focus on the creating and communicating process so she carefully designed activities and resources to minimize student efforts with searching and sorting. First, she defined the research problem carefully. Students were to write at least eight entries in the diary of their person—two from before the war, two from life in the ghetto, two from life in the concentration camp, and two from life after the war. The identification card clearly provided each student with information as to their person's whereabouts during those times. Second, she identified a set of questions that students needed information to answer. Her list of questions included (1) What was the weather like in each of those places? (2) What was the geography of each place including population, interesting places, and cultural events? (3) What historical events occurred during that time? (4) What was it like living in the ghetto? (5) What was it like living in a concentration camp? and (6) What happened in postwar Europe? Third, she located a set of resources that students would use. These included CD-ROMs like the *Encarta Encyclopedia,* a world atlas, and MacMillan's *Library Reference Historical Atlas of the Holocaust* as well as books and reference material selected by the school's librarian and placed in her classroom, and a set of appropriate Internet sites. Ms. Chase talked with students about Internet etiquette and ethics. She told them of the "hate" sites on the Internet and the sites that tried to prove there was no Holocaust. She told students she had sorted through the sites, judging them for their relevance and reliability. Last, she constructed worksheets for students to use that would summarize researched information relevant to each of the questions at each of the locations where their victims had resided.

Ms. Chase reserved the school's computer lab for five days and placed the books provided by the librarian on a resource table in the lab. Students spent those days using the resources Ms. Chase had identified to find information related to the worksheets and questions. She told students they could collaborate and share information, that researching did not have to be a lonely and individual task. It was amazing how small groups formed and disbanded as the experiences of each of their victims changed. She was a bit shocked when Rudolpho shouted, "Hey, did anyone go to that Auschwitz place?" But his call resulted in the identification of five other students, and those students clustered together around one computer to search for information about the weather. While visiting the Holocaust Memorial Museum Web site (http://www.ushmm.org/index.html), Jennifer and Mary discovered information about the Nazi Olympics in Berlin in 1936. Their people had lived in Berlin before being forced into one of the ghettos. Beginning with the same address, Jonathan and Marguarite found information on the Nuremburg Code and Human Rights.

When students returned to the classroom after their week in the lab, Ms. Chase described the next phase of their project. "We are going to create a Holocaust diary and publish the diary entries of our Holocaust victims," she told her classes. In order to do this, we have to first design our diaries. She asked students to identify the theme of each entry and supporting information that would make the entry both more interesting and more historically correct. Jennifer decided one of her entries for life before the war would tell about the day her victim passed the stadium where the 1936 Olympics were happening. Along the way, her victim would pass one of the Berlin theaters. She would have to get a little more information so she could tell about which play was being performed. Alex decided that his victim would find and read a copy of the Nuremburg Code as he trudged home after the war. As students began to near the end of their design of each entry, Ms. Chase suggested that the entries would be more interesting if they include simple black-and-white line drawings. She asked students to design not draw the illustrations they would use. Jonathan decided his victim had a flair for political cartooning and created an idea for a cartoon to accompany each entry that made a political statement. Rudolpho's victim had been a biology teacher before the war. He designed a series of drawings of plants that reflected the mood of each entry. Before the war, his plants would have flowers and leaves. For the entries while his victim was in the concentration camp, the plants would be lifeless, brittle trees. The drawings for life after the war would be of plants just beginning to bud.

Ms. Chase's students returned to the computer lab to encode their designs and complete any research they needed. She showed students how to use a simple graphics program to complete their drawings and how to save each drawing on a disk. Her students already knew how to use a word processor. They wrote and edited each journal entry, saving it to disk. When they had encoded their entries and drawings, Ms. Chase showed students how to use a desktop publisher available on the lab's computers. She asked them to use a template she had created to assemble their entries and drawings. The template used a two-column layout with a bold line across the top of the page. When all the diaries had been assembled and printed, students were organized into teams of three and asked to share their diaries. It was the responsibility of each group member to provide feedback and editing suggestions. As students read the diaries, they chuckled over Jonathan's caricature of Hitler at the head of his army. They shed tears as Jennifer's victim told of the day at Treblinka when her son had been taken to the gas chamber.

When all the diaries had been revised and reprinted, Ms. Chase placed them in a bound book made available to students in the school library. Students asked if they could keep their identification cards and collected 50 cents each to send to the Holocaust Museum. Ms. Chase's goals were met. Students had learned about the consequences of intolerance on the lives of real people. They had learned about the history of the Holocaust. They had honed their abilities to create and communicate with information using the DEAPR process.

BRINGING IT ALL TOGETHER

As educators work to design learning opportunities for students to become effective users of information, there are times when it is appropriate to design learning opportunities that focus on various aspects of the information-using process. Thus, Mrs. Williams designed a lesson that focused her students' attention on searching for information, particularly on the design of effective search strategies. Her lesson de-emphasized sorting and judging information. Creating and communicating were left to students to do as they chose. Mr. Jeffryes, on the other hand, focused the design of his lesson on sorting and judging information. He completed the search aspect of the process for students, identifying a series of appropriate Internet sites and focused the creating and communicating activities on narrow projects such as designing a rubric, completing a grid, and writing an essay. The essence of his lesson lay in the contrasting information sources he provided students and the focusing of his lesson on using a set of criteria to sort through and judge the information contained in those sites. Ms. Chase designed her lesson to emphasize the creating and communicating process. She narrowed the topic for her students and specified the information for which students had to search. Because of the imaginative and largely open-ended nature of the assignment, there was not a significant need for students to be concerned with the reliability and validity of their information sources. Instead, Ms. Chase's lesson focused on the creative use of information to create an imaginative yet personalized identification with the victims of the Holocaust and to express students' developing connection with the victims through diary entries.

There are other times, however, when the design of learning opportunities must engage students with the entire process. It is important that students supplement their emerging skills with the searching, sorting, and creating and communicating subsets of the information-using process with experiences designed to allow them to merge and experiment with the SSCC information-using process as a whole. Even though it is possible to embed this process in activities such as writing research papers, role playing, designing hypermedia stacks, and preparing for formal presentations, an instructional strategy—an activity structure (Harris, 1998b)—called a WebQuest is a powerful way to design learning opportunities that bring the whole process together.

WebQuests

Developed by Bernie Dodge (http://edweb.sdsu.edu/people/bdodge/Professional. html), a WebQuest is an inquiry-oriented activity in which some or all of the information students interact with comes from the Internet. There are at least two kinds of WebQuests: a short-term WebQuest and a longer-term WebQuest. The goal of a short-term WebQuest is knowledge acquisition and integration. At the end of a short-term WebQuest, a learner will have interacted with a significant amount of new information and made sense of it. A short-term WebQuest is designed to be completed in one to three class periods. The instructional goal of a longer-term WebQuest is the extension and refinement of knowledge. After completing a longer-term WebQuest, a learner would have analyzed a body of knowledge deeply, transformed it in some way, and demonstrated an understanding of the material by creating something that others can respond to. A longer-term WebQuest will typically take between one week and a month in a classroom setting.

WebQuests of either short- or longer-term duration are deliberately designed to make the best use of a learner's time. There is questionable educational benefit in having learners surf the Internet without a clear task in mind, and most schools must ration student connect time. To accomplish efficient interaction with information in order to solve a problem, a WebQuest should contain at least the following elements:

- An introduction that sets the stage and provides some background information.
- A task that is doable and interesting.
- A set of information sources relevant to solving the task. These information resources may include classroom, library, and Internet resources. Many of the resources embedded in a WebQuest are anchors that point to World Wide Web documents and databases. Because pointers to resources are included in a WebQuest, learners are not left to wander through "cyberspace."
- A description of the process learners should use to accomplish the task. The process should be broken into clearly described steps.
- Some guidance on how to organize students' time and resources as well as information.
- A conclusion that brings closure to the quest, reminds learners what they have learned and accomplished, and perhaps encourages them to extend the experience (http://edweb.sdsu.edu/...6/About_WebQuests.html).

Optional, but noncritical attributes of a WebQuest include designing the Web-Quest based on group activities, wrapping motivational elements around the basic structure by giving learners a role to play, a simulated personae, or an authentic audience, and creating tasks that are interdisciplinary. Whether or not these optional features are added to the critical attributes listed previously, thinking skills associated with WebQuests include comparing, classifying, inducing, deducing, analyzing, constructing, abstracting, and analyzing perspectives.

Ms. Sprague sat pondering. The end of the school year was nearing, and she wanted to design a final learning opportunity for her students that would be interesting and challenging. She reviewed the school year in her mind. She and her students had participated in a long space unit. The unit had culminated in students dividing into small groups, studying one of the other eight planets in the solar system, and preparing a brief on adaptations that would need to be made if humans were to settle on that planet. While they were preparing their briefs, students had also participated in literature groups, reading science fiction stories about extraterrestrial life. Ms. Sprague's students were very interested in thinking about life other than that on Earth.

Next, students had studied the biological systems of life-forms. As a final challenge for that unit, Ms. Sprague had had a package delivered to class from a research institute in her state telling students about a message from space. The scientists' letter told the students they thought the message was about a faraway life-form. The package had included small bags of lego-like components the scientists thought were the body parts of the life-form. They asked students to assemble those parts into viable life-forms and write descriptions of the forms in terms of the biological systems. Students had completed the activity by drawing representations of their space creatures to scale. The scientists' letter told them each of the components had been built to a scale of 1 to 13. The cute little lego-like space creatures turned out to be 5 to 7 feet tall depending on how students had assembled the parts. Students had called these life-forms the Zerkonians.

As part of their social studies curriculum, students had been studying the state of New Mexico. They had explored the state's history, its government, and its cultures. Embedded throughout all the units, Ms. Sprague had designed lessons that focused students' attention on the process for using information. They had worked with the Internet, the library, and a range of informal information sources. They had learned to use a variety of software tools to organize and present information. During Ms. Sprague's Friday morning current affairs lessons, students had talked about judging information for its validity and reliability and talked about sorting through all the information available to them to determine what was important and useful and what was not. What she needed now was a lesson to end the year that tied all these threads together.

An idea finally occurred to her. She would create a WebQuest and post it to the school district's Web site. Her students could use the Internet connections in the computer lab to access the WebQuest. In designing her WebQuest, Ms. Sprague wanted to end the year with a unit on contemporary New Mexico. In this way, her students would bring their study of New Mexico to a close by exploring the state as it exists today. She would use their interest in extraterrestrial beings as well as their knowledge of biological systems and space as a framework. And, the WebQuest would bring together all that students had learned about the process of using information. Students would be searching a large and varied set of information resources available in their classroom, in the school library, and on the Internet. The WebQuest identified a number of sites that students could use to collect information. Any boldface word or phrase in the WebQuest represented a link to a set of sites related to that word or phrase. For example, when students clicked on **Car Rentals—Information and Reservation,** they could connect to Web sites such as Thrifty Car Rental (http://www.thrify.com). When they clicked on **Native American Places of Interest,** they could select to visit the Pueblo Cultural Center's home page and go from there to a Web page on each of New Mexico's pueblos (http://hanksville.phast.umass.edu/defs/independent/PCC/PCC.html#toc). When they clicked on **Hotel/Motel Accommodations,** they could check on accommodations provided by a variety of hotel/motel companies including Best Western (http://bestwestern.com/best.html). The Zerkonian Web page is located at http://mason.gmu.edu/~pnorton/Zerkon.html and presented in Figure 7.1.

On Monday morning, five weeks before school ended for the year, students arrived at class to find a huge banner across the front of the room. The Zerkonians

zerkon.html - Microsoft Internet Explorer provided by StarBand

File Edit View Favorites Tools Help

Back • ➡ • ⊗ ⊡ ⌂ | Search Favorites History | ⧉ • ⬛ W • ⬛ ⬙ ⬙

Address http://mason.gmu.edu/~pnorton/Zerkon.html ▼ Go Links »

President Bush's Web Site:

The Zerkonians Are Coming!

Introduction

Humans have long awaited news of life in outer space. Scientists have looked for evidence of life on planets other than Earth. Science fiction writers have tried to imagine what it would be like if we encountered new life-forms. Moviemakers have created movie extravaganzas like *Independence Day*. Well, news has finally arrived. The Zerkonians are coming!

President Bush has just released a letter to all students announcing the arrival of space creatures called Zerkonians. The Zerkonians have beamed a message to Earth that they will be arriving in the United States very soon. They have sent a request to the White House asking for a range of possible guided tours of each of the 50 states in the United States. They would like to receive at least six different plans from each state so that they can review them, ask questions about them, and decide which tour they would like to take of each state. The Zerkonians, of course, will pay for their tour of each state so they need to know not only about the tour schedule but also about the cost of each tour.

What's Known About the Zerkonians' Visit

The Zerkonians will be on Earth for 200 days—that is the sequence of available descent and launch windows. They have requested that they be permitted to see each state in the United States. That works out to four days in each state. They will be arriving at the New Mexico/Arizona border west of Gallop at 9:00 A.M. They need to be at the Las Cruces/El Paso border at 9:00 A.M. the morning of the fifth day ready for a four-day tour of Texas.

Wishes for Visit: While in each state, the Zerkonians have asked to see an example of at least one of each of the following: an example of a traditional industry, an example of a new electronic-based business, a scientific endeavor, something related to the three cultures of New Mexico, something to do with political life, something to do with each state's history, something to do with religion and/or religious ceremony, something geological, something environmental, and the opportunity

FIGURE **7.1**

A ZERKONIAN WEBQUEST

Source: Screenshot reprinted with permission from Microsoft. All rights reserved.

FIGURE 7.1 (*CONTINUED*)

to purchase souvenirs. In addition, some Zerkonian attributes you need to be aware of include:

Sleep/Wake Patterns: The Zerkonians' biorhythms cycle in nine-hour blocks. Thus, they are awake for six hours; then asleep for three; then awake for six hours; then asleep for three hours. They will be starting a wake period when they arrive in your state. They do not need time for elaborate preparations for their waking or sleeping periods, but they do need to lay down to sleep.

Nutrition: The Zerkonians eat one meal during each waking period, preferably at the wake period's beginning. They like, but do not demand, a short snack before sleep. The Zerkonian diet is somewhat flexible. However, they do require one meal once in every three waking periods that provides some sort of seafood, and one meal once in every three waking periods that is high in fat.

Hygiene: One time during their visit in your state, the Zerkonians must have the opportunity to bathe and eliminate. In order to accomplish these functions, the Zerkonians must remove their outer protective covering. This can be done only when they are submerged in at least 30 feet of water. In between times, the Zerkonians will need access once in every three waking periods to nitrous oxide (laughing gas) that they will insert underneath their protective covering. All other considerations must be dealt with as they arise during the course of the trip. We are aware of no other requirements for which special preparation must be made.

The Task

President Bush is asking you, on behalf of your country, to assist him. He is asking you and three of your classmates to prepare a guided tour to show the Zerkonians your home state. Of course, your tour will have to be designed to meet all the Zerkonians' needs. It should include stops that meet all the Zerkonians' requirements for the kinds of things they would like to see as well as meeting their sleep/wake patterns and their nutritional and hygiene needs.

Carefully read all the steps to creating a prospectus included in THE PROCESS before you begin. When you have read through all the steps, use an idea processor like the Inspiration program on your classroom computers to plan out all the things you need to do and decide who in your group is going to be responsible for each part of your prospectus. When you have charted all the components and determined who is going to be responsible for each, arrange a group meeting with your teacher to explain your plan. Then, begin researching and planning a tour of New Mexico for the Zerkonians. Your tour will be presented to the Zerkonians as a tour prospectus.

FIGURE **7.1** (*CONTINUED*)

The Process

Steps to Complete a Tour Prospectus for the Zerkonians:

Step 1: Construct your Inspiration organization plan and have it approved by your teacher.

Step 2: Create a chart that identifies the exact times that relate to the sleep/wake patterns of the Zerkonians.

Step 3: Using your research skills, create a list of all the places in New Mexico that you might take the Zerkonians. Make sure you identify plenty of options to meet the Zerkonians' requirements for the kinds of things they would like to see.

Step 4: Using your research from Step 3, create a tour for the Zerkonians. Be sure that they visit at least one place that meets each of their requirements. Be sure you plan stops for nutritional breaks, hygiene breaks, and sleeping breaks. In New Mexico, you can plan to travel about 50 miles in one hour. Be sure that you include travel time from place to place.

Step 5: Prepare a trip prospectus for the Zerkonians. Use the following outline for creating your prospectus:

   a.) A cover for your prospectus. Use any graphics program you choose.
   b.) A table of contents (a word processor works here).
   c.) A text-based overview of the trip. Capture your clients' attention. Include an outline of the trip indicating sleep/wake times, bathing opportunities, and times when fat and seafood will be available (a word processor works here).
   d.) A graphic overview of the trip. Use a scanned image of a map of New Mexico, a graphics program, or create a flowchart using a program like Inspiration.
   e.) A chronological description of the stops on the trip. Tell the Zerkonians where they will be going, what they will see, and some interesting information about each stop on the tour (a word processor works here).
   f.) A detailed cost analysis with all expenses included. Include a total for the trip as well. A printed copy of a spreadsheet would work well here.
   g.) A visual presentation of the highlights of your tour. ClarisWorks Slide Show or a PowerPoint presentation would work well here.

FIGURE 7.1 (*CONTINUED*)

Step 6: Be prepared to make a presentation to the Zerkonians. Ask your teacher when the presentation and a copy of your prospectus should be ready.

Resources

A variety of resources are available to you to assist in completing your tour prospectus.

Library Resources

You may request a pass from your teacher to go to your school library. The librarian has been told about your project and will help you if you ask.

Computer Resources

A wide range of software resources are available on the classroom computers including several graphics programs, Inspiration, PowerPoint, and the ClarisWorks and Microsoft integrated packages.

Internet Resources

The following boldface topics are buttons to a variety of Internet Resources that you can use to gather information. Each button takes you to a list of sites on various aspects of the broader category identified by the button title.

CityNet—Find Information about Cities Worldwide
Car Rentals—Information and Reservations
Hotel/Motel Accommodations—Information and Reservations
National Parks, Monuments, and Forests
Scientific and Research Sites in New Mexico
Native American Places of Interest
Additional Sites of Interest Related to Different Cities in New Mexico
Automobile Manufacturers

Learning Advice

For your team's project to really come together, it is important to create an overall plan first, clearly deciding exactly all the things that must be done and who will take the lead in making sure that they get done. Present your plan to your teacher who will help you make sure you have identified all the things you need to do and realistically divided responsibility for those things among your group members.

Even though you assign responsibility for the finished product to different people in your group, it will take a lot of close group work and sharing of information. Many of the items in the process will need to be completed and agreed upon by the whole group. This will take detailed and supported discussion among all your team members.

Conclusion

Plan a presentation and be prepared to present to the Zerkonians about the tour you have planned for them. The Zerkonian representatives will be joining us for the presentations.

Done   Internet

Are Coming, it shouted. As students settled into their seats, the questions began. "When?" "Where?" "How do you know?" "Because I received a letter this weekend," Ms. Sprague responded. "From who?" they yelled. "Read it to us," they pleaded. So, Ms. Sprague read them a letter from President Bush telling the students that he had received information that the Zerkonians were coming to visit the United States. The letter asked them to please help make the Zerkonians' visit a pleasant one by creating a tour of their state for the Zerkonians. The students knew the letter was another of Ms. Sprague's tricks, but her tricks always led to interesting learning. Besides, the students knew that the Zerkonians were really coming even if they were not coming from space. The letter ended by referring them to a World Wide Web address. Ms. Sprague could hardly coax students to get through the morning business and pledge before they set out for the lab.

Once in the school's lab, students eagerly located the Web site listed in the President's letter and studied the WebQuest. The class had a discussion about the WebQuest. Ms. Sprague helped them understand exactly what the task and the process were. She told the class that after lunch a travel agent was coming to visit to show them examples of a tour prospectus. Sure enough, after lunch a travel agent visited the class, showing students what a table of contents, a text-based overview, a graphic overview, a chronological description of stops, a budget analysis, and a presentation were. The travel agent brought examples for students to look at that included a trip to Europe she had planned for a family of four and a trip to Asia she had planned for a study group from the local university.

For the next four weeks, students worked diligently on their tour prospectus. As Ms. Sprague watched, she was able to observe students searching through the online and off-line resources. She was able to observe as they sorted through all the information. After all, in four days, students could not take the Zerkonians to every geological point of interest in New Mexico. They had to carefully sort through their choices and judge them against the time constraints of the visit and all the constraints posed by the Zerkonians' strange sleep/wake patterns and hygiene and nutritional needs. She watched as they carefully created images, text, and numeric solutions to problems and as they crafted their creations into a form that would communicate to the Zerkonians the wonderful trips they were planning. The WebQuest had embedded the SSCC Process, and Ms. Sprague's students did well.

And, the Zerkonians did arrive on the designated date. Ms. Sprague made arrangements with students in an introduction to computers for teachers course at the local university to dress up as space aliens. Two of the prospective teachers from the university class reviewed a group's prospectus, participated in a teleconference with that group, listened to their videoconference presentation, and asked questions about their prospectus. Each group from Ms. Sprague's class had the opportunity to present and converse with two Zerkonians. The university students did a wonderful job of playing space aliens and even created very funny and clever answers to Ms. Sprague's students' questions about what it was like to be a Zerkonian. It was the perfect way to end the school year.

Information and the Virtual Classroom

In Chapter 5—Designs for Problem Solving—we introduced Harris's (1998b) notion of activity structures—flexible frameworks that instructional designers can use to generate powerful learning environments. In the previous section of this chapter, we presented an activity structure we have found particularly useful—the WebQuest. To this structure, Harris has added five additional Internet-based structures to use when designing opportunities for students to refine their information-using abilities. These five information collection and analysis structures include information exchanges, database creation, electronic publishing, telefieldtrips, and pooled data analysis. We will also share one of Harris's examples of each structure, but we want to echo Harris's caution. These examples are presented to illustrate the structure not to be a "plug and play" solution for your own classroom. Challenge yourself to think of ways in which you can use the frameworks to design your own learning opportunities.

Information Exchanges.   Information exchanges engage students in intrinsically interesting, authentic cultural interchange. These exchanges can involve many classes and are particularly appropriate for telecomputing tools because participating students become creators, consumers, and critics of the information they share. David Warlick's yearly *Global Grocery List Project* (http://www.landmark-project.com/ ggl.html) invites students from around the world to find and share the prices for items on a common, virtual shopping list. Individual classes can then use the resulting price lists to discover which items are more or less expensive in which places. Once they have identified pricing patterns, students can research and discuss reasons for the differences.

Database Creation.   Some projects involve students from a wide range of places in both the collecting and organizing of information. As the amount of information from the varied sources is shared, students must decide how to organize the information so that it can be manipulated. Databases are the result. Many projects support adding additional information each year and soon present students with opportunities to interpret information for patterns over time. One long-running database creation project is *KidLink's Multicultural Calendar* (http://www.kidlink.org/KIDPROJ/MCC/). The project began in 1994. Since then, students from many different countries have contributed information about holidays in their own countries. Records in the database encourage students to report specific information—month, holiday, user-supplied keywords, and author. Harris (1998b, p. 6) states: "This rich and well-organized collection of student-produced information has many possible uses in the classroom."

Electronic Publishing.   High-speed Internet access and the growing number of Internet authoring tools have made electronic publishing projects possible for students in all grade levels. The appeal of an international audience is a powerful experience. The challenge is making sure that a wide audience is aware and has access to students' publications. There are many publishing projects that students can participate in. One of the best-known examples is *MidLink Magazine* (http://longwood. cs.ucf.edu/~MidLink/), a quarterly e-zine for students ages 10 through 15. Harris (1998b, p. 7) describes the February and March 1997 edition.

> . . . contributors encouraged readers to think about dreams for peace in honor of Dr. Martin Luther King, Jr. Other sections in the publication included an egg hunt, a haiku exchange with students in Japan, and a virtual quilt that invited visitors to 'curl up by the fire . . . and drink a cup of hot chocolate with your cyberfriends.' The quilt was virtually created with student-contributed squares and stories that represented their countries, states, and territories.

Telefieldtrips.   Telefieldtrips help students experience information from a distance. Telefieldtrips open the virtual door to rich multimedia experiences. So far, there are two types of telefieldtrips. The first is where students take a local field trip and then share their experiences directly with other students electronically. Often, remote classes submit questions that on-site participants try to answer. One example is the Hong Kong International School's *Virtual China* (http://www.kidlink.org/ KIDPROJ/VChina97/). This weeklong telefieldtrip included a group of seventh graders who visited southern China by bicycle and another group that studied in the ancient capitol city of Xi'an. Both groups kept in touch with preregistered classes using both e-mail and a question forum hosted by the KIDPROJ site.

The second, more popular, type of telefieldtrip is a virtual expedition. Organized around research or historical projects usually undertaken by adults, online participants experience the expedition electronically. Sometimes these online participants remotely join the inquiry process. One of the best-known examples is *MayaQuest* (http://www.classroom.com/login/landing.jhtml;jsessionid=KEMYNQ3FK5KP3QF IAJICFEQ?_requestid=58126). Classes that subscribe to the project interact with explorers traveling in the rain forests and Mayan ruins and help them solve the problems they encounter in their work.

Pooled Data Analysis.   In the virtual activities representative of this activity structure, students in various remote locations gather and share similar data from different locations and then analyze the patterns that emerge from the combined samples. In the simplest of these activities, students electronically issue a survey, collect responses, analyze results, and share their findings. Pooled data analysis activities have also included examples where students collect environmental data at many different sites, then combine and analyze the data to reveal patterns that solve environmental challenges. *EnvironNet*-sponsored projects (http://earth.simmons.edu/) are among the best designed and best supported (Harris, 1998b).

In this chapter, we explored the contemporary information environment, focusing on the information explosion and the dangers of information overload. We saw how this information environment challenges educators to design learning opportunities for students to master information-using skills within the framework of an integrated and a process approach. Information skills were described as (1) the ability to search for relevant information based on an understanding of which resources yield what kinds of information, (2) the ability to sort through and judge information for its reliability, validity, and relevance, and (3) the ability to create and communicate the ways in which information has been used to solve problems and inform the conduct of life. In the next chapter, we will explore the importance of designing learning opportunities that help students participate in virtual, collaborative, cooperative, and democratic communities.

Before moving on to Chapter 8, we recommend that you go to the FACTS Web-Based Design Tool site (http://www.norton.wadsworth.com) and click on the Design Mentors puzzle piece. This chapter's Design Mentors demonstrate how Brooks White and Allan Sutton consider how they can support students' abilities to search, sort, create, and communicate as they develop their information using skills. It is interesting to note the differences in Ms. White's and Mr. Sutton's approach. Information using is an overt part of Mr. Sutton's design as students work as detectives. For Ms. White's students, information using is a covert part of her design. Ms. White's students are refining their search, sorting, creating, and communicating skills even though they are not receiving direct instruction. After you have studied the Design Mentors, you might find it helpful to return to the opening page of the Web site and complete Design Challenge Seven. You can also examine some of the Design Examples and see how they reflect the considerations discussed in this chapter.

CHAPTER IDEAS

- More information has been produced in the last 30 years than in the previous 5,000 years. A thousand new book titles are published each day throughout the world, and the total of all printed knowledge is doubling every eight years. Information in the sciences doubles approximately every 5.5 years. Electronically stored information available online has grown an astonishing 700 percent between 1980 and 1990. The information age forces us to face massive amounts of information transmitted at accelerating speeds.
- What is most needed now is not more information but the power to manage the information we already have.
- In a society where information is becoming our most important resource, educators are faced with the problem of designing learning opportunities for students that assist them to make sense of the complex information environments they encounter.
- Information skills should not be taught in isolation. The skills program must be fully integrated with the school's curriculum. In addition, essential information skills encompass more than just location of and

access to sources. The skills curriculum should emphasize general information problem-solving and research processes and the specific skills within these general processes.

- Using an integrated approach to teaching information skills refers to the teaching of such skills in the context of subject area curriculum and classroom learning. This approach requires that instruction be tied to real needs. This is a major change from traditional, often isolated, bibliographic instruction, which frequently takes place independent of any classroom activities or assignments. Integrated instruction gives students skills for coping with topics of study and life situations.

- Traditionally, teaching students to cope with information focused on skills related to sources: locating, accessing, and using a variety of information sources. These isolated, library-dependent skills were frequently taught out of subject context, without any formal, articulated curricular framework. In recent years, a newer approach to skills instruction has emerged, one that centers on a process approach to information skills.

- A process approach does not depend on any particular source or library. Instead, the emphasis is on developing transferable cognitive skills that should increase students' effective use of information in general as well as their use of specific libraries, reference materials, online databases, and Internet sources.

- The process of being an information user is not linear. Problems are defined not as first steps in the information-using process, but within the frame of disciplinary and interdisciplinary inquiry. Problem definition is not the first step in the process of using information, but the reason one seeks to use information.

- Not all aspects of a process for effective use of information can be mastered or learned within one curricular unit. There may be times when a design for learning to be an information user is best focused on one aspect of the process for using information rather than on the entire process.

- Process skills for effective information use are best embedded in three general categories of activity—searching for information, sorting and judging information, and creating and communicating ideas and concepts as the result of information use (SSCC). Each of these activities can be supported by a range of tools, related to a particular problem arising within the domain of particular content areas, and embedded within designs for learning knowledge, literacy, and problem-solving abilities.

- Skills associated with effective searching include the ability to develop a broad overview of a topic, to integrate broad concepts by developing a basic understanding of words and related concepts that expand the topic, to locate information providers, to identify information resources and tools, and to search for relevant information. These skills are elaborated and extended by the development of the ability to narrow the topic, to develop specific questions and a thesis, and to plan a search strategy.

Effective searchers learn to identify the location and function of information resource facilities.

- Effective searchers recognize that the development of an appropriate search strategy lies at the core of effective searching. They know how to conduct browsing searches, hypertext searches, hierarchical searches, or analytical searches. They have learned to clearly define the kind of information they need, the most likely sources for such information, and an appropriate search strategy.

- To be an effective sorter, students must be prepared to judge the validity of the information they have gathered or encountered in the conduct of their lives. Cross-media checking (same medium, but different source) and intermedia confirmation (different medium) are among the most reliable strategies for verifying information. Thus, sorters use cross-referencing to sort and judge information.

- Good information sorters assess information for its reliability, validity, and usefulness as well as use information to develop personal meaning. Among the many subskills used by effective sorters are paraphrasing, inferring, drawing conclusions, comparing and contrasting, determining credibility, understanding cause and effect, connecting concepts, determining patterns, trends, similarities, and differences, and detecting bias.

- Students must learn processes for using information that lead to the creation and communication of ideas. To use information to create, students must be fluent at combining disparate information in order to generate knowledge, to find solutions, and to make decisions.

- The process skills associated with using information to effectively create concepts, ideas, and knowledge are integrally linked to the communication process. In the process of structuring communication in ways that permit others to understand and interact with emerging ideas, students must bring order to the disorder of isolated pieces of information.

- To be an effective communicator, students must learn to share both raw information and the results of their creating. They must be presented with opportunities that lead to proficiency with the kinds of communication skills required by the social dialogue. In the act of using information to design effective communication, students need to learn to choose an appropriate style, format, and medium.

- Just as the overall information-using process can be represented by the acronym SSCC, the creating and communicating part of that process can be represented by the acronym DEAPR—designing, encoding, assembling, publishing, and revising.

- As educators work to design learning opportunities for students to become effective users of information, there are times when it is appropriate to design learning opportunities that focus on various aspects of the information-using process. There are other times, however, when the design of learning opportunities must engage students with the entire process. A WebQuest is one powerful way to design learning opportunities that bring the whole process together.

DESIGNS FOR COMMUNITY

So many of the students in my eighth-grade math class are having trouble even though I am spending a lot of time preparing good lectures and selecting reinforcing homework assigned from their textbooks. Students today seem to have more trouble learning mathematics than in the past. Some of my students are new to this country and maybe their lack of English makes things especially hard for them. Or, perhaps, all the time students spend watching television and playing computer games makes them less willing to absorb lectures. Maybe assuming that students' learning depends primarily on individual initiative, aptitude, and hard work is a poor assumption. Whatever the reason, I am just not satisfied with what and how my students are learning.

Several days ago, I was thinking about my students' disappointing performance as I hurried to the hospital after school to visit a friend. When I arrived, my friend was in the X-ray department so I wandered down to the cafeteria for some coffee. As I walked through the hospital, I noticed that everywhere I looked people were working in small groups. No one was sitting in rows of desks, raising their hands, and listening to only one person. Two nurses were bent over a chart near a doctor discussing a case. Other nurses at the nursing station were individually jotting down notes on charts, but even they stopped frequently to consult with another nurse or aide about what they were writing. They were using computers to look up information, telephones to clarify problems, and adding machines for complex calculations. I had never really noticed before how different work in the world is from what work in school is. I'm thinking of giving my students math problems related to the world of work and then encouraging them to solve those problems in small groups. Maybe there is something to the things I had been reading about classrooms as communities of learners.

Paula Froud
Middle School
Math Teacher

Traditional views of learning hold that all learning and knowledge happens in the heads of individuals. More recent views recognize the contributions of tools, people, beliefs, practices, and attitudes to cognition and learning. Learning is not an isolated event; it is the result of collective actions and experiences embedded in local settings and cultural contexts. Schools should be communities where students learn to learn. In this setting, teachers are models of intentional learning and self-motivated scholarship, both individual and collaborative. Graduates of such communities are lifelong learners who have learned how to learn in many domains. In a community of learners, teachers and students are role models not "owners" of some aspect of knowledge. They are acquirers, users, and extenders of knowledge in a sustained, ongoing process of understanding.

Today's students must learn to draw on the strengths of communities and be prepared to contribute to these communities. They must learn the social skills necessary for working within communities. This chapter explores five categories of community interactions. It presents examples of how teachers have designed opportunities for learning that both help students learn the rules associated with the patterns of organization embedded in each form of interaction and allow students to draw on the strengths of these interactions to become learners. The chapter begins with a discussion of community and its role in learning and then examines (1) communities of diverse learners, (2) cooperative communities, (3) collaborative communities, (4) democratic communities, and (5) virtual communities.

COMMUNITIES OF LEARNERS

In today's challenging and evolving world, the goals of schooling are changing. As we have seen in previous chapters, it is no longer enough for students to be able to read and write print. They must be able to use a varied set of symbolic forms, discourse forms, and cognitive processes. It is no longer possible for students to know everything there is to know. Instead, they must understand the structures and processes associated with disciplinary knowledge and learn to "do" the disciplines—to act as historians, scientists, economists, and politicians. They must learn to be problem-solvers, using a range of cognitive strategies to shape the conduct of their lives. It is no longer students' primary task to locate information. Students must learn to be searchers, sorters, creators, and communicators.

As the goals of schooling move beyond mastery of discrete skills and traditional conceptions of the academic disciplines, what should constitute authentic learning in the classroom? Brown (1992) and Scardamalia and Bereiter (1991) argue that schools should be communities where students learn to learn. In this setting, teachers are models of intentional learning and self-motivated scholarship, both individual and collaborative. Graduates of such communities are lifelong learners who have learned how to learn in many domains. These "intellectual novices" are students who, although they may not possess the background knowledge needed in a new field, know how to go about gaining that knowledge. These learning experts are prepared to be inducted into the culture of practice they choose and have the background to select among several alternative practitioner cultures (Brown, Bransford, Ferrara, & Campione, 1983). In a community of learners, teachers and students are role models not "owners" of some aspect of knowledge. They are acquirers, users, and extenders of knowledge in a sustained, ongoing process of understanding. Students become apprentice learners,

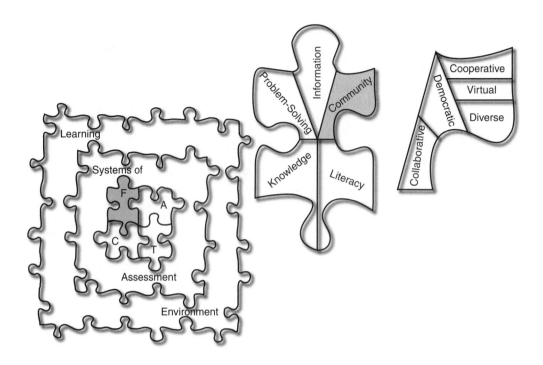

learning how to think and reason in a variety of knowledge domains, using the power of others to support individual and collective goals.

Attributes of Communities

A community of learners depends on community of kinship, place, and mind. Community of kinship emerges from the kinds of relationships among people that create a unity of being, similar to that found in families and other closely knit collections of people. Community of place emerges from the sharing of a common habitat or locale for sustained periods. Community of mind emerges from the bonding of people around common goals, shared values, and shared conceptions of being and doing (Tonnies, 1957). Together, the three kinds of community represent webs of meaning that link diverse groups of people by creating among them a sense of belonging and a common identity as human beings capable of affection and caring for others as well as themselves (Sergiovanni, 1994). "America's future," writes Corrigan (1995, p. 2), "depends on the ability of its citizens to create healthy, humane communities and on the commitment of its leaders to act on the values embodied in such communities."

A classroom climate that fosters a community of learners is built on four main qualities. The first is an atmosphere of individual responsibility coupled with communal sharing. Students and teachers each have "ownership" of certain forms of expertise but no one has it all. Responsible members of the community share the expertise they have or take responsibility for finding out about needed knowledge.

Through a variety of interactive formats, the group uncovers and delineates aspects of knowledge possessed by no one individual. The second is respect among students, between students and teachers, and among members of the extended community of experts. Respect is earned by responsible participation in a genuine knowledge-building community. Students, teachers, and extended community members take turns and listen to one another. Third, a community of discourse is established in which constructive discussion, questioning, and criticism are the mode rather than the exception. Meaning is negotiated and renegotiated as members of the community develop and share expertise. The group comes to construct new understandings, developing a common mind and a common voice. Fourth, a community of learners shares rituals—patterns of organization and interaction. These rituals are few and are practiced repeatedly so that students, teachers, and observers can tell immediately what format the class is operating under at any one period of time. The ritualistic nature of the community's activities enables students to make the transition from one pattern to another quickly and effortlessly. As soon as students recognize a particular pattern, they understand the role expected of them and can navigate between activities with ease (Brown, et al., 1993).

Cognition and Community

The traditional view of cognition rests on a view of intelligence framed by three basic characteristics. First, intelligence is a single, general problem-solving ability generalized from setting to setting. Second, intelligence is located inside the head of each individual. Third, the intelligence of each individual is relatively stable from one situation and setting to another. This view, however, is being challenged. Hatch and Gardner (1993) suggest that factors or forces at three different levels— personal, local, and cultural—contribute to create cognition in the classroom. They envision the personal, local, and cultural forces at work in any situation as interacting to shape the activity and skills of all learners. Changes in the forces at any one of these levels contribute to changes both in what learners do and in what they are capable of doing.

Cultural forces are the institutions, practices, and beliefs that transcend particular settings and affect a large number of individuals. Cultural forces have three principal effects on behavior. These forces influence the kinds of skills people can exhibit, the way those skills are developed, and the purposes to which those skills are directed. Thus, for example, children in American classrooms who use their spatial skills for imaginative drawing might use their spatial skills for navigation, tracking, or some other culturally valued activity if transported to another culture. Even in a culture like China where drawing is valued, children are taught to meticulously copy a picture according to a teacher's instructions instead of encouraged to use drawing to express themselves more freely. Such differences in classroom activities contribute to differences in artistic development (Gardner, 1989) as well as differences in academic achievement (Stevenson, Lee, & Sigler, 1986).

Local forces focus on those resources and people who directly affect the behavior of an individual within a specific local setting such as the home, the classroom, and the workplace. When the role of local forces in cognition is acknowledged, it becomes apparent that little is accomplished by individuals who work in isolation. Instead, individuals depend on a wide variety of tools, people, and other resources to help carry out their activities. These "facts of the environment" function to both shape and support the kinds of activities and skills in which individuals can engage. At this level, it is proper to think of intelligence as shared by individuals and all the human and nonhuman resources they use.

The attributes and experiences students bring with them to learning are the personal forces. While traditional models of intelligence and learning have focused on general problem-solving ability, they have failed to take into account the wide variation in people's abilities and the vast array of individual differences that influence the development of those abilities. From a more pluralistic perspective, both genetic proclivities and personal experiences within a given culture influence the activities in which students choose to become involved and the abilities they subsequently develop. Although the interconnectedness of genetic proclivities and personal experiences is difficult to unravel, it is possible to identify them as personal forces that influence children and are carried from one local setting to another.

Intelligence, then, is enmeshed in all of a person's activities and embedded in the settings and cultures in which those activities are carried out. Cultural, local, and personal forces are interdependent. An individual's intelligences, interests, and concerns are formed in interactions with peers, family members, and teachers, constrained by available materials, and influenced by cultural values and expectations (Hatch & Gardner, 1993). Educators who seek to design opportunities for students to learn must, therefore, recognize the role of personal, local, and cultural forces in shaping the learning community. They must both use the power of that community to support learning and help students learn to participate in and contribute to that community.

TECHNOLOGY IN DIVERSE CLASSROOMS

Today's classrooms are a microcosm of an ever-increasing world of diversity. In the year 2010, one-third of the nation's children will live in just four states—California, Texas, New York, and Florida—with "minority" children becoming the majority in these school populations (Hodgkinson, 1992). By the year 2020, one-half of the nation's school children will be non-European American (Au, 1993), and one-quarter will be Hispanic (Darder, Ingle, & Cox, 1993). Yet, even though classroom populations reflect this changed world, the curriculum used in most schools is based on materials and instructional strategies developed in the first half of the twentieth century when nearly three-fourths of all students were European Americans (Pallas, Natriello, & McDill, 1989) and the country's human resource needs were the product of an industrial rather than an information age. This curriculum is inappropriate in both content and activities for today's and tomorrow's student populations and is often in direct conflict with many students' cultures and community lives (Darder, Ingle, & Cox, 1993).

Many teachers lack strategies for incorporating the richness available within diverse cultures to build, rather than stifle, student learning (Au, 1993). Many still possess attitudes that consciously or unconsciously see culturally or linguistically different students as lazy rather than as students whose knowledge and skills may be hidden by various barriers. While some educators have characterized the "at-risk" student as lacking a broad range of learning abilities, others argue that the curriculum is deficient, providing only limited avenues for learning to which some students may not have access (Joyce, Weil, & Showers, 1992). As Toffler (1983) asked:

> Today as industrialized civilization passes into history, powerful voices demand to know whether the emergent civilization will find room in it for the millions, indeed, billions on the earth who today are discriminated against, harassed or oppressed because of their racial, ethnic, national or religious backgrounds. Are the poor and powerless of the past going to stay that way, viewing the future, as it were, through bullet-proof glass—or will they be welcome in the new civilization we are creating?

Technology can be used to oppress. In the Philippines in 1986, Acquino's "peoples' power movement" might not have succeeded in overthrowing the old dictatorship without the support of the world powers watching on television. Romanian leaders were aware of the potential power of technology to the extent that every typewriter in that country had to be registered with the government. In Russia, copy machines were kept under lock and key and sheets of paper numbered and accounted for. For many years, it was illegal to bring microcomputers into the Soviet Union. The telephone system in East Berlin was intentionally limited to the technology of the 1930s so that the secret police could easily listen to conversations. In 1981, telecommunications in Poland was still simple enough that the government was able to isolate its people from the rest of the world in order to crack down on Solidarity, a popular peoples' movement.

Technology can also be used to liberate. In 1991, enough technology had been smuggled into the Soviet Union—fax machines, modems, and microcomputers—that when the old-line Communist party tried to overthrow Gorbachev they were unable to isolate Russia from the rest of the world. Faxes were sent; desktop-published posters appeared in the subways; and television broadcasts around the world helped Yeltsin to stop the coup. Technology presents us with a double-edged sword. Its power to oppress or to liberate pivots on who has access and how that technology is used.

While technology can be liberating and can provide the tools needed for diverse students to succeed in school, technology has not been used well with diverse populations nor is it shared equally by students. Fears that technology is potentially just another tool for the oppression of underrepresented and female students are not unfounded. Educators' assumptions about the use of technology with certain groups of students serves to place many students at a disadvantage (Harrington, 1993). Research suggests that educational computer use is much less frequent among groups other than White males and high-ability-level students. It is "indisputable that the classroom computer is not shared equally" (Skelle, 1993, p. 15).

Students of Lower Socioeconomic Status

Tracking remains an implicit part of the curriculum and, in general, students in high-achievement classes use computers quite differently from those in low-achievement classes. Levy, Navon, and Shapira (1991) found that in those schools where the majority of students are of lower social economic status (SES), drill and practice programs comprised the highest percentage of computing assignments. Drouyn-Marrero (1989) found that Anglo students were given significantly more access to computers in schools than Hispanic and African American students. Dutton, Rogers, and Jun (1987) surveyed the uses of computers with poor students and compared them with those provided to wealthier students and concluded that wealthier students direct the computer while poor students are directed by it.

Minority Students

Hunt and Pritchard (1993) report that fewer than 25 percent of teachers currently teaching minority students use technology in their teaching. Teachers report modifying instruction for limited-English speakers, but they do not report modifications involving the use of technology. Even when teachers report regular classroom access to computers and use them regularly with their students, more than half of them report never using computers with language minority students. Those who do use computers with language minority students state that these students use computers mostly for drill and practice in language arts and mathematics.

Contrary to popular myth, drill and practice for students who are not doing well in school may be especially demoralizing. In a study of elementary students, Hativa (1988) reported a differential impact of drill and practice programs for lower-achieving as compared with higher-achieving students with higher-achieving students receiving more benefit. Likewise, the kinds of drill and practice programs that direct these low-achieving and poor students present special problems for those who need to learn English as well as content. These students tend to get stuck in loops, and because their problem may be language rather than conceptual understanding, they do not receive the benefit they should from these programs. Nord (1986) has developed successful interactive multimedia environments for language learning in Japan. He argues that language learning is an interactive process in which content must be placed in context. It is difficult for either textbooks or drill programs to provide a context for learning language. However, technology tools tied to new teaching strategies can provide interactive, context-rich multimedia environments supportive of communicative language learning (Mergendoller & Pardo, 1991).

Questions of Equity

Problems of equity are influenced by issues related to gender, race, and socioeconomic status. Researchers have found that girls continue to receive less attention from classroom teachers than boys and are less likely to enroll in higher-level mathematics, science, and technology courses. Girls have less access to computers than boys (Stanford Research Institute, 1992). African American girls have fewer interactions with teachers than White girls, even though they attempt to initiate interactions more often (American Association of University Women Educational Association, 1992). Girls from low-income families face additional obstacles because SES, more than any other variable, affects access to school resources and educational outcomes.

Despite trends in the misuse of technology and schools' seeming unwillingness to alter instruction to meet the needs of increasingly diverse student populations, different instructional approaches and appropriate uses of technology can be effective in promoting learning among traditionally underrepresented students. Teachers can design learning experiences that are responsive to the needs of diverse students, that create communities of learners, and that use technology to liberate rather than oppress.

Tapping Funds of Knowledge

Students in diverse communities have vast "funds of knowledge" related to science, mathematics, and social studies (Moll & Greenberg, 1992; Goldenberg & Gallimore, 1991). In fact, all students possess a rich social network that could be supportive of learning. However, these "funds" remain largely untapped in schools where children's knowledge and aptitudes are hidden behind cultural, ethnic, or linguistic barriers. This is especially true in the areas of mathematics and science where ethnically diverse students consistently perform significantly less well than same-grade White students (National Assessment of Educational Progress, 1990). Many children living in the rural Southwest, for example, are engaged in raising animals and crops, building shelters, assisting in family stores and businesses, and repairing equipment. Yet, this knowledge rarely finds its way into the science or mathematics classroom.

All children need to see people from diverse cultures valued in the materials they work with in schools. A new kind of curriculum is needed—a curriculum grounded in an instructional approach that considers students' diverse languages and cultures as valuable sources of knowledge. How do educators choose culturally relevant learning experiences for students? One way is to focus on universal themes: survival, justice, conflict resolution, friendship, or betrayal. Such themes reflect the questions that touch the human condition and provide a way to cross cultures as different perspectives within each group bring life to students' inquiry. Literature drawn from many cultures can provide a rich resource for exploring universal themes.

Another way to decide what content to use in the development of thematic units is to look to the latest standards and frameworks developed by national curriculum leader groups such as the National Council of Teachers of Mathematics (1993) or the American Association for the Advancement of Science (1993). In standards-based instruction, teachers are advised to teach big ideas and unifying themes. In mathematics class, children are encouraged to explore patterns, ratio, and measurement as opposed to filling in another worksheet with limited correct answers. The new science themes of interaction, scale, and change provide a rich framework for thematic lesson development.

Mrs. Barresas attended a workshop last summer called The Arid Lands Project. When she returned to her fourth-grade classroom, she used her new knowledge to design a unit on plants. She hoped that her students, some who were Native American, some who were Hispanic, and others who were White, would realize that contrary to popular myth, there are many varieties of plants and animals living in the local desert. In addition, Mrs. Barresas was determined to create learning experiences for students that were sensitive to the multicultural "funds of knowledge" her students brought to the classroom. She began the unit on a Friday afternoon. Mrs. Barresas and her students watched a rented video version of Walt Disney's *A Far Away Place*. It tells the story of two White children and a young African bushman who are forced to flee across the Kalahari Desert. As the children watched, they were amazed at the young bushman's knowledge of the desert. He knew where to find water, food, and medicinal plants. The bushman showed the other two how to use animals for food and clothing. After a long discussion with the children, Mrs. Barresas asked them what they might need to learn to survive if they were forced to live off the land around them.

The students seemed fairly certain that they did not have the knowledge they would need but agreed it might be important someday. As their curiosity and enthusiasm grew, Mrs. Barresas suggested that each of her students adopt a square meter of land in the fields close to the school and another square meter at home. The students could carefully observe both pieces of land to learn about plants and animals that might be found there. She also asked students to interview their families and relatives to learn about plants that might be useful as medicine and food. Last, she consulted the school librarian and, together, they identified a collection of stories, legends, and myths from the children's cultures. Some could be read by children; others would be shared during story time. The children would write their own as they learned new stories from their families.

Twice a week for several weeks, the children were given time during the school day to carefully observe their land. Mrs. Barresas helped students to note changes in plants and to identify traces of animal life in their adopted square meter of land. Students used cameras to take pictures of important changes in their two pieces of land or events they observed happening on their land. They also took notes and drew pictures of things they observed and the things they learned from members of the community about nutritional and medicinal uses of plants. When the children found an especially rich source of information about desert plants, the teacher and a small group of children went to interview the community person, taking along the camera and a tape recorder.

At the end of the observation and research period, Mrs. Barresas and the students created a multimedia database that included the children's photographs and drawings, taped interviews, and research notes. The power of the multimedia database permitted students to build a single "bank" of knowledge using a variety of symbolic forms. Students used the audio capabilities of the computer to record and save their voices and their families' voices. Using a graphing program, they included data about temperatures and plant growth, experimenting with different kinds of graphs and using different formats and colors. Carlos discovered a way to show the extreme differences between the early morning temperature on his land at home and the afternoon temperature on his land at school. He designed a chart using a red line for the afternoon temperatures and a blue line for the morning temperatures.

Once the database was complete, Mrs. Barresas and her students watched *A Far Away Place* again. When it ended, Mrs. Barresas challenged her students to divide into groups of five and create a script that would tell a survival story about the arid lands that surrounded their homes. The final scripts would be performed as readers' theater. Each story was to contain elements similar to those found in the video. The characters in their story had to use plants and animals for food, clothing, and medicine. Their characters had to cope with at least one weather change and at least one danger from either plants or animals. Once students were clear about the elements that were to be included in their stories, Mrs. Barresas reminded them that the multimedia database they had created could serve as a reference. She then stepped back and watched the scripts grow and change as students worked to tell a story of survival in the arid lands.

******

Mr. Gray had been doing oral histories with his students for several years and had recently been given two new and powerful computers for use in his high school social studies class. He decided to give students the opportunity to integrate their histories this year using the hypermedia capabilities of the computer instead of asking them to create written reports as he had done in years past.

The students were divided into small groups and given the task of interviewing people who had lived in the early days of their Utah town. As a class, they decided to ask these people about several main topics including education, business, religion, family life, and community events. Students were provided with tape recorders and cameras for conducting their interviews and the use of a scanner. In addition, students used the school and local library as well as the library's Internet access to find additional information about the history of their community.

When students neared the end of their initial information gathering, they began using a hypermedia program called HyperStudio to design a "stack" that began with a scanned picture of the person they had interviewed. Additional cards were created and added to the stack. Each card contained information they had collected during their interviews or supporting information they had found during their research time. The cards were then connected to other cards using small icons that signaled a "button." Each button acted as an electronic connection between the current card and a related card. When students had finished making cards and linking those cards with buttons, they had a web of electronic information. Someone "reading" each HyperStudio "stack" might select a button and hear a short segment from the recorded interview or see a picture of an artifact saved by the interviewee. Another button might lead the "reader" to a text field where they could read about related history, a description of a related craft, or perhaps find a list of additional things to read.

Mr. Gray was amazed at how much the students enjoyed working with this new media. Their writing was much longer than in previous years and, once they discovered how to link one card to another, they kept adding new cards, going back and interviewing additional people, or consulting the library to clarify facts.

Mrs. Barresas's project was designed to integrate the science of arid lands (physical, life, and earth), related mathematics, and the history of life on these lands around a universal idea: how to survive. In contrast to traditional science curricula, the project's materials presented a highly diverse set of elements—modern science and ancient mythology, computer-based learning and mud-under-the-fingernails exploration, the Navajo student who herds sheep through eerie land formations on Saturdays and the Rio Grande Hispanic student who glides down colonial side streets on a skateboard, the environmentalist and the agricultural scientist, the rancher and the medicine man. Mr. Gray's oral history unit did likewise. His students used the members of their own community as their primary source. They asked questions about the human experience in all its intricate glory instead of studying economics or politics or religion as an isolated collection of facts, removed from human experience.

Both Mrs. Barresas and Mr. Gray selected a variety of technologies to bring the world into the classroom. They understood that print is only one way of experiencing reality and that print in English for limited-English-speaking students is not always the best way. They recognized the power in a picture or a video of the real thing and that students appreciate hearing the diverse languages and sounds of their surrounding community. They understood that the power of the new technologies to store print, video, sound, and images and create a world of diverse resources facilitated students' ability to create new products and insights.

LEARNING IN COLLABORATIVE AND COOPERATIVE COMMUNITIES

According to Johnson and Johnson (1994), there are three types of goal structures in classrooms:

1. Students work in a competitive classroom in order to receive limited rewards (As);
2. Students pursue individualized learning programs to achieve mastery of a series of preset criteria; and
3. Students work cooperatively in small groups to accomplish shared learning goals. Within these learning structures, members seek rewards that are beneficial both to themselves and to their group.

Teachers make decisions about whether and when they want students to pursue individualistic, competitive, or cooperative goals. Different goal structures are appropriate depending on the intended student outcomes, the type of student-teacher interaction desired, the amount of peer assistance required by the task, and the type of evaluation planned. Collaborative and cooperative small-group learning strategies support cooperative goals and are an important component of designing learning opportunities for students that promote the development of community.

Learning to work together is at the heart of family life, government, and even the evolution of the human species. Diamond (1989) writes that if there were any single moment when we could be said to have become human, it was at the time that *Homo sapiens* learned to cooperate. In a world increasingly characterized by pluralism, rapid change, and conflict, cooperation may be our most important survival skill.

There are two distinct approaches to the development of group learning in classrooms. These approaches are called *collaborative* and *cooperative learning*. Notions about collaborative learning first developed within the arts and humanities settings in universities and colleges and have since become important in business and in K–12 education. Notions about cooperative learning draw primarily on insights from educational psychology and group learning theory and have been most practiced in precollege settings (Mathews, Cooper, Davidson, & Hawkes, 1995).

In general, *collaborative learning* refers to the design of learning opportunities in which students with differing levels or areas of expertise assist each other. In collaborative learning, the goal is for students to either combine expertise to accomplish a mutual goal or for more expert students to teach others. *Cooperative learning* refers to learning that brings students with similar expertise together. The goal of cooperative learning is to build collective knowledge and use that emerging expertise to solve a problem. Both strategies are useful for the K–12 classroom teacher interested in designing opportunities for students to learn to profit from and contribute to their various communities.

Research on both collaborative and cooperative learning suggests that both strategies are generally positive, especially for students who have not previously been successful in traditional classrooms (Johnson & Johnson, 1994; Joyce, Weil, & Showers, 1992). In general, both collaborative and cooperative learning stimulate cognitive complexity and provide a positive social climate. In both situations, there is increased participation by the learner especially if students are coached in helping behaviors (Ross, 1995). Additionally, when students have opportunities and the need to articulate concepts and problems, student achievement increases (Nattiv, 1991). And, finally, students gain an appreciation for the diversity of viewpoints. While both these strategies result in similar learning benefits, there are differences between cooperative and collaborative learning strategies, especially in relation to the composition of the group, the degree of training required for group work, the level of interdependence desired in the learning outcome, and the different ways in which teachers are involved with each type of group.

Cooperative Learning

Cooperative learning rests on the assumption that students working as a team toward a common goal learn better than students working by themselves (Ladestro, 1989). The idea is to create an environment in which students want each other to succeed and work to motivate and teach each other in order to accomplish shared goals. Students are required to present their ideas to each other and to work through differences of opinion. They are actively involved in thinking about course content and using that content to accomplish the group goal. Typically, cooperative groups are heterogeneous or mixed with respect to ability, gender, and ethnic group. Positive academic achievement (Johnson & Johnson, 1987), improved self-esteem (Foyle, Lyman, & Thies, 1991), improved social skills (Slavin, 1991), and improved race relations (Slavin, 1990) are all associated with cooperative learning experiences.

Cooperative learning requires positive interdependence. *Positive interdependence* means that each member of the group is actively involved and committed to the group's success. When students freely make appropriate decisions that empower them to be successful in their relationships with others, positive interdependence emerges. When positive interdependence exists, students have the subjective experience of "being on the same side" and behave cooperatively toward each other.

An important part of the process of learning to be a member of a cooperative group is the debriefing that happens after a cooperative activity. Groups need to talk about what interactions went well and where improvements might be made. Teams should be encouraged to assess their teamwork. Students make greater improvements in their interaction skills when they take time to reflect on and review their actions, setting goals for improvement (Nattiv, 1991).

Successful cooperation does not occur without some planning and training. Teachers must do more than form groups and tell students to work together. They must teach social skills. Johnson, Johnson, and Holubec (1991) suggest three activities for promoting the social skills necessary for successful cooperation. First, teachers need to help students understand what the positive cooperative social skills look or sound like. Second, students need to practice these cooperative skills. Role playing is an effective way to learn social skills as students take turns practicing how they might respond to teacher-created scenarios. Third, students need to reflect on their use of these social skills. They need to discuss how well the targeted skills are being implemented in their group.

> Penny Garcia's students had had many opportunities to cooperate when they were working with software in their biweekly trips to the computer lab. Ms. Garcia actively encouraged students to work in groups of two or three when they were using some of the problem-solving software programs. During a unit on plants, Mrs. Garcia had paired students in the lab to cooperatively discover how water, acidity, light, and temperature interacted to influence plant growth using a program by Sunburst Communications called Botanical Gardens. It had been fun to watch how when one group figured out how to combine the elements to make a particular plant grow to its maximum, they jumped for joy and divided up to show other groups what they had learned. It was now time to extend these cooperative behaviors to larger groups, to a longer-term project, and to ongoing classroom activities, not just computer lab activities.
>
> After doing some planning, making arrangements, and gathering resources, Mrs. Garcia called her students together. "You know that empty room down the hall," she asked. "Let's turn it into a Colonial Museum in time for Thanksgiving." Students thought that was a great idea. Several days later, the class took a field trip to a local museum to investigate what kinds of exhibits museums had and how those exhibits were organized. Students learned about exhibits that displayed crafts and artwork. They learned about labeling exhibits and placing descriptions of how those exhibits reflected the life of people during those times. When they returned to the classroom, the class broke into small groups to list the kinds of exhibits they thought their Colonial Museum should have. The lists of each group were compiled, and students made decisions about what exhibits would go into their museum. They decided on a newspaper exhibit that would display the front

page of various newspapers related to important historical events, an arts and crafts display with examples of various colonial crafts, a display on each of the colonies with famous leaders, places, and economic activities of each, a recreational display, and a display of home life in the colonies. The class divided into groups of four. Each group chose two colonies, a craft, an important event, and a sport or an aspect of home life.

The small groups began to cooperatively research each of these areas. They decided exactly what they would produce for the museum and set about creating their displays. One group made candlestick holders from small paper plates and spray paint. Other groups created quilts, weavings, and apple dolls. All these projects would be displayed in the arts and crafts section of their museum. Each group created the front page of a newspaper reflecting the historical event they had chosen. They used a desktop publishing program and printed their papers on 14-by-17-inch paper. Soon, the newspaper section was filled with newspapers declaring "Indians Board Ship, Destroy Tea," "Revere Rides All Night," and "Colonists Tell George to Leave." The home life section began to display student drawings of family settings drawn with graphics programs and printed in color. A small box was placed near this display with copies of a Colonial Cookbook created by one group using a word processor. Visitors to the museum were encouraged to take one and try some of the recipes. Small three-dimensional dioramas began to appear of colonial children playing stickball, blacksmiths sweating over hot fires, and men meeting in rooms late at night to produce anti-British pamphlets.

Students worked together, checking one another's products for historical accuracy, coordinating the displays so that there were no duplicates, helping groups that were falling behind, and organizing the museum so that all the displays were clearly and easily visible. A large banner appeared across the doorway of the once-empty room declaring "Mrs. Garcia's Fifth Grade Presents A Colonial Museum." Invitations were sent to all the students' families inviting them to come see the museum and to have lunch in the Media Center. The invitation assured everyone that the feast would include only authentic colonial foods. Parent volunteers prepared dishes using the recipes from the cookbook. At least one visitor accompanied every student. Sometimes it was a parent; other times it was a grandparent or an important neighbor or relative. After lunch, students led their visitors through the museum, pointing out interesting things that others had contributed and what they had contributed. Over the next several days, the Colonial Museum was visited by every class in the school. "What a monumental cooperative effort," reflected one visitor to the museum.

Collaborative Learning

Classroom social interactions can influence learners in powerful ways. Just as cooperative learning activities build shared goals and mutual systems of interaction, collaborative learning activities provide opportunities for more experienced and skilled students to demonstrate to less experienced and skilled students how they think and learn. In collaborative learning relationships, more experienced students become advisors or consultants for less experienced students. This form of group learning is different from cooperative learning because it assumes some difference in skills and does not assume that individuals work together continuously (Kafai &

Harel, 1991). The exact nature of the interactions between novice and expert are varied. In some group interactions, older students are assigned to assist younger students (cross-age tutoring). Other times, same-age students who have already mastered a learning goal are assigned to assist classmates (peer tutoring). When experienced practitioners are paired with novice practitioners, mentoring or apprenticeship relations are established. In yet another model of collaborative learning—the jigsaw approach (Aronson, et al., 1978), novices come together to identify a common goal. They then break apart to study as individuals or join other groups in order to gain needed expertise. Finally, students return to their original group with newly acquired expertise, teach others what they have learned, and collectively combine their expertise to accomplish their shared goal.

In collaborative learning situations, students are often attempting to help others work with skills that they themselves have only marginally mastered. Collaborative learning situations provide opportunities for these students to revisit familiar material and move from a superficial level of knowledge to understanding. Explaining something to someone else, providing explanations, and responding to questions requires a "depth of understanding that students may not impose on themselves as learners" (Grabe & Grabe, 1996, p. 67). Collaborative learning requires students to enter the culture of teaching. Thus, novices benefit from the expertise of fellow students, while experts strengthen their knowledge and skills through the act of sharing their expertise.

Barb Pena and Susan McKinney are team teachers in a middle school. They teach an eighth-grade social studies/science two-hour block. To show the students a connection between the two disciplines, the teachers planned an Environmental Conference. Parents, community members, and a representative from the Governor's Office would be attending. To prepare for the big event, Mrs. Pena and Mrs. McKinney assigned environmental issues to groups of five students. The issues included a stalled nuclear waste disposal site in the southern part of their state, a mining problem in the northern part of their state, the severe water shortage crisis in their own community, and a groundwater problem associated with a manufacturing plant in a nearby community. Students were challenged to cooperate in their small Research Groups to investigate their issue, to identify political and economic problems associated with the issue, and to study the science concepts related to their issue. Using a specific framework presented to each group, Mrs. Pena and Mrs. McKinney challenged the Research Groups to prepare a presentation to be given at the Environmental Conference that explained their issue, taught the audience about the related science concepts, and detailed a strategy for resolving the problem.

About a third of the way into the time allotted for preparing for the Conference, six classroom computers and six video cameras arrived. These had been ordered as part of a grant that Mrs. Pena and Mrs. McKinney had submitted. They would be the perfect tools for preparing the presentations. Students could create graphic slide shows to support their talks. They could use the desktop publishing and word processing programs for preparing written reports and brochures. Students could create short videos as well as prepare spreadsheets for creating charts and graphs. The problem Mrs. Pena and Mrs. McKinney confronted though was how to teach students to use these tools and still be ready for the Conference.

Mrs. Pena suggested a collaborative approach to solving the dilemma. The teachers assigned each member of a Research Group to a new Technology Group. Thus, one member from each Research Group was assigned to a video group. One member from each Research Group was assigned to a slide show group. One member from each Research Group was assigned to a desktop publishing group. And so forth. While one of the teachers monitored the work of the Research Groups, the other one taught the different Technology Groups to use a particular tool. For four days, the video group met to learn how to operate the video cameras, how to do in-camera editing, and how to storyboard a video. For four days, the desktop publishing group learned how to import text files and graphic files. They learned about the basic principles of layout and design. They learned the specific details of how the desktop publishing program worked. For four days, the spreadsheet group learned how to organize data in a spreadsheet format and how to construct graphs from the data. They learned to save the resulting graphs as a file so that they could be loaded into the desktop publisher and/or the slide show program. When members of each Technology Group returned to their Research Group, members of the Research Group had to teach the returning member the things they had learned during that member's absence.

As the Research Groups began to organize the results of their research into presentation form, the group member who had attended each of the Technology Groups was responsible for heading up that phase of the presentation. They served as their group's expert, teaching others how to use the tool and answering questions. It was amazing to Mrs. Pena and Mrs. McKinney how smoothly the presentation materials were created. They were asked very few questions about how a particular technology worked. As they reflected on the process, they were confident that this collaborative approach to sharing expertise worked better than if they had tried to teach the whole class how to use each technology. The Environmental Conference was a huge success, and participants remarked on the high quality of the videos, slide shows, written reports, and graphs used by students.

LEARNING IN DEMOCRATIC COMMUNITIES

Some believe that democracy is nothing more than a form of federal government and thus is not a concern of schools and other social institutions. Others believe that democracy is a right of adults, not of young people. And still others believe that democracy simply cannot work in schools. Others (i.e., Apple & Beane, 1995), however, are committed to the idea that a democratic way of life is built upon opportunities to learn about what it is and how to lead it. They believe that schools, as a common experience of most all young people, have an obligation to introduce the democratic way of life. As Green (1985, p. 4) writes: "Surely it is an obligation of education in a democracy to empower the young to become members of the public, to participate, and play articulate roles in the public space."

Democracy works in multiple ways in social affairs. Most of us were taught that democracy is a form of political governance involving the consent of the governed and equality of opportunity. For example, we learned that citizens may directly and fully participate in such events as elections while being represented in other matters by those we elect to federal and state offices. Less explicitly, we were taught the foundations of a democratic way of life (Beane, 1990). These conditions and their extensions through education are the central concerns of democratic communities, both in and out of school. Important foundations for democratic communities include:

1. The open flow of ideas, regardless of their popularity;
2. Faith in the individual and collective capacity of people to create possibilities for resolving problems;
3. The use of critical reflection and analysis to evaluate ideas and policies;
4. Concern for the welfare of others and the "common good";
5. Concern for the dignity and rights of individuals;
6. An understanding that democracy is not so much an ideal as a set of values that guide our life as a people; and
7. The organization of social institutions to promote and extend the democratic way of life.

If people are to secure and maintain a democratic way of life, they must have opportunities to learn what that way of life means and how it might be led (Dewey, 1916). Yet, democratic schools, like democracy itself, do not happen by chance. They result from explicit attempts by educators to design learning opportunities that bring democracy to life. The design of opportunities to learn the democratic way of life focuses on the creation of structures and processes by which school life is carried out and the creation of a curriculum that gives students democratic experiences (Apple & Beane, 1995).

The structures and processes created in democratic learning communities prize diversity. Such communities include people who reflect differences in age, culture, ethnicity, gender, socioeconomic class, aspirations, and abilities. These differences enrich the community and the range of views it might consider. While democratic learning communities prize diversity, they also have a sense of shared purpose. Democracy is not seen as simply a theory of self-interest; seeking the common good is a central feature. For this reason, democratic communities of learners are marked by an emphasis on cooperation and collaboration rather than competition. Learners see their well-being and success tied to relationships with others, and arrangements are created that encourage learners to seek to improve the life of the community by helping others. These structures and processes constitute a kind of "hidden" curriculum by which people learn significant lessons about justice, power, dignity, and self-worth (Apple & Beane, 1995).

A democratic curriculum emphasizes access to a wide range of information and the right of those of varied opinion to have their viewpoints heard. Educators who design opportunities for students to experience and learn to participate in democratic communities help learners seek out a range of ideas and voice their own ideas. Learners learn to become critical readers of their society. They are encouraged to ask questions. Helping students to understand the different ways in which events can be interpreted or problems solved leads to learners who appreciate different interpretations and helps develop a richer and more ethically committed sensitivity to the societies around them.

In a community of democratic learners, no one individual claims sole ownership of knowledge and meaning. A democratic curriculum includes not only what adults think is important but also embraces the questions and concerns that learners have about themselves and their world. "A democratic curriculum invites young people to shed the passive role of knowledge consumers and assume the active role of 'meaning makers' " (Apple & Beane, 1995). It recognizes that learners acquire knowledge by both studying external sources and engaging in complex activities that require learners to construct their own solutions to collective problems. This process, however, is not simply a participatory conversation about just anything. Rather, it is directed toward intelligent and reflective consideration of problems, events, and issues that arise in the course of collective living. A democratic curriculum involves continuous opportunities to explore such issues, to imagine responses to problems, and to act upon those responses.

> Elaine Wilkerson was sure there was more that she could do in her third-grade classroom to promote the foundations of a democratic way of life than giving good citizenship certificates, having students elect class officers, and assigning weekly jobs to students. There must be a way that third graders could experience a curriculum that encouraged them to seek ways to improve the life of their community. As Mrs. Wilkerson was reading the community newspaper one night, she happened on an article describing the efforts of a local community planning committee to finish the design of a new community library. The article announced that the committee had contracted with a consulting company to assist them in their efforts. Among the aspects of the library left to be planned was a proposed children's reading room. "Why," thought Mrs. Wilkerson, "couldn't my third-grade students serve as consultants for the children's reading room?" The next morning Mrs. Wilkerson shared the article with her class and inquired if they thought it would be possible for them to become consultants. The class heartily endorsed such an activity and agreed to invite the planning committee to visit their class. Three of the five committee members visited the following week to explain the library project, share a sample proposal prepared by a professional consulting firm, and formally request the children's help.
>
> In preparation for creating a proposal, Mrs. Wilkerson's class studied communities, community service, community planning, and libraries. They looked at fire departments, police services, garbage and water systems, and finally focused on libraries. The community served as content. Students read the chapters in their social studies book on communities and community members. They listened as Mrs. Wilkerson read stories during Read Aloud time about firefighters, police, and stories about other children participating in their communities. Students used Tom Snyder's simulation, Choices, Choices: Taking Responsibility, to experiment with talking about decision making, values, and compromise. Students learned to present ideas by making three-dimensional models of their version of a children's reading room. They learned to use calculators to construct their cost analysis. (Students did not know how to multiply, but a few lessons with a calculator and they understood the principle of multiplication.) Students learned to use a database to

survey other children in the school about their opinions. They learned to use a simple computer graphing program to present the results of their surveys. They learned to use a simple desktop publishing program to prepare professional proposals. Students learned about square feet and marked off the tiles in the cafeteria to get a sense of the dimensions of the reading room. They studied their school library, learning about the kinds of books and magazines and reference materials that were there. They began an independent reading program to help them compile a list of recommended books that might be placed in the reading room.

Groups of four students formed a consulting company. They named their company. They created business cards and a letterhead using a computer program called Print Shop Deluxe. With Mrs. Wilkerson's assistance, students analyzed the sample professional proposal left by the planning committee. They created a proposal format that included biographical statements about the consulting company members, a summary description of their proposed reading room, a floor plan for the reading room, a list of books recommended for the reading room, a cost analysis section including prices for books, equipment, and furniture for the reading room, and the results of their survey of opinions about the reading room. As the students' proposal neared completion, they built three-dimensional models of their plans, prepared charts for use during their presentations, and planned and practiced what role each member of the consulting committee would take and what each of them would say.

Time was reserved in the school's media center, and the planning committee was invited to come hear their proposals. This time all five committee members were able to attend. Each group presented their formal presentation covering all aspects of their proposal, showing their floor plans, and making their recommendations. After all the presentations were completed, students took their bound proposals, floor plans, three-dimensional models, and prepared charts to individual tables, and the committee members circulated among the groups asking questions of each group. Three weeks later, the Committee Chairperson returned to Mrs. Wilkerson's class to tell the students about the finalized plans for the reading room.

Students were amazed as the Committee Chairperson told them about the final plan. They had become part of their community. The plan reflected their ideas. The children's reading room would include lots of beanbag chairs and comfortable places to read. The children had told the Committee they thought a reading room needed more than just tables and chairs. A section of the reading room would be set aside as a writing center where students visiting the library could write and illustrate stories of their own and leave them for other visitors. A special area would be set aside with Braille books and books on tape for children with disabilities. A magazine rack would be set just outside the reading room with reading material for adults. As one of the student consulting groups had recommended, the rack would give parents something to read while they waited for their children.

Mrs. Wilkerson's students were very proud of their contribution. Mrs. Wilkerson was very proud of her students. They had learned they had the power to participate in solving real community problems. They had learned to openly share their ideas and to arrive at compromises as they constructed their proposals. They had learned to gather opinions from community members using a survey, to critically reflect on the survey results, and to analyze information to evaluate ideas and recommendations. Students had acted as members of a democratic society and had experienced their own power to shape their community.

LEARNING IN VIRTUAL COMMUNITIES

The notion of classrooms as communities of learners is no longer restricted to the confines of the four walls of the classroom. Communities of learners can now be virtual communities. The concept of virtual communities first introduced by Rheingold (1993) refers to social aggregations that emerge on the Internet when enough people carry on public discussions long enough, with sufficient human feeling, to form webs of personal relationships in cyberspace.

People in virtual communities use words and images on screens to exchange pleasantries and argue, engage in intellectual discourse, conduct commerce, exchange knowledge, share emotional support, make plans, brainstorm, gossip, find friends, and create a little art and a lot of idle talk. People in virtual communities do just about everything people do in real life, but they leave their bodies behind.

Designing Virtual Online Learning Communities

Accompanying growth in Internet access in K–12 classrooms is an increase in the availability of electronic tools and environments that support Web-based collaboration. Early collaborative projects based primarily on e-mail have now expanded to Web environments that support the development of ongoing learning communities. In fact, researchers (e.g., Bonk & King, 1998; Dede, 1996; Odasz, 1994; Reil & Fulton, 1998; Harris, 2000; Coulter, Feldman, & Konold, 2000) agree that the potential for learning on the Web is greatest when students are involved in online learning communities. Although much recent work on electronic learning communities has centered on the development of distributed learning and distance education at the college and university level, Harris (1998b) has identified three broad "telecollaboration" categories of K–12 online community learning: Interpersonal Exchanges, Information Collection and Analysis, and Problem Solving. Harris (1998a) has further divided these three categories into a number of "activity structures." Harris (1998b) defines activity structures as flexible frameworks that instructional designers can use to generate powerful learning environments. She has identified 18 telecollaborative activity structures. We will only discuss some of them, but you can access her online article at http://www.iste.org/L&L/archive/vol26/no1/feature/index.html. Like Harris, we will provide examples, but remind the reader that the examples are intended not as "plug and play" solutions but as illustrations of the main concept—the design framework. Challenge yourself to think of ways in which you can use the frameworks to design your own learning opportunities.

Keypals.   Keypal exchanges are similar to more conventional pen pal activities.

Dorothy Johnson teaches fourth grade in a predominantly Hispanic school in the Southwest. Her brother, Harold, teaches fifth grade in an inner-city school in the

Southeast. Ninety percent of his students are African American. They often use e-mail to share their teaching experiences, both their successes and their challenges. One thing that has frequently been part of their conversations is the "minority" composition of their classes. They have come to recognize that although their classrooms reflect students who are considered ethnically diverse, their classrooms are not really culturally diverse. They are, in fact, quite homogeneous. Dorothy and Harold wondered how they might teach their students to appreciate and understand the cultural diversity of their nation.

Dorothy had an idea. Why not use e-mail to foster cross-cultural understanding? Harold e-mailed Dorothy a list of his students, and she paired one of his students with one of hers. Students in both classrooms wrote and sent a short introductory e-mail message to their virtual pen pal. Their students were quite excited to receive an e-mail message from students in another state. Harold and Dorothy proposed to their students that they write their pen pals' biographies using e-mail to gather information. They read sample biographies to their classes and created webs for the kinds of information that might be useful for writing a biography. Over the next six weeks, students in the two classes exchanged e-mail messages. While they were collecting information to write their biographies, each class planned and prepared a videotape about their class, their school, and their community. The videotapes were exchanged. When students finished their biographies of their e-mail partners, the two classrooms exchanged biographies. It was interesting to see how the virtual pen pals wrote about one another's lives and customs.

Electronic Appearances.   Electronic appearances are guest appearances by specially invited experts. Generally, such appearances are one-time events. While electronic appearances are possible with e-mail and asynchronous conferencing tools, most are done with real-time text-chat programs like Blackboard's Virtual Classroom or videoconferencing programs such as CU-SeeMe.

Telementoring.   When exchanges with subject-matter experts become more extended, the activity structure can be described as telementoring. With this structure, Internet-connected specialists serve as electronic mentors to students who want to explore specific topics.

Jill Snyder is the New Mexico coordinator for the Adventures in Supercomputing (AiS) project. This project supports teachers and students in New Mexico high schools who study computer programming and computational science. Computational science is the study of using mathematical models encoded in computer programs to solve problems. Students in AiS classes learn to program using a variety of computer languages and then identify and research a problem that can be solved by creating a mathematical model. Based on their research, students create and program a mathematical model that results in problem solutions. Sample AiS problems include population problems, environmental problems like water flow or water use, and wildlife management problems. The work of AiS classrooms culminates in a yearly AiS Fair at a central location in the state. Prior to the Fair, students present a scientific paper. At the Fair, students present their work, creating displays that identify their problem, their research, their mathematical models, and the resulting solutions. Expert judges review the papers and the displays, providing feedback to all projects and presenting awards for excellence.

An integral part of the AiS project is the role of expert mentors. The project provides telecommunications capability to all AiS classrooms, and students are encouraged to use this capacity to seek the advice of experts. AiS teachers are skilled in helping students with programming challenges, but they are not experts in the problem areas students selected. The successful selection of problems that can be solved with mathematical models and the creation of mathematical models depends on interactions with experts. Students are helped to identify experts by exploring Internet sources related to their problem and by researching scientific journals. When students locate experts in related fields, they are encouraged to e-mail or phone these experts. Sometimes students interact only once with an expert, obtaining the answer to specific questions. Other times, students develop ongoing relationships with experts in their problem area, asking for advice, soliciting expert review of their work in progress, or editorial review of their paper. One of Jill Snyder's roles as coordinator of the project is to help students locate, contact, and interact with these expert mentors. Teachers and students unanimously agree that the role of the mentor is invaluable and that a relationship exists between the quality of interactions with expert mentors and the quality of the final project. In this virtual scientific community, teachers and students are able to push their learning and their problem-solving abilities far beyond the limitations of their classrooms.

Impersonations.   With the impersonation activity structure, at least one participant in an online group communicates as a character. For instance, the education director at Monticello, Thomas Jefferson's home, impersonates that president by answering students' questions using e-mail. It is also possible for one group of students to impersonate another while responding to e-mail inquiries. Norton and Sprague (2001) tell of students in a fifth-grade classroom who impersonated famous colonial public figures while answering questions from fourth graders who were writing biographies about colonial figures.

Electronic Publishing.   High-speed Internet access and the growing number of Internet authoring tools have made electronic publishing projects possible for students in all grade levels. The appeal of an audience beyond those in any single classroom is a powerful experience. The challenge is making sure that a wide audience is aware and has access to students' publications.

> Sponsored by AT&T Learning Networks, Learning Circles bring classrooms from around the world together to form a community of learners around a shared theme and goal. The Learning Circles Teachers' Guide can be found on the Internet at http://www.att.com/education/lcguide. Learning Circles promote theme-based project work integrated with the classroom curriculum. Working with Learning Circle partners, students develop important interpersonal skills as well as develop and share knowledge related to the Circle's theme. A Learning Circle is created by a team of six to eight classrooms joined in the virtual space of an electronic classroom. The group remains together over a three- to four-month period working projects drawn from the curriculum of each of the classrooms. At the end of the time, the group collects and publishes its work. Most of the Learning Circle activities take place using e-mail and teleconferencing.
>
> The first phase of a Learning Circle involves getting to know the partners. Classroom surveys about students, their school, and their community are shared.

Classes exchange additional information such as class photos and other materials that are helpful for classrooms to get to know each other. Once students and teachers are acquainted, the groups move on to complete a project based on a mutual theme. Learning Circle themes have included places and perspectives (history, geography, and social studies classes), global issues (government, politics, environmental studies, and writing classes), energy and the environment (science and social studies classes), and mind works (creative writing, literature, and social studies classes).

The Circle working cooperatively on energy and environment, for instance, focuses student attention on how energy needs interact with the stability of the environment. Students explore the fragile balance between the economics of modern technology and the health and future of their planet. Students explore issues from energy consumption to environmental ethics. Working in teams, students study the basic forces of nature by sharing local information and experimental observations. The goal of the Learning Circle is to extend the learning that takes place in the curriculum of each class by exchanging data, analysis, and information. Students are encouraged to sponsor projects that are likely to be affected by differences in local environmental conditions such as identifying particles in lakes and streams, measuring the amount of sunlight, and comparing fuel efficiency and water usage. Students offer ideas for experiments, use of materials, or discuss explanations or interpretations of the findings reported by one of the Learning Circle classes. Students work together to explore nuclear energy, problems of toxic waste, contamination of groundwater, degradability of different materials, benefits and problems associated with the use of plastics, and problems caused by agricultural pests and pesticides. The work of the Learning Circle culminates in student publication of an issue of the *Energy and Environment Newsletter* describing their Learning Circle projects.

Peer Feedback Activities. In this activity structure, participants offer consecutive responses to other students' ideas or expressions. Peer feedback activities can be organized as electronic writer's workshops, electronic debates, or the like. One example for young learners is the MindsEye Monster Exchange Project (http://www.monsterexchange.org) where

> . . . children draw original monsters and use words to describe them. These descriptions are then e-mailed to students in other schools who read the descriptions and then draw what they think the described monsters look like. Both sets of pictures and the descriptions are then displayed in the project's "Monster Gallery," and students communicate with each other about the similarities and differences between the first and second drawings. (Harris, 1998b, p. 10)

Parallel Problem Solving. In parallel problem-solving activities, classes devise solutions to commonly shared problems and then share their results. "Such rich and varied problem solving and discussion of multiple problem solving methods are becoming quite popular among telecollaborating classes" (Harris, 1998b, p. 10). The Midi Music Relay (http://www.kidlink.org/KIDPROJ/midi/) is one example of parallel problem solving.

Social Action Projects. Social action projects help learners understand and take action to help solve authentic global challenges. Social action projects focus on real and immediate problems and often propose that students take action to help solve a problem, rather than simply stop learning once they understand it. Many examples of social action projects are sponsored by I°Earn (http://www.iearn. org/iearn/).

In this chapter, we have explored the ways in which learning and cognition are developed and shared within the context of communities of learners. Rather than portraying learning as a solely individual act, we have emphasized the social nature of learning. To facilitate the process of designing learning opportunities for students that not only rely on the power of communities of learners but also help students develop the ability to be constructive participants within communities, we explored five patterns of community interactions: communities of diverse learners, cooperative communities, collaborative communities, democratic communities, and virtual communities. The next chapter looks at systems of assessment that support the design of learning opportunities consistent with models of learning presented in this and previous chapters.

Before turning our attention to systems of assessment, however, it is time to rejoin Brooks White and Allan Sutton as they elaborate on their design. We recommend that you go to the FACTS Web-Based Design Tool site http://www. norton.wadsworth.com and click on the Design Mentors puzzle piece. This chapter's Design Mentors demonstrate how Brooks White and Allan Sutton think about how to help their students be positive and competent community members. Considering issues related to the community is fundamental to both Mr. Sutton's and Ms. White's designs. It is interesting to note that issues related to participating in a democratic community are in the forefront of Ms. White's design. Helping students develop competence at participating in a community is more a function of the overall climate and structure of Mr. Sutton's design as opposed to something taught overtly. After you have studied the Design Mentors, you might find it helpful to return to the opening page of the Web site and complete Design Challenge Eight. You can also examine some of the Design Examples and see how they reflect the considerations discussed in this chapter.

CHAPTER IDEAS

- Schools should be communities where students learn to learn. In this setting, teachers are models of intentional learning and self-motivated scholarship, both individual and collaborative. Graduates of such communities are lifelong learners who have learned how to learn in many domains.
- In a community of learners, teachers and students are role models not "owners" of some aspect of knowledge. They are acquirers, users, and extenders of knowledge in a sustained, ongoing process of understanding. Students become apprentice learners, learning how to think and reason in a variety of knowledge domains, using the power of others to support individual and collective goals.

- A community of learners depends on community of kinship, place, and mind. Together the three kinds of community represent webs of meaning that link diverse groups of people by creating among them a sense of belonging and a common identity as human beings who are capable of affection and caring for others as well as themselves.
- A classroom climate that fosters a community of learners is built on four main qualities: an atmosphere of individual responsibility coupled with communal sharing, respect among students, between students and teachers, and among members of the extended community of experts, a community of discourse that honors constructive discussion, questioning, and criticism, and shared rituals—patterns of organization and interaction.
- The traditional view of cognition rests on a view of intelligence framed by three basic characteristics. First, intelligence is a single, general problem-solving ability generalized from setting to setting. Second, intelligence is located inside the head of each individual. Third, the intelligence of each individual is relatively stable from one situation and setting to another. This view, however, is being challenged.
- Factors or forces at three different levels—personal, local, and cultural—contribute to cognition in the classroom. These forces interact to shape the activity and skills of all learners. Changes in the forces at any one of these levels contribute to changes both in what learners do and in what they are capable of doing.
- Intelligence is enmeshed in all of a person's activities and embedded in the settings and cultures in which those activities are carried out. Cultural, local, and personal forces are interdependent. An individual's intelligences, interests, and concerns are formed in interactions with peers, family members, and teachers, constrained by available materials, and influenced by cultural values and expectations.
- Today's classrooms are a microcosm of an ever-increasing world of diversity. Yet, the curriculum used in most schools is based on materials and instructional strategies developed in the first half of the twentieth century when nearly three-fourths of all students were European Americans and the country's human resource needs were the product of an industrial rather than an information age. This curriculum is inappropriate in both content and activities for today's and tomorrow's student populations and is often in direct conflict with many students' cultures and community lives.
- Despite trends in the misuse of technology and schools' seeming unwillingness to alter instruction to meet the needs of increasingly diverse student populations, different instructional approaches and appropriate uses of technology can be effective in promoting learning among traditionally underrepresented students. Teachers can design learning experiences that are responsive to the needs of diverse students, that create communities of learners, and that use technology to liberate rather than oppress.

- All children need to see people from diverse cultures valued in the materials they work with in schools. A new kind of curriculum is needed— a curriculum grounded in an instructional approach that considers students' diverse languages and cultures as valuable sources of knowledge. One way to design opportunities for learning in classrooms of diverse students is to focus on universal themes: survival, justice, conflict resolution, friendship, or betrayal.

- Teachers make decisions about whether and when they want students to pursue individualistic, competitive, or cooperative goals. Collaborative and cooperative small-group learning strategies support cooperative goals and are an important component of designing learning opportunities for students that promote the development of community.

- There are two distinct approaches to the development of group learning in classrooms. These approaches are called collaborative and cooperative learning. In general, collaborative learning refers to the design of learning opportunities in which students with differing levels or areas of expertise assist each other. Cooperative learning refers to learning, usually within a single classroom, that brings students with similar expertise together.

- Cooperative learning rests on the assumption that students working as a team toward a common goal learn better than students working by themselves. The idea is to create an environment in which students want each other to succeed and work to motivate and teach each other in order to accomplish shared goals.

- Classroom social interactions can influence learners in powerful ways. Just as cooperative learning activities build shared goals and mutual systems of interaction, collaborative learning activities provide opportunities for more experienced and skilled students to demonstrate to less experienced and skilled students how they think and learn. In collaborative learning relationships, more experienced students become advisors or consultants for less experienced students.

- Many people believe that democracy is nothing more than a form of federal government and thus is not a concern of schools and other social institutions. Yet, democracy works in multiple ways in social affairs.

- Important foundations for democratic communities include the open flow of ideas, faith in the individual and collective capacity of people to create possibilities for resolving problems, the use of critical reflection and analysis to evaluate ideas and policies, concern for the welfare of others and the "common good," concern for the dignity and rights of individuals, an understanding that democracy is not so much an ideal as a set of values that guide our life as people, and the organization of social institutions to promote and extend the democratic way of life.

- If people are to secure and maintain a democratic way of life, they must have opportunities to learn what that way of life means and how it might be led. Yet, democratic schools, like democracy itself, do not happen by chance. They result from explicit attempts by educators to design learning opportunities that bring democracy to life. The design of opportunities to learn the democratic way of life focuses on the creation of structures and processes by which school life is carried out and the creation of a curriculum that gives students democratic experiences.

- The notion of classrooms as communities of learners is no longer restricted to the confines of the four walls of the classroom. Communities of learners can now be virtual communities. The concept of virtual communities refers to social aggregations that emerge on the Internet when enough people carry on public discussions long enough, with sufficient human feeling, to form webs of personal relationships in cyberspace. Teachers are using the Internet to design opportunities for learning that extend the community of the classroom to the community of the world.

DESIGNING SYSTEMS OF ASSESSMENT

I remember hearing a speaker at a conference on school restructuring who talked about what she called the Nintendo Principle. *This principle states that every instructional activity should have embedded within it enough feedback so that students always know how they are doing. The idea, of course, comes from watching young people engaged in learning as they manipulate variables in computer games to meet the game goals. User engagement results from the continuous feedback that occurs as players are allowed to rapidly try out different actions. The most engaging games come with complex problems that can be solved by the player in a variety of different ways.*

I often think of this principle when I design learning opportunities for my students and attempt to devise ways to provide feedback as part of instruction. I have learned to design learning situations where students can constantly adjust and improve their work before it becomes something for me to grade. I find teaching to be a lot more enjoyable when I do not carry home piles of papers to grade. I recently reflected on how far my idea of continuous instructional assessment is from the increasing external pressure we feel to prepare students to perform well on yearly standardized tests.

**Laura Hernandez,
Mentor Teacher
El Paso Collaborative
for Academic
Excellence**

To a large extent testing drives the curriculum. Teachers and schools are experiencing increasing pressure to perform well on high-stakes standardized tests (Educational Testing Service [ETS], 2000). At the same time, these tests are being criticized for a number of reasons, perhaps most significantly, in terms of whether they are measuring the new kinds of learning foundations required for students to do well in a communicative, rapidly changing global society. Until students are evaluated in ways aligned with the learning goals reflected in new understandings about teaching and learning—constructivism, situated cognition, distributed expertise, and problem-based learning—efforts at changing the learning opportunities available to students will have limited success.

The purpose of this chapter is to suggest ways to assess student learning in alignment with the design models introduced in this book. Various assessment strategies and tools are described in relationship to student learning. Systems of assessment are an integral part of expanding classroom learning activities. This chapter summarizes systems of assessment and suggests practical strategies for teachers to use as part of implementing new designs. The chapter begins with a discussion of the changing nature of assessment and the influence of technology on the assessment process. It then explores systems of assessment as they relate to new interpretive tools made possible with technology including the use of rubrics, portfolios, expanded audiences for assessment, and possibilities for increased interaction with students' work.

THE EVALUATION OF AN INNOVATION

Nancy and Maria are college professors who work at a small university in the East and were invited to evaluate a four-year teacher-based innovation designed to improve student learning at the elementary level. Nancy and Maria learned as much as they could about the goals of the project. They learned that it involved efforts to align mathematics instruction with the new National Council of Teachers of Mathematics (NCTM) Standards through an emphasis on mathematical thinking, problem solving, and the use of technology. Increased student performance in mathematics was to be measured using the district-required standardized test.

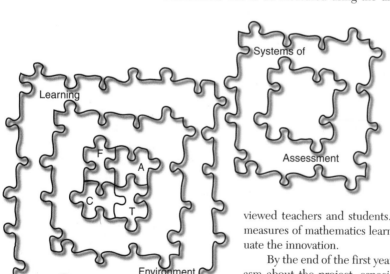

The professors worked closely with the district project directors who were providing ongoing professional development for teachers in mathematics teaching, cooperative learning and the integration of technology. In addition to the directors' support, each of the 36 teachers in the project received five computers and appropriate software for their rooms. The evaluators observed in classrooms and frequently interviewed teachers and students. They also developed additional measures of mathematics learning designed specifically to evaluate the innovation.

By the end of the first year, the teachers expressed enthusiasm about the project, especially the use of computers. They commented that the computers made math more fun, provided support for both individual and group learning, and helped learners who needed multisensory approaches to math. When one teacher was asked if computers helped children learn mathematics, she commented:

> . . . just walk through any classroom that has more than one child on a computer and your questions will be answered. There is no doubt that two minds are better than one when you see this happening. . . . There is no need to justify an answer if there is no one to question it and peers certainly question! (Uslick & Walker, 1994, p. 14)

Several teachers expressed surprise that many of their low-achieving students were often the most skilled at using the computer. Observations confirmed that with increased cooperative learning and computer support, teachers began to spend more time asking questions, looking for patterns, and generally supporting mathematical thinking. Observations and discussions with teachers indicated that they were moving from a dependency on textbooks to the use of a problem-solving approach. One teacher commented on "her new and different role as a teacher, especially her ability to make a child think."

As the innovation continued with growing observational evidence of its effectiveness, frustration grew with the original goal of evaluating the project using the district's standardized test. Teachers began to realize that the test was not measuring what they were teaching and asked for information on alternative forms of assessment, such as portfolios or performance tasks. The evaluators looked to the research. They discovered that other writers had commented on the lack of higher-level thinking required by standardized achievement tests (Romberg & Wilson, 1992; O'Connor & Brie, 1994). Nancy and Maria also found a study supported by the National Science Foundation that reported "only 3 percent of the questions on standardized mathematics exams test conceptual knowledge and only 5 percent test for problem-solving and reasoning skills" (NCTM, 1993, p. 7). After four years, it was concluded that the project was successful in changing beliefs, curriculum, instruction, and assessment in mathematics. Positive factors influencing this success focused on teacher- and student-centered uses of technology and cooperative learning within the new math curriculum. Those involved concluded that the existence of the standardized district exam actually served to limit their reform efforts and that until required assessments begin to reflect new designs for learning, sustained innovation in education is unlikely to succeed.

Educational practice has a long tradition of assessment—the process of identifying, documenting, and judging learning outcomes. In fact, the practice of testing is a deeply ingrained educational idea. The old adage "If it can't be tested, it isn't worth teaching" reflects beliefs about learning and teaching that have long been held by some educators (Hart, 1994, p. 14). Yet, this belief can severely limit curriculum to what can be easily tested not what is deemed important for students to learn. Testing has a profound effect on what and how teachers teach, what is studied, and what kinds of skills and knowledge are valued (Eisner, 1994b; Eisner, 1998; Kohn, 1999).

Teachers have become accustomed to depending on assessment strategies determined by those outside the classroom. They often doubt that the assessments they design are as important or valued as district- or state-mandated standardized tests. After all, many decisions that affect students' lives such as admission into special programs, promotion, and graduation depend more on the outcomes of standardized state or district tests than on input from the teachers.

TRADITIONAL ASSESSMENT PRACTICES

Whether created by large organizations for state and national assessment or by teachers for their own classroom use, traditional assessment strategies focus predominantly on short-item, multiple-choice formats designed to assess the facts and skills students have learned. These assessment practices are based on a view of learning identified in Chapter 2 as the efficiency model. This model is sometimes called the transmission model of instruction and assessment. Transmission models are based on assumptions that learning involves the accumulation of particular sets of facts and skills; teaching involves the transmission of facts and skills by an expert; and assessment involves an accounting of whether the desired facts and skills have been acquired (Cognition and Technology Group at Vanderbilt, 1996).

These assumptions are consistent with the psychology of learning known as behavioral learning theory. As we saw in Chapter 2, behaviorists theorize that all learning, even complex learning, can be broken down into small units of information and taught and tested in this way (Skinner, 1958). They believe that all people store this information in a similar linear fashion and that ideal paths for learning any subject can be developed. If the teaching of content is broken down into objectives and each objective is taught in a linear, sequential fashion, behaviorists believe that student learning can best be assessed by measuring small units of behavior. Based on the Skinnerian idea that learning is the result of external reinforcement from the environment not internal processing by the learner, traditional assessment focuses on the product of learning not the process.

The view of assessment inherent in the transmission model and the assembly line metaphor have found their most robust expression in standardized testing, both norm-referenced and criterion-referenced testing. A norm-referenced test is a standardized assessment designed to place a student or group of students in rank order compared with other test-takers of the same age and grade. On norm-referenced tests, the "questions are not chosen to reveal what a student knows or can do so much as how an individual student's performance compares with the performance of his or her peers" (Hart, 1994, p. 5). Some norm-referenced testing may be useful for comparing districts, schools, or programs, but the results of most norm-referenced tests provide little useful information about individual students and, therefore, are of little use to teachers or parents (Corbett & Wilson, 1993; Darling-Hammond, 1997; Kohn, 1999). Oakes and Lipton (1999, p. 222) conclude

> These tests have one element in common. Tests proceed from an assumption of a test giver—powerful with knowledge and licensed to judge others—and a test taker—without power and submitting to judgment. In this respect, conventional tests are consistent with traditional behavioral and transmission models of learning.

In theory, criterion-referenced tests may be more useful for the classroom teacher. A criterion-referenced test is designed to reveal what an individual student knows, understands, or can do in relation to specific objectives. Criterion-referenced tests can provide information on each student's strengths and weaknesses. However, with the exception of several enhanced multiple-choice tests that require students to synthesize information or understand charts before selecting an answer, criterion-referenced multiple-choice tests do not measure higher-level thinking or the learning processes used by the student. Bloom (1984), who led the effort to develop a taxonomy of cognitive abilities, noted that as much as 80 to 90 percent of the short answers required on standardized tests continue to be at the recall or knowledge level. In addition, many criterion-referenced tests are normed and used to compare groups of students or school performance rather than provide specific information about individual students (Austin Independent School District, 1993).

The use of standardized tests is increasing. According to the U.S. Congress, Office of Technology and Assessment [OTA] (1992), revenues from standardized tests doubled between 1960 and 1989 while enrollment in schools only increased by 15 percent. The Educational Testing Service (ETS) itself suggested that there is "too much testing of the wrong kind; too little of the right kind in K–12 education" (ETS, 2000) (http://www.ets.org/research/pic/testing/tmt2.html). The ETS suggests that in the 1980s and 1990s it was elected officials—governors and state legislators—not educators, who continued to press for more testing and that the original purpose in using standardized tests—evaluating programs and sampling student learning—has been lost in a political bandwagon. Many voices in the evaluation field are now questioning the increased use of standardized, norm-referenced testing as the primary source for making decisions about student placement, grading, and achievement or the effectiveness of educational programs.

The problem of standardized testing is compounded for students from low socioeconomic and minority cultural groups who are more negatively affected by these tests than students from the dominant culture (Lacelle-Peterson & Rivera, 1994; Lam & Gordan, 1992; Cummins, 1996). A variety of factors influence lower test scores for students who are not proficient in English including stylistic and interpretive language differences, time pressure, and cultural differences (Garcia & Pearson, 1993; Geisinger & Carlson, 1992; Harmon, 1995). Since classrooms are becoming increasingly diverse (Lam & Gordan, 1992; "New America," 2000), it is important that the assessments used are supportive of education for all students. Wilson and Davis (1994) suggest "standardized exams measure the kinds of knowledge that are becoming steadily less relevant to our definition of education" (p. 140). Darling-Hammond (1997, p. 241) suggests "Focusing on testing without investing in organizational learning is rather like taking a patient's temperature over and over again without taking the necessary steps to promote greater health."

In spite of the problems with standardized testing, it remains a reality for schools and teachers. We recognize the urgent need to attend to student performance on these tests. We also recognize that school administrators and teachers often fear that a concentration on deeper knowledge and the development of higher-level thinking skills may interfere with standardized test performance. We believe this fear to be unfounded. Recent studies support the finding that teaching conceptually and involving students in higher-level thinking applications can result in higher achievement scores on standardized tests. For example, Wenglinsky's (1998) comprehensive study of the use of technology and its relationship to student achievement scores found that students whose teachers used technology to support problem solving had significantly higher scores in mathematics in grades 4 and 8 than students whose teachers used technology for drill and practice.

THE ALTERNATIVE ASSESSMENT MOVEMENT

Teachers who view learning from a constructivist perspective emphasize different elements for assessment than those used in standardized tests. These teachers notice the knowledge and skills their students bring to class, observe how students interact and solve problems, and then provide multiple ways for students to learn and demonstrate their learning. They often focus on students' in-class work and ask students to tell them how they solved a problem or what their intention is as they write or work on projects.

Educational assessment in the twenty-first century looks quite different from the assessment practices of the past couple of decades. Newer forms of assessment (preparing portfolios, conducting experiments, conversations about student work, and rubric assessment) measure higher-level cognitive skills. Current use of the term "educational assessment" rather than "educational testing" highlights the two important shifts taking place in the field of assessment. First, there is a shift from an emphasis on facts and skills to an emphasis on higher-order thinking; second, there is a shift from the standardized testing formats to multiple forms of assessment (Linn, 1995; Montgomery, 2000). Those involved with the alternative assessment movement believe, "if it's worth learning, it is worth assessing."

There is no single agreed-upon definition of *alternative assessment*. It has been described as an alternative to standardized testing and all of the problems found with standardized, multiple-choice testing (Huerta-Macias, 1995). Knapp and Glenn (1996, p. 64) state, "assessment is alternative when the tasks used in testing are equal or similar to the best tasks found in instruction." It is also alternative when students are engaged in "using knowledge and skills to solve the kinds of problems and do the kinds of things students will face in the world outside school." Hart (1994) prefers the term *authentic assessment*, which she defines as "assessment that both mirrors and measures students' performance in 'real life' tasks and situations" (p. 105). For example, if we want students to communicate effectively in writing, the authentic way to assess them is to evaluate actual samples of their writing.

Terms like *alternative assessment*, *authentic assessment*, and *performance-based assessment* are used synonymously to mean variants of performance assessments that require students to generate rather than choose a response (Herman, et al., 1992). By whatever name, these types of assessments require students to actively accomplish complex and meaningful tasks, integrating prior knowledge, recent learning, and relevant skills to solve realistic problems. A variety of assessment forms include performance assessment, portfolio assessment, informal assessment, situated or contextualized assessment, and assessment by exhibition (Garcia & Pearson, 1993).

First, process is viewed to be as important as product and students' explanations of how they developed, changed, or created a product as important as the product itself. A second characteristic of alternative assessment strategies is that they are instructionally based and relatively nonintrusive. There is no separate block of time for assessment. Learning activity is not stopped as students spend time testing. Instead, assessment is built into the instructional tasks students are performing and used as criteria for continuously improving that performance.

embedded

A third characteristic of alternative assessment is the effort to find assessment strategies that provide students with expanded opportunities to demonstrate what they know. Students are evaluated on what they can produce, explain, or show rather than on what they can recall or reproduce. Learning is assessed as a holistic act with assessment focused on a wide range of processes and products rather than on small bits of behavior.

The alternative assessment movement is shifting attention from behavioral to cognitive views of learning and assessment, from paper-pencil tasks to authentic tasks, from single occasions for assessment to examining samples of student work over time, from a focus on unitary visions of learners to viewing learners as multidimensional, and from an exclusive emphasis on individual assessment toward group assessment. Eisner (1998, pp. 140–148) suggests eight criteria for creating and appraising new assessment practices in education:

1. Tasks used to assess what students know and can do need to reflect the tasks they will encounter in the world outside schools, not merely those limited to the schools themselves;
2. Tasks used to assess students should reveal how students go about solving a problem, not only the solutions they formulate;
3. Assessment tasks should reflect the values of the intellectual community from which the tasks are derived;
4. Assessment tasks need not be limited to solo performance;
5. New assessment tasks should make possible more than one acceptable solution to a problem and more than one acceptable answer to a question;
6. Assessment tasks should have curricular relevance, but not be limited to the curriculum as taught;
7. Assessment tasks should require students to display a sensitivity to configurations or wholes, not simply to discrete elements; and
8. Assessment tasks should permit students to select a form of representation they choose to use to display what has been learned.

Aligning Instruction, Curriculum, and Assessment

Throughout this book, we have explored current and emerging theories about learning and teaching—the multidimensional nature of human potential, constructivist learning, situated cognition, distributed expertise, and problem-based learning. Designing learning opportunities for students consistent with these perspectives depends, in part, on our ability as educators to embed these opportunities in appropriate systems of assessment. If, for instance, we design problem-centered learning opportunities for students but hold them accountable for only factual knowledge, students will soon recognize the discrepancy between our actions and our assessments and learn to value their ability to accumulate information over their ability to solve problems. "The ways in which curriculum, instruction, and assessment are linked reflects the overall climate or community of the classroom" (Cognition and Technology Group at Vanderbilt, 1996, p. 818).

In constructivist classrooms, assessment takes various forms, promoting a multiplicity of goals including but not limited to content knowledge. Assessment takes place in many contexts and includes individual and group work, aided and unaided responses, and short and long time periods. Open discussions of performance criteria and standards of excellence among teachers, students, and even parents characterize the constructivist classroom. Assessment is an integral part of instruction not a function added after the fact.

Putting Teachers At the Center of Assessment

Teachers have long been attuned to the process of instruction—how a lesson is going, who is having difficulty, who is paying attention, how a certain group is working—and have adjusted their plans and activities in response to their observations. Similarly, most teachers use a range of strategies to gather information to determine how well students are learning. What is new about principles associated with the alternative assessment movement is that teachers are being encouraged to make explicit and formal what they have previously done implicitly and informally. Teachers are being encouraged to articulate their instructional goals more clearly, to align their teaching practices with current views of meaningful teaching and learning, to gather evidence to guide instruction, and to combine assessment strategies into a comprehensive system of assessment designed to capture multiple forms of learning. Teachers' roles as assessors of learning are changing.

In many cases, learners are asked to help define the task to be evaluated and the conditions under which the evaluation is to occur. Teachers find this easier to do if they, themselves, are involved in classes and workshops that require them to participate in the process of assessing their own work. Teachers need practice, not only in meeting a list of desired outcomes but also in explaining how they learned and how they overcame barriers in problem-solving situations. These types of professional development opportunities help teachers design similar types of learning environments for their students.

> Teachers who were themselves learning to use new multimedia tools to design projects were asked how they would evaluate these projects if they were to ask their students to complete similar projects. At first, they were baffled by the question. As they began to think and talk about how to evaluate their students' work, one group of teachers favored using a point system tied to a list of criteria while another group suggested using a holistic rubric. These teachers had experience evaluating their own work as graduate students using both checklists and rubrics. The teachers arguing for a checklist with points thought this would make it easier

to calculate grades. Those who wanted rubrics suggested that a rubric might provide a more holistic view of students' work than a checklist. Others suggested options including using a narrative form of evaluation, simply talking with the students about how they thought they were doing, asking students to evaluate themselves, or asking students to evaluate one another's work.

Teachers agreed that these alternative assessment strategies seemed more appropriate for assessing the type of learning they were facilitating than traditional testing techniques, but many questions remained. How were they going to learn about all the different types of assessments that were possible? When should they use a rubric or a portfolio? What kinds of rubrics were possible? When is performance assessment appropriate? If students are involved in assessment, how objective would students really be about their own work? Should students be allowed to evaluate other students? How could teachers help parents to understand these newer forms of assessment? What does an A or a B really mean anyway—to students, teachers, administrators, and parents? The issues seemed complex, and teachers asked for more time to learn about alternative assessment.

ALTERNATIVE ASSESSMENT STRATEGIES

Assessment of student work requires multiple forms of assessment—a system of assessment. Educators need opportunities to assess development of students' background knowledge. Standardized tests and teacher-made objective tests serve well to learn about the facts, definitions, and content inherent in student learning. Educators need opportunities to assess students' development over time. They also need opportunities to assess how students define and understand their own learning. Portfolio assessment can support both student learning and assessment of student learning over time. Educators need opportunities to assess student problem-solving abilities, and the ways in which student problem-solving takes on visible form through their productions. Rubrics can support thoughtful and comprehensive assessment of students' individual and collective productions.

Using Rubrics for Assessment

Criteria used for judging student performances lie at the heart of alternative assessment. In the absence of criteria, assessment tasks remain just that, tasks or instructional activities. According to Arter and McTighe (2001, p. 4), performance criteria are guidelines, rules, or principles by which student responses, products, or performances are judged. They describe what educators and parents look for in student performances or products to judge quality. These criteria also make public guidelines for students to use as they think through their own performances.

Criteria communicate goals and achievement levels. They make public what is being judged and the standards for acceptable performance. Developing rubrics is a way to publish performance criteria and make evaluation explicit. Public discussion of criteria for quality informs students and parents of what students are expected to be able to do and know in relation to the curriculum. For students, making these criteria public at the beginning of an instructional unit allows students to guide their own learning, judge their efforts, and make improvements before they are evaluated. Discussions of criteria also help students see the perspectives of their teachers, their peers, and sometimes even the experts in a particular field. The process of developing performance criteria rubrics often helps teachers become clearer about what criteria are appropriate for demonstrating learning and how they might want to change instruction to ensure the attributes being measured are also taught.

Scoring rubrics are descriptive scoring schemes developed by teachers or other evaluators to guide the analysis of the products or processes of students' efforts (Brookhart, 1999). A rubric is a particular format for a criteria—it is the written version of the criteria. The best rubrics "are worded in a way that covers the essence of what we, as teachers, look for when we're judging quality, and they reflect the best thinking in the field as to what constitutes good performances" (Arter and McTighe, 2001, p. 8). These rubrics are sets of criteria for scoring student performance on tests, portfolios, writing samples, presentations, products, or other performance tasks. Sometimes individual teachers develop rubrics for classroom tasks. Sometimes groups of teachers develop rubrics to articulate grade level, disciplinary, or schoolwide expectations. Sometimes teachers and students or teachers and parents develop rubrics.

Holistic and Analytic Rubrics.   There are many different types of rubrics. One common distinction is that made between holistic and analytic rubrics. A holistic rubric is used when there is an overlap between different factors and when the intention is to evaluate the product as a whole. Holistic scoring involves giving an overall evaluation of a product or performance without analyzing individual strengths and weaknesses. Holistic rubrics are often used when the purpose is to get a quick overall evaluation of the student's abilities. Figure 9.1 contains a rubric used for evaluating final essay exams at the college level. The purpose of this rubric is to provide a fairly quick evaluation of a whole piece of writing at the end of a class. While it is a public rubric that can guide students in preparing for the final written exam, it is not intended to help students continuously improve their writing or to guide teachers modifying their instruction.

An analytical assessment rubric focuses attention on the different parts or components of a learning task. An analytical rubric helps students and teachers analyze the strengths and weaknesses of a student product. Generally, an analytical rubric uses a point scale to differentiate between levels of performance. Often, rubrics use a five-point scale with clear criteria listed for writing of a high (5), middle (3), or low (1) criteria for each category of performance. This scale provides a clear picture of what an average response is, what high and low responses are, and the distance between these. Figure 9.2 presents part of an analytical writing assessment rubric known as the *Six-Trait Analytical Writing Model*—the part designed to assess word choice. This rubric attempts to capture the complexity of good writing and provides scoring rubrics in six different areas of writing assessment: ideas and content, organization of the writing, voice, word choice, sentence fluency, and conventions (mechanics and spelling). It is available online from the

4 points	Outstanding Rating	Addresses the topic in depth Shows understanding of the topic, discusses implications and interrelationships Uses scholarly information or references to support generalizations Contains theoretical and research information Projects originality in terms of freshness of ideas and voice of writer Provides a feeling of conviction and demonstrates insight Gives pertinent support (examples, details, reasons) that provide credibility Flow of ideas is easy to follow, transitions are well written Includes a summarization or conclusion
3 points	Satisfactory Rating	Addresses the topic satisfactorily Shows understanding of the topic Uses scholarly information or references to support generalizations Makes points explicit with details, elaboration, and/or examples Projects writer's voice Information presented is relevant Sticks to the topic
2 points	Unsatisfactory Rating	Partially addresses the topic Reflects only partial understanding of the topic Some detail, elaboration, or support for ideas Loose organization, hard to follow
1 point	Fail	Does not address the topic Contrived, filling up space Illogical or irrelevant ideas Only personal opinion, no support from literature Poor writing interferes with understanding meaning

FIGURE **9.1**

RUBRIC FOR HOLISTIC SCORING OF FINAL ESSAY EXAMS

Northwest Regional Lab (www.nwrel.org/eval/toolkit98/traits/) and is being used in various districts as part of a comprehensive effort to improve student writing. Figure 9.3 presents another analytical rubric developed by Wiburg (1987) to assess the impact of computer tools on students' writing in the area of social studies.

General and Specific Rubrics.   Rubrics may also be general or specific. A general rubric is used to identify a broad category of tasks. For example, if a course such as a speech class is meant to develop a student's oral presentation skills, a general rubric can be used to evaluate oral presentations. However, if the oral presentations are meant to demonstrate how well the student understands the history of an event in a social studies class or the plot and characters of a book in a literature class, different task-specific rubrics need to be designed for each presentation. Sometimes an analytic rubric can be designed in which one part evaluates the student on general presentation skills while another part evaluates the student's

5   *Words convey the intended message in a precise, interesting, and natural way*
- Words are **specific** and **accurate:** it is easy to understand what the writer means.
- The language is **natural** and never overdone: phrasing is highly **individual.**
- **Lively** verbs energize the writing. **Precise nouns and modifiers** create pictures in the reader's mind.
- **Striking words and phrases** often catch the reader's eye—and linger in the reader's mind.
- **Clichés and jargon** are used sparingly, only for effect.

3   *The language is functional, even if it lacks punch; it is easy to figure out the writer's meaning on a general level*
- Words are almost always **correct and adequate:** they simply lack flair.
- **Familiar words and phrases** communicate, but rarely capture the reader's imagination.
- **Attempts at colorful language** come close to the mark, but sometimes seem overdone.
- Energetic verbs or picturesque phrases **liven things up now and then:** the reader longs for more.

1   *The writer struggles with a limited vocabulary, searching for words to convey meaning. The writing reflects more than one of these problems:*
- Language is so **vague** (e.g., It was a fun time. She was neat, It was nice, We did lots of stuff) that only the **most general message** comes through.
- Persistent **redundancy** distracts the reader.
- **Jargon or clichés** serve as a crutch.
- **Words are used incorrectly,** sometimes making the message hard to decipher.
- Problems with language **leave the reader wondering** what the writer is trying to say.

Note: Certain words have been bolded and their further definition is available to help teachers guide instruction and to help students understand the criteria.

FIGURE **9.2**

WORD CHOICE

Source: Reproduced with permission of Northwest Regional Education Laboratory (NWREL), Portland, Oregon.

understanding of the assigned content area. It is often useful to ask students to help in the development of such an analytic rubric.

A group of middle school students in a rural border community in New Mexico are developing multimedia history presentations. The small town of Columbus, in which the students are working, is famous for what is known in this country as the Mexican Invasion of 1916. At that time, members of the Mexican army under Pancho Villa crossed the border into Columbus. The class is fortunate to have access to a small local museum that has maintained pictures and documents related to this event. There is also a rare 16-millimeter film available for viewing at nearby Pancho Villa State Park. The films and documents represent both the North American and the Mexican point of view.

Rate the following items from 0 to 2, with 0 being an absence of a criterion and 2 being complete satisfaction of the criterion. A 1 indicates a rating halfway between 0 and 1.

0 = failure to meet criteria
1 = meets some of the criteria
2 = fully meets or exceeds the criteria

A. Appeal of the piece of writing
    1. Voice—Is there a lively interesting voice?
    2. Interest—How interested are you in reading it?	

B. Convergent production
    1. Organization—Is there a clear, coherent message?
    2. Controlling Idea—Does the piece support a controlling idea?
    3. Information—Is it relevant, concrete, and specific?	

C. Divergent production
    1. Is the piece of writing original?
    2. Is there an unusual use of text or graphics?	

D. Effective integration of text and graphics
    1. Are the graphics appropriate to the text?
    2. Do the graphics enhance the meaning of the text?	

Total Score _____

FIGURE **9.3**

PRODUCT ASSESSMENT SCALE FOR COMPUTER-GENERATED WRITING

Pancho Villa claimed that he had paid a large amount of money to the local hardware store in Columbus in exchange for ammunition and that the ammunition had never been delivered. In addition, he claimed to have large amounts of money in the Columbus bank, which he had not been allowed to withdraw. From Pancho Villa's point of view, his crossing the border with his army was not an invasion but an effort to obtain what was his. In contrast, the settlers in Columbus saw Villa's army as an invasion.

Students soon understood the problems relating to the interpretation of history as they began to design their local history projects. Students had previously been given help in planning electronic presentations using a storyboard format and had learned how to use the different functions of the authoring software available in their classroom. Students found the work interesting. The controversy about the invasion and the availability of real historical records, in both print and on film, stimulated questions and discussion and provided opportunities to "do" history.

After students had been working for a while, Mrs. Gonzales called the students together and asked them to think about how their projects should be evaluated. What would a good presentation look like? What criteria should be used to evaluate their work? Students first suggested some concrete criteria related to multimedia skills. They suggested that each stack should have a title card, at least four more content cards, and a reference card. The cards should be linked correctly, and the buttons used to link cards should work. Students felt it was important to use all the different capabilities of multimedia. Specifically, students felt that the research of each group should be presented in formats that included print, pictures, sound, and a scanned image or video sequence.

Mrs. Gonzales recorded all their ideas. She next encouraged them to look beyond the form. What should the content be like? What would they, as readers, viewers, and listeners, find interesting? What is important about studying history? Most students thought the different points of view on the border skirmish would be interesting. They suggested that each stack represent at least two points of view and that these views should be well supported by research. Students also felt it was important that the two points of view be presented without bias. Their point of view, they felt, should be presented separately from the two points of view and clearly identified as "their" viewpoint. Students felt it was important that text be precise. Too many words on each screen made the messages unclear. They felt the main messages on each card should be clear, concise, and easy to understand. Finally, they thought the pictures and sounds should support the words expressed in print and make those ideas easier to understand. If the pictures were not related to the words, they confused the reader.

Mrs. Gonzales combined all their ideas into a rubric and posted that rubric on a large bulletin board. Students referred to it frequently as a guide for the design of their multimedia history presentations. Occasionally, they asked students from other groups or Mrs. Gonzales to clarify the criteria and help them apply it to their presentations. When all the multimedia presentations were finished, Mrs. Gonzales distributed a printed version of the rubric and asked students to use it to provide feedback to the different groups. She used it herself to provide students with her feedback. Several students were so excited about their presentation that they invited their parents to attend. Mrs. Gonzales asked these parents to use the rubric. The day after the last presentation was complete, Mrs. Gonzales provided copies of the completed rubrics to the appropriate groups. She asked them to collaboratively write an assessment of their presentation, including a description of the process of construction and a description of what they would change. Students used the copies of the rubric assessment to help them reflect on their presentations. These final, collaborative reflections would be stored in their electronic portfolio along with the multimedia version of their presentation.

Developing Rubrics.   There are several different strategies we would recommend to teachers interested in developing their own rubrics. If a teacher or group of teachers have a clear idea of what a high-quality product should look like, such as an A paper or an A performance, they can begin by writing down their criteria based on experience. They will need to clearly define the criteria using language that specifies the desired outcome in concrete terms. It is not enough to say that students should demonstrate creativity in their story writing. The rubric writers will need to define what creativity looks like. Does it mean the story has originality and contains unique elements? Is it important that the reader can hear the unique writer's voice? It is important for designers to avoid vague terms.

Designers need to decide if the rubric will be a holistic rubric, one that looks at the whole product, or an analytic rubric that provides subsections that examine different aspects of the product or performance. Often teachers will divide a rubric related to learning a content area into a content learning part (content) and a publication part (form). When teachers want to develop a rubric that can be used to guide teaching and learning over time in a complex area of learning such as problem solving, a general, analytical rubric is usually the most helpful.

Developers of rubrics also need to decide what kind of scale they want to use in the rubric. Do they want a scale of 1 to 4—a typical range for many rubrics—or is the task so complex that a scale of 1 to 6 or more is needed. Arter and McTighe (2001) provide examples of a six-point mathematics problem-solving scale, a six-point primary reading scale, and an 11-point developmental writing continuum rubric. Readers of this text should explore the many different types of rubrics available for guidance on scoring scales.

After specifying what a high-level product should look like, it is necessary to build criteria for a middle-level and a low-level product. This will help in determining the criteria for a low, average, or high performance, process, or product and how they relate to each other. Sometimes rubrics only report the high (5), middle (3), and low (1) performance criteria and then ask scorers to place student work that does not fit at those levels in between at a 4 or a 2. After developing the rubric, teachers should try out a rubric, using it to evaluate student work and modifying it when characteristics that seem important in the student work are not included in the rubric or when aspects of the rubric do not seem helpful in evaluating the work.

A second way to begin developing a rubric is to look at student work. This might be a way to start when teachers are not clear on what criteria is important or are inexperienced in articulating important criteria. Teachers can begin by describing what they think is A work, C work, and work that fails to meet the desired criteria. In the mathematics professional development community, increasing emphasis is put on having teachers look at student work, not only in terms of designing criteria for evaluating it but also in terms of finding out what they can about how students solve problems and think about mathematics. Looking at student work provides an excellent opportunity to think about the many different ways that students solve problems or create products. Insights gained from examining student work can be very helpful in designing classroom assessments.

Teachers designing a rubric by looking at and sorting student work can then begin to list criteria that seem most relevant at each level of the work. Teachers might also want to consider alternative ways that students have solved problems or presented information and find ways to include a range of different, but *good* answers in their evaluation. This follows Eisner's (1998) recommendation that students should be able to demonstrate their understanding using different forms of representations. It also supports what we know about the importance of providing alternative solutions in order to gain higher-level thinking skills.

In general, rubrics should include:

1. One or more traits or dimensions that serve as the basis for judging students' responses;
2. Definitions and examples to clarify the meaning of each trait or dimension;
3. A scale of values (or a counting system) on which to rate each dimension; and
4. Standards of excellence for specified performance levels accompanied by models or examples of each level (Herman, Aschbacher, & Winters, 1992).

Teachers should also note that they do not have to start from scratch. There are now sites on the Web that provide multiple examples of excellent rubrics that can be modified by the teacher, school, or district. Examples are especially useful when developing rubrics that reflect some of the new learning foundations such as participation in communities or management of information. A list of recommended Web sites is included in Figure 9.4.

Using Portfolios for Assessment

A portfolio is a systematic and selective collection of student work that has been assembled to demonstrate the student's motivation, academic growth, and/or level of achievement. In addition, portfolios are at their best when they contain students' reflections on why the works contained in a portfolio are representative of what a student has learned. When students write about the products in their portfolio, portfolios become more than collections of student work; they become reflections of what students have learned.

Montgomery (2000) identifies three main types of portfolios:

- **Product Portfolios:** Portfolios that contain products that are judged to be the students' best work. These are often called Display Portfolios, Best Work Portfolios, or Achievement Portfolios.
- **Process Portfolios:** Portfolios that contain work that provides evidence of how works evolved and were refined. These are sometimes called Effort Portfolios. Contents of this kind of portfolio might include all drafts leading to a completed product.
- **Progress Portfolios:** Portfolios that compare identical work samples over time in order to show student improvement (Montgomery, 2000, pp. 79–80).

Portfolio assessment is most common in instances where much of the work is in written or artistic forms, but portfolios can contain video- and audiotapes, computer programs, photographs, or virtually any product that serves to highlight learning. Portfolios should contain carefully selected samples of students' work, students' comments about their work, and various types of assessments from teachers, students, parents, community members, classroom visitors, and students' peers. Samples of student work contained in a portfolio should have assessment instruments (e.g., a completed rubric, teacher comments, and objective tests) attached to them (Slavin, 1994).

The most common type of portfolio is the product portfolio. It reflects the original purpose of portfolios as used by artists, writers, and any individual wanting to give the viewer a sense of the range and quality of the individual's work. Students at any age are capable of selecting their best work and helping to define why it is their best work. They also benefit from discussion of their work with their teachers, parents, and other school personnel including principals and peers.

Ann Ciconnetti in Wooster, Ohio, has been using pizza boxes for her fourth-grade students as places for them to collect their best work. She has organized the portfolio

The Staff Room   http://www.odyssey.on.ca/~elaine.coxon/rubrics.htm
    Provides a range of rubrics in all subject areas as well as rubrics for process skills such as research or information management.

Understanding Rubrics   http://www.middleweb.com/rubricsHG.html
    Demonstrates how rubrics can use qualitative descriptions to assess levels of quality.

RubricStar   http://rubistar.4teachers.org/
    This site helps teachers create their own rubrics. It provides criteria and scoring options for specific projects. The newsletter, rubric maker, and the criteria interface are helpful.

Blue Web'n Site Evaluation Rubric
http://www.kn.pacbell.com/wired/bluewebn/rubric.html
    Provides a simple yet effective rubric for building an educational Web site.

Kathy Schrock's Rubrics List
http://school.discovery.com/schrockguide/assess.html#rubrics

Cooperative Learning Rubrics   http://www.phschool.com/professional_
development/assessment/rub_coop_process.html
    Available from Prentice Hall as a PDF file. Includes forms that can be filled in by teachers.

Chicago Public Schools
http://intranet.cps.k12.il.us/Assessments/Ideas_and_Rubrics/Create_Rubric/Step_1/
Dimensions_of_Scoring/dimensions_of_scoring.html
    List of criteria that can be used in rubrics for different subject areas.

FIGURE **9.4**

WEB-BASED RESOURCES FOR DESIGNING RUBRICS

process around six-week increments at the end of which she spends some time doing individual conferences with the students about their work. She makes this student conference time possible by planning a daily activity center time during which students read books, complete activity center projects, work on the classroom computers, or meet with her to discuss their portfolio. The students have been asked to pick out their best work each week and to write about why they think it is their best work. From time to time, Ann adds her own examples of student work to the pizza box. During student conferences, Ms. Ciconnetti and the student together write a letter home describing what is in the portfolio and what the contents demonstrate about the abilities of the student. The pizza box is then taken home and parent(s) or guardian(s) are asked to look at the pizza portfolio with their children. Parents are asked to add their comments to the contents of the pizza box and return both to the teacher. Ms. Ciconetti repeats this portfolio production several times during the year giving herself a break in between these six-week sessions and student conferencing periods.

Often the development of a portfolio is a joint activity between teacher and student. Teachers might suggest certain categories such as "the piece I am most proud of," "something I really struggled to learn," or "my attempt to do something different." Teachers should also require that certain standard items be included. At University Heights High School, students must demonstrate mastery of seven domains of learning: effective expression and communication, self-awareness and self-esteem, taking responsibility and preparing for the future, social interactions and effective citizenship, critical thinking and problem solving, cultural and historical involvement, and valuing and ethical decision making. To graduate, students must successfully prepare and present portfolios in each of these areas. Any piece included in their portfolio must be accompanied by a "cover letter" that expresses the students' beliefs about how the work represents what they learned and accomplished (Clarke & Agne, 1997).

Another type of portfolio focuses more on process and is often called a process portfolio. It allows teachers and students to evaluate the whole of a learning process or to evaluate progress in a specific area such as writing, problem solving, or the development of skills in multimedia presentations. DeFina (1992) suggests teachers help students complete a writing process portfolio. The portfolio would include examples of each of the stages of the writing process. It might include activities such as list making, brainstorming, pictures used to stimulate writing, or graphic organizers to represent the prewriting process. It might then include a first draft, notes from peer or teacher meetings on editing, and various revisions. Finally, examples of published works would be included. Teachers should always conference with students to help them select work that demonstrates their growth not only for writing but for areas such as problem solving and understanding new concepts.

Creating Electronic Portfolios

With the availability of technology, students can prepare electronic portfolios that include not only computer-generated work such as word processing, multimedia products, and spreadsheets but also work that has been selected and scanned in for inclusion in the portfolio. An electronic portfolio is a convenient way to store information and to save it over the years as well as to build in electronic links between samples of work related on some criteria. If a school has a high-performance network, students may also be able to save work into a central file server from any class or location (including work at home) for use later in an electronic portfolio. To meet the needs of parents that may not have access to computers, it is possible to capture an electronic portfolio onto videotape that can be played at home on the VCR.

Technology and portfolio assessment are ideally suited to each other. Products generated with technology ranging from word processing documents to major student-created multimedia projects can be components of a portfolio. Technology can also provide an environment for constructing portfolios. Web-based environments, hypermedia programs, or specially prepared portfolio programs like Grady's Portfolio can be used to store and organize student work and might include work samples of text, scanned images of artwork, and audio clips of oral reading. Comments should be attached to work samples by students, teachers, and parents (Barrett, 1994). These electronic portfolios have clear advantages over their physical counterparts. These advantages include: (1) An electronic portfolio lets students trace their development along different paths, using one body of illustrative work. (2) An electronic portfolio allows easy editing so students can add or link new productions as they complete them. (3) An electronic portfolio promotes browsing by reducing bulk (Clarke & Agne, 1997).

Joanne Keane teaches in the program for four-year-olds at her school. This program is designed to provide educational programs for young students with disabilities. The program is part of the special education program provided by the district and supported, in part, by federal funds. The 11 children in this program have disabilities that range from mild cerebral palsy to severe communication disorders. Ms. Keane's educational goals center on helping students' development readiness skills so that when they enter the academic program they will be better able to profit from their experiences. Goals center on gross and fine motor coordination, social skills, independence skills, language development, and concept development.

Ms. Keane is responsible for creating, implementing, and assessing individualized educational plans for each student. She uses a series of behavioral and developmental checklists and readiness tests for initial assessment, for ongoing progress reports, and for year-end evaluation. Over the years, she has discovered that these instruments are inadequate. Abstract marks on paper do not communicate to parents what their students are actually able to do and what progress they are making. Ms. Keane was convinced that samples of students' work, pictures, and short video segments would be much better at expressing students' levels of achievement. But it had seemed impossible to manage and present such a variety of samples.

While involved in a four-semester graduate program focusing on the integration of technology to support teaching and learning, Ms. Keane became familiar with several hypermedia programs. She thought, perhaps, these programs might provide an environment for presenting and managing a more diverse array of information about her students. On the advice of her instructor, she previewed several programs designed to support electronic portfolios, but none of the ones she looked at seemed to meet her particular needs. Instead, she designed a portfolio template using Toolbook that better met her assessment needs (see Figure 9.5). She copied the template 11 times, saving each copy of the template in a file labeled with the student's name.

Ms. Keane's template included an opening card where she could place a digitized picture of the student taken at the beginning of the year and again at the end of the year. Also included on this card was a text field where she could enter basic information about a student. A button in the right corner connected to a card that listed all the developmental competencies that were part of her curriculum. She linked an invisible button to this linking button and collected language samples from students. On the second card with the list of developmental competencies, she constructed buttons for each competency that connected to a description of that competency and sample behaviors deemed desirable for entrance into the academic program of the school. From the description of each competency, she created a button that led to information relevant to the particular level of the student. Her buttons linked to appropriate video segments, scanned images of checklists and readiness tests, digitized pictures, and scanned samples of student work. Another button linked to a card with an empty, scrolling text field. This was for entering the individualized plan for a student. A final button connected to a duplicate of this card that would be used at a later time to provide updated information.

During the first month of school, Ms. Keane used one of the school's video cameras and the school's digitizing camera to record images of students working at centers. Her classroom was structured to rotate students through a series of learning centers each day. Each learning center was developed to target one of the competency areas in her curriculum. As she observed children through the lens of the

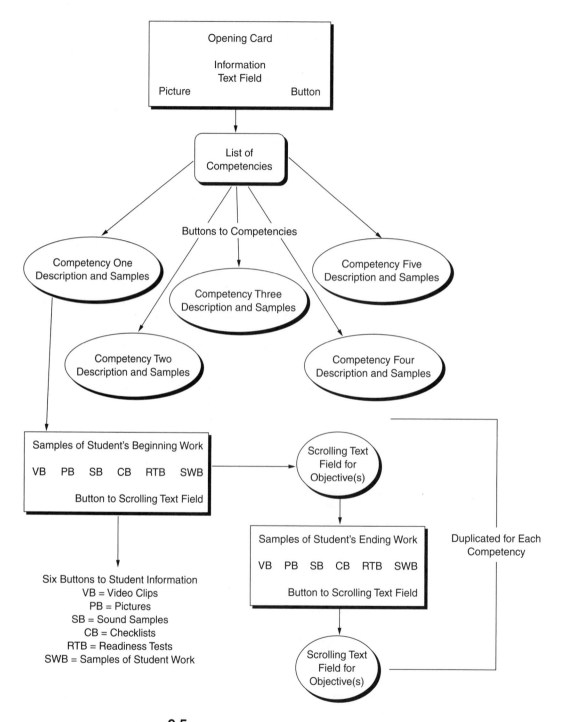

FIGURE **9.5**

MS. KEANE'S ELECTRONIC PORTFOLIO TEMPLATE

cameras working independently, with each other, or with her classroom aide, she was able to notice and jot notes about her observations that specified appropriate samples of students' abilities. She also completed the checklists and readiness tests she usually used. She reviewed her notes and selected pictures or video clips to connect to the buttons in each student's electronic portfolio. She scanned student work and her checklists and readiness tests and embedded them in the electronic portfolio also. Since she had already created the template, it was not a difficult process.

When it came time to meet for an IEP (individualized educational plan) meeting that included parents, the speech and occupational therapists, and the special education director, Ms. Keane simply loaded the student's electronic portfolio on a computer in the meeting room, and those at the meeting used the electronic portfolio and the samples of the student at work to discuss how the needs of each child might best be met. When everyone was ready, Ms. Keane simply clicked on the button leading to the blank text field, and the group created an objective for each of the competency areas. The entire process was repeated in March to review progress, compare information from the beginning of school with that gathered in March, update objectives, and begin planning for next year. Everyone who attended the IEP meeting agreed that the electronic portfolio helped them understand what the student could do, how students' behaviors in class were not always the same as those observed in their own settings, and how well the process of reviewing the portfolio supported insightful planning for the student.

Ms. Keane was so excited about her electronic portfolios she told everyone about them. Her instructor at the University asked her to present one of the portfolios in class. She obtained permission to share one of them from a student's parents. Her fellow students were as impressed by the results as those at the IEP meeting had been. Her presentation sparked the interest of one of the middle school participants in the program. He asked her to present an electronic portfolio to his fellow "family group" teachers. These middle school teachers asked many questions of Ms. Keane and finally decided that they wanted their middle school students to create electronic portfolios. Only, they decided, students in their family group would create their own portfolios. Being older, the middle school teachers felt it was important that their students participate in decisions about what represented their learning.

◦◦◦◦◦◦

Jamie Cohen teaches third grade in Manassas Park, Virginia. Her school district encourages portfolio evaluation so Ms. Cohen has created a PowerPoint template for her students to use. Students save their work in folders on the school's network throughout the nine-week grading period. Then, during the last week of the grading period, Ms. Cohen makes sure students have plenty of time to look through their work and select a sample in each of the subject areas as well as a free time activity. Students place their selections into the portfolio template and write reflections about why they chose the sample. When parents come for end of semester conferences, they begin by reviewing their child's portfolio. They are asked to attach a note to the portfolio. When parents have finished reviewing the electronic portfolio, they conference with Ms. Cohen. During the conference, Ms. Cohen and the parents frequently refer back to samples included in the electronic portfolio. Sample slides from Ms. Cohen's portfolio template are printed in Figure 9.6.

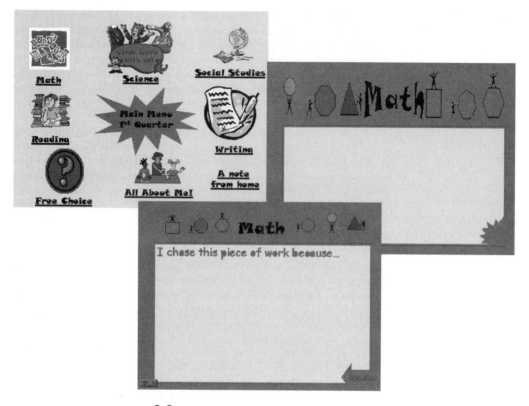

FIGURE **9.6**

SAMPLE SLIDES FROM MS. COHEN'S POWERPOINT PORTFOLIO TEMPLATE
Source: Screenshot reprinted with permission of Microsoft Corporation.

Portfolios are not just for young learners. Doctoral students in the Graduate School of Education at George Mason University are required to design a portfolio as part of their studies. The Ph.D. in Education Portfolio is an organized, yet *selective* collection of documents designed to facilitate a student's academic and professional development and to provide a basis for evaluating degree progress. The portfolio represents the scope and depth of a student's goals, plans, and accomplishments in coursework, independent study, research, internships, and other advanced learning activities. The portfolio thus provides both a vehicle for self-reflection and a comprehensive record of a doctoral student's experiences and ongoing progress toward his or her academic and professional goals. Students use the portfolio to:

1. *Define* and clarify academic and professional *goals;*
2. *Formulate* specific *plans* to achieve those goals through coursework, research, and field-based activities;
3. *Reflect* upon the process and results of their learning activities;

4. *Modify goals and plans* as needed based on reflective self-evaluation and feedback from faculty advisors; and
5. *Demonstrate readiness* to proceed to the dissertation phase of the doctoral program.

As students progress through the program, they periodically meet with their doctoral advising committee to review goals, plans, and accomplishments, and to discuss possible modifications and additional work needed to facilitate continued progress in the doctoral program. When a student has completed the coursework phase of the program, a final meeting is held with the advisory committee. This meeting is the context for conducting the Comprehensive Portfolio Assessment, a formal evaluation of a student's readiness to proceed to the dissertation phase of the Ph.D. in Education program (analogous to the traditional doctoral comprehensive exam). Guidelines for the Ph.D. Portfolio can be found at http://gse gmu.edu. A sample of a completed doctoral portfolio can be found at http://www.sg-systems.com/gmu_portfolio.

Expanding Assessment Audiences

Technology affords expanded opportunities for the assessment of student work by wider audiences. Projects range from student-made newspapers and books to multimedia development of home pages for the World Wide Web. Research on student assessment by distant audiences has been quite positive. For example, Allen and Thompson (1994) examined the effects of a computer-mediated, networked learning environment on the writing of fifth-grade students who used word processing to write collaboratively over an eight-week period. The 93 fifth-grade students, 45 males and 48 females, all had access to and were comfortable using technology for writing. Half of these students were randomly assigned to an experimental group. This group had access to a telecommunication network that allowed them to send their work via e-mail to an audience of readers, in this case, students preparing to be teachers in a college of education. The college students read and responded, via e-mail, in a supportive fashion to the students' writing. The other half of these elementary students, the control group, had the same assignments as the experimental group, had equal access to computers for writing, but did not have access to an audience via e-mail. Instead, the classroom teachers responded to their writing as usual.

The researchers were interested in whether or not students with the distance audience would write longer and/or higher-quality texts, whether their attitudes about writing would change, and whether there would be a gender difference in writing when using the network. Using a holistic writing scale, student writing was evaluated by three college writing instructors. Each scorer read all of the texts, assigned each a score, and the researchers averaged these scores. Text length was calculated, and students were given an attitude survey before and after the eight-week experiment. The experimental group had significantly higher scores on both the quality of the writing and the length of writing. There were no differences on the attitude survey and no gender differences. Both girls and boys in the experimental group did better than boys and girls in the control group.

Technology makes it much easier for the classroom teacher to bring the world into the classroom and provide an expanded audience for assessment. The audience for student learners might be another classroom, interested partners from education or business, or college students in a teacher education program.

Laurie Gould's ninth-grade Earth Science students received a letter from the National Earth Science Week Organizing Committee (NESCO) requesting help. The letter asked students to research and prepare a PowerPoint presentation on each of the five physiographic provinces of Virginia. The slide shows were to be presented before a committee of Virginia scientists and evaluated for their appropriateness for use at an upcoming National Conference. Students divided into five groups, each group selecting one of the provinces. As students began their research and preparation of the slide show, they examined geological features, availability of resources, and environmental issues related to their province. With the structure provided by this authentic problem/request, students participated in a variety of background-building activities including lab experiments, textbook assignments, videos, and Web-based research. They used spreadsheets, databases, word processors, and Web-page editors to analyze and prepare information to be presented in their slide shows. As the three weeks neared an end, students practiced their presentations and took an objective knowledge test. Ms. Gould used High Plains Regional Technology in Education Consortium's (HPR°TEC) Web site and the QuizStar (http://www.hprtec.org) option to construct an online quiz. Next, students completed a survey about their experiences during the Unit designed. Finally, the panel of "expert scientists" arrived. In her Action Research Paper, Ms. Gould wrote:

> The panel of scientists that visited was recruited from the Minerals Management Service in Herndon, Virginia. The group included an oceanographer, an environmental scientist, a petroleum engineer, and a geologist. Prior to attending the presentations, one of the panel experts expressed concern over assigning the students a "fake" problem. He felt that students would be upset by the fact that all of their hard work was for nothing. He worried that this would affect students' self-esteem and motivation to work on other class projects. The experimenter addressed these concerns through email communications, and the scientist reluctantly agreed to play along. After participating in the panel, he was thrilled to see that students did not seem to care that the problem and panel were "authentic" but not "real." At the conclusion of the experience, he said, "All teachers should design lessons this way. The kids were so enthusiastic. All we ever hear about in the news is the negative aspects of public education. Why don't we hear about things like this?"
>
> Overall, the panel was extremely impressed by the efforts of students and their communication skills. They reported that the entire project was very much like what they do in their work world. One scientist said, "I am going to use some of these PowerPoint techniques in a presentation I am currently working on." Another scientist asked, "Did the students take a required computer class to learn to use the software before

this project?" (They had not.) One of the most exciting outcomes of this project was the establishment of a mentoring program between this agency and the science students at Park View. (Gould, 2000, p. 32)

✧✧✧✧✧✧

Alma Jackson teaches desktop publishing (DTP) and business principles at a Northern Virginia high school. Instead of teaching these courses as separate contents, she designed a unit to combine the contents. She redesigned her units around a problem-centered, authentic, constructivist approach. Her first unit was designed to teach about businesses structured as sole proprietorships as well as desktop publishing design and production principles. The unit began with a visit from several local real estate agents who shared presentations on their work responsibilities, the legal and organizational structures of their sole proprietorships, and marketing and advertising materials commonly produced as part of real estate marketing.

After the agents' visits, Ms. Jackson used her school's internal student e-mail system to send a number of e-mails from potential real estate customers. After a variety of background-building activities related both to understanding sole proprietorships and desktop publishing design and production principles, students would begin the "work" portion of class by signing into their e-mail accounts. Over the course of the unit, students found it necessary to produce business cards, letterheads, advertisements, notepads, brochures, floor plans, amenities/features sheets, townhouse tear-offs, and a newsletter in order to respond to all the e-mails. As students worked to produce these materials, they were organized into a "real estate" portfolio, and students included short reflections about what they had learned about marketing, business, and desktop publishing while producing the products. Midpoint in the unit, students helped Ms. Jackson create a rubric for assessing the portfolios. Criteria were categorized around desktop publishing design principles, effectiveness of communication, and appropriateness of material. Students continually referred to these criteria as they responded to e-mails and produced materials. When the portfolios were completed, four real estate agents were invited to assess the portfolios. The agents were asked to use the rubric.

In her Action Research Paper, Ms. Jackson wrote:

> On a student survey, students indicated that they looked forward to having their portfolios evaluated by the professionals and valued the comments that were given. Interesting to note, students indicated that after the professionals reviewed their work, and once given time to make corrections, only 11% felt they were not prepared to present their portfolios for possible employment opportunities (p. 18). . . . After completing the evaluation process, the real estate agents orally discussed how impressed they were with the quality of student work and were impressed with the unit as a whole. Many expressed how much education had changed and how they would like to be a student in the DTP class. One agent wrote, "Great project. The kids did a great job! The portfolios were easy to follow and very organized. Not too much information. Good use of color in plans. We need more agents. Plenty of jobs for these students! Well done." (Jackson, 2000, p. 20)

Creating New Knowledge and Publishing Students' Work

Technology affords students opportunities not only to have knowledge delivered to them but also to create knowledge themselves. In 1997, Wiburg coordinated a project in New Mexico in which students were engaged in using technology tools to study and publish information about their local community.

> In the Nuestra Tierra Project at Onate High School in Las Cruces, New Mexico, students were using technology to learn about their local environment. John Sandin, a doctoral student and college history teacher at New Mexico State University, had been working with students at risk of school failure that had experienced little or no previous success in history classes. He had been successful in engaging these students in conversations about what really happened in New Mexico during the last 100 years—cowboy fights with Native populations, conflicts between Mexico and the U.S. government, and continuous battles over the U.S.–Mexico border.
>
> Students became so interested they each chose an area to research using both traditional print examples and the Internet access that was available in their school. Because so little was available in print about southern New Mexico history, they decided to make their own publication on the history of Mesilla, the old town near their high school. John arranged a walking tour for the students. They interviewed people, took digital photos, discussed issues, and were sometimes overheard remarking that they were now surprised that history was actually interesting.
>
> The result of their work became a hypermedia essay developed both in HyperStudio (1993) and then as a home page on the World Wide Web. Students from social studies, science, and English classes all participated in this project. Later, the English students published an additional virtual tour related to famous ghost stories in the state. Because they live in a bilingual community, their work was translated into Spanish by the Spanish class, and the Internet site can now be read in both Spanish and English (http://www.cahe.nmsu.edu/uswest).

Student knowledge contributions are not limited to history. For example, students in an elementary school in New Jersey spent many hours observing and describing specimens of flies delivered to them by scientists at nearby Hoffstra University (Condon, 1994). The scientists simply did not have the human resources to catalog the many fly specimens they had gathered in South America. As a result of their work, the children actually discovered a new kind of fly! Using technology, students can make genuine contributions to a field of study, whether it is examining millions of insects for entomologists or making information about the history of small, rural communities accessible to the residents of the area. When students publish their work, they contribute to the knowledge base of a community. As they begin to see themselves as doing science, history, writing, and mathematics in ways that are useful for both themselves and others, students who formally could not find themselves in school are discovering their own capabilities and potential. Seeing the results of their work through the eyes of others helps students assess their own capabilities.

TECHNOLOGY AND ALTERNATIVE ASSESSMENT

Using technology supports the development of alternative assessment and assists in making it both more accessible and affordable in educational settings (Sheingold and Frederiksen, 1994; Wall, 2000). Sheingold and Frederiksen (1994, p. 131) argue that technologies can be enlisted, designed, and developed that allow educators to engage in more authentic and complex learning activities. These technologies can facilitate portable and replayable copies of student achievements, store libraries of examples, provide tools for interpreting students' work, publish selected works, and expand assessment communities by enlisting more participants.

Recording and Observing Process

One of the central tenets of alternative assessment considers student learning and problem-solving processes to be as important as student products. Yet, process by definition is dynamic, contextualized, internal, and generally develops over sustained periods of time. Technology permits educators to observe and record student processes. For instance, extensive editing of student writing samples is cumbersome if students are required to recopy each draft. When teachers or other students read drafts and mark sections for elaboration, students must recopy the draft in order to embed an elaboration. Using word processors, students can edit their writing repeatedly. Teachers or other students can read the electronic file, using all capital letters to embed reactions and suggestions. Students can respond to the comments and seamlessly insert, revise, and correct. To maintain a record of the editing process, they need only save each new version with a new file name. Teachers can easily compare successive drafts, examining the processes students used to improve their writing. Some word processors even allow teachers to compare the word, line, and paragraph features of successive documents.

When Ms. Angell and Mr. Shepard (Chapter 4) asked students to summarize the process they used to research, write, and pass their legislation by creating a hypermedia stack, they were able to see what students had learned about the legislative process and to pinpoint any errors in student understanding. Perhaps more important, students were able to articulate what they had learned and to reflect on what they had learned. When their hypermedia stacks were reviewed at the lunchtime Open House, many of the visitors asked them questions about their hypermedia stacks and further prompted students to assess their learning. When Mr. Harvey (Chapter 5) asked students to compare their journal article analyzing the Donner Party members most likely to survive with the journal article published in *Discover* magazine, he was prompting students to assess the outcomes of their problem solving. Students who had reported generalizations in their article that appeared in the original article were able to validate their analytical skills and those who reported generalizations that did not appear in the article were able to validate their divergent thinking or challenge and rethink their problem solving.

As students are engaged in complex, problem-solving environments, teachers can shift the complex job of structuring problem-solving activities from the teacher to computer programs. This is referred to as "off-loading." Off-loading parts of the teaching task to distributed resources enables teachers to focus on modeling complex cognitive processes and supporting learners as they attempt to replicate and master these complex processes. When parts of the teaching task are off-loaded to distributed resources, teachers have increased opportunities to work with students as cognitive mentors or to observe students as they problem solve.

One day while visiting a student teacher, Anne Fisk found the student teacher with a group of fourth-grade students in the computer lab using Sunburst Communications' The Factory, a problem-solving program. When using The Factory, students arrange a series of machines in such a way that running a blank square through the machines results in a design that matches a given model. Students' goal is to construct a sequence of machines that produce a product that matches a computer generated sample. Students may choose from three levels: easy, medium, and hard. As Ms. Fisk observed students, she noticed that students were arranging representational machines that could turn, stripe, or punch the raw material in the correct sequence, leading to the desired product. She also noted that students were working in pairs at the computers and were quite engrossed in the task. A low buzz of self-talk, typical of children engaged in challenging problem solving, was everywhere.

Observing the children, it occurred to Anne that assessing students and teachers in computer-rich, problem-solving situations would be a different process from observing teachers as they presented before the class. In this new situation, while students were problem solving, there was actually time for the student teacher and the supervisor to walk around and listen to the students talk to each other and to themselves. Anne and her student teacher were able to observe problem-solving strategies. Time to observe children and to observe for the desired learning was available. Opportunities abounded to spend time with those having trouble or to provide elaboration and discussion with other children. Teachers had become cognitive mentors; they were able to record comments and processes that students were using in order to monitor student learning. Assessing the teaching competence also shifted. Instead of assessing presentation skills or classroom management skills, Ms. Fisk could focus on the student teacher's mentoring skills, her questioning skills, and her observation skills.

New Interpretive Tools

Technology is not just a means for learning. It also provides a new set of interpretive tools that support careful interpretation of student problem solving. Examining the links that students create in a hypermedia stack, for instance, permits teachers and parents to explore the kinds of connections and relationships students are and are not making. Examining student chat logs, bulletin board posting, e-mail, or electronic journals provides valuable insight into students' thinking and communication abilities. Examining how students use spreadsheets and databases to solve mathematics and science problems provides a window into the ways students structure a problem and pursue problem solutions. Video recordings of student performances or of students at work can create flexible, replayable environments for observing student learning. New technology environments can support interactive, multimedia portfolios. Telecommunications tools like e-mail, videoconferencing, and Web pages can support invitations to multiple assessment audiences by making student work and interactions with students over distance and time feasible.

> Children in Mr. Reyes's room developed original plays to explain some of the mathematics operations they were learning. Mr. Reyes, with the help of the students, videotaped each of the plays so that he and his students could observe students' mathematical thinking. One group tackled fractions, determined once and for all to show others why a larger denominator makes a smaller fraction. Their play involved the cutting up of cookies and the wisdom of understanding fractions if one wanted to eat a lot of cookies. Another group set about demonstrating the relationship between area and perimeter by fencing in two imaginary gardens and deciding which shape would provide the most space for vegetables. A third group had the challenging task of explaining how there could be more than 100 percent of something using liquids and containers and comparing increases in volume. Because videotapes existed of each group's performance, Mr. Reyes and his students did not have to be satisfied with the original live performance.
>
> In fact, Mr. Reyes used the tapes as a sort of first draft of their mathematical explanations. Students looked at the tapes many times, repeating parts as needed. They were given the opportunity to change any parts of their play and to improve their explanations, actions, or props. Students' revised performances were taped. The final tape was assessed by the teacher, students, and parents. With presentations and student work recorded as video, assessments did not have to be superficial or arbitrary. Arguments over points could be clarified by replaying episodes several times as decisions were made about what was clear, what needed improvement, which actions were confusing, and which student explanations made a mathematical idea clear. Reviewing the first taped performance helped students assess their explanations of mathematical processes. Reviewing the final versions helped Mr. Reyes and parents assess the depth of understanding achieved by students.

As expectations of what students need to know and be able to do change, questions arise about how these desired learning goals should be assessed. Technology can help people to build and apply interpretive frameworks for viewing performance. It provides multimedia environments in which students can demonstrate their knowledge in a much broader way including the use of graphics, voice, print, video, and sound or music. In addition to supporting the diversity of the students we teach, these multiple forms of representation support both broader and deeper thinking. The designs for literacy, knowledge, thinking, community, and using information that have been introduced in this book are of little value if assessment continues to be based on older efficiency models of education. If students are encouraged to become active constructors of knowledge but graded only on memory and recall, students will not learn to value their growth as independent learners.

A variety of alternative assessment strategies including rubrics, portfolios, peer critiques, exhibitions, and performance assessment, supported by technology applications, can provide designs for assessment compatible with emerging educational goals. As educators begin to change their assessment practices to value higher-level thinking and group collaboration, they are likely to make much progress in implementing new teaching and learning processes. The final chapter of this book explores how educators can create learning environments that construct, select, and communicate these processes.

Before you move on to the final chapter, we recommend that you rejoin Brooks White and Allan Sutton as they begin to put the final touches on their design by adding a system of assessment that complements rather than clashes with their design. Use the FACTS Web-Based Design Tool site (http://www.norton.wadsworth.com) and click on the Design Mentors puzzle piece. In this chapter's Design Mentors, Brooks White and Allan Sutton wrestle with planning a system to assess student learning. Both of them learn, as they reflect on their goals and the activities they have chosen for students, that no single assessment strategy will allow them to understand the range of learning outcomes possible. After you have studied the Design Mentors, you might find it helpful to return to the opening page of the Web site and complete Design Challenge Nine. You can also examine some of the Design Examples and see how they reflect the considerations discussed in this chapter.

CHAPTER IDEAS

- Educational practice has a long tradition of assessment—the process of identifying, documenting, and judging learning outcomes. In fact, the practice of testing is a deeply ingrained educational idea. Testing has a profound effect on what and how teachers teach, what is studied, and what kinds of skills and knowledge are valued.

- Whether created by large organizations for state and national assessment or by teachers for their own classroom use, traditional assessment strategies have focused predominantly on short-item, multiple-choice formats that attempt to assess the facts and skills students have learned. Traditional assessment focuses on the degree to which students are in fact acquiring the skills and knowledge at an efficient rate as they proceed along the assembly line of grades.

- Even though schools must be accountable for student learning, shifts in understandings about what schools should teach and how students should be taught and assessed call into question traditional standardized tests.

- Standardized testing is not likely to be discontinued in schools, in large-scale assessments, or in credentialing examinations. Yet, objective forms of assessment such as multiple-choice tests will need to be balanced in school, state, employment, and national testing programs by more direct measures of assessment such as writing tasks, performance tests, computer simulation exercises, hands-on projects, and portfolios of work.

- Terms like alternative assessment, authentic assessment, and performance-based assessment are used synonymously to mean variants of performance assessments that require students to generate rather than choose a response. By whatever name, these types of assessment require students to actively accomplish complex and meaningful tasks, integrating prior knowledge, recent learning, and relevant skills to solve realistic problems.

- Several common characteristics permeate all alternative assessment efforts. First, process is viewed to be as important as product and students' explanations of how they developed, changed, or created a product as important as the product itself. A second characteristic of alternative assessment strategies is that they are instructionally based and relatively nonintrusive. A third characteristic of alternative assessment is the effort to find assessment strategies that provide students with expanded opportunities to demonstrate what they know.

- In constructivist classrooms, assessment takes various forms, promoting a multiplicity of goals including but not limited to content knowledge. Assessment is not limited to scheduled, timed, paper-pencil tasks for individuals to perform alone. Assessment takes place in many contexts and includes individual and group work, aided and unaided responses, and short and long time periods. Open discussions of performance criteria and standards of excellence among teachers, students, and even parents characterize the constructivist classroom. Assessment is an integral part of instruction not a function added after the fact.

- Teachers are being encouraged to articulate their instructional goals more clearly, to align their teaching practices with current views of meaningful teaching and learning, to gather evidence to guide instruction, and to combine assessment strategies into a comprehensive system of assessment designed to capture multiple forms of learning. Traditional teacher skills such as the ability to observe student learning, to ask questions that facilitate student understanding of their work, and to provide individualized and meaningful feedback about a student's progress are newly valued as powerful assessment abilities.

- Criteria used for judging student performances lie at the heart of alternative assessment. In the absence of criteria, assessment tasks remain just that, tasks or instructional activities. Scoring criteria make public what is being judged and the standards for acceptable performance. Criteria communicate goals and achievement levels.

- Regardless of who is involved in developing the rubric, the criteria identified by a rubric should be made public and should be discussed with students. Public discussions help students to internalize the standards and "rules" they need to become independent learners. Public discussion of quality and criteria inform students during the formative period of instruction, not simply at the end of a unit or course when it is too late to make improvements.

- A portfolio is a systematic and selective collection of student work that has been assembled to demonstrate the student's motivation, academic growth, and/or level of achievement. Portfolios should contain carefully selected samples of students' work, students' comments about their work, and various types of assessments from teachers, students, parents, community members, classroom visitors, and students' peers.

- Technology affords expanded opportunities for the assessment of student work by wider audiences. Technology makes it much easier for the classroom teacher to bring the world into the classroom and provide an expanded audience for assessment. The audience for student learners might be another classroom, interested partners from education or business, or college students in a teacher education program. This distance audience expands teaching, learning, and assessment opportunities.

- There is growing evidence that technology can support the development of alternative assessment and assist in making it both more accessible and affordable in educational settings. Technologies can be enlisted, designed, and developed that allow educators to engage in more authentic and complex learning activities, to have portable and replayable copies of student achievements, to use libraries of examples and tools for interpreting students' work, to expand the assessment community by enlisting more participants, and to publish selected works.

- Technology affords students opportunities not only to have knowledge delivered to them but also to create knowledge themselves. When students publish their work, they contribute to the knowledge base of a community.

- Technology permits educators to observe and record student processes. It provides a new set of interpretive tools that allow interested parties to carefully interpret student problem solving.

DESIGNING LEARNING ENVIRONMENTS

As part of a two-year grant to teach teachers in rural areas about technology, I frequently do workshops with my friend, Barbara Copeland, a multimedia developer at the university. One of the more challenging aspects of this work is that we never know what kind of computer lab we might walk into. Therefore, we have developed a wide range of lessons, doable on old or new machines. Yet, even when our materials and approaches are the same, we experience mixed success in different locations. We have finally concluded that the way in which the computer classroom is designed is what often determines the difference.

In some rooms the computers are lined up close together in rows. There is very little room between each computer or between each row of computers and the row behind it. There is no room for small groups of students to work together—a strategy we frequently use in introductory technology workshops. In these types of classrooms, it is difficult for us to get to students to assist them. There is room in the front of these rooms to present, but there is no room to teach—to work with students in collaborative relationships as meaning is constructed.

On the other hand, we have encountered classrooms that seem to be set up to support collaborative work. There is room around each computer to put books and materials and for several students to work together on the machine. Since we like to pair students for introductory projects and also like to be able to move around and work easily with groups, our introductory lessons always seem to go better in this second type of classroom. In general, working with teachers in flexible, collaborative settings simply feels better.

Mary Saxton
High school art and
computer teacher

Throughout the history of educational reform a great deal of attention has been paid to teaching, learning, and the curriculum. Yet, little attention has been focused on the effects of teachers' decisions related to designing places to learn (the physical environment), selecting knowledge environments to support learning goals (software), and establishing a climate of values consistent with learning outcomes (the emotional environment). Although businesses spend much money and effort to design environments that facilitate desired customer and employee behaviors, efforts in education have not always been as serious or sustained. If we want to design learning environments that support students to do more than take notes and recite facts, educators must pay careful attention to the ways in which they design learning environments— physical, intellectual, and emotional. This chapter explores (1) arranging the physical spaces in which teaching and learning occur, (2) provisioning classrooms with tools that promote important learning goals, and (3) creating classroom climates that model and teach values. The chapter concludes by examining the interactions of these considerations as they are reflected in three case studies.

LEARNING ENVIRONMENTS ARE INSTRUCTIONAL STRATEGIES

Today is Maria's first day at the new child care center. She had trouble sleeping last night because she was so excited she was finally going to "school." Her mother had hired a baby-sitter to stay with her last year, but now that she was three and a half, she was tired of spending each day with Lucy, even though Lucy was nice and took her for walks and read stories to her. She was ready to play with other children, discover new toys, and see new places.

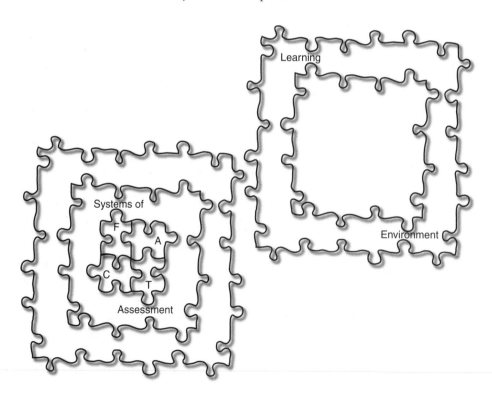

Maria's mother parked the car right in front of the colorful preschool building and walked toward Sunshine School. The child care center looked inviting from the outside. A wall-size mural of children, balloons, and cartoon animals surrounded the front door through which they entered. Inside was a hall and a counter. The room smelled of the wet coats that hung from hooks high above Maria's head. It had been raining as it so often did in the Northwest. Maria's mother put the paperwork she had filled out down on the counter. It was a convenient height for adults, but Maria could not see anything but the bottom of a shelf that stuck out just above her head. She knew there was a room with a window behind the shelf, because she could see light. But there was no way to tell what her mother could see. She wondered if the window looked out on trees in a park or onto one of the busy streets near by. Maria waited patiently, assuming she would soon be in a room more suited to her size and interests.

The teacher who was greeting parents came out from behind the counter and entered the hall through a door next to the counter. She knelt down to greet Maria and led mother and daughter down another long hall. Again, the windows were high, and Maria could not see out of them. Only a few of the pictures on the wall were low enough for Maria to see. She had to tilt her head back to see the others, and she felt like she might fall over or run into something. Eventually, Maria, her mother, and the teacher came to a door that opened into a room full of three-year-olds. Children were sitting in the corner listening to a teacher reading a story. There were pillows spread around the room, and some of the furniture was small. Maria could see the tops of tables now. The room was lined with shelves stuffed with supplies and toys, but only things on the lower shelves were visible to Maria. These seemed to be mostly boxes full of blocks, clay, material, and other things to be used for classes. When Maria asked her mother about the boxes, her mom mentioned storage—whatever that was. Maria touched the boxes. She guessed they were not supposed to be opened by children, because she could feel the tape on the top of each box. Maria reached for her mother's hand. She wasn't sure she was going to like this place.

Learning environments are instructional strategies. Teachers' choices about the types and organization of learning environments are choices about what and how students will learn. Piaget recognized this when he wrote, "Teaching means creating situations where structures can be discovered: it does not mean transmitting structures which may be assimilated at none other than a verbal level" (quoted in Gebhardt-Seele, 1985, p. 48).

Maria Montessori was, perhaps, the first educator to develop a pedagogy that focused on the learning environment as an instructional strategy. She suggested that a teacher's role is to observe students as they interact with the natural environment and then design and modify learning materials so that these materials support children's natural curiosity (Montessori, 1912). Her work with children in the slums of Italy was a powerful demonstration of the strength of her ideas. Even children with little previous education who were sufficiently supported by a well-organized and developmentally appropriate environment soon became self-motivated learners. Montessori wrote:

Education is not something which the teacher does, but it is a natural process which develops spontaneously in the human being. It is not acquired by listening

to words, but in virtue of the experiences in which the child acts on his environment. The teacher's task is not to talk, but to prepare and arrange a series of motives for cultural activity in a special environment made for the child. (quoted in
Gebhardt-Seele, 1985, p. 49)

All learning takes place in a context. The design of that context, the learning
environment, is as important as the designs teachers create for literacy, problem-
solving, knowledge, community, and information use. And, if the decisions teachers make about the learning environment are inconsistent with the designs they
create to meet learning goals, the impact of these learning opportunities will be less
powerful and important for students than teachers might hope.

Constructing Learning Environments

Much effort and money is spent to create business environments that facilitate specific kinds of behavior. Months of study and work occur before a supermarket or
clothing store is designed, built, and opened. The lighting, the placement of displays and furniture, and proposed movement patterns are all carefully researched
so that the building is designed in just the right way. After all, if the building does
not encourage and support the behaviors desired by the business, customers and
employees might not act in ways that support the business's goals.

Yet, in education, with the possible exception of early childhood programs, little thought has been focused on various aspects of the learning environment. Almost all classrooms are still boxlike. At the front of the box is a space for teaching
from which information can be delivered as efficiently as possible. Students often
sit in individual chairs, separated into rows that, by design, discourage conversation. Just enough desk space is provided for each individual to take notes or complete assignments delivered from the front of the room. There is often only a single
door into the box. Learners entering the room must generally pass by the
teacher/lecturer in order to take a seat in one of the rows. Sometimes bookshelves
or storage spaces are provided along the sides of the boxlike room. The lighting is
often fluorescent and views from windows are restricted in an effort to eliminate
distractions from outside the room.

This apparently passive learning environment is really not passive at all. Its
arrangement and the presence or absence of materials and tools speak loudly to
students about what is expected, what is valued, and how students are to act. It is
an important and active part of the teaching/learning process. The boxlike classroom suggests that most conversation should be with the teacher not with peers. It
suggests that individual work is valued more than collaborative work. It suggests
that quiet, paper-and-pencil tasks are most valued.

Look at any classroom, even without students present, and you can tell what the
teacher thinks is important. Is there evidence of student-centered and problem-
centered activity? What role does technology play in the classroom? Do the computers sit in a corner covered with plastic or is there evidence of their use (schedules,
directions for computer-based activities, and computer-generated products)? What
kinds of materials are displayed on the walls? How much of the work on the walls

and tables is produced by children? Can you tell from what you see what concepts are currently being studied, or are there old posters on the walls that display seemingly unrelated ideas? If there are pictures of people doing science or business or mathematics, are they representative of our diverse culture? Are men and women in the pictures portrayed in stereotyped activities or are men and women shown in a variety of collaborative roles? Do the materials displayed reflect the demographics of the current classroom population or some imaginary world familiar to the readers of "Dick and Jane"?

The design of places to learn must be rethought if educators are to respond to the learning needs of today's third-stage technology users. Some have started that process. For example, when Governor Caperton became Governor of West Virginia, he chose to spend school reform money on the redesign or replacement of his state's rundown and obsolete schools. In doing so, he moved the debate about restructuring beyond isolated arguments about schedules, standards, and methods and recognized the symbolic importance of the school building as a place in the life of a community. He believed that if people could take pride in their local schools, they would also value the learning that occurs there.

Schools and our experiences of school as a place to learn and grow have deep emotional meaning. Whether students' feelings are positive or negative, their memories of the schools and neighborhoods in which they grow up have a powerful influence on who they become. As Meek (1995, p. 13) writes:

> A school building, its playgrounds and playing fields, its bus lanes and bathrooms, is replete with coaching and interactions. We inhabit schools when we are young and impressionable, when our minds are busy with the tasks and issues of deep meaning. For these two reasons, the school as a place is fertile ground for the creation of deep meaning, and therefore of symbolic importance in the hearts and minds of people.

Fiske (1995) reinforces Meek's notion of the importance of place when he advocates redesigning school buildings. He asserts that since American school architecture is deeply rooted in nineteenth-century values and reflects a transmission model of learning, successful reform of the system of primary and secondary education depends on giving serious thought to the overall design of the learning environment. In fact, as much as 25 percent of learning can be accounted for by examining the qualities of the external environment of schools (Draves, 1995). Taylor (1993) believes that school buildings should be thought of as three-dimensional textbooks. For example, he writes, halls can become both vertical and horizontal learning surfaces with graphics, displays of student work, presentations of puzzling problems, and mini-museum exhibits for which the students act as curators. Windows can become demonstration centers for the science of light and the study of the changing angles of the sun as it relates to seasons. Teachers, instead of working in isolation in their rooms, can better develop collaborative, interdisciplinary learning experiences for students if schools include professional clusters of offices where teachers meet.

After reviewing the research on the impact of architectural design on learning, Lackney and Moore (1994) developed 27 design suggestions organized into four areas: planning issues, building organizing principles, characteristics of individual spaces, and critical technical details. All of the characteristics were weighted in terms of importance, with the most important being: (1) smaller schools, (2) smaller classrooms, (3) team-building, clustered classrooms and offices, (4) flexible, adaptive facilities, (5) controlled indoor climate, and (6) natural full-spectrum lighting. In sum, they recommend that builders of educational facilities redesign traditional isolated boxlike classrooms into team suites that include teacher offices equipped with professional office equipment, team work space, and a variety of different-size classrooms ranging from large meeting spaces to smaller classrooms for quiet study and work.

DESIGNING PLACES TO LEARN

Teachers may never have the opportunity to design an entire school building, but they daily make decisions about the organization of their classroom environment. And these decisions are decisions about what and how students will learn.

> Mrs. Schley designed her classroom to include a large open space in the middle. She intended this to be a quiet meeting space for children each morning. She soon observed, however, that when children entered this large space they always began joyfully running, jumping, dancing, and wrestling. Quite in contrast to her intentions, this was certainly not the sort of behavior she had expected for a quiet, orderly opening of school. Instead, Mrs. Schley found herself spending the early morning chastising students not welcoming them to another day of learning. "What a terrible way to begin each day," she thought.
>
> After some serious reflection, it occurred to Mrs. Schley that as students encountered this open space each morning, it invited them to do what children always do with open spaces. It invited them to move, to physically interact, and to enjoy the freedom of an open space. Her design of a quiet place was really a design that promoted the very behaviors she sought to avoid. Realizing this, she was able to solve the problem by changing the learning environment. After the space was redesigned, students entered the room more thoughtfully than before, filing by bookshelves with interesting displays related to concepts they would be studying. Students always stopped to touch and consider these displays. Sometimes they paused to ask questions or discuss things with each other. Soon, they were able to recognize these displays as harbingers of exciting things to come. After passing these displays, students reached a cozy rug and pillow-lined corner in which they could settle quietly for their morning meeting.

Mrs. Schley had learned the important lesson expressed by Loughlin and Suina (1982): Environmental messages can urge movement, call attention to some learning materials but not others, encourage deep or superficial involvement, and invite children to hurry or move calmly. Environmental arrangements can also promote independence and self-direction, encourage use of skills, and lengthen or shorten attention span. The environment sends messages, and learners respond.

Teachers, when designing physical learning environments, need to analyze two categories of environmental problems (Loughlin and Suina, 1982). The first category of problems relates to those that are caused by commission such as inappropriate patterns of spatial organization, inadequate provisioning, or poorly arranged materials. Mrs. Schley's original design is an example of problems that result from commission. The second category of problems focuses on those problems that are caused by omission, inadequacies in the learning environment revealed by desired learning that does not occur. For example, when a teacher observes that students are not writing, it is probably because the writing materials are stored out of sight and out of reach. When students are not asking questions about the water cycle during the rainy season, it is probably because there is no visible stimulus that prompts inquiry about the weather. If classroom books are located in an out-of-the-way corner or behind a screen, students are not likely to examine the books or select one to read. If students do not seem interested in the plants on the window, it is probably because there are no accompanying tools, materials, or information to encourage repotting, identification, propagation, or recording growth under various conditions.

The arrangement of furniture and materials, the kinds of tools available to students, and the use of time influence student learning. These factors also influence the quality of the relationships between student and student and student and teacher. The choices teachers make about the ways they construct learning environments influence the types of relationships probable in classrooms. Manke (1994) studied three teachers' classrooms in order to discover possible relationships between these teachers' organization of space and time and the teacher-student power relationships in their classrooms. She made extensive and detailed observations of classroom interactions in two fifth-grade classes and one first-grade class. The classrooms ranged from an environment in which students had almost no opportunity to move about to a class in which students made choices of activities during most of the day. The amount of time devoted to highly structured versus loosely structured activities also varied among the three classrooms.

Her study revealed three interesting consequences associated with the decisions these teachers had made when constructing the learning environment. First, the culture of each classroom was deeply influenced by the teachers' decisions about the arrangement of time and space. The consequences of these teachers' decisions could be seen by observing what students considered proper behavior in different settings. In the more structured classrooms, students had learned that they must sit facing forward and look only at their own books during a lesson. In the less structured room, children had learned the rules for quietly choosing which activity center to use during free time. Second, regardless of the arrangement of the classroom and the schedule, students tended to push the teachers' rules to assert more of their own power. Students need a sense of control and influence as well as a sense of limits and expectations. The design of learning environments should make efforts to respond to these needs. Third, interviews with teachers revealed that their choices about the arrangement of space and time were deeply embedded in their beliefs about how children learn best. In classrooms that were highly structured with little student movement and rigid time restraints, teachers viewed learning as an individual act. The curriculum was viewed as a series of skills, sequenced by their difficulty, presented to students at predetermined times, and then practiced as students completed assignments. In loosely structured classrooms with flexible patterns of movement and time arrangements, teachers expressed beliefs about the social nature of learning. The curriculum was seen as a whole with problems and themes used to organize student learning. These classrooms allowed learners to assume greater responsibility for their learning then in the more highly structured classrooms.

The kinds of designs for learning presented in previous chapters are more consistent with loosely structured classrooms. When learning is understood as the result of what learners construct and when cognition is understood as the interaction of activities, tools, and culture, places for learning support this view by structuring learning environments rich in materials, varied in the kinds of physical arrangements in which students work, and flexible in the arrangement of time. Mr. Wild has created such an environment.

Richard Wild is the Chapter One teacher in a middle school. His school uses a block scheduling pattern, which means students are scheduled to attend Mr. Wild's class for a two-hour block of time. He is charged by the school, the community, and the mandates associated with receiving Chapter One federal funds to teach reading and language arts. He has redefined these subject matter areas as literacy. He values conceptions of literacy that were expressed in Chapter 3 of this book and has designed his classroom environment to support this view of learning (Figure 10.1).

His classroom has a space where the whole class can gather for student presentations, for short teacher presentations, demonstrations, and project planning, and for whole-group activities. A projecting monitor is located in this area. There is a small area with beanbag chairs and a small carpet. Students gather here for quiet, individual reflection and study, or occasionally for small-group planning. Another area has tables and chairs configured to easily accommodate groups of three or four students. In one corner of the room is a television and VCR set, not on a tall cart but on a low table. Sometimes students sit on the floor; other times they bring chairs. The remote control is readily accessible so students can take control of the video presentation. Students know that television watching does not have to be only linear. Another part of the class is organized to accommodate the three classroom computers. There is plenty of space around each computer for groups of students to work together. The computers are connected to the school-wide network so that students may access the Internet. A sign-up sheet is located near each computer so students can arrange times to work. There are a series of cubbyholes near the door where students can store personal materials or group projects in process. There are two video cameras in an open cupboard area. There is a sign-up sheet nearby.

A quick glance around the classroom gives one a good indication of the kind and quality of literacy being produced. Examples of student writing are everywhere. Displays are not limited to print; there are also pictures, maps, desktop-published newspapers, ideas from the Internet, graphical organizers, and charts. Tools for recording, illustrating, and writing are visible everywhere. There are containers of markers, shelves with a variety of paper, tape recorders, video cameras, computers, reference materials, and software manuals. Students make use of these tools as they need them. There are classroom experts and their expertise listed on a classroom chart. Others can arrange help when they need it. The ways in which Mr. Wild has constructed his classroom learning environment ensure that his students have easy

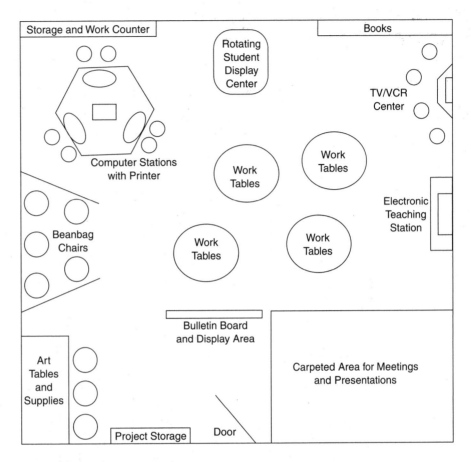

FIGURE **10.1**

MR. WILD'S CHAPTER ONE CLASSROOM

and continuous access to communication tools, spaces for using these tools, interesting things to read and write about, and spaces for sharing and displaying their work. Planning and recording their work is a normal part of every learning activity for students. Physical space, especially around computers, is provided for students to write, record, outline, plan, and arrange the materials they are using. Vertical space is used for students to record ideas, check out materials, or post their work. There are clipboards available for additional writing and planning space.

INTELLECTUAL LEARNING ENVIRONMENTS

The time has come to reconceptualize teaching and learning (Jonassen, 1994; Wilson, 1995). Hannafin (1994), for example, argues that while instruction as operationalized for more traditional models of teaching and learning may be effective for defined outcomes, it is relatively ineffective for deeper learning. "Advanced knowledge invariably requires insights and knowledge that cannot be taught algorithmically" (p. 52). Traditional models are highly prescribed, externally directed, content-driven, and represent a view of knowledge as external to the learner. Constructivist learning requires the kinds of flexible learning environments created when teachers provision their classrooms with tools that prompt students to organize and create knowledge.

The intellectual learning environments educators select to structure student learning are deeply influenced by their views of knowledge (Wilson, 1995). For instance, if knowledge is viewed as a quantity of content waiting to be transmitted, instruction becomes a product to be delivered, and teachers select intellectual learning environments that transmit content. If educators consider knowledge as enculturation or adoption of a group's ways of seeing and acting socially-negotiated meaning, instruction requires participation in a community's everyday activities. When educators focus on the later view of learning, they recognize that the intellectual learning environments they select combine to create "a place where learners may work together and support each other as they use a variety of tools and information resources in their pursuit of learning goals and problem-solving activities" (Wilson 1995, p. 28) instead of creating a place where learning is individual, isolated from its use, and skill-oriented. Thus, considerations about learning environments include more than the construction of physical spaces for learning; careful attention must be also be directed toward the selection of intellectual learning environments as well.

Carefully selected intellectual learning environments represent "comprehensive systems that promote engagement through student-centered activities, including guided presentations, manipulation and explorations among interrelated learning themes" (Hannafin, 1994, p. 51). The newer electronic technologies, when understood as intellectual environments, can function as comprehensive systems of learning that support new visions of the teaching/learning process.

As we have discussed many times throughout this book, the choices educators make about what tools will be available to learners influence the kinds of intellectual activities in which learners will engage. A learner's interaction with these tools models, engages, and challenges the user to think in certain ways. These tools create learning environments just as surely as desks, chairs, and chalkboards create learning environments. When learners interact with these environments, they begin to see reality differently simply because these environments structure knowledge and activity in particular ways.

When teachers select intellectual learning environments, they must consider the properties—affordances—of particular systems, recognizing that various environments make some activities easier and some activities more difficult. Each environment creates a mind-set—a way of thinking about that environment and the activities that are relevant in that environment. A place of learning that has been provisioned with only one or two varieties of intellectual learning tools facilitates only one or two kinds of intellectual activity. A place of learning that has been provisioned with a variety of learning tools is a place that facilitates and values a wide range of intellectual activity.

Like physical learning environments, intellectual learning environments are not passive. They are an important and active part of the teaching/learning process. Look at any classroom, even without students present, and you can notice the kinds of intellectual activities deemed important for learners by identifying the kinds of intellectual environments present. Do you see only textbooks or do you see a variety of reference books? Do you see a variety of different kinds of paper—some large, some lined, some colored—or only neatly stacked spiral notebooks? If the classroom has a computer, turn it on. What kinds of computer programs are available? Is there only a word processor and a few drill and practice programs? Is the computer only a "dumb" terminal connected to a schoolwide Integrated Learning System? Is there an Internet browser like Netscape or Microsoft Explorer? Is there a telephone to support a wide range of connections outside the classroom or is there only an intercom button to call the school office? How about a television monitor and a videocassette recorder? Are they part of the ongoing flow of learning activities or are they hidden in closets or permanently placed high up on the wall?

The Cognition and Technology Group at Vanderbilt (CTGV) (1996) suggests that intellectual learning environments created must be thought of not in terms of how they should be used but in terms of how they shape and interact with learning goals and learning environments. Early uses of technology, suggest the CTGV, were based on the transmission model of learning and were designed to make existing models of teaching and learning more efficient. Technology applications that were consistent with transmission models of learning were easily moved into classrooms. Applications consistent with this model were simply assimilated into existing classroom practice. They required little if any reassessment of the standards by which teachers selected learning environments.

More recently, however, technology use in education is being shaped by shifts in thinking about learning and education, directing attention to the ways in which technology can be used to design intellectual learning environments that reflect constructivist models of learning. These uses of technology, however, are not easily assimilated into traditional classroom practices. Instead, classrooms must be transformed (e.g., Bereiter, 1994; Bransford, Goldman, & Vye, 1991; Pea, 1992) and that transformation happens at multiple levels. Thus, reports the CTGV, challenges increase as one moves from attempts to transform only part of the school day to attempts to transform the entire nature of schooling. These transformations include attempts to build innovative linkages between schools and the home and the community as well as transform what happens in classrooms.

When teachers confront these transformative challenges and begin to think of technology not as teaching machines but as important mediating tools that impact the interaction of teachers, students, and content, selecting intellectual learning environments becomes a complex process. Just as constructing physical learning environments depends on beliefs about the teaching/learning process, decisions that guide the selection of appropriate intellectual environments should be based on teachers' beliefs about teaching and learning. Traditional considerations for selecting technology applications have focused on factors such as ease of use, dependability, attractiveness of the screen presentation, quality of graphics and sound, ability for modification by the teacher, and similar technical characteristics.

While these factors are important and can be included when selecting technological applications, it is far more important to assess the pedagogical approach that underlies the design of a particular technology application. Can you tell when viewing a program if the application is intended to teach students specific content-related facts and concepts, or is it designed to provide a rich environment in which students construct their own understandings of content through exploration, interaction, and creation?

Selecting Appropriate Intellectual Learning Environments

A critical look at software is especially important as educators become inundated with enormous amounts of new software. For instance, multimedia software has been shown to enhance education. Studies have shown that when teachers select multimedia learning environments, they can increase learning in mathematics and science, create a more student-centered learning environment (O'Connor, 1993), and help students learn a second language more effectively (Sprayberry, 1993). On the other hand, a five-year study conducted by the Center for Children and Technology suggests how easy new video and imaging technologies have made it to manipulate reality. "We have seen up close that multimedia technologies can sometimes make it even harder for kids to sort out reality and fiction, thanks to the power of the medium and the way multimedia designers play fast and loose with the accuracy of the images they choose" (Brunner and Tally, 1994, p. 16). There has been little opportunity for educators to gain experience in how to effectively use and critically evaluate this new media.

Educators are currently bombarded with all types of multimedia and a daunting variety of new multimedia technologies—interactive video, CD-ROM, DVI, CD-I, hypermedia, hypertext, and virtual reality. Any number of programs on the market are called multimedia or hypermedia simply because they include visuals, text, and/or color. Yet, many multimedia programs are still based on models that emphasize overly simplified notions of learning. Many programs do not provide problem-rich video and computer-based resources to encourage generative learning and cooperative work by students. Often, these learning environments are designed in ways that capitalize on the technical possibilities of multimedia but do not consider pedagogical issues. They manipulate reality, provide all kinds of "bells and whistles," and seem "high-tech" but fail to create productive learning environments. Educators must learn to judge and select tools that afford activities that support learning goals rather than for their seeming technological sophistication. This process has traditionally been referred to as software evaluation.

Learner-based tools should be selected for the ways in which they help students learn. In these environments, the quality of the product is not as important as how well the tool supports the learning process. When teachers ask students to create a multimedia stack to show what they have learned, they do not expect the product to look like a commercial multimedia product. Rather, they want this tool to become an intellectual learning environment that supports students as they organize their thinking, prioritize the most important facts and ideas, and create vivid pictures and/or sounds that help students remember and organize their learning. Instead of focusing attention on the technical capabilities of multimedia authoring, questions educators might ask when they are selecting learner-based intellectual learning environments include:

1. Does this learning environment provide students with a choice in the goal of the activity and/or strategies to meet the goal?
2. Does this learning environment encourage prediction and successive approximations to solving problems or creating a desired product?
3. Does this learning environment provide feedback to students that is informational rather than judgmental?
4. Does this learning environment have easy-to-start aspects for the novice user as well as a "high ceiling" for more experienced learners so that they can continue to use the tool in increasingly more sophisticated ways?
5. Does the structure of the learning environment focus on learning and problem-solving processes rather than product?
6. Does the learning environment facilitate a three-way interaction between teacher, student, and computer? (Bull & Cochran, 1991)

Wiburg (1995), after reviewing the research on multimedia and learning, suggested a series of questions that teachers should ask when selecting multimedia learning environments. We believe that these questions generalize to the selection of all intellectual learning environments—textbooks, videos, software applications, or audiotapes. Combined with the preceding questions posited by Bull and Cochran, these questions represent the important considerations teachers can use to select intellectual learning environments.

1. What is the theoretical approach to learning that is guiding the design of this learning environment? Is it behavioristic, presenting information in small pieces and containing reinforcement aimed only at the individual learner or is the theoretical approach consistent with constructivist notions of learning, providing opportunities for students to investigate and interact with rich problems?
2. Does the learning environment support opportunities for groups of students to discuss and think about content?
3. Is the learning environment well organized? Is it easy to navigate? Are there clear pathways to locating necessary information? If the learning environment has different parts, are the functions and uses of each of the parts clear?
4. Are there a variety of ways to use the learning environment including an opportunity to make choices about the kinds and levels of learner control?
5. Are there a variety of different perspectives presented for concepts taught? Are students encouraged to critically evaluate information regardless of whether that information is presented as images, sounds, or text?
6. Are opportunities provided within the structure of the learning environment for students to construct their own links between different kinds of information?

⚬⚬⚬⚬⚬⚬

When we visited Mr. Wild's classroom, we noticed that he had selected a wide range of intellectual learning environments for his students. Software available on the classroom computers included applications for word processors, databases, spread-sheets, graphics, desktop publishers, and telecommunications tools. Mr. Wild had found an integrated software package such as Microsoft Works or ClarisWorks that made it easy for students to integrate text, graphics, spreadsheets, databases, and telecommunications. He had a desktop publishing program. He told us he particu-larly liked The Writing Center and The Bilingual Writing Center, both published by The Learning Company. He felt these desktop publishing programs were more de-velopmentally appropriate for his students than more complex desktop publishing programs like Adobe's PageMaker and Microsoft's Publisher. Computer resources for his students also include a multimedia authoring tool. He had chosen Roger Wag-ner's HyperStudio, again because he felt it was more developmentally appropriate for his students than HyperCard, Linkways, or Toolbook. These computer environ-ments were part of the larger collection of intellectual learning environments that included a variety of books, videos, cameras, recorders, pencils, and pens.

Mr. Wild's students use graphics with text whenever it is appropriate. Mr. Wild is always asking students to examine their choices critically. He often asks if their choices of pictures, charts, or graphs enhance their communication or if another image might make their meaning clearer. Students are beginning to ask those kinds of questions of each other. He has selected intellectual learning environ-ments that allow students to digitize pictures, manipulate them in graphics pro-grams, and either embed them in other documents or print them out. Sometimes students download pictures from the Internet, but Mr. Wild discourages this and encourages students to create their own visual images. He has found that when students create their own images they are more successful at communicating their ideas as opposed to adopting or adapting others' ideas.

On the day that we visited, we observed two students working together at one of the classroom computers. They were creating an interactive map as part of their multimedia report about an inventor they had been researching. They had started with a picture of the world and then placed a button on the country where their inventor lived. As we questioned them about the large butcher paper flowchart on the floor near where they worked, they told us that the next button they planned to construct would take the user from the map of their inventor's country to a close-up image of the inventor's birthplace. They also planned additional buttons that would link to the inventor's discoveries. Next to the maps and pictures the stu-dents had included in the design of their hypermedia stack were text fields where they were writing about their inventor.

As we listened to the students from a polite distance, it was obvious that stu-dents had learned to be aware of the special skills each student contributed to the projects. Susan asked Jose to draw a better engine for her invention picture. Sal asked Maria to help him find information in the dictionary. Several of the students decided that a short animation would help them show how their invention worked. They checked the chart of "experts," noticed that Tracy had recently mastered an-imation techniques, and asked her to help them when she was able.

Anyone who visits Mr. Wild's classroom can easily recognize the ways in which Mr. Wild's careful selection of intellectual learning environments fits smoothly with the way he has constructed the overall physical learning environment. Both support and suggest learning opportunities to students in his room that are consistent with his view of teaching and learning.

THE ENVIRONMENT AS A CLIMATE OF VALUES

Critics of traditional models for designing learning environments express concern that principles about the value of learning and about values important for learners actually detract from learners' ability to fully participate in today's society and that they do, in fact, interfere with their learning. Toffler (1980), for instance, writes that current educational practice is built on the factory model. Mass education, he asserts, which teaches basic reading, writing, and arithmetic, a bit of history and other subjects constitutes the "overt curriculum." Beneath it, however, lies an invisible or "covert curriculum" that is far more basic. It consists of three courses: one in punctuality, one in obedience, and one in rote, repetitive work. This cluster of overt and covert curriculums is the result of an industrialized society's demand for workers who are willing to take orders from a management hierarchy without questioning.

John Gatto (1992), on the occasion of being named 1991 New York State Teacher of the Year, expressed his frustration with the covert curriculum embedded in the design of traditional learning environments when he told his audience that the structure of schooling leads to lessons in confusion, class position, indifference, emotional dependency, intellectual dependency, provisional self-esteem, and that "one can't hide." He writes:

> Everything I teach is out of context. I teach the un-relating of everything. I teach dis-connections. . . . I teach that students must stay in the class where they belong. . . . I teach children not to care too much about anything, even though they want to make it appear they do. . . . when the bell rings I insist they drop whatever it is we have been doing and proceed quickly to the next work station. . . . By stars and red checks, smiles and frowns, prizes, honors, and disgraces, I teach kids to surrender their will to the predestined chain of command. . . . Successful children do the thinking I assign them with a minimum of resistance and a decent show of enthusiasm. . . . My kids are constantly evaluated and judged. . . . I teach students they are always watched, that each is under constant surveillance by myself and my colleagues. There are no private spaces for children, there is no private time. (pp. 12–17).

Although Gatto's indictment of the covert curriculum of values communicated by traditional learning environments may be harsh, critics like Gatto illustrate the importance of recognizing that how learning environments are designed conveys fundamental lessons about the way to learn, about the value of learning, about being a member of one's community, and about who we are as individual learners. These lessons of the covert curriculum are at least as important, if not more important, than the overt curriculum of orbiting planets, wars fought, or computer programming. Educators who plan to design learning environments for today's students must design for the whole of learning—the covert as well as the overt. They must recognize that much of learning is social, that learning is not for later life but for living, and that students are not vessels to be filled but constructors of their knowledge. They must create values environments that promote problem solving, cooperation, communication, critical thinking, and learning how to learn.

The Values Environment

For teachers interested in designing learning environments, attention must be paid to the psychological as well as the physical needs of students. Research on affective, social, and emotional learning declined somewhat during the 1980s after an avalanche of interest in the 1970s. However, there has been a revival of interest in the affective component of education, particularly the interaction between the social and emotional climate of the classroom and student learning (Brandt, 1996, p. 9). Those who tried to improve schools through the redesign of schedules, standards, and instructional strategies have found that not only must more attention be paid to the physical and intellectual learning environment of students, attention must also be paid to the values environment in which students learn.

However, responsibility for establishing a climate of values does not belong to the school alone. Values do not start and stop at the classroom door. Any values climate created in classrooms must include the community in both the design of its schools and in the development of the activities that occur in school. For children to succeed in school, they must feel valued and feel that their families and experiences are also valued. They must see connections between what they are asked to do in school and what they experience doing at home (Moll, Amanti, Neff, & Gonzales, 1992). Only then will students feel invited to learn. Resources for the development of positive values climates for learning are available within the multicultural education movement (Lee, 1994); the new content standards that include "habits of mind" and values as well as conceptual knowledge (AAAS, 1993); and reform movements related to school improvement efforts (Wallace, 1993; Re-Learning, 1995)

Comer's (1996) school development program is one of the most vivid examples of the growing interest in merging affective and social learning with cognitive growth. In these programs, psychologists work in teams with teachers, administrators, parents, and community members to plan and implement school improvement designs. The mission of these programs, according to Comer, is to use child development and relationship theories in a way that improves academic achievement and psychosocial functioning in schools.

Based on a review of work by Comer and others, the following teacher actions are recommended for the creation of positive and productive values environments. These include: (1) developing learning activities that are meaningful to students; (2) emphasizing task completion rather than relative performance; (3) using cooperative and collaborative learning; (4) contextualizing learning in ways that relate to real-world problems; (5) designing problem-centered approaches; (6) emphasizing respect for each individual; (7) using democratic processes; and (8) providing as much authentic communication as possible. In short, classrooms must communicate values environments in which children feel a sense of welcome and belonging, in which their ideas are valued, and where participation is continually encouraged.

EXPLORING THREE SCHOOLWIDE LEARNING ENVIRONMENTS

When technology money became available at Parkhurst Elementary School, teachers on the technology committee made a series of decisions about the ways in which they would use the money to construct learning environments for students. The first year they spent the money purchasing a computer for each teacher and eight computers for the school library. Parent volunteers helped wire the school for Internet access and for a schoolwide e-mail system. Most teachers placed their computer on their desk, using the computer for "teacher" work—grades, notes to parents, worksheets, administrative communications, accessing lesson ideas and teaching materials, and test making. Occasionally, students were permitted to use this teacher computer to check for missing assignments or as an electronic encyclopedia.

The eight computers that were placed in the library were used primarily as an electronic card catalog. Students were able to use a districtwide resource locator called Athena. It was often frustrating because the resources they were able to locate were often not in the school's library. When one of us made arrangements to use the library's computers for a workshop, we discovered that the Paint program that came with the Windows operating system had been removed from all the computers. The librarian told us that students were coming in and playing with it. "That," she reported, "was not what libraries were for." When asked about the three Macintosh computers with signs covering the monitor stating that the computers were out of order, the librarian told us that someone had installed a video game on those computers. A group of fifth-grade boys had discovered the game and were coming to the library during lunchtime to play. "They simply make too much noise, and libraries are not for game playing," reported the librarian. "I just label them as out of order and the boys leave."

The second year when more money became available the technology committee decided to create a school computer lab. Twenty-four computers were placed on tables lined up in rows. When we observed the lab, we noticed five rows of four computers, all facing toward the front of the room where a white board and lectern were located. The tables were so high that for all but the bigger fifth graders, when students sitting at the computers looked up all they could see was the monitor. They could not see the teacher at the front of the room. The spaces between the rows and the tables were nearly impassable. It was almost impossible to reach individual students working at the computers. Students worked alone. The only time they were paired was if there were not enough computers.

Each class in the school was scheduled for two 45-minute "computer times." The school purchased a large integrated learning system that students could use during their computer times from funds available the second year. However, teachers soon became disillusioned with this system. Students found it boring, and it was nearly impossible for teachers to monitor the individual progress of each student. Teachers used funds available the third year to buy a software library of games that taught skills, tool software like word processors, information CDs like electronic encyclopedias, and special-topic CDs on animals and plants. Soon, teachers began using each class's assigned computer time to teach students how to use computers. They focused on asking students to use programs that taught keyboarding skills. They had students bring their writing to the computer lab and taught them to use the word processor to type in their stories and print them out. They asked students to look up information on CDs to complete worksheets on the states, the presidents, animals, and the like. At the end of three years, the teachers at Parkhurst Elementary School felt they had a school well equipped with technology.

What do students learn at Parkhurst Elementary School? Since over half of the school's computers are largely unavailable to students, students learn that computers are adult tools with little relevance to the work of students. The learning environments teachers have selected for students at Parkhurst Elementary are tools of transmission not tools of construction. Even though students use a variety of technology in their nonschool environments, the kinds of technology applications for learning are limited at school. Students learn that computers are tools to be learned about not with. Computers are not fun; they are sources for locating noncomputer information; they do things "to" you not "for" you or "with" you. The learning environments the teachers have constructed send messages to students that learning is individual and repetitious. Students learn that they are not in control of their learning; they are not meaning makers but meaning receivers. Teachers know all there is to learn, and students must just figure out what is in the teacher's head. Decisions that have resulted in this design communicate a set of values—the covert curriculum—that students are valuable if they can store large amounts of information. They are valuable if they follow directions and avoid exploration. They are valued for their individual achievements, not for the contributions they make to their community or the decisions they make about their own learning.

Teachers at Jackson Middle School began their design of learning environments in much the same way as teachers at Parkhurst Elementary School. But as they reflected on the learning that their decisions were promoting, they began to reassess their practices. The computers that originally sat on teachers' desks and the computers that had been placed in two computer labs—one for open use and one for teaching computer applications classes—were clustered into groups of four. These clusters were placed on movable carts, and teachers checked them out for extended periods of one to three weeks and brought the computers into their classrooms.

The availability of these computers and the limitations for their use that resulted from the short 50-minute periods led teachers to rethink the ways in which time was managed at their school. Teachers divided into "family" groups of four teachers. Each family assumed responsibility for 90 students and made decisions about time based on the work of the family at any given time. This permitted students to work on projects and problems in sustained ways. Because these choices about the construction of learning environments led to students working in groups, teachers soon learned to select learning environments that were sufficiently complex and flexible so that students were challenged to use these tools in complex ways. Without a learning environment that permitted students to learn about these environments as a whole group, teachers began constructing learning environments that facilitated small-group instruction. Students who mastered the ways in which particular learning environments could be manipulated became teachers.

The messages communicated to students through the decisions teachers at Jackson Middle School made about the learning environments they constructed for students were very different from the messages communicated to students at Parkhurst Elementary. The ways in which learning environments were constructed and selected at Jackson supported collaborative learning. Learning was viewed as the social construction of knowledge. Students began to see knowledge as connected across the disciplines, not as isolated facts that might be of use at some later date. Students learned that they were responsible for their learning and the learning of their peers. They learned that tool use, learning activity, and content were interconnected with the development of competence in literacy, knowledge, problem solving, community, and information use.

The learning environments at Jackson Middle School communicated to students that they were valued as interdependent learners. They were valued for their creativity, their problem solving, and their initiative. They learned they were responsible for learning the things valued by the school community, which included teachers, parents, members from the larger community, and the students themselves. When students came to school, they experienced a sense of excitement about learning, a sense of belonging to a community of thinkers, and a sense of their place in a broader context.

> Teachers at Cibola High School designed learning environments for their 2,000 students from two perspectives. They first agreed on a basic set of environments that would be used schoolwide. They created two computer labs. They agreed all computers would be networked and connected to the Internet. They agreed to create a demonstration classroom with a presentation station and student desks. And, they agreed to place 12 networked computers in the school library. Ms. Chase (see Chapter 7) taught at this school and used this resource for her Holocaust unit.
>
> The technology committee with input from all the teachers selected a set of universal intellectual learning environments that were predominantly tool applications. All school computers shared a common word processor, desktop publishing program, and software packages that integrated a spreadsheet, a word processing, and a database program as well as a common hypermedia and Web-based editing (Web page development) program.
>
> Teachers agreed that use of the computer labs and the library computers would be on a sign-up basis. Lab and library computers would be used for short-term, whole-group instruction in which strategies for manipulating particular applications were presented to students. Students would apply this knowledge to projects and problems within teachers' individual classrooms. Teachers could also sign up for short-term use of these labs for final production times. When students had used the classroom learning resources and were nearing completion of a large project, teachers would use the lab environments for sustained, whole-group completion of work.
>
> The second perspective used at Cibola High School focused on designing learning environments that met the needs of particular programs. Individual departments created plans, presented them to the technology committee, and received allocations of technology resources. The Business Department decided on a computer lab near the business classrooms. This lab was set up using more traditional considerations for the design of learning environments. Teachers in the

Business Department believed that each student needed access to an individual computer in order to learn keyboarding, secretarial, and accounting skills. Mrs. Dobson, the accounting teacher, has recently begun to design learning opportunities for students that are case-based and collaborative. She is beginning to question the validity of the Business Department's choices.

The Art, Math, and Journalism departments pooled their resources to create a flexible computer environment with workstations, space for collaborative project planning, a video editing system, and a high-end graphics and production station. They selected an advanced desktop publisher, several program languages, and advanced graphics programs in addition to replicating the basic tools provided on all school computers. This lab was used to schedule students who participated in advanced classes offered by these departments. Two periods were dedicated for the Computer Art courses, one period was designated for the Yearbook program, another period was scheduled for the school newspaper class, and two periods were set aside for the supercomputing, computational science classes.

Each department in the school except for Business, Art, and Journalism purchased minilabs. These clusters of four computers were shared by department members on an as-needed basis. Along with the standard technology applications used schoolwide, each department selected simulations, databases, and other applications appropriate to their disciplines. The Science Department, for instance, purchased microcomputer-based learning labs that provided sensors and software for conducting experiments on such phenomena as light, temperature, and acidity. The Social Studies Department selected a range of simulations that engaged students in exploring the interactions of disciplinary structures. The Math Department purchased programs like the Geometry Supposer and Logo. Most departments purchased two television and VCR systems.

What did students at Cibola High School learn? They learned that the work of a community happens in varied environments. They learned that tools are used in different ways to achieve different goals and that some values and habits shift a bit depending on the goal. They learned that learning environments can reflect their nonschool environments. They learned to participate in a variety of flexible communities as they learned a variety of things. Some of their learning experiences reflected traditional transmission models and some reflected more constructivist approaches. As they moved among these environments, they learned to value their own capacities for adapting.

The Web-Based Design Tool site (http://www.norton.wadsworth.com) is available to you even though you have now finished reading the book. We hope that you find it useful as you continue to design opportunities for students to learn. We have included a final set of Design Mentors so that you will be able to see the ways in which Brooks White and Allan Sutton planned for the physical, intellectual, and values environments to support their designs. In addition, these Design Mentors show how Ms. White and Mr. Sutton translated their designs into action plans as they created a schedule for instruction. After you have studied these final Design Mentors, you might find it helpful to return to the opening page of the Web site and complete Design Challenge Ten.

Throughout this book, we have explored concepts and stories about principles for designing learning opportunities for students that recognize the electronic technologies as integral parts of the teaching/learning process, that are based on constructivist, situated, and problem-based models of learning, and that recognize the interrelatedness of the foundations of learning, content, tools, and activities within well-designed systems of assessment and learning environments. We hope that this exploration of teaching with technology has helped you to envision ways in which you might design learning opportunities for your students.

CHAPTER IDEAS

- Learning environments are instructional strategies. Teachers' choices about the types and organization of learning environments are choices about what and how students will learn.
- Learning takes place in a context. The design of that context, the learning environment, is as important as the designs teachers create for literacy, problem-solving, knowledge, community, and information use. And, if the decisions teachers make about the learning environment are inconsistent with the designs teachers create to meet learning goals, the impact of these learning opportunities will be less powerful and important for students than teachers might hope.
- The physical learning environment is not passive. It is an important and active part of the teaching/learning process. Look at any classroom, even without students present, and you can tell what the teacher thinks is important.
- Teachers, when designing physical learning environments, need to analyze two categories of environmental problems. The first category of problems involves those caused by commission, such as inappropriate patterns of spatial organization, inadequate provisioning, or poorly arranged materials. The second category of problems involves those caused by omission, inadequacies in the learning environment revealed by desired learning that does not occur.
- The arrangement of furniture and materials, the kinds of tools available to students, and the use of time influence student learning. These factors also influence the quality of the relationships between student and student and student and teacher.
- Considerations about learning environments include more than the construction of places for learning. Carefully selected intellectual learning environments are comprehensive systems that promote engagement through student-centered activities, including guided presentations, manipulation and explorations among interrelated learning themes. The newer electronic technologies, when integrated into the physical learning environment, can function as comprehensive systems of learning that support new visions of the teaching/learning process.
- The choices educators make about what information tools will be available to learners influence the kinds of intellectual activities learners will engage

in. Whatever the intellectual tool, human interaction with these tools models, engages, and challenges the user to act in certain ways. These tools create intellectual learning environments just as surely as desks, chairs, and chalkboards create physical learning environments.

- Each intellectual learning environment creates a mind-set—a way of thinking about that environment and the activities that are relevant in that environment. A place of learning that has been provisioned with only one or two varieties of learning tools facilitates only one or two kinds of intellectual activity. A place of learning that has been provisioned with a variety of learning tools is a place that facilitates and values a wide range of intellectual activity.

- Learner-based tools should be selected for the ways in which they help students learn. In these intellectual learning environments, the quality of the software per se is not as important as how well the tool supports the learning process.

- Critics of traditional learning environments illustrate the importance of recognizing that how learning environments are designed conveys fundamental lessons about the way to learn, about the value of learning, about being a member of one's community, and about who we are as individual learners. These lessons of the covert curriculum are at least as important, if not more important, than the overt curriculum of orbiting planets, wars fought, or computer programming. Educators who plan to design learning environments for today's students must design for the whole of learning—the covert as well as the overt.

- For teachers interested in designing learning environments, attention must be paid to the psychological as well as the physical needs of students. Because emotional abilities are prerequisite to everything else schools are trying to teach, the curriculum must include well-planned programs for teaching social and emotional skills.

- Responsibility for establishing a climate of values does not belong to the school alone. Values do not start and stop at the classroom door. Any values climate created in classrooms must include the community in both the design of its schools and in the development of the activities that occur in school. For children to succeed in school, they must feel valued and feel that their families and experiences are also valued. They must see connections between what they are asked to do in school and what they experienced doing at home.

Bibliography

Ackerman, E. (1995). Construction and transference of meaning through form. In L. P. Steffe & J. Gates (Eds.), *Constructivism in education* (pp. 341–354). Hillsdale, NJ: Lawrence Erlbaum Associates.

Allen, G., & Thompson, A. (1994). *Analysis of the effect of networking on computer-assisted collaborative writing in a fifth-grade classroom.* Paper presented at the annual meeting of the American Educational Research Association. (Information Analyses No. ERIC ED373777)

American Association for the Advancement of Science (AAAS). (1993). *Benchmarks for science literacy.* New York: Oxford University Press.

American Association of University Women Educational Foundation, *How Schools Short-change Girls: The AAUW Report.* NY: Marlowe and Co., 1992.

American Association of School Librarians. (1998). *Information power: Building partner-ships for learning.* Chicago: American Library Association.

American Library Association (ALA); Association for Educational Communications and Technology. (1988). *Information power: Guidelines for school library media pro-grams.* Chicago: American Library Association.

Ames, S., Angle, M., Brubaker, S., Mahan, J., Marchand, D., Walker, D., O'Neil, S., & Pappas, M. (1995). *Teaching electronic information skills: A resource guide for grades K–5.* McHenry, IL: Follett Software Company.

Apple, M. W., & Beane, J. A. (1995). *Democratic schools.* Alexandria, VA: Association for Supervision and Curriculum Development.

Aries, P. (1962). *Centuries of childhood: A social history of family life.* New York: Vintage Press.

Aronson, E. (1978). *The jigsaw classroom.* Beverly Hills, CA: Sage.

Arter, J., & McTighe, J. (2001). *Scoring rubrics in the classroom: Using performance criteria for assessing and improving student performance.* Thousand Oaks, CA: Corwin Press.

Au, Kathryn H. (1993). *Literacy instruction in multicultural settings.* Fort Worth: Har-court Brace College Publishers.

Au, W. K., Horton, J., & Ruba, K. (1987). Logo, teacher intervention, and the develop-ment of thinking skills. *The Computing Teacher, 15*(3), 12–16.

Austin Independent School District. (1993). *TAAS* [On-line]. Retrieved August 1996 from the World Wide Web: http://www.austin.isd-tenet.edu/taas/taas.html

Baron, J. B., & Sternberg, R. J. (1987). *Teaching thinking skills.* New York: Freeman.

Barrett, H. (1994). Technology-supported assessment portfolios. *The Computing Teacher, 21*(6), 9–12.

Beane, J. (1990). *Affect in the curriculum.* New York: Teachers College Press.

Bereiter, C. (1994). Implications of postmodernism for science, or, science as progressive discourse. *Educational Technology, 29,* 3–12.

Berliner, D., & Biddle, B. (1995). *The manufactured crisis: Myths, frauds, and the attack on America's public schools.* New York: Longman.

Bloom, B. S. (1956). *The taxonomy of educational objectives: Classification of educational goals.* New York: Longmans, Green.

Bloom, B. S. (1984). The 2 sigma problem: The search for methods of group instruction as affective as one-on-one tutoring. *Educational Leadership, 13*(6), 4–16.

Bloom, B. S., Madaus, G. F., & Hastings, J. T. (1981). *Evaluation to improve learning.* New York: McGraw-Hill.

Blythe, T. (1998). *The teaching for understanding guide.* San Francisco, CA: Jossey-Bass.

Bolter, J. D. (1984). *Turing's man: Western culture in the computer age.* Chapel Hill, NC: University of North Carolina Press.

Bonk, C., & King, K. (1998). *Electronic collaborators: Learner-centered technologies for literacy, apprenticeship, and discourse.* Hillsdale, NJ: Lawrence Erlbaum Associates.

Brandt, R. (1990). On knowledge and cognitive skills: A conversation with David Perkins. *Educational Leadership, 47*(5), 50–53.

Brandt, R. (1996). Overview: Climate in the classroom and in the community. *Educational Leadership, 54,* 1, 5.

Bransford, J. D., Goldman, S. R., & Vye, N. J. (1991). Making a difference in people's abilities to think: Reflections on a decade of work and some hopes for the future. In L. Okagaki & R. J. Sternberg (Eds.), *Directors of development: Influences on children* (pp. 147–180). Hillsdale, NJ: Lawrence Erlbaum Associates.

Bransford, J., Sherwood, R. D., Hasselbring, T. S., Kinzer, C. K., & Williams, S. M. (1990). Anchored instruction: Why we need it and how technology can help. In D. Nix & R. Spiro (Eds.), *Cognition, education, multimedia: Exploring ideas in high technology.* Hillsdale, NJ: Lawrence Erlbaum Associates.

Bronowski, J. (1977). *A sense of the future.* Cambridge, MA: MIT Press.

Brookhart, S. M. (1999). *The art and science of classroom assessment: The missing part of pedagogy.* (ASHE-ERIC Higher Education Report Vol. 27, No. 1). Washington, DC: The George Washington University, Graduate School of Education and Human Development.

Brooks, J. G., & Brooks, M. G. (1999). *In search of understanding: The case of constructivist classrooms* (Rev. ed.). Alexandria, VA: Association for Supervision and Curriculum Development.

Brown, A. L. (1992). Design experiments: Theoretical and methodological changes in creating complex interventions in classroom settings. *Journal of the Learning Sciences, 2*(2), 141–178.

Brown, A. L. (1994). The advancement of learning. *Educational Researcher, 23*(8), 4–12.

Brown, A. L., Ash, D., Rutherford, M., Nakagawa, K., Gordon, A., & Campione, J. C. (1993). Distributing expertise in the classroom. In G. Salomon (Ed.), *Distributed cognition: Psychological and educational considerations* (pp. 188–228). New York: Cambridge University Press.

Brown, A. L., Bransford, J. D., Ferrara, R. A., & Campione, J. C. (1983). Learning, remembering, and understanding. In J. H. Flavell & E. M. Markman (Eds.), *Handbook of child psychology: Vol. 3. Cognitive development* (4th ed., pp. 77–166). New York: Wiley.

Brown, A. L., & Campione, J. C. (1994). Guided discovery in a community of learners. In K. McGilly (Ed.), *Classroom lessons: Integrating cognitive theory and classroom practice* (pp. 229–272). Cambridge, MA: MIT Press.

Brown, J. S., Collins, A., & Duguid, P. (1989). Situated cognition and the culture of learning. *Educational Researcher, 18,* 32–41.

Bruner, J. (1960). *The process of education.* Cambridge, MA: Harvard University Press.

Bruner, J. (1986). *Actual minds, possible worlds.* Cambridge, MA: Harvard University Press.

Bruner, J. (1990). *Acts of meaning.* Cambridge, MA: Harvard University Press.

Bruner, J. (1996). *The culture of education.* Cambridge, MA: Harvard University Press.

Brunner, C., & Tally, B. (1994). Teaching visual literacy. *Electronic Learning, 14*(3), 16–17.

Bull, G., & Cochran, P. (1991). Learner-based tools. *The Computing Teacher, 18*(7), 50–53.

Bureau of State Library, Division of School Library Media Services, Pennsylvania Department of Education. (1988). *Integrating information-management skills: A process for incorporating library media skills in content areas.* Harrisburg, PA: Pennsylvania Department of Education.

Chi, M. T. H., Glaser, R., & Rees, E. (1981). Categorization and representation of physics problems by experts and novices. *Cognitive Science, 5,* 121–152.

Clarke, John H. (1990). *Patterns of thinking.* Needham, MA: Allyn and Bacon.

Clarke, J., & Agne, R. (1997). *Interdisciplinary high school teaching.* Needham, MA: Allyn and Bacon.

Clements, D. H. (1997). (Mis?)constructing constructivism. *Teaching Children Mathematics, 4,* 198–200.

Cobb, P. (1994). Where is the mind? Constructivist and sociocultural perspectives on mathematical development. *Educational Researcher, 23*(7), 13–20.

Cognition and Technology Group at Vanderbilt. (1990). Anchored instruction and its relationship to situated cognition. *Educational Researcher, 19*(5), 2–10.

Cognition and Technology Group at Vanderbilt. (1996). Looking at technology in context: A framework for understanding technology and education research. In D. Berliner & R. Calfee (Eds.), *Handbook of educational psychology.* New York: Simon & Schuster-Macmillan.

Collins, A., Brown, J. S., & Newman, S. E. (1989). Cognitive apprenticeship: Teaching the crafts of reading, writing, and mathematics. In L. B. Resnick (Ed.), *Knowing, learning, and instruction: Essays in Honor of Robert Glaser.* Hillsdale, NJ: Lawrence Erlbaum Associates.

Comer, J. (1996). Yale Child Study Center School Development Program overview. Retrieved January 1997 from the World Wide Web: http://infor.med.yale.edu/comer/ overview.html.

Committee for Economic Development. (1985). *Investing in our children.* Washington, DC: Committee for Economic Development.

Corbett, H. D., & Wilson, B. (1993). *Testing reform and rebellion.* Norwood, NJ: Ablex.

Corrigan, D. (1995). *Teacher education and interprofessional collaboration: Creation of family-centered community-based integrated service systems. Teachers for the new millennium: Five views on teacher education.* Washington, DC: American Association of Colleges for Teacher Education.

Coulter, B., Feldman, A., & Konold, C. (2000). Rethinking online adventures. *Learning and Leading with Technology, 28*(1), 42.

Cromer, J. (1984). *High-tech schools: The principal's perspective.* Reston, VA: National Association of Secondary School Principals.

Cuban, L. (1986a). Persistent instruction: Another look at constancy in the classroom. *Phi Delta Kappan, 68*(1),7–11.

Cuban, L. (1986b). *Teachers and machines: The classroom use of technology since 1920.* New York: Teachers College Press.

Cuban, L. (1990). Reform again, again, again. *Educational Researcher, 19*(1), 3–13.

Cummins, J. (1996). *Authentic assessment for English language learners: Practical approaches for teachers.* In J. M. O'Malley & L. V. Pierce (Eds.). Menlo Park, CA: Addison-Wesley.

Cummins, J. (1996). *Negotiating identities: Education for empowerment in a diverse society.* Los Angeles: California Association for Bilingual Education.

Darder, A., Ingle, Y. R., & Cox, B. G. (1993). *The policies and the promise: The public schooling of Latino children.* Claremont, CA: Thomas Rivera Center.

Darling-Hammond, L. (1997). *The right to learn: A blueprint for creating schools that work.* San Francisco, CA: Jossey-Bass Publishers.

Dede, C. (1996, April). The transformation of distance education to distributed learning. *Learning and Leading in Educational Technology, 23*(7), pp. 25–30.

DeFina, A. (1992). *Portfolio assessment: Getting started.* New York: Scholastic Professional Books.

Dewees, K. (1987). *The effect of teaching library skills using "The Pooh Step-by-Step Guide for Writing the Research Paper" at Lieder Elementary School in the Cypress Fairbanks Independent School District: A research report.* Master's seminar research report, Prairie View A&M University. (Information Analyses No. ERIC ED 284577)

Dewey, J. (1916). *Democracy and education.* New York: Macmillan.

Dewey, J. (1933). *How we think* (Rev. ed.). Boston: Heath.

Diamond, J. (1989). The great leap forward. *Discover, 10*(5), 50–60.

Diamond, J. (1992). Living through the Donner Party. *Discover, 13*(3), 100–107.

Doyle, C. S. (1992). *Outcome measures for information literacy within the National Educational Goals of 1990.* Final Report to National Forum on Information Literacy: Summary of Findings. (Information Analyses No. ERIC ED 351033)

Draves, W. (1995). *Energizing the learning environment.* Learning Resources Network (LERN), 1550 Hayes Drive, Manhattan, KS 66502.

Drinan, J. (1990). The limits of problem-based learning. In D. Boud & G. Feletti (Eds.), *The challenge of problem-based learning.* New York: St. Martin's Press.

Drouyn-Marrero, M. A. (1989). Computer access, social interaction, and learning in a bilingual-multicultural setting. (Doctoral dissertation, University of Massachusetts). *Dissertation Abstracts International, 50,* 3871A.

Duffy, T. M., and Cunningham, D. J. (1996). "Constructivism: Implications for the design and delivery of instruction." In D. H. Jonassen (Ed.), *Handbook of Research for Educational Communications and Technology* (pp. 170–198). New York: Simon & Schuster-Macmillan.

Durant, W. (1939). *The story of civilization: Part II—The life of Greece.* New York: Simon & Schuster.

Dutton, W. H., Rogers, M. E., & Jun, S. (1987). Diffusion and social impacts of personal computers. *Communication Research, 14*(2), 219–250.

Educational Testing Service (ETS). (2000). *Too much testing of the wrong kind: Too little of the right kind in K–12 education.* Available online at http://www.ets.org/research/pic/testing/tmt2.html

Eisenberg, M. B. (1991, June 28). *From information skills to information literacy.* Presentation at the American Association of School Librarians Preconference, Atlanta, GA.

Eisenberg, M. B. (1992, Winter). Current themes regarding library and information skills instruction: Research supporting and research lacking. *School Library Media Quarterly* (Winter 1992), 103–109.

Eisenberg, M. B., & Berkowitz, R. E. (1988). *Curriculum initiative: An agenda and strategy for library media programs.* Norwood, NJ: Ablex.

Eisenberg, M. B., & Spitzer, K. L. (1991). Skills and strategies for helping students become more effective information users. *Catholic Library World, 63*(2), 115–120.

Eisenstein, E. L. (1979). *The printing press as an agent of change.* Cambridge, MA: Cambridge University Press.

Eiser, L. (1986, March). Problem-solving software: What it really teaches. *Classroom Computer Learning.*

Eisner, E. W. (1994a). *Cognition and curriculum re-considered.* New York: Teachers College Press.

Eisner, E. (1994b). *The educational imagination: On the design and evaluation of school programs* (3rd ed.). New York: Macmillan.

Eisner, E. W. (1998). *The kinds of schools we need: Personal essays.* Portsmouth, NH: Heinemann.

Erlich, K., & Soloway, E. (1984). An empirical investigation of the tacit plan knowledge in programming. In J. Thomas & M. L. Schneider (Eds.), *Human factors in computer systems.* Norwood, NJ: Ablex.

Fardouly, N. (1998). *Instructional design of learning materials.* Available online at http://www.fbe.unsw.edu.au/learning/instructionaldesign/materials.htm

Fiske, E. (1995). Systemic school reform: Implications for architecture. In A. Meek (Ed.), *Designing places for learning* (pp. 1–10). Alexandria, VA: Association for Supervision and Curriculum Development.

Flavell, J. H. (1976). Metacognitive aspects of problem solving. In L. B. Resnick (Ed.), *The nature of intelligence.* Hillsdale, NJ: Lawrence Erlbaum Associates.

Fosnot, C. T. (1989). *Enquiring teachers and enquiring learners: A constructivist approach for teaching.* New York: Teachers College Press.

Foucault, M. (1976). *The archeology of knowledge.* New York: Harper & Row.

Foyle, H., Lyman, L., & Thies, S. (1991). *Cooperative learning in the early childhood classroom.* National Education Association Publication.

Freud, S. (1961). *Civilization and its discontents.* James Strackey (Ed.). New York: W. W. Norton.

Gagne, R. M. (1965). *The conditions of learning.* New York: Holt, Rinehart and Winston.

Gagne, R. M. (1987). *Instructional technology: Foundations.* Hillsdale, NJ: Lawrence Erlbaum Associates.

Garcia, G. E., & Pearson, P. D. (1993). Assessment and diversity. *Review of Research in Education, 20*(1), 337–389.

Gardner, H. (1983). *Frames of mind: The theory of multiple intelligences.* New York: Basic Books.

Gardner, H. (1989). *To open minds: Chinese clues to the dilemma of contemporary education.* New York: Basic Books.

Gardner, H. (1990). Teaching for understanding and beyond. *Teachers College Record, 96*(2), 198–218.

Gardner, H. (1991). *The unschooled mind.* New York: Basic Books.

Gardner, H. (2000). *The disciplined mind.* New York: Penguin Books.

Gatto, J. T. (1992). *Dumbing us down: The hidden curriculum of compulsory schooling.* Philadelphia, PA: New Society Publications.

Gebhardt-Steele, P. (1985). *The computer and the child—A Montessori approach.* Rockville, MD: Computer Science Press.

Geisinger, K. F., & Carlson, J. F. (1992). *Assessing language-minority students.* Washington, DC: ERIC Clearinghouse on Tests, Measurement, and Evaluation. (Information Analyses No. ERIC ED 356232)

Gilder, G. (1989). *Microcosm: The quantum revolution in economics and technology.* New York: Simon & Schuster.

Glaser, W. (1986). *Control theory in the classroom.* New York: Harper & Row.

Goldenberg, C., & Gallimore, R. (1991). Local knowledge, research knowledge, and educational change: A case study of early Spanish reading improvement. *Educational Researcher, 20*(8), 2–14.

Goleman, E. (1997). *Emotional intelligence: Why it can matter more than IQ.* New York: Bantam Books.

Goodman, K. S. (1984). Transactional psycholinguistic model: Unity in reading. In A. C. Purvis & O. Niles (Eds.), *Becoming readers in a complex society.* Yearbook of the National Society of the Study of Education, Part I. Chicago: University of Chicago Press.

Gould, L. (2000). *The impact of the Virginia Earth Science Challenge (VESC) on the learning of high school earth science students.* Unpublished Master's Action Research Project. Fairfax, VA: George Mason University.

Gowin, D. B., & Novak, J. D. (1984). *Learning how to learn.* New York: Cambridge University Press.

Grabe, M., & Grabe, C. (1996). *Integrating technology for meaningful learning.* Palo Alto, CA: Houghton Mifflin.

Gray, L., & Reese, D. (1957). *Teaching children to read.* New York: Ronald Press.

Grayson, D. K. (1990). Donner party deaths: A demographic assessment. *Journal of Anthropological Research, 46*(3), 223–242.

Greenberg, J. (1990). *Problem-solving situations* (Vol. 1). Corvallis, OR: Grapevine Publications.

Gumperts, G. (1987). *Talking tombstones and other tales of the media age.* New York: Oxford University Press.

Handler, M. G., and Dana, A. S. (1998). *Hypermedia as a student tool: A guide for teachers* (2nd ed.). Englewood, CO: Libraries Unlimited.

Hannafin, M. (1994). Emerging technologies, ISD, and learning environments: Critical perspectives. *Educational Technology Research and Development, 40*(5), 49–53.

Hanson, N. R. (1970). A picture theory of theory meaning. In R. G. Colodny (Ed.), *The nature and function of scientific theories* (pp. 233–274). Pittsburgh: University of Pittsburgh Press.

Harman, D. (1987). *Illiteracy: A national dilemma.* New York: Cambridge Book Company.

Harmon, M. (1995). The changing role of assessment in evaluating science education reform. In R. G. O'Sullivan (Ed.), *American Evaluation Association: Vol. 65. Emerging roles of evaluation in science education reform* (pp. 31–52). San Francisco, CA: Jossey-Bass.

Harrington, H. (1993). *Technology and teacher education annual 1993* (pp. 25–27). Charlottesville, VA: Association for Advancement of Computers in Education.

Harris, J. (1998a). Wetware: Why use activity structures? *Leading and Learning with Technology, 25*(4), 13–18.

Harris, J. (1998b). Curriculum-based telecollaboration: Using activity structures to design student projects. *Leading and Learning with Technology, 26*(1), 6–13.

Harris, J. (1998c). *Virtual architecture—Designing and directing curriculum-based telecomputing.* Eugene, OR: International Society for Technology in Education.

Harris, J. (2000). Online to learn or in line with standards? An illusory dilemma. *Leading and Learning with Technology, 28*(1), 10–15.

Harris, S. (1996). Bringing about change in reading instruction. *The Reading Teacher, 49*(8), 612–618.

Hart, D. (1994). *Authentic assessment: A handbook for educators.* Menlo Park, CA: Addison-Wesley.

Hatch, T., & Gardner, H. (1993). Finding cognition in the classroom: an expanded view of human intelligence. In G. Salomon (Ed.), *Distributed cognitions: Psychological and educational considerations* (pp. 164–187). New York: Cambridge University Press.

Hativa, N. (1988). Computer-based drill and practice in arithmetic. Widening the gap between high-achieving and low-achieving students. *American Educational Research Journal, 25*(3), 366–397.

Herman, J. L., Aschbacher, P. R., & Winters, L. (1992). *A practical guide to alternative assessment.* Alexandria, VA: Association for Supervision and Curriculum Development.

Hirsch, E. D. (1996). *The schools we need and why we don't have them.* New York: Anchor Books.

Hodgkinson, H. L. (1992). *A demographic look at tomorrow.* Washington, DC: The Institute for Educational Leadership. (Information Analyses No. ERIC ED 359087)

Holmes, E. D. (1997, May). The spreadsheet absolutely elementary! *Leading and Learning with Technology, 24*(8), 6–12.

Huerta-Macias, A. (1995). Alternative assessment: Responses to commonly asked questions. *TESOL Journal, 5*(1), 8–11.

Hunt, M. (1982). *The universe within.* New York: Simon & Schuster.

Hunt, N., & Pritchard, R. (1993). Technology and language minority students: Implications for teacher education. In *Technology and teacher education annual 1993* (pp. 25–27). Charlottesville, VA: Association for Advancement of Computers in Education.

Hunter, C. S., & Harman, D. (1979). *Adult illiteracy in the United States: A report to the Ford Foundation.* New York: McGraw-Hill.

Irving, A. (1985). *Study and information skills across the curriculum.* Portsmouth, NH: Heinemann.

Jackson, A. (2000). *Desktop publishing multimedia presentations in a problem-centered environment.* Unpublished Master's Action Research Project. Fairfax, VA: George Mason University.

Jaynes, J. (1976). *The origin of consciousness in the breakdown of the bicameral mind.* Boston: Houghton Mifflin.

Johnson, D. W., & Johnson, R. T. (1987). *Learning together and alone* (2nd ed.). Englewood Cliffs, NJ: Prentice-Hall.

Johnson, D. W., Johnson, R. T., & Holubec, E. (1991). *Cooperation in the classroom* (Rev. ed.). Edina, MN: Interaction Book Company.

Johnson, R., & Johnson, D. (1994). *Learning together and alone* (4th ed.). Boston: Allyn and Bacon.

Johnson-Laird, P. (1989). Reasoning by model: The case of multiple quantification. *Psychological Review, 96*(4), 658–673.

Jonassen, D. (1994, April). Thinking technology: Toward a constructivist view of instructional design. *Educational Technology, 30*(9), 34–37.

Jonassen, D. H. (1996). *Computers in the classroom: Mindtools for critical thinking.* Englewood Cliffs, NJ: Prentice-Hall.

Jonassen, D., Peck, K., & Wilson, B. (1999). *Learning with technology: A constructivist perspective.* Upper Saddle River, NJ: Prentice-Hall.

Joyce, B., Weil, M., & Showers, B. (1992). *Models of teaching* (4th ed.). Boston: Allyn and Bacon.

Kafai, Y., & Harel, I. (1991). Children learning through consulting. In I. Harel & S. Papert (Eds.), *Constructivism* (pp. 110–140). Norwood, NJ: Ablex.

Kandel, E. (1992). The biological basis of learning and individuality. *Scientific American, 267*(3), 78–86.

Kleibard, H. M. (1995). *The struggle for the American curriculum.* New York: Routledge.

Knapp, L., & Glenn, A. (1996). *Restructuring schools with technology.* Boston: Allyn and Bacon.

Kohn, A. (1999) *The schools our children deserve: Moving beyond traditional classrooms and "tougher standards."* Boston: Houghton Mifflin.

Kuhlthau, C. C. (1985). *Teaching the library research process.* West Nyack, NY: The Center for Applied Research in Education.

Lacelle-Peterson, M., & Rivera, C. (1994). Is it real for all kids? A framework for equitable assessment policies for English language learners. *Harvard Educational Review, 64*(1), 55–75.

Lackney, J., & Moore, G. (1994). *Design patterns for educational facilities: Translating research into prototypical school designs.* (Information Analyses No. ERIC ED 380865)

Ladestro, D. (1989). Teaching tolerance. *Teaching and Learning/Curriculum, 23*–24.

Lam, T., & Gordon, W. (1992). State policies for standardized achievement testing of limited English proficient students. *Educational Measurement: Issues and Practices, 11*(4), 18–20.

Large, P. (1984). *The micro revolution revised.* Totowa, NJ: Rowman and Allenheld.

Larkin, J. H., McDermott, J., Simon, D. P., & Simon, H. A. (1980). Modes of competence in solving physics problems. *Cognitive Science, 4,* 317–345.

Lave, J. (1988). *Cognition in practice: Mind, mathematics, and culture in everyday life.* Cambridge, England: Cambridge University Press.

Lee, C. (1994). *Multicultural education: Challenges to administrators and school leadership.* Urban Education Program, Urban Monograph Series. Washington, DC: Office of Educational Research and Improvement.

Levy, D., Navon, D., & Shapira, R (1991). Computers and class: Computers and inequality in Israeli schools. *Urban Education, 25*(4), 483–499.

Linn, R. L. (1995). High-stakes uses of performance-based assessments: Rationale, examples, and problems of comparability. In T. Oakland & R. K Hambleton (Eds.), *International perspectives on academic assessment* (pp. 49–73). Boston: Kluwer Academic Publications.

Loughlin, C. E., & Suina, J. (1982). *The learning environment: An instructional strategy.* New York: Teachers College Press.

Madaus, G. F. (1991). The effects of important tests on students: Implications for a national examination system. *Phi Delta Kappan, 73*(3), 226–231.

Mager, R. (1962). *Preparing instructional objectives.* Palo Alto, CA: Fearon Publishers.

Manke, M. (1994). *Teachers' organization of time and space as an aspect of the construction of classroom power relationships.* Paper presented at the annual meeting of the American Educational Research Association. (Information Analyses No. ERIC ED 379217)

Marshall, S. (1993). *Wingspread Conference Report: Problem-based learning.* Aurora, Il: Center for Problem-Based Learning.

Matthews, R., Cooper, J., Davidson, N., & Hawkes, P. (1995). Building bridges between cooperative and collaborative learning. *Change, 27*(4), 34–37.

McGee, L. M., & Tompkins, G. E. (1995). Literature-based reading instruction: What's guiding the instruction? *Language Arts, 72,* 405–414.

Means, B. (1994). Introduction: Using technology to advance educational goals. In B. Means (Ed.), *Technology and educational reform* (pp. 1–21). San Francisco: Jossey-Bass.

Meek, A. (Ed.). (1995). *Designing places for learning.* Alexandria, VA: Association for Supervision and Curriculum Development.

Meier, D. (1996). The big benefits of smallness. *Educational Leadership, 54*(1), 12–15.

Meier, D. (2000). *Will standards save public education?* Boston: Beacon Press.

Mendelsohn, P., & Dillenbourg, P. (1994). Implementing a model of cognitive development in an intelligent learning environment. In S. Vosniadou, E. DeCorte, &
H. Mandl (Eds.), *Technology-based learning environments: Psychological and educational foundations* (pp. 72–78). Berlin: Springer-Verlag.

Mergendoller, J., & Pardo, E. (1991). *An evaluation of the MacMagic Program at Davidson Middle School.* (Information Analyses No. ERIC ED 351143)

Miller, J. (1985). *The effect of computer-assisted problem-solving instruction on the academic achievement of elementary students.* Unpublished doctoral dissertation, United
States International University, San Diego.

Moffett, J. (1968). *Teaching the universe of discourse.* Boston: Houghton Mifflin.

Moll, L., Amanti, C., Neff, D., & Gonzales, N. (1992). Funds of knowledge for teaching:
Using a qualitative approach to connect homes and classrooms. *Theory Into Practice,
31*(2), 132–141.

Moll, L., & Greenberg, J. B. (1992). Creating zones of possibilities: Combining social contexts for instruction. In L. Moll (Ed.), *Vygotsky and education: Instructional implications and applications of socio-historical psychology* (pp. 319–348). New York:
Cambridge University Press.

Montessori, M. (1912). *Dr. Montessori's own handbook.* New York: Schocken Books.

Montgomery, K. (2000). *Authentic assessment: A guide for elementary teachers.* New York:
Longman.

Naisbitt, J. (1982). *Megatrends: Ten new directions transforming our lives.* New York:
Warner Books.

Naisbitt, J. (1982). In R. S. Wurman (Ed.), *Information anxiety.* New York: Doubleday.

National Assessment of Educational Progress. (1990). Washington, DC: Office of Educational Research and Improvement, U.S. Department of Education.

National Commission on Excellence in Education. (1983). *A nation at risk.* Washington,
DC: U.S. Department of Education.

National Council of Teachers of Mathematics. (1989). *Curriculum and evaluation standards for school mathematics.* Reston, VA: Author.

National Council of Teachers of Mathematics. (1993). *Standards for teaching mathematics.* Reston, VA: Author.

Nattiv, A. (1991). *Synthesis of research on cooperative learning.* Presented at the Association for Childhood Education International Convention, San Diego.

Neuman, W. R., Just, M. R., & Crigler, A. N. (1992). *Common knowledge: News and the
construction of political meaning.* Chicago: University of Chicago Press.

The New America. (2000, September 18). *Newsweek, 137*(19) 48.

Newell, A., & Simon, H. (1972). *Human problem solving.* Englewood Cliffs, NJ: Prentice-
Hall.

Nord, J. (1986, September). Language as an interactive process. *Nagoya University of
Commerce Bulletin, 31,* 275–316. (Information Analyses No. ERIC ED 284419)

Norman, D. (1982). *Learning and memory.* New York: W. H. Freeman.

Norman, D. (1993). *Things that make us smart: Defending human attributes in the age of
the machine.* New York: Addison-Wesley.

Norton, P. (1985). Problem-solving activities in a computer environment: A different angle of vision. *Educational Technology, 25*(10), 35–41.

Norton, P. (1997). Using technology to learn about technology. In J. Clarke & R. Agne (Eds.), *Interdisciplinary high school teaching* (pp. 191–204). Needham Heights, MA: Allyn and Bacon.

Norton, P., & Angell, C. (1986). Computers aren't crazy: Reading and the four C's. *The New Mexico Journal of Reading, 6*(3), 5–8.

Norton, P., & Harvey, D. (1995). Information knowledge: Using databases to explore the tragedy at Donner Pass. *Leading and Learning with Technology, 23*(1), 23–25.

Norton, P., & Heiman, B. (1988). Computers, literacy, and communication disordered students: A research study. *Educational Technology, 27*(9), 36–41.

Norton, P., & Resta, V. (1986). Investigating the impact of computer instruction on elementary students' reading achievement. *Educational Technology, 26*(3), 35–41.

Norton, P., & Sprague, D. (2001). *Technology for teaching.* Needham, MA: Allyn and Bacon.

Oakes, J., & Lipton, M. (1999). *Teaching to change the world.* Boston: McGraw-Hill.

O'Connor, J. (1993). *Evaluating the effects of collaborative efforts to improve mathematics and science curricula.* Paper presented at the annual meeting of the Educational Research Association. (Information Analyses No. ERIC ED 357083)

O'Connor, J., & Brie, R. (1994). The effects of technology infusion on the mathematics and science curriculum. *Journal of Computing in Teacher Education, 10*(4), 15–18.

Odasz, F. (1994). Online teaching: A significant new pedagogy, the community as a K–100 university. *Ed Journal, 8*(1), 1–4.

Office of Technology Assessment. (1993). *Adult literacy and new technologies: Tools for a lifetime.* Washington, DC: U.S. Government Printing Office.

Ohanian, S. (1999). *One size fits few.* Portsmouth, NH: Heinemann.

Pagels, H. (1988). *The dreams of reason.* New York: Simon & Schuster.

Pallas, M. M., Natriello, G., & McDill, E. I. (1989). Changing nature of disadvantaged population: Current dimensions and future trends. *Educational Researcher, 19*(5), 16–22.

Papert, S. (1996). *The connected family: Bridging the digital generation gap.* Marietta, GA: Longstreet Press.

Patel, V. L., & Groen, G. J. (1986). Knowledge-based solution strategies in medical reasoning. *Cognitive Science, 10,* 91–116.

Pea, R. D. (1992). Augmenting the discourse of learning with computer-based learning environments. In E. DeCorte, M. C. Linn, H. Mandl, & L. Verschaffel (Eds.), *Computer-based learning environments and problem solving* (pp. 313–344). New York: Springer.

Pea, R. D. (1993). Practices of distributed intelligence and designs for education. In G. Salomon (Ed.), *Distributed cognitions: Psychological and educational considerations* (pp. 47–87). New York: Cambridge University Press.

Pellegrino, J., & Dillon, M. (Eds.). (1991). *Instruction: Theoretical and implied perspectives.* New York: Praeger.

Perelman, L. (1992). *Schools out: Hyperlearning, the new technology, and the end of education.* New York: William Morrow.

Perkins, D. N. (1986). *Knowledge as design.* Hillsdale, NJ: Lawrence Erlbaum Associates.

Perkins, D. N. (1992). Technology meets constructivism: Do they a marriage make? In T. M. Duffy and D. H. Jonassen (Eds.), *Constructivism and the technology of instruction: A conversation* (pp. 45–55). Hillsdale, NJ: Lawrence Erlbaum.

Perkins, D. (1995). *Software goes to school: Teaching for understanding with new technologies.* (Information Analyses No. ERIC ED 390664)

Perkins, D. N., & Salomon, G. (1989). Are cognitive skills context-bound? *Educational Researcher, 18*(1), 16–25.

Perkins, D. N., Schwartz, S., & Simmons, R. (1991). Toward a unified theory of problem-solving: A view from computer programming. In M. Smith (Ed.), *Toward a unified theory of problem-solving.* Hillsdale, NJ: Lawrence Erlbaum Associates.

Perkins, D., Schwartz, J., West, M., & Wiske, M. (Eds.). (1995). *Software goes to school: Teaching for understanding with new technologies.* London: Oxford University Press.

Perlis, A. (1985). Quoted in P. McCorduck. *The universal machine: Confessions of a technological optimist.* New York: McGraw-Hill.

Plato. (1928). The *works of Plato.* Irwin Edman (Ed.). New York: Simon & Schuster.

Polin, L. (1992). Subvert the dominant paradigm. *Research Windows, the Computing Teacher, 19*(8), 6–7.

Polya, G. (1957). *How to solve it: A new aspect of mathematical methods* (2nd ed.). Garden City, NY: Doubleday.

Postman, N. (1979). *Teaching as a conserving activity.* New York: Delacorte Press.

Postman, N. (1982). *The disappearance of childhood.* New York: Delacorte Press.

Postman, N. (1986). *Amusing ourselves to death.* New York: Viking Press.

Postman, N. (1993, Winter). Technology as dazzling distraction. *TECHNOS, 2,* 24–26.

Reil, M., & Fulton, K. (1998, April). *Technology in the classroom: Tools for doing things differently or doing different things.* Paper presented at the annual meeting of the American Educational Research Association, San Diego.

ReLearning. (1995). *Information on this national reform effort.* Available from ReLearning New Mexico, 1300 Camino Sierra Vista, Santa Fe, NM 87501. Director, Pedro Attencio.

Resnick, L. (1987). Learning in school and out. *Educational Researcher, 18*(4).

Rheingold, H. (1993). *The virtual community.* Reading, MA: Addison-Wesley.

Rich, E. (1983). *Artificial intelligence.* New York: McGraw-Hill.

Rogers, M. (1987, February 9). Now, "artificial reality." *Newsweek,* 56–57.

Romberg, T. A., & Wilson, L. D. (1992). Alignment of test with the standards. *Arithmetic Teacher, 40*(1), 18–22.

Rosen, H. (1985). *Stories and meanings.* Portsmouth, NH: Heinemann Educational Books.

Ross, J. (John). (1995). Effects of feedback on student behavior in cooperative learning groups in a grade 7 mathematics class. *The Elementary School Journal, 96*(2), 125–143.

Rybczynski, W. (1983). *Taming the tiger: The struggle to control technology.* New York: Viking Press.

Salomon, G. (1991). Learning: New conceptions, new opportunities. *Educational Technology, 31*(6), 44.

SCANS Report (Secretary's Commission on Achieving Necessary Skills). (1991). *What work requires of schools.* Washington, DC: U.S. Department of Labor.

Scardamalia, M., & Bereiter, C. (1991). Higher levels of agency for children in knowledge building: A challenge for the design of new knowledge media. *Journal of the Learning Sciences, 1,* 37–68.

Scardamalia, M., Bereiter, C., & Lamon, M. (1994). The CSILE Project: Trying to bring the classroom into world 3. In K. McGilly (Ed.), *Classroom lessons: Integrating cognitive theory and classroom practice* (pp. 201–228). Boston: MIT Press.

Schank, R. (1977). *Scripts, plans, goals, and understanding: An inquiry into human knowledge structures.* Hillsdale, NJ: Lawrence Erlbaum Associates.

Schoenfeld, A. H., & Herrmann, D. J. (1982). Problem perception and knowledge structure in expert and novice mathematical problem solvers. *Journal of Experimental Psychology: Learning, Memory, and Cognition, 8,* 484–494.

Schramm, W. (1960). *New teaching aids for the American classroom.* Stanford, CA: Institute for Communication Research.

Scollon, S., & Scollon, R. (1984). Run Trilogy: Can Tommy read? In H. Gollman, A. Oberg, & F. Smith (Eds.), *Awakening to literacy.* Portsmouth, NH: Heinemann Educational Books.

Sergiovanni, T. J. (1994). Organizations or communities? Changing the metaphor changes the theory. *Educational Administration Quarterly, 30*(2), 214–226.

Sheingold, K., & Frederiksen, J. (1994). Using technology to support innovative assessment. In B. Means (Ed.), *Technology and education reform: The reality behind the promise* (pp. 111–132). San Francisco: Jossey-Bass.

Shenk, D. (1997). *Data smog: Surviving the information glut.* New York: HarperCollins Publishers.

Shinn, J. (1986). *The effectiveness of word processing and problem solving computer use on the skills of learning disabled students.* Unpublished doctoral dissertation, United States International University, San Diego.

Sivin-Kachala, J., & Bialo, E. R. (1996). Educational technology, teaching, and the development of complex skills. *Edutopia, 2*(2), 5, 9–10.

Skelle, R. (1993). Technology and diversity: Resolving computer equity issues through multicultural education. *Technology and Teacher Education Annual 1993.* Charlottesville, VA: Association for the Advancement of Computers in Education.

Skinner, B. F. (1954). The science of learning and the art of teaching. *Harvard Educational Review, 24*(2), 86–97.

Skinner, B. F. (1958). *The behavior of organisms.* New York: Appleton-Century-Crofts.

Slavin, R. E. (1990). *Cooperative learning: Theory, research, and practice.* Englewood Cliffs, NJ: Prentice-Hall.

Slavin, R. E. (1991). Are cooperative learning and "untracking" harmful to the gifted? *Educational Leadership, 48*(6), 68–70.

Slavin, R. (1994). *Educational psychology: Theory and practice* (4th ed.). Boston: Allyn and Bacon.

Smith, F. (1990). *To think.* New York: Teachers College Press.

Sprayberry, R. (1993). *Using multimedia to improve the aural proficiency of high school students of Spanish.* Practicum report, Nova University. (Information Analyses No. ERIC ED 358735)

Stanford Research Institute. (1992, December). *Using technology to support educational reform.* Report prepared by SRI and EDC for the Office of Educational Research and Improvement, U.S. Department of Education. Available for $10 from SRI International, Room BS178, 333 Ravenswood Ave., Menlo Park, CA 94025.

Stepien, W. (1997). Quoted in J. Clarke & R. Agne. *Interdisciplinary high school teaching.* Needham, MA: Allyn and Bacon.

Stepien, W., Gallagher, S., & Workman, D. (1993). *Problem-based learning for traditional and interdisciplinary classrooms* (Draft manuscript from authors). Aurora, IL: Illinois Mathematics and Science Academy, 1500 W. Sullivan Road.

Sternberg, R. (Ed.). (1982). *Handbook of human intelligence.* New York: Cambridge University Press.

Sternberg, R. (1985). *Beyond IQ: A triarchic theory of human intelligence.* New York: Cambridge University Press.

Stevenson, H. W., Lee, S. Y., & Stigler, J. W. (1986). Mathematics achievement of Chinese, Japanese, and American children. *Science, 231,* 693–699.

Stoll, C. (1995). *Silicon snake oil: Second thoughts on the information highway.* New York: Doubleday.

Stripling, B. K., & Pitts, J. M. (1988). *Brainstorms and blueprints: Teaching library research as a thinking process.* Littleton, CO: Libraries Unlimited.

Sutcliff, R. (1994). *The Sword and the Circle.* London: Puffin Books Limited.

Swerdlow, J. (1995). Quiet miracles of the brain. *National Geographic, 187*(6), 2–19, 24–41.

Tapscott, D. (1998). *Growing up digital.* New York: McGraw-Hill.

Taylor, A. (1993). How schools are redesigning their space. *Educational Leadership, 51*(1), 36–41.

Thorndike, E. L. (1921). *Elementary principles of education.* New York: Macmillan.

Tickton, S. G. (Ed.). (1970). To improve learning: An evaluation of instructional technology. In *Part I: Report of the commission on instructional technology (McMurrin Report).* New York: R. R. Bowker.

Toffler, A. (1980). *The third wave.* New York: William Morrow.

Toffler, A. (1983). *Previews and premises.* Toronto: Bantam Books.

Tonnies, F. (1957). *Community and society [Gemeinschaft und gellschaft].* C. P. Loomis (Ed.). New York: Harper & Row. (Original work published in 1887)

Tucker, M., & Codding, J. (1998). *Standards for our schools.* San Francisco, CA: Jossey-Bass.

Tyler, R. W. (1975). Educational benchmarks in retrospect: Educational change since 1915. *Viewpoints, 51*(2), 11–31.

Uslick, J., & Walker, C. (1994). *An evaluation of an innovation: Standardized test scores were not valid indicators of success.* Paper presented at the annual meeting of the American Educational Research Association. (Information Analyses No. ERIC ED 372099)

Valenza, J. K. (1996). Information literacy is more than computer literacy. Philadelphia Online's School Crossings. *http://crossings.phillynews.com/archive/k12/infolit4_16.htm*

Van Haneghan, J., Barron, L., Young, M., Williams, S., Vye, N., & Bransford, J. (1992). The Jasper Series: An experiment with new ways to enhance mathematical thinking. In D. F. Halpern (Ed.), *Enhancing thinking skills in the sciences and mathematics.* Hillsdale, NJ: Lawrence Erlbaum Associates.

Von Glasersfeld, E. (1995). A constructivist approach to teaching. In L. Steffe & J. Gale (Eds.), *Constructivism in education* (pp. 3–16). Hillsdale, NJ: Lawrence Erlbaum Associates.

Vygotsky, L. S. (1978). *Mind in society: The development of higher psychological processes.* Cambridge, MA: Harvard University Press.

Wall, J. (2000). *Technology-delivered assessment: Guidelines for educators traveling the technology highway.* ERIC/CASS Digest. Available online at http://ericir.syr.edu/plumb-cg/obtain.pl

Wallace, J. (1993). *Building bridges: A review of the school-college partnership literature.* Denver: Education Commission of the States. (Information Analyses No. ERIC ED 365199)

Watson, J. (1925). *Behaviorism.* New York: The People's Institute Publishing Company.

Wenglinsky (1998). Does it compute? The relationship between educational technology and student achievement in mathematics. Available online at http://www.ets.org/research/pic/dic/preack.html

White, T. (1960). *The making of a president, 1960.* NY: Atheneum Publishers.

White, T. (1964). *The making of a president, 1964.* NY: Atheneum Publishers.

White, T. (1968). *The making of a president, 1968.* NY: Atheneum Publishers.

White, T. (1972). *The making of a president, 1972.* NY: Atheneum Publishers.

Whitehead, A. N. (1929). *The aims of education.* New York: Macmillan.

Wiburg, K. (1987). The dance of change: Integrating technology in schools. *Computers in Schools, 13*(1 and 2), 171–184.

Wiburg, K. (1995). Becoming critical users of multimedia. *The Computing Teacher, 21*(5), 59–61.

Wilson, B. (1995). Metaphors for instruction: Why we talk about learning environments. *Educational Technology, 35*(5), 25–30.

Wilson, K. G., & Davis, B. (1994). *Redesigning education.* New York: Henry Holt.

Young, M. F., & Kulikowich, J. M. (1992). *Anchored instruction and anchored assessment: An ecological approach to measuring situated learning.* Paper presented at the annual meeting of the American Educational Research Association. (Information Analyses No. ERIC ED 354269)

Index